Business & Administration

Student Handbook
Level 2

By
Anthony Lapsley

Published by CfA

© CfA 2011

Registered charity number 1095 809

Published 2011

First published 2005

ISBN 978-0-9567738-0-7

CfA is committed to providing and promoting
relevant business skills and knowledge to all
types of organisations, to make sure employees
have the required skills to excel and develop
throughout their careers.

Cover design by Consider Creative
Additional graphics and design by Method UK and AyDesignWorks
Printed and bound by Mail Options Ltd.

Microsoft product screen shots reprinted with permission from Microsoft Corporation.

www.cfa.uk.com

Introduction

computer they need a comfortable and supportive chair to avoid back injuries. Desks will also house day-to-day items: pens, pencils, post-it notes, paperclips, elastic bands, notebooks, tacks, pins, stapler and staples etc. Some organisations have a clear-desk policy, which means everything that has been on the desk during the working day has to be tidied away at the end of the day so the desk is clear of any material.

Personal computers (PCs) or laptops

This is the main piece of office equipment that every employee will use. It will be set up with software which will allow an employee to write letters, sort and store documents, prepare presentations etc. It may also be connected to the Internet, which allows employees to search for information outside of the organisation - subject to certain restrictions, depending on organisational policy. Computers may be PCs that come with an external hard drive or laptops that come with a built-in hard drive. There are a number of electronic devices that can be connected externally to a PC:

- Printers - Provide a hard, paper copy of the information held on a PC

- Scanners - Used to enter text or images of data into a PC from a hard copy

- Speakers or earphones - Allow audio to be heard, though most PCs will have built-in speakers

- Memory sticks - Allow information to be stored as a back-up to a PC's hard drive. They are portable and allow information to be transported outside the organisation by an employee

- Projectors - Allow images to be projected onto a wall or screen for an audience to view either at meetings or presentations, including conferences etc.

- Digital cameras - Download images of data onto a PC

It is essential to use technology in a sustainable way. To make sure a business is sustainable and to lessen the carbon footprint of an organisation, PCs should:

- Set monitors to switch off after periods of inactivity, rather than relying on a screen saver

- Be set to go into **standby mode** after 10 minutes of inactivity
- Be set to **hibernate mode** after 30 minutes of inactivity
- Be switched **off** if they are sitting inactive for long periods
- Be switched off at the end of every day, including other peripheral devices, e.g. printers

The above may vary depending on the program the organisation has chosen to use.

• ACTIVITY 2

What are some of the electronic devices that can be attached to a PC? Why would these electronic devices be used?

Telephones

Most employees will have a telephone on their desk. These will vary in the functions they are programmed to deliver depending on the system being used by an organisation. Some of them can be quite complex in the functions they offer. Many managers will also have a mobile phone, e.g. BlackBerry, iPod, which can function as a PC and provide instant access to their internal and external customers. They also allow the user to send text messages and leave voice messages.

Calculators

These can carry out a wide range of calculations. This function is also built into a PC and other electronic equipment, where it is easy to keep a record of the calculation.

Shared office equipment

Shared office equipment is office equipment that everyone in the office will share and use depending on their needs. It is office equipment that every employee will have access to. This may have a dedicated team to organise and manage some of the resources for its use. The types of shared office equipment are:

Printers / photocopiers

An employee's PC will be connected to the office printer / photocopier. Most offices will have a combined printer / photocopier, but they can be separate. A combined printer / photocopier will print documents or copy documents. Depending on the complexity of the printer / photocopier, it can provide many functions that are fast and cost-effective, e.g. giving all employees a code number to access printing, which then allocates the printing to specific cost centres. Using a PC program, print jobs can be tailored to an employee's needs, e.g. print on both sides of the paper etc. Photocopiers have many functions, which include:

- Enlarging copies
- Reducing copies
- Producing multiple copies
- Collating and stapling documents
- Producing double-sided copies
- Producing colour copies

Some managers may have a private printer in their office to allow them to print off private and confidential material

Before starting a print run, make sure the printer / photocopier is stocked with paper and has sufficient toner or print cartridges.

• ACTIVITY 3

What functions can a printer / photocopier perform?

Fax machines

A fax machine transmits a copy of an original document via a telephone line to a receiver. To use a fax machine the required fax number is dialled and the start button pressed. A copy of the original will appear at the other end of the transmission to the receiver. Most fax machines will automatically print incoming faxes. As with printers / photocopiers, make sure the fax machine is stocked with paper and has sufficient toner or print cartridges. A PC can be set up to fax directly to a fax machine rather than printing out and using a fax machine - this saves time and paper.

Shredders

Shredders are used to manage the disposal of private and confidential documents, which cannot just be thrown away or recycled. With identify theft on the rise, it is critical to shred sensitive documents. A shredder will cut the paper into strips or squares, which makes it difficult to reassemble. Care must be taken not to get clothing or hair trapped in a shredder. Shredders can vary in the number of pieces of paper it can shred.

• ACTIVITY 4

Which piece (s) of office equipment would be used to?

1 Add together a table of figures

2 Produce 500 copies of a letter

3 Stamp envelopes and parcels

4 Bind a document in plastic covering

Specialised office equipment

Specialised office equipment may not be used very often or by many employees within the business, or it may require specialised skill and knowledge to use. This kind of office equipment may have a dedicated team to organise and manage resources for its use.

Digital projectors

A digital projector will only be used for meetings or presentations where it is important to share detailed information with an audience. This is usually attached to a PC. A digital projector, also called a digital projection display system, is a specialised computer display that projects an enlarged image onto a screen. A digital projector may also project three-dimensional (3-D), interactive, full-motion audio-visual files on a PC screen.

Videoconferencing

Videoconferencing is a communications technology that is used to integrate video - the visual image - and voice to connect users from different locations with each other in real time. It allows the transmission of natural conversations. Communications can be as simple as a conversation between two people at different sites or involve several sites and

groups of people in large rooms. Videoconferencing can also be used to share documents and information displayed on a computer screen and whiteboards. To use a videoconferencing system, the following components are required:

- **Video input** - Video camera or webcam
- **Video output** - Computer monitor, television or projector
- **Audio input** - Microphones, CD / DVD player, cassette player or any other source of preamp audio outlet
- **Audio output** - Usually loudspeakers associated with the display device or a telephone
- **Data transfer** - Analogue or digital telephone network, LAN or Internet

Audio teleconferencing

Audio teleconferencing, or a conference call, is a telephone call that connects users in different geographical locations in real time. Conference calls may be designed either for all users to participate in or limited to a few users. Participants in a conference call will join in by dialling a given number which will then have access codes that need to be dialled in. This will connect to a 'conference bridge', which is a specialised type of equipment that links telephone lines. Businesses usually use a specialised service provider which maintains the conference bridge or provides the phone numbers and PIN codes that participants dial to access the meeting or conference call. As well as using normal telephones, there are also specially designed phones for conference calling. Whoever organises a conference call will need to make sure that all users know in advance the time of the conference call, the telephone number to call and the PIN numbers to use. They will usually give users an emergency telephone number to use in the event of any problems.

• ACTIVITY 5

When would audio-teleconferencing and videoconferencing be used?

Franking machines

Franking machines are issued with a licence from Royal Mail. Franking is a quick and easy way to manage an organisation's mail. It can save time and money. It can also project a more professional image of a business. It can be paid for using credit with Royal Mail, as and when

it is needed by a business. Franking machines can be used by any type or size of business. There are no restrictions on minimum or maximum postage volumes and there are discounts for franked mail per item. Franking machines can be used to post items using most Royal Mail services, including First Class, Second Class, Recorded Delivery, Special Delivery, Cleanmail, Mailsort, ParcelForce Worldwide Services, International Signed For, Airmail etc. Franking machines vary in size and type. Franked mail can be handed in at a local Post Office or Mail Centre, posted in a franked postbox or picked up by Royal Mail. Care must be taken when using a franking machine, as any mistakes cannot be corrected. Once the franking is printed, the credit has been used. Always check before processing the frank that the correct amount of postage is used.

• ACTIVITY 6

When would a franking machine be used?

Whiteboards
Whiteboards are a quick and easy way to demonstrate points or take notes during a meeting or brainstorming sessions. Whiteboards have various accessories depending on the model of whiteboard being used, e.g. erasers and markers. Whiteboards can be wall mounted or come with stands and wheels. The type of whiteboard required will depend on the office and resources.

Laminators
A laminator will protect a document by encasing it between two pieces of plastic which are sealed together. The document will be protected from water damage, tearing etc. Examples of items that may be laminated include telephone lists, training notes, glossy prints, photos, maps etc. Laminators may be either manual machines or electric automatic machines capable of producing bulk laminates.

Binding machines
A binding machine will bind together pages of a document for presentation to an audience at

a meeting. The bound document presents a professional finish to a document. There are many different types of binding machines, including coil, comb, click, strip, thermal and wire. Different binding machines can bind different numbers of sheets.

Using office equipment

Office equipment should be used as efficiently as possible. If a piece of office equipment is unfamiliar, either ask for help from someone who knows how to use it or ask the specific team who may have overall responsibility for the equipment or read through the manufacturer's manual.

The manufacturer's manual will outline the best way of using the office equipment. Reading the manual is not the last resort to figure out how to make a machine work. A lot of time can be saved by reading the manual before starting to use the office equipment. A manual will also contain vital safety and operating information. If this information is ignored, it may cancel the warranty if something goes wrong. There may also be a number of functions or time-saving features that will not be discovered by chance. Keep the manual close to the piece of office equipment so it can be referred to. The manufacturer's manual will also set out how to maintain the office equipment. If it is a complex piece of office equipment, specific training may be required. Only use specific office equipment when fully competent to do so.

The manual will also outline how to deal with specific problems related to the office equipment. This may include a helpline number to call or addresses of service centres. Report any problems to the office manager first. Office equipment should only be repaired by qualified service engineers.

Most office equipment will need some resources. These may include:

- **Paper** - This comes in a range of quality and is measured by weight. It includes headed, letter, copy and photographic paper. Use the right quality of paper for the intended audience

- **Envelopes** - Letters to external addresses will need good-quality envelopes, e.g. with transparent windows to show the address typed on the letter. Internal memos may be sent using internal envelopes which can be used a number of times. Always consider the right size of envelope for what is being sent. Documents with several pages should be placed flat in an envelope

- **Cartridges** - Used in ink-jet printers. They come in black, multicolour, single-colour and photo-quality versions
- **Toner** - Used in laser printers and photocopiers, available in black and single-colour versions
- **Ribbons** - Used in dot matrix printers, printing calculators, fax machines and typewriters
- **Labels** - Used in franking machines for letters and parcels which are too bulky to frank. Computer printers use address labels, file labels etc. Specially printed labels are used in laminators to create security passes, visitor passes etc.
- **Pouches** - Used in laminators to protect the contents
- **CD-ROMs / DVDs** - Used to store information

• ACTIVITY 7

What are the common resources used in an office?

The manufacturer will recommend particular resources to be used with their machine. These should be used wherever possible. Use of non-standard resources may also cancel the manufacturer's warranty or stop the equipment working as well as it can.

A well-maintained piece of office equipment will always perform better than one that is not maintained well. Always make sure that the health and safety procedures for each piece of office equipment are followed. This will make sure that the piece of office equipment is kept in good condition. This will also help to minimise injury, minimise repair or replacement costs and make sure the office equipment is ready for the next user to use.

Try to minimise the production of unwanted copies of materials when using any piece of office equipment. Check the functions of a piece of office equipment will produce the required results. Perhaps the biggest source of waste in most organisations is paper. Before initiating a print run, print off one copy of the page and check it. If satisfied with the quality of the print then go ahead and print a large number of copies.

Resources for office equipment can be expensive, so make sure as few resources are wasted as possible. Careful storage will also prevent waste through damage. Almost all waste produced by using office equipment can be recycled, e.g. pieces of A4 paper can be cut in half or quarters and used as notepads. In some cases this saves money on new products or replacements.

It is important to use a piece of office equipment for the purpose for which it has been designed. Despite the best intentions to follow a manual and accept advice from office colleagues, problems can arise:

- **The piece of office equipment does not work -** If it is an electric piece of office equipment, check to make sure it is switched on. Check the mains are switched on as well. If it is still not working, look on the piece of office equipment to see if it is indicating where the problem is occurring. If so, follow the instructions it is giving. Many printers / photocopiers will give a step-by-step process of where the problem is occurring and what to do to eliminate it, e.g. with paper jams. If following the steps does not resolve the problem, consult with the office manager. It may have broken down and the manufacturer will need to send out a technician to fix it. Never attempt to repair a piece of office equipment, particularly if it is electrical or electronic

- **No paper in the paper bins -** Check the printer / photocopier to make sure is the paper trays are fully stocked

- **Printing may be corrupted because the printer / photocopier has run out of ink -** Replace the ink cartridge. Check with the office manager for advice on how to install a new ink cartridge

- **Use of incorrect resources for a piece of equipment, which disables it -** Stop the piece of equipment immediately and review what has happened. If unable to fix the problem, consult with the office manager or technical support team

• ACTIVITY 8

What are some common problems found when working with office equipment?

As a first resort to resolving any problems with office equipment, check the manufacturer's manual, as it will troubleshoot problems and offer solutions for how to deal with them. If this still does not provide a solution, consult with the office manager or technical support team. When using office equipment make sure that all the instructions on how to use the equipment are known. If not, either check the manufacturer's manual or consult with the office manager. Any job needs to be completed in accordance with organisational procedures, to the standard of work required and agreed with the person for whom the work is being done. If not, this can lead to a waste of resources, time and money. It will also undermine confidence in the ability to perform tasks using office equipment in the future.

If any agreed task which is to be completed using office equipment is not going to be met on time, for whatever reason, it should be reported immediately so a new priority can be agreed. Doing this helps to maintain confidence in a team. It can also be a lesson learned, which can be followed by other team members in the future, empowering employees to take more responsibility for their own learning.

After using office equipment

After completing any piece of work using office equipment leave the equipment in good working order and ready for the next user to use:

- Do not leave a paper jam in a printer / photocopier for the next user to resolve

- Take the original documents out of the photocopier

- Do not leave paperclips or pieces of paper on the photocopier

- Replace the telephone handset on its base

- Leave the franking machine set on the minimum value

- Make sure paper is stored flat and tidily

- Refill the printer / photocopier with paper, if required

- Replace an ink cartridge

- Make sure the meeting room has been cleared of teleconferencing or videoconferencing equipment

If a resource runs out, make sure the person who is responsible for ordering replacements has been told to order more of that resource. It is important to know who this person is in the office. This may require some observation well in advance of a task, e.g. if a print run is planned tomorrow and there is only one ream of paper left.

All office equipment will operate better if it is kept clean. Office equipment should be kept clean enough to meet health and safety requirements. Some will have self-cleaning functions. Most will have instructions in the manual on how to keep them clean. Follow these instructions to keep the equipment clean and hygienic. Care should be taken when cleaning particular pieces of office equipment. For example, do not attempt to clean electrical equipment using water. Office equipment such as telephone handsets and keyboards need to be cleaned with antiseptic wipes. This prevents germs being transferred from one person to another.

Always think ahead.

Keep the work area clean and tidy. A clean and tidy work area is motivating to work in and healthier than a dirty / untidy one.

Testing your knowledge

1. Why is it necessary to read the manual before operating office equipment?

2. Why should a franking machine always be reset after use?

3. Why must some documents be shredded before recycling?

4. Which resources can be recycled?

5. Why is it important to keep waste to a minimum?

6. Why do equipment manufacturers recommend particular resources for their machines?

7. Why is it important to leave the work area ready for the next user?

8. Why should office equipment be kept clean and hygienic?

9. When a new piece of office equipment is delivered, what is the first thing that should be done?

10. Where is the best advice found on how to use a new piece of equipment?

Skills

You may be familiar with some pieces of office equipment, having worked with them in previous jobs. However, you will need to check the office equipment models you will be working with, particularly if they are different from the models you have had previous experience of. Check with your office manager if there are any differences and what the implications of these differences are. If you are coming across new pieces of office equipment of which you have no experience, make sure you ask your manager to cover these either in your induction or additional training. Use the manufacturer's manual or any organisational procedures that might have been prepared to review how to operate office equipment you will operate.

• ACTIVITY 9

Keep a work diary over the period of a month, recording which office equipment you have used and the training you have received. If there is any equipment in your office that you have not been trained to use, speak to your supervisor about getting trained to use it.

Review the office space to find out where the office equipment you will be working with is situated. Is the work area safe, clean and tidy? If not, make sure it is before commencing your operations, as working in a positive environment will make the task more enjoyable. Make sure all the manufacturer's manuals or organisational procedures are accessible for each piece of office equipment.

• ACTIVITY 10

Find all the operating manuals for the office equipment in your office. If there are any missing, ask your supervisor if you can order a copy.

When asked to undertake a task using a piece of office equipment, make sure you clearly understand what it is you have to do. Check the deadline you have for the task. You need to know if you are producing a finished article or a rough draft for internal use. If you know exactly what standard of work is required you will be able to check for yourself whether you have met it, e.g. are copies required in colour or black and white / should copies be single- or double-sided? This will make sure you take as little time as possible executing the task and use as few resources as required.

Minimise the amount of waste produced at all times. Do dummy runs to test out how effectively the piece of office equipment you are using is operating. Make any adjustments or replacements or report any problems. If the task is going to be delayed, check back with the person who gave you the task to let them know and make alternative arrangements. Remember to shred any confidential documents before recycling.

Deal with any problems as they arise by either following instructions of the office equipment or reporting them to the appropriate authority. When completing a task using a piece of office equipment make sure you keep it clean and hygienic and ready for use by the next user.

• ACTIVITY 11

Get your supervisor to record how well you use the below, if these are used in your organisation:

- A computer to send emails, search the Internet and produce letters
- The messaging function on a telephone
- A photocopier to make copies, enlarge and reduce copies
- A printer to use double-sided printing
- A franking machine using different Royal Mail services
- A calculator to work out costs
- A laminator to cover documents etc.
- A binding machine to bind together documents

Testing your skills

1. What office equipment is used in your office?
2. Which pieces of office equipment do you regularly use?
3. Where are the manufacturers' manuals or organisational procedures kept for pieces of office equipment?
4. Who do you ask if you do not understand a manufacturer's manual?
5. Which pieces of equipment do you need authority to operate?
6. Who do you report to if office equipment breaks down?
7. Where are the resources stored for office equipment?
8. Where do you find the postage costs for outgoing mail?
9. Why should paper be stored flat?
10. How do you restock paper and toner in a photocopier, printer and fax machine?
11. How do you keep office equipment clean and hygienic?

Ready for assessment?

To achieve this Level 2 unit of a Business & Administration qualification, learners will need to demonstrate that they are able to perform the following activities:

1. Located and selected office equipment needed for a task

2. Used office equipment following the manufacturer's and organisational guidelines

3. Used office equipment, minimising waste

4. Kept office equipment clean and hygienic

5. Dealt with office equipment problems, following the manufacturer's and organisational procedures

6. Referred problems, if required

7. Made sure final work products met agreed requirements

8. Made sure products were delivered to agreed timescales

9. Made sure office equipment, resources and the work area were ready for the next user

You will need to produce evidence from a variety of sources to support the performance requirements of this unit.

If you carry out the 'ACTIVITIES' and respond to the 'NEED TO KNOW' questions, these will provide some of the evidence required.

Links to other units

While gathering evidence for this unit, evidence **may** also be used from evidence generated from other units within the Business & Administration suite of units. Below is a **sample** of applicable units; however, most units within the Business & Administration suite of units will also be applicable.

QCF NVQ
Communications
Communicate in a business environment (Level 2)
Make and receive telephone calls
Use electronic message systems
Core business & administration
Manage own performance in a business environment (Level 2)
Improve own performance in a business environment (Level 2)
Work in a business environment (Level 2)
Work with other people in a business environment (Level 2)
Customer service
Handle mail
Document production
Produce documents in a business environment
Prepare text from notes

SVQ
Communications
Prepare to communicate in a business environment
Make and receive telephone calls
Use electronic message systems
Core business & administration
Agree how to manage and improve own performance in a business environment
Undertake work in a business environment
Work with other people in a business environment
Customer service
Handle mail
Document production
Produce documents in a business environment
Prepare text from notes

2

Maintain and issue stationery stock items

MAINTAIN AND ISSUE STATIONERY STOCK ITEMS

'Maintain and issue stationery stock items' is an <u>optional</u> unit which may be chosen as one of a combination of units to achieve either a Qualifications and Credit Framework (QCF), National Vocational Qualification (NVQ) or Scottish Vocational Qualification (SVQ).

The aims of this unit are to:

- Understand procedures for maintaining and issuing stationery stock items

- Know how to handle, store and dispose of stationery stock items

- Understand problems that may occur with maintaining and issuing stationery stock items and how to deal with them

- Understand how to make recommendations for improving stationery stock handling

- Be able to maintain stationery stock levels

- Be able to issue items from stationery stock

- Be able to deal with unwanted or damaged items of stationery stock

- Be able to make recommendations to improve stationery stock handling

To achieve the above aims of this unit, learners will be expected to provide evidence through the performance of work-based activities.

Knowledge

Organisations will need to provide their employees with supplies of required stationery stock items to meet their demands for conducting business. Stationery covers a wide range of materials, from paper clips to reams of paper to ink cartridges for office printers. Depending on the size of an organisation, there should be some repository for housing all the stationery stock items employees will use, e.g. a large stationery stock room, a cupboard. Very large organisations may have a dedicated stationery department that will manage the stationery resources for the organisation across different geographical locations.

• ACTIVITY 1

What is stationery?

Stationery stock items should be arranged to provide easy access not only to those who want to use stationery but to those who maintain the volume of stationery stock items. Whoever maintains the stationery items for a business will need to make sure that their stationery room / cupboard is always:

- Fully stocked
- Stocked with the required stationery items
- Replenished when stocks are low
- Kept clean and tidy

Each of the above components will help the employee to maintain stationery requirements to meet the requirements of the employees in a business. While it is important for the stationery person to manage a fully stocked stationery room / cupboard, it is equally important to educate employees on how their stationery needs can be met, e.g. if an employee is doing a very large print run of delegate packs for a conference, they need to check with the stationery person that there are sufficient supplies of paper to complete the run while, at the same time, allowing other members of the office to complete their business printing tasks.

• ACTIVITY 2

How should a stationery room / cupboard be organised?

Stationery stock items should be available to meet the needs of a business. Depending on the size of an organisation, the person who is responsible for maintaining all stationery stock items will need to take stock of all stationery stock items that they are responsible for managing, which is called **stocktaking**. Stocktaking is basically counting all the stock that a business is holding at any given time. Stocktaking should provide

a clear and accurate record of stock levels for all stationery items. The person responsible for stocktaking will make reports recording this information, which can be used for accounting purposes or to continue to monitor stock. All businesses should carry out some form of stationery stocktake, as frequently as required, to make sure stationery stock levels are properly monitored.

A business should always have total control of its **inventory** of stationery stock items to maintain and keep stock levels under control. Taking correct inventory control can be the making or breaking of a business. It is easier to order or reorder stationery stock items more easily and efficiently if accurate records of stationery stock levels are kept. The inventory of stationery stock items can then track which items are in high demand, to make sure that these items are replenished, and destock those items that are used infrequently or may be dead stationery stock items, e.g. letterhead paper which may have the old brand logo of an organisation which is no longer relevant - this stock could either be recycled or used as notepads throughout the organisation. If stock levels get out of control to the extent that it is not known what stationery stock items exist, it could damage the flow of business within an organisation, which could affect the reputation of an organisation. Stationery stock inventories should record all stationery items accurately and legibly, if records are kept manually, in the event that the person responsible for maintaining stationery stock levels is absent from the workplace.

• ACTIVITY 3

What is a stationery stock inventory used for?

A fully inventoried stock of stationery items will allow the person who is managing the maintenance of stationery stock items to **order** the specific requirements of a business, to avoid the production of waste and conform to the environmental policies an organisation has in place. To manage stationery costs, this may mean that some requests for stationery items will not be sanctioned. This usually occurs when a **supplier** of stationery items requires orders to have minimum volumes, which, if large, may be prohibitively expensive for a business, especially when the stationery stock item is limited in use.

Most organisations will have a preferred stationery supplier that they will normally order from. Suppliers will vary in range from a small bespoke stationery business to a larger supplier who will supply not only stationery stock items but all office furniture requirements and other accessories. Again, depending on the size of an organisation, their procurement department will probably have negotiated which stationery supplier to order from based on the business case of the organisation. In very large organisations, where they have an independent stationery department to cater for the needs of the organisation across different locations, orders will be placed through this department.

Ordering stationery stock items may occur:

- **Cyclically** - Depending on the size of the organisation, ordering stationery may occur every week, month etc., based on stock item movement which has been analysed over years of use, which highlights periods when high volumes of specific stock may be required

- **On demand** - Stationery may be ordered on a needs basis when requested by employees

• ACTIVITY 4

How often could organisations order stationery stock items?

When preparing to make an order, the person maintaining the stationery will usually notify either the organisation or individual departments that they will be ordering stationery stock items at a particular time in order for employees to identify individual requests for stock items. This practice will vary depending on the size of an organisation. Orders may be produced automatically using electronic alerts to the stationery stock supplier. This is more likely to happen in large organisations where stationery stock items may be controlled electronically. Or stock may be ordered manually either by telephoning or electronically ordering with the stationery supplier. When ordering stationery stock items always check that:

- Correct **volumes** of stock items have been ordered. Always make sure that there is sufficient stock to meet the requirements of the business. If too much stock is ordered it may not be possible to store it adequately, which could result in stock being damaged or ruined. Too much stock could also be a drain on the stationery budget, which may prevent orders of more important stationery stock items. Too little stock may jeopardise the successful day-to-day running of business activities within an organisation

- Correct **size** of stock has been ordered
- Correct stock items, **code numbers**, have been ordered
- The correct **price** has been charged
- The **date of delivery** has been agreed
- The form **invoices / bills** will take and period of payment. Alternatively, a business may require the issuing of receipts, particularly if they are able to claim back VAT

• ACTIVITY 5

What should be checked when ordering stationery stock items?

It is important that an order is double-checked to make sure that the order meets the business needs of a business. Ordering stationery stock items, like most functions carried out in a business, requires planning. For example, if a board meeting is coming up, plan for sufficient letterheaded paper and envelopes to alert stockholders. Orders of stationery should also take into account an organisation's **environmental policies**, e.g. an organisation may decide that its employees can only use recycled paper rather than high-quality paper for printing, unless for high profile documents, or clip small bundles of paper together not using staples.

Once the order has been **delivered** it should be checked to make sure that all stationery items that were ordered have been delivered on time, in the correct quantity, quality maintained, using the correct brand etc. If there are any **problems** encountered as a result of any of these areas not being satisfied, the stationery items should not be opened or used and the supplier should be notified - some deliveries of stationery items may take place in the delivery bay of an organisation, print room etc., or the person to whom they should have been delivered was not available so they could not be checked in situ. Arrangements should then be agreed for their replacement. An organisation may have specific arrangements to follow in the event of problems with the supply and delivery of stationery items, which should be adhered to.

• ACTIVITY 6

What problems could occur with the delivery of stationery stock items?

Stock items should then be organised in the stationery stock room / cupboard so that they are available and accessible to the stocktaker and employees. The supplies should be checked to make sure that there are no damages. If there are any damaged stationery items, these should be reported to the supplier as soon as possible, so that they can be replaced. Most organisations will have service agreements in place with their suppliers in the event of damage or delay to orders.

Special care should be taken when **storing** the delivery of stationery items. For example, boxes of paper housing five reams of paper will be heavy and bound with plastic tape. These boxes should be lifted and carried using organisational **health and safety guidelines**. In this particular example, bend the knees and not the back to pick up the box and do not carry it by the plastic tape.

Organisations may provide gloves to keep hands free from dirt / cuts / bruises. For large deliveries into a warehouse where the stationery stock items have been delivered on palettes, these will either have to be unpacked or moved about by pallet jacks. Training should be given to people using specialist equipment to move stationery stock items about the workplace to preserve the safety of people's lives and the fabric of an organisation's building (s). To assist with the inventory of stationery stock items, they should be stored methodically, allowing easy access to them. The stationery store area should be kept clean and tidy at all times.

Stationery stock items will then be issued depending on organisational procedures, e.g. employees may have access to take stationery stock as required or it will only be handled by the person responsible for handling stationery stock items. The latter case is probably better as they can keep a keener eye on stationery stock levels in their stationery storeroom / cupboard. Some organisations may have cost centres against which they will charge specific departments or teams for the issuing of stationery stock items. Stationery stock items will be coded and costed against these departments. In some cases, the initial order may have to be countersigned by a manager, particularly if the cost of the order is very large.

There should be a system of recording all the information from what has been ordered, delivered, stored, issued etc. This can be done either manually or using electronic means. It should be accurate and meaningful and add to the goals of the business.

There is a great variety of ways that stationery stock items can be maintained and managed by different organisations. As suppliers use more and more technology, organisations will need to consider how they may want to deliver this function in the future. Costs will also need to be managed. Reviews should take place to analyse the total costs of stationery items used in an organisation and seek ways to reduce these by reviewing the different service agreements that other stationery suppliers can offer. Every opportunity is an opportunity which can be used to improve the ordering, delivery, storing, issuing, stocktaking and disposing of unwanted or damaged stationery stock items.

Testing your knowledge

1. Why should stationery stock items be arranged methodically?

2. What is meant by stocktaking?

3. When is the best time to stocktake?

4. What is an inventory?

5. When should an order of stationery stock items be made?

6. What is the purpose of having environmentally friendly polices to govern the way stationery stock items are managed and maintained?

7. What is the best way to store stationery stock items?

8. What is the best way to issue stationery stock items to employees?

9. Why do organisations have a health and safety policy on lifting heavy items?

Skills

There is a great variety of ways an organisation will manage and maintain the ordering, delivery, storing, issuing, stocktaking and disposing of unwanted or damaged stationery stock items. As with any function undertaken in an organisation, your role is to be a part of maximising the profitable output of your organisation. So it is important that if this function falls within your area of responsibility that you conform to your organisation's policies and procedures. As with most things in any business, it is imperative to keep costs down and, therefore, stationery stock items should only be ordered when they are required within the business. Identify what stationery stock items are most frequently used and therefore need replenishing. You could identify these items on a list which is automatically ordered every week, fortnight, month etc., so you do not have to think about these items. These items could also be organised in a different way in your stationery storeroom / cupboard.

• ACTIVITY 7

Outline how you make an order and what you do to make sure it has been delivered as ordered.

Acquaint yourself with the different suppliers you use, if you use a variety of suppliers. Review the quality of the service that they are providing from time to time - can it be improved? Does the service contract with the supplier need to be renegotiated? Discuss this with your supervisor / manager, as they will probably have the authority to agree any changes you think are appropriate. Your role is not only to monitor the current volume of stationery stock items that you manage and maintain but also to consider ways of improving the service you provide, e.g. minimising costs. This could be done, e.g. by monitoring who uses stationery the most and how often the stationery stock items they use need replenishing to keep stock full.

To manage the volume and quality of stocks of your stationery you should undertake a stocktake of your inventory of stock items. Again, this may need to conform to the requirements of organisational policy and procedures. Make sure that your stationery room / cupboard has been organised so it is easy for you and your clients to manage. It should be done at regular intervals so you can manage costs, damage, disposal etc., of stationery stock items. Use the source of information you have collected from this stocktake to analyse the movement of stationery stock items you manage and maintain. Are there any trends that stand out on how often you reorder particular items? Are there damages with the same stock item? Do these occur with the same supplier, if your company uses more than one supplier?

Make sure that when you place an order that you are placing the correct order. Check through everything that you are ordering to make sure you have the correct volumes, quality etc. Before you order, how do you alert other employees that you are about to make an order? Do you visit department heads to make an announcement or send out an email alert? When an order is being delivered make sure that all items you have ordered have been delivered and in good quality. Resolve any problems as they arise or refer them to the appropriate authority. If an order is late, contact the supplier (s) to find out what the problem is. Issue all stationery stock items as required and in line with your organisation's policies and procedures.

• ACTIVITY 8

Keep a log of the different problems that you have encountered managing and maintaining stationery stock items. How did you resolve these problems? Did any of them lead to identifying ways of improving how you facilitate this function?

Keep records accurate, up to date and available to those who have been authorised access to this information.

Dispose of unwanted or damaged stationery stock items as required and in line with organisational policies and procedures. Use recycling where appropriate.

With the information you have acquired from managing and maintaining the stock of stationery items, look at ways of improving the service you provide. Discuss your ideas with your supervisor / manager to see how feasible and viable they are.

Testing your skills

1. What are your organisational policies for managing and maintaining the ordering, delivery, storing, issuing, stocktaking and disposing of unwanted or damaged stationery stock items?

2. How do you know when to place an order for stationery stock items?

3. How often do you stocktake stationery stock items?

4. How do you stocktake stationery stock items?

5. How do you order stationery stock items?

6. What do you do in the event of an incorrect delivery of stationery stock items?

7. What do you do when you find that damaged stationery stock items have been delivered?

8. What have you done to improve the ordering, delivery, storing, issuing, stocktaking and disposing of unwanted or damaged stationery stock items?

Ready for assessment?

To achieve this Level 2 unit of a Business & Administration qualification, learners will need to demonstrate that they have performed the following activities:

1. Maintained stationery stock items to required levels

2. Handled and stored stationery stock safely and securely, having maintained their condition and followed organisational procedures

3. Carried out stocktakes as instructed and reported problems

4. Ordered stationery stock from suppliers within limits of own authority

5. Chased up orders with suppliers

6. Checked incoming deliveries against orders and reported any problems

7. Kept up-to-date, accurate and legible records of stationery stock delivered and held

8. Issued stationery stock items as requested, having followed organisational procedures

9. Kept up-to-date, accurate and legible records of stationery stock items issued

10. Disposed of unwanted or damaged stationery stock items safely, having followed organisational procedures and legal requirements

11. Identified and recommended ways in which systems for receiving, issuing and disposing of stationery stock could be improved, as required

You will need to produce evidence from a variety of sources to support the performance requirements of this unit.

If you carry out the 'ACTIVITIES' and respond to the 'NEED TO KNOW' questions, these will provide some of the evidence required.

Links to other units

While gathering evidence for this unit, evidence **may** also be used from evidence generated from other units within the Business & Administration suite of units. Below is a **sample** of applicable units; however, most units within the Business & Administration suite of units will also be applicable.

QCF NVQ
Communications
Communicate in a business environment (Level 2)
Core business & administration
Manage own performance in a business environment (Level 2)
Improve own performance in a business environment (Level 2)
Solve business problems (Level 2)
Work with other people in a business environment (Level 2)
Customer service
Provide reception services

SVQ
Communications
Prepare to communicate in a business environment
Core business & administration
Agree how to manage and improve own performance in a business environment
Plan how to solve business problems
Work with other people in a business environment
Customer service
Provide reception services

3

Use a diary system

USE A DIARY SYSTEM

'**Use a diary system**' is an <u>optional unit</u> which may be chosen as one of a combination of units to achieve either a Qualifications and Credit Framework (QCF), National Vocational Qualification (NVQ) or Scottish Vocational Qualification (SVQ).

The aims of this unit are to:

- Understand a diary system

- Understand how to use a diary system

- Be able to use a diary system

To achieve the above aims of this unit, learners will be expected to provide evidence through the performance of work-based activities.

Knowledge
Definition of a diary system
A diary system is used in a business environment to assist with the **planning** and **organising** of activities and resources performed and used by employees. Activities may include attending meetings, internal, external or virtual; attending conferences; allocating time to travel; due dates for reports; routine daily activities etc., while resources may include scheduling the delivery of stationery stock items; stocktaking etc. A diary system is a tool that enables **time management**. Time management is a skill used to manage time as a resource. It enables employees to **prioritise** tasks and objectives to complete projects within agreed timescales.

• ACTIVITY 1

What is time management?

Using a diary system gives the user a complete picture of everything that is planned to be done at all times, e.g. during the day, over a week, throughout a month. It allows users to stay up to date and avoid scheduling conflicts. Every day, working in a business, employees will find that they have to change their plans - change is the only constant in an organisation. This may have an impact on the activities that users have scheduled in their diaries. It is essential that changes to scheduled activities are identified. Changes to diary entries should then be communicated to all relevant users. This will avoid confusion and time wasting.

Diary systems may be implemented either individually or on behalf of someone else, e.g. as a personnel assistant looking after the daily activities of their supervisor / manager. There are various types of diary systems, depending on the information that needs to be kept.

• ACTIVITY 1

Why is a diary system used?

Electronic diary system

An electronic diary is currently the most frequently used diary system. Most users will have a personal computer (PC) with a calendar function. Alternatively, web-based diaries are available in the form wireless mobile devices, e.g. 'BlackBerrys', 'iPods'. The technology to access PC information from a mobile phone has become commonplace, which

is supported by a server which connects everyone within a business, enabling them to plan and organise appointments and meetings between users.

An electronic diary system is based in real time. It provides the most up-to-date information in a user's system. It allows users to access other users' diaries to check their availability and invite other users to an appointment or meeting. This also allows users to identify conflicting arrangements and save time by adjusting their invitations. Users can also be connected to databases so they have easy access to telephone numbers, etc. The advantages of using an electronic diary system are:

- Faster to use

- Easier to use

- Cheaper to use

- Software will update new functions as technology advances

- Will update information immediately in real time. Invitations are updated into the diary system automatically

- The system is not paper based, so it reduces paperwork and allows invitations to be changed easily, clearly and efficiently

- There is an automatic reminder system, displayed on a screen, which will inform the user that an appointment is approaching. This function can be modified to a user's requirements, e.g. five-minute reminder, one-day reminder

- It is 'virtual', which allows users' diaries to be shared between multiple users across different geographical locations. However, access to diary pages can be restricted using a password -protection function, so that confidential information cannot be seen by unauthorised people

As with all electronic appliances, there is the risk of a system failure, which could result in all of the information becoming unavailable or lost. There is also the danger of an electronic system being open to hacking. While a desktop computer is not portable, there are sufficient portable electronic appliances available to users, if they  have the authority to use such appliances. While computer literacy has increased over the past decade, some potential users may not have the required level of skill and knowledge to use an electronic diary system, and training will be required to enable potential users to use an electronic diary with skill.

• ACTIVITY 3

What are some of the advantages and disadvantages of using an electronic diary system?

Some of the functions of an electronic diary system are:

- Shows entries by day, week, work week or full week or month

- Views all appointments, recurring appointments, events, annual events, by category

- Allows groups to be created for recurring appointments or meetings

- Creates an address book of contact names and telephone numbers
- Uses all the functions that a software program offers, e.g. Microsoft

Paper-based diary

A paper-based diary system can be used in exactly the same way as an electronic diary to plan and organise appointments or meetings and action activities. Diary entries can be made accurately and preferably in pencil, to allow changes to be made easily and clearly. Paper-based diary systems are not as flexible or as efficient as an electronic-based diary system.

The disadvantages of using a paper-based diary system are:

- It does not allow other users instant access to diary entries, if at all. Other users are unable to monitor your activities, so they are unable to make amendments to activities as they change, particularly changes at short notice
- It may contain confidential or highly classified information which, in the event of being lost or stolen, may be read by unintended audiences, which could jeopardise the security of a business
- It is restricted by size, so this limits the amount of information that can be recorded on each page
- It does not link with other information stored or circulated in an organisation
- If it gets lost there may be no back-up, unlike an electronic diary system
- Legibility

• ACTIVITY 4

What is the difference between an electronic diary system and a paper-based diary system?

A wall planner

This form of diary system usually covers a whole year, with spaces for each day. It may be laminated, which allows amendments to be made easily using the correct type of pen. Alternatively, coloured stickers

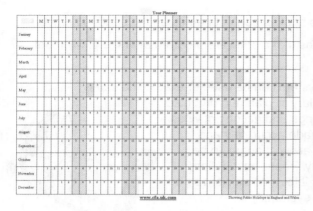

www.cfa.uk.com

Showing Public Holidays in England and Wales

can be attached to the planner to give a graphic display of information. Wall planners are used for long-term planning, e.g. staff holidays, sickness, event planning. The recording of different types of information will allow users to see at a glance whether too many people are on holiday at the same time. Wall planners are also useful for displaying deadlines for projects and planning promotions or events. As wall planners are a very public record of past, current and future events, confidential information will probably not be displayed, unless it is in a room that has restricted access.

Users should be aware of the dangers of maintaining two or more versions of a diary system. It may be convenient, from the point of view of being able to carry the paper version and still have all the advantages of the electronic system; however, it is vital that any changes made to one are made to the other as soon as possible, to avoid confusion.

Testing your knowledge

1. What are the different types of diary systems that can be used?

2. What are the major differences between an electronic diary system and a paper-based diary system?

3. What is the purpose of having a wall planner?

4. What procedures should be in place to notify attendees of diary entry amendments?

5. What problems may occur when amendments are made to a diary using different diary systems?

6. Why should amendments be updated to a diary system as soon as possible?

7. What steps would be taken to deal with diary system problems?

8. What is the purpose of keeping a diary system up to date?

9. Why should security implications be taken into account when organising a diary system?

Skills

Diary entries

When making a diary entry it is important to enter information accurately and clearly. Check the information obtained for a diary entry to confirm the information is correct or to clarify any points. The following aspects of an appointment or meeting are required to make a diary entry:

*   Purpose
*   Date
*   Time
*   Location

- Attendees
- Duration

The user must make sure that the diary entries are kept up to date. Users must also make sure that diaries are stored securely or only allow access to nominated users.

Changes to diary entries

If users' plans change, it may be necessary to make a change to a diary entry. It is important to make sure that all relevant information is obtained to make the necessary amendments to a diary entry. If electronic diaries are not used, requests for amendments to diary entries may be made by telephone, fax, email, letter or verbally. It is important to confirm that all intended amendments have been fully understood to make the requested changes.

Some requested changes may appear to be minor, e.g. amending an appointment from 09.00 to 10.00, but the impact could be significant. The change could have major implications for existing commitments, as all other appointments for the rest of the day could be delayed or may have to be rescheduled for another day. Original plans will need to be checked to identify what other appointments / meetings will be affected by a requested change to a diary entry. If a requested change will have implications for existing diary entries, alternative arrangements will have to be made.

The efficient planning and organising of a diary system is a vital part of contributing to the smooth running of a work environment and, indeed, the whole organisation. Keeping a diary is not a trivial part of your daily routine. Imagine the chaos there would be in a work environment if everybody had to remember where they should be, when they should be there and what they should be doing at any given time. Whichever type of diary system is used, organising the amendments to diary entries and making sure that everybody has the latest diary entry information is an important responsibility.

• ACTIVITY 5

The HR manager has telephoned to say that she will not be in today due to illness. She has a number of appointments in her diary. What methods would you use to rearrange her diary?

Prioritising changes to diary entries

A number of requests to amend existing diary entries may be received simultaneously. These will need to be prioritised to make sure that diary amendments are made to imminent events first. Some requested changes may not be that straightforward to amend. They may be dependent on the importance and / or urgency of a requested change. In some circumstances, it may result in a refusal to attend an amended invitation.

Communicating changes to diary entries

When recording agreed changes in the diary, remember to amend anything that is affected by later arrangements. Delete appointments that have been cancelled. It is a waste of time and resources, as well as embarrassing, to turn up to a meeting when it has been cancelled. An electronic planner will allow the user to update other people's diaries automatically.

It is important to communicate the agreed schedule alterations on time, if an electronic diary system is not being used, and to the appropriate people who will be affected by the amendments. This may be done by various forms of communication, e.g. telephone, fax, email. It needs to be completed even where networked diary software is in place. An electronic diary system will send a diary alert to make users aware of an impending appointment. An electronic diary alert can be customised to let users know of an appointment in advance, e.g. in five minutes, thirty minutes, four hours.

The method of communication will vary depending on who the user is communicating with. Further consideration will also be given to issues of security and confidentiality, e.g. arranging meetings that involve royalty, politicians or celebrities. Other types of meetings which may be considered as high security and confidential are:

- Disciplinary or grievance interviews

- Research and development meetings discussing new products and services

- Appraisal meetings

A diary must be kept up to date or it serves no purpose. People rely on the information in a diary, e.g. telephone numbers, notes for a meeting, the email invitation to attend a meeting / appointment. This information is what a user needs to plan and organise their daily work. It helps them to organise activities for future work activities. Make sure all changes are made as soon as possible after they have been agreed. Check regularly. If a mistake occurs, investigate the reason for the error and take steps to prevent it from reoccurring.

• ACTIVITY 6

Keep a work diary over the period of a month, recording amendments you have made to your diary system.

Solving problems

If there is a conflict of diary entries, refer to the original plans to identify alternative arrangements. This may require the user to contact a number of users to advise them that the arrangements have had to be amended and to negotiate other schedules with them. This may require some tact and diplomacy to avoid giving the impression that something more important has come up.

• ACTIVITY 7

You are responsible for keeping the diary of the Sales Manager of a building contractor. The diary below is his current schedule for 21st July.

At 16.00 on 20th July, the Managing Director's secretary calls to advise that the meeting scheduled for 09.30 tomorrow has been rearranged for 11.00.

The meeting for the MRA has been organised for the past six weeks and they are a valued supplier.

- How would you deal with the alteration to the schedule?
- Would the meeting at 16.00 be publicly displayed? What would you do?
- How could the planned meeting due to take place at 17.30 be displayed in the diary system?

Thursday 21st July:
09:00
Budget meeting with MD (MD's Office)
10:00
11:00 Client meeting at MRA
12:00
13:00 Lunch with John Smith (John's office)
14:00 Finance meeting with Mable
15:00 Sales Dept meeting (Matthew Jones Office)
16:00 Disciplinary Hearing with Jane Butters
17:00
Drinks With Sam and James

Testing your skills

1. How do you use an electronic diary system?
2. How do you use a paper-based diary system?
3. How do you use a wall planner to organise staff holidays?
4. Whose diary are you responsible for organising, if required?
5. What confidential information do you deal with that goes into a diary system?
6. What types of diary systems does your organisation use?
7. How do you deal with problems relating to diary systems?

Ready for assessment?

To achieve this Level 2 unit of a Business & Administration qualification, learners will need to demonstrate that they are able to perform the following activities:

1. Obtained the information needed about requested diary entries
2. Made diary entries accurately and clearly
3. Prioritised requested changes
4. Identified the implications of any changes for existing entries
5. Solved problems by negotiating alternative arrangements
6. Recorded agreed changes in the diary
7. Communicated agreed changes to those affected
8. Kept the diary up to date

Remember that you will need to produce evidence from a variety of sources to support the performance requirements of this unit.

If you carry out the 'ACTIVITIES' and respond to the 'NEED TO KNOW' questions, these will provide some of the evidence required.

Links to other units

While gathering evidence for this unit, evidence **may** also be used from evidence generated from other units within the Business & Administration suite of units. Below is a **sample** of applicable units; however, most units within the Business & Administration suite of units will also be applicable.

QCF NVQ
Communications
Communicate in a business environment (Level 1)
Communicate in a business environment (Level 2)
Communicate in a business environment (Level 3)
Make and receive telephone calls
Provide reception services
Core business & administration
Manage own performance in a business environment (Level 2)
Improve own performance in a business environment (Level 2)
Work in a business environment (Level 2)
Work with other people in a business environment (Level 2)
Solve business problems (Level 2)

SVQ
Communications
Understand how to communicate in a business environment
Prepare to communicate in a business environment
Communicate in a business environment (Level 3)
Make and receive telephone calls
Provide reception services
Core business & administration
Agree how to manage and improve own performance in a business environment
Undertake work in a business environment
Work with other people in a business environment
Plan how to solve business problems

4 Take minutes

TAKE MINUTES

'Take minutes' is an optional unit which may be chosen as one of a combination of units to achieve either a Qualifications and Credit Framework (QCF), National Vocational Qualification (NVQ) or Scottish Vocational Qualification (SVQ).

The aims of this unit are to:

- Understand the task of taking minutes at meetings
- Understand the role of the chair and other formal responsibilities in meetings
- Know how to take minutes at meetings
- Be able to prepare for taking minutes
- Be able to minute meetings

To achieve the above aims of this unit, learners will be expected to provide evidence through the performance of work-based activities.

Knowledge
What are minutes?
Minutes are an official written record of the discussion and outcomes agreed from a meeting. Minutes are a **reference tool** for participants and non-participants of a meeting. A meeting is arranged to bring together at least two people for the purpose of:

- **Solving or resolving business problems -** These may range from research and development or sorting out issues to dealing with difficult employees in the workplace
- **Sharing information -** Providing a platform for the giving or receiving of information, e.g. explaining new policies within the organisation, learning new procedures
- **Decision-making -** Identifying available options, seeking authorisation for the delivery of an option before implementing it
- **Developing -** New systems, ideas, practices or processes

• ACTIVITY 1

What is the purpose of taking minutes at a meeting?

Minutes can be taken for the following types of meetings:

- **Formal -** These types of meetings may include: board meetings; annual general meetings (AGMs); public forums, e.g. shareholder meetings; conferences; appraisal meetings; disciplinary hearings or team meetings. Generally, formal meetings are arranged for more than four people who need to inform others of decisions agreed at a meeting. The format for taking minutes will involve a lot of detail, not necessarily word for word, though this will depend on the reason for taking the minutes. This will vary, depending on the legal or regulatory necessity of attributing who contributed to the discussion and decisions taken. In some instances, it is a legal requirement to record the outcomes of a meeting, e.g. a public board meeting

- **Informal -** These types of meetings may include: one-to-one meetings or impromptu meetings. The format is less formal and may only record agreed actions to be taken

Formal Meeting

Informal Meeting

Minutes may be issued and made available to the public, if this is a legal requirement for the organisation, or only available as a private record, e.g. within an organisation where commercial decisions are too sensitive to share publicly. Decisions that are made and the issues discussed during a meeting are crucial to the continued productivity of a business. It is important to keep a record of decisions and discussions in an **organised** and **methodical** fashion. While it may not be a legal obligation to maintain minutes, it is considered good practice to maintain them as verification of a collaborative approach to the decision-making process within an organisation.

The **Freedom of Information Act 2000** provides public access to records created by a Board and its employees, which includes minutes from a meeting. However, there are exemptions from the Act which allow non-disclosure of either full or partial information, depending on the commercial sensitivity of the information recorded in the minutes.

The **Data Protection Act 1998** sets out the rules for processing personal information, facts and opinions about the individual. It applies to paper records and those stored on computers. The Act refers to 'personal data', i.e. data about identifiable living individuals. The rules of good information handling, known as the data protection principles, state that data / information must be processed:

- Fairly and lawfully
- For limited purposes
- Adequately, relevantly and not excessively
- Accurately
- So that it is not kept for longer than is necessary
- In line with the data subject's rights
- Securely
- So that it is not transferred to countries without adequate data protection

Information / data recorded as a result of taking minutes should take account of these principles, to protect all employees and the commercial interests of an organisation.

• ACTIVITY 2

How should minutes comply with relevant legislation and organisational processes?

Documents and terms used during a meeting

Most meetings will either provide documents to attendees in advance or they will be tabled, see Table 4.1. below, on the day of the meeting. Documents are an essential means of providing information to members of a meeting and are provided to enrich discussion. Documents should provide all of the information from which meeting attendees are able to take actions and make decisions.

The types of documents that may be included at a meeting are:

- **Working documents** - Documents which specifically target the subject area for which attendees have been invited to discuss and make decisions on. This could include guidelines; arrangements for the meeting, e.g. an agenda; Terms of Reference (ToR); Memorandum of Understanding (MoU)

- **Background papers** - Documents which provide an update on issues previously discussed at a meeting. They may also be documents that offer a history or context within which meeting attendees will be informed to enable them to discuss agenda items

- **General information documents** - Documents of various types, e.g. reports from international meetings

- **Starter papers** - Documents which allow the discussion and development of ideas

- **Briefing notes** - A short summary of key issues that may be discussed at a meeting

- **Papers produced during the course of a meeting**

Like many aspects of business, there is a degree of jargon connected with the running of meetings. A minute taker will need to be familiar with most of the terms listed in Table 4.1. below, depending on the level of formality of the meeting. This glossary is not exclusive, as there are more terms, particularly Latin terms, that are used in the context of a meeting.

WORD / PHRASE	MEANING
Ad hoc - Latin	For the purpose of
Adjourn	Continue the meeting at a later time / date
Adopt minutes	Minutes signed off by the meeting attendees and chairperson
Advisory	Provide advice
Agenda	Schedule of items to be discussed at the meeting
Agenda item	Individual topic for discussion
AGM	Annual general meeting
Any other business	Unidentified agenda items raised at the end of a meeting
Apologies	A reason for not attending a meeting

Attendance list	List of attendees at a meeting
Bye-laws	Rules to regulate activities
Casting vote	Used if votes are equally divided
Chairperson	Person given the authority to lead the meeting
Consensus	General consent of meeting members - no formal vote taken
Convene	Call a meeting
Executive	The power to act on decisions taken
Extraordinary meeting	A non-routine meeting convened for a specific purpose
Ex officio - Latin	Given power or rights because of the office held
Guillotine	Cut short a debate
Intra vires - Latin	Within the power of the meeting
Lie on the table	Consider an agenda item at the next meeting
Motion	Name given to a proposal being discussed at a meeting
Opposer	Person who speaks against a motion
Point of information	Focus on a relevant fact
Point of order	Notice of a breach of rules or procedures
Proposal	Item submitted for discussion at the meeting
Proxy	On behalf of another
Quorum	Minimum number of people in attendance for a meeting to begin
Refer back	Return to a previous item for discussion
Resolution	Passing of a motion
Seconder	Person who supports the proposer's motion
Secretary	Administrator of the meeting
Standing orders	Rules of procedure
Table	Introduce a document at the meeting
Taken as read	Assumes meeting members are aware of this
Unanimous	Everybody in favour

Table 4.1. Glossary of terms used in the context of meetings

Roles and responsibilities of meeting officials

To achieve the successful performance and conclusion of a meeting, expectations of the meeting attendees need to be managed. Attendees need to have a clear understanding of their role and responsibility in agreeing to attend a meeting. If not, the meeting will be difficult to manage, raising challenges for all in attendance.

Some of the roles and responsibilities of those attending a meeting are listed below:

Chairperson

The chairperson has a number of roles to which they must attend to, including planning, coordinating, managing, facilitating, leading and contributing to the meeting. Their responsibilities also include having to:

- **Plan and coordinate the meeting in line with agreed processes** - This may include: writing meeting objectives, negotiating meeting time and date with attendees, booking the venue, inviting attendees, inviting special guests and planning catering, if required. This function will also involve working closely with the minute taker

- **Manage the meeting process** - By making sure all meeting roles are assigned and expectations clearly communicated. Prepare the agenda and any other resources in time to address the agenda items. Make sure all attendees are able to attend at the agreed time

- **Facilitate and lead the meeting** - By directing the meeting process by keeping to the agenda and agenda items. Guide and lead discussions, making sure all attendees are given the opportunity for equal participation. Make sure the agenda runs to the agreed time schedule. Manage attendee participation in discussions, making sure that no one attendee dominates discussions. Maintain respect for all contributions to the agenda items

- **Contribute ideas and strategies to discussions** - Including brainstorming and short presentations and workshops

Secretary

The role of the secretary starts before the meeting and continues during and after the meeting, while making sure that all components of the meeting are successful. This role may include the responsibilities of the minute taker. The secretary is responsible for:

Effective Communications

- Maintaining of an up-to-date distribution list for the organisation

- Being the first point of contact for the organisation

- Filing all necessary information, if a registered body

Treasurer

The role of the treasurer is to make sure that the appropriate financial records and procedures are in place. Their responsibilities include:

- Producing financial reports

- Arranging an external audit - As provided for by the organisation's roles

- Presenting accounts at the AGM

Minute taker

Like the chairperson, the minute taker has a number of roles to fulfil, some of which will be undertaken in partnership with the chairperson. Roles performed by the minute taker include: working with the chairperson to sign off the meeting process and documentation, co-ordinating the agenda, writing the agenda, writing the minutes during the meeting, transcribing the minutes, disseminating the minutes and, if appropriate, facilitating discussion during the meeting. The minute taker is responsible for:

- **Working in partnership with the chairperson** to achieve the aims of the meeting. This will take place over three phases:

  - Before the meeting: make sure all the administration for the meeting and minute taking is in place

  - During the meeting: keep the meeting on track and pick up signals / cues from the chairperson throughout the meeting

  - After the meeting: sign off minutes and any lessons to be learned from the delivery and management of the meeting

- **Planning, designing and finalising the agenda** in line with agreed meeting protocols. Invite attendees to contribute to the agenda items. Send the provisional agenda to attendees for their confirmation. Design content for the final agenda, including new items and items carried forward from the previous meeting. Send the final agenda to the meeting attendees

- **Recording key discussion and action points during the meeting** and to take notes throughout the meeting which conform to the organisation's minute-taking principles. Liaise with the chairperson and attendees to check that the minutes are an accurate reflection of the discussion that took place at the meeting. Finalise the transcribed minutes and disseminate them to all those invited to the meeting, including those who sent apologies, creating a full and accurate record of the meeting

Timekeeper

The role of the timekeeper is to make sure all agenda items are discussed sufficiently within the time constraints of the meeting. This role may not be specifically allocated, but undertaken by either the chairperson or the minute taker. The responsibilities of the timekeeper include:

- **Assisting the chairperson** to maintain the meeting in line with the agenda item timings and make sure the meeting stays on track and within time

- **Informing the meeting / chairperson when five minutes is remaining on each agenda item**

Facilitator

The role of the facilitator is to inform meeting attendees of progress within specific projects. The responsibilities of a facilitator include:

- **Planning and managing** - Specific special projects, as required

- **Leading and facilitating** - Workshops within the meeting

- **Recording and managing** - The progress of special projects

- **Managing team communications** - In relation to special projects, to make sure that all project members are kept informed of progress and know their roles and responsibilities within the project

Meeting participant

The role of the meeting participant is to contribute to the design and creation of the final agenda, contribute to discussions and brainstorms throughout the meeting and be a member of a project (s), as required. Their responsibilities include:

- **Contributing appropriate items** - To the meeting agenda

- **Contributing to discussions** - Brainstorming, strategic planning and special projects during the meeting

- **Undertaking assigned special project tasks**

- **Reading meeting minutes** - Before they are finalised. Keep up to date with team and business information, strategic planning and special project initiatives

• ACTIVITY 3

Compare and contrast the roles and responsibilities of a meeting secretary and a minute taker.

Approach to taking minutes

The format for taking minutes may vary from organisation to organisation. This will depend on the purpose of the meeting, the degree of formality the minutes should take or the '**house style**' of the organisation.

The minutes taken at a meeting will start as **rough notes**. These rough notes will be recorded as a result of discussions throughout the meeting, and will need to be **clear** enough for them to be transcribed after the meeting. As a rule, the minute taker should:

- Leave enough space between each line of the notes, to enable additions if the meeting returns to an earlier topic

- Identify decisions or 'action points' that have been agreed. Record the reasoning behind the decisions and agreed action points. If alternatives were suggested, record why these were agreed to be unsuitable

- Focus on points made for and against a proposal or idea and the reasons to support these points

- Record points, not people, and focus on the ideas, arguments and facts. Identify who has said what and if this is the agreed procedure. This could be done by adding names after the heading of the item being recorded: divide the page in half, so one column records who has agreed to the decision and who will action them, or insert the relevant names against the corresponding agenda item

- Record all the necessary information and no more

- Assume that people reading the notes will not necessarily know what is being discussed. Notes should begin with appropriate 'background notes' to the item being recorded. Do not refer to 'they', 'them' etc., but specify who each of these individuals or groups of individuals are

- Write the minutes as soon as possible after the meeting, when the information is still fresh in their mind

By following these guidelines, it will help to avoid some of the **difficulties** that may be encountered, where:

- The discussion jumps from one item to another without any resolution or agreement regarding future actions

- All members of the meeting are talking at once. This makes it difficult for the minute taker to follow and decide what is relevant to record and what has been agreed

- Discussions may be long and meander from topic to topic, making it difficult to recognise which bits of the discussion should be recorded

- The attention of the minute taker is distracted by getting involved in the discussion while taking notes

- The minute taker may be nervous

Avoiding Difficulties
To **avoid some of these difficulties**, the minute taker should make sure that:

- The meeting is run well. The chairperson should organise the meeting so that it keeps to the agenda and allocated time. The chairperson should ask for the co-operation of the meeting members and will:

  - Record when a member of the meeting wishes to make a contribution to the discussion. They will then be nominated by the chairperson to make their contribution once the previous speaker has finished. Only one voice will then be heard at any one time

  - Remind those attending the meeting that an accurate record of the meeting cannot take place if everyone is talking at once

  - Remind those attending the meeting to follow the agenda

  - Clarify points of discussion and the actions agreed

  - Check with the minute taker when an important or controversial decision has been agreed

- The minute taker should consider when they wish to join in any discussions. If there is an important discussion which affects the minute taker directly, they could ask either the chairperson or another member of the meeting to continue their notes for this part of the meeting

- For long discussions, the main points should be picked out and summarised to those attending the meeting for their agreement, e.g. 'There was a long discussion about ... and the following points and decisions were made ...'

- The agenda is discussed with the chairperson before the meeting - the clearer the minute taker is about the content of the meeting, the easier it is to record it

- Rough notes are checked with the chairperson, immediately after the meeting, for accuracy and detail

- The minute taker realises that confidence and perfection come with practice. It will become easier to minute meetings the more practice they have

- The minute taker has access to previous notes at the meeting in case any questions are asked about previous decisions

For rough notes to be **meaningful**, the minute taker will **NOT** write everything down. Use a tape recorder instead, as this will lead the minute taker to:

- Waste their time

- Lose track of discussions

- Disrupt the discussion by asking to backtrack, which will interrupt the attendees' train of thought

- Focus on agreed **actions** and **whose** task it is to carry this out

Listening

Listening, in the context of taking notes and transcribing them into minutes, is probably the most important aspect of taking minutes. In a sense, it is an 'art' that needs to be honed and articulated to help the minute taker maximise the quality of the notes they record. Listening at a meeting is different from everyday listening in conversation. Here are some ideas on how to improve listening:

- **Active listening skills -** If clarification is required, ask the speaker to say more. Give feedback or paraphrase what was discussed. Use physical signals to show interest. Maintain eye contact with the speaker

- **Identify personal filters and triggers** - Everyone is a product of their upbringing, culture, life experiences etc. This can sometimes be an obstacle to being an effective listener. When listening, try to remain open to what is being heard. Pay attention to the triggers in the verbal communication process that prevent listening to the real message

- **Explore the listening habits of the minute taker and other members of the meeting**

- **Listen without formulating a response to the speaker too soon** - Listeners think about 500 words per minute. The normal speaking rate is about 125 to 150 words per minute. That creates a lot of room for communication to break down or for the mind to wander! Try to listen to everything that is being said. Listen to the entire discussion, then respond. Do not fill the extra spaces with personal thoughts and / or responses to what is being said. Valuable  information may be missed because the minute taker has moved on to a new topic without the speaker

- **Listen with empathy** - Empty the mind and focus on actively listening. Empathy shows respect for what others are experiencing

- **Be aware of the speaker's non-verbal communication** - Up to 75% of all communication is non-verbal. Does the speaker's vocal tone match the words being used? Are the speaker's movements consistent with the message the words are conveying? Is the verbal communication consistent with the non-verbal communication?

- **Create an environment that optimises listening** - Remove distractions to allow members of the meeting to be fully present in the moment. Use 'do not disturb' signs on the meeting-room door; close windows to minimise noise; switch off telephones; switch off 'BlackBerrys' and switch off equipment that is making a noise

• ACTIVITY 4

What strategies could you use to improve your listening?

To listen fully means to pay close attention to what is being said beneath the words. You listen not only to the 'music', but to the essence of the person speaking. You listen not only for what someone knows, but for what he or she is.

- Peter Senge

Style of minutes

This will vary from organisation to organisation. The style of minutes adopted depends on the **'house style'**, the level of **formality** required and to whom the minutes are to be **distributed**. The minute taker's aim is to transcribe **rough notes** into minutes that are:

- **Brief** - The audience reading the minutes do not have a great deal of time. Despite being short, the minutes should reflect an accurate record of the meeting

- **Relevant** - The purpose of the meeting and the agenda items that were discussed, noting decisions taken, action points, motions passed, names of attendees etc. Focus on conclusions, not gossip and controversy, and avoid ambiguity

- **Accurate** - Record a balanced and impartial account of the meeting

- **Simple** - Do not complicate the use of language, format etc., and provide a good overview of the meeting. **Plain English** is a good style to follow

Written in language that is clear, concise and unambiguous - Use of language should be accessible to the audience and not overly formal for those who are going to read the minutes. Minimise the use of jargon, acronyms and abbreviations. If this cannot be avoided because of the nature of the subject matter, add a glossary as an appendix to the minutes

- **Grammatically correct** - As a rule, minutes should be written in the 'simple past tense': 'Mr Johnson noted ...' or 'AJ noted ...' etc. Make sure spelling is correct and conforms to English standards

- **Reader friendly** - To assist the reader with their understanding of the topics discussed and recorded in the minutes

- **Written in a style which is consistent throughout** - Grammatical form should not change throughout the document, e.g. from 'simple past tense' to 'simple present tense'; narrative form, which may vary in style, versus bullet points / numbering of items

- **Text formatted in the agreed font etc.** - Agree style, size, spacing, layout of pages and any special effects to be incorporated in the minutes

Format of minutes

The minutes should be based on the agenda items, and this format may vary from organisation to organisation. Formats of minutes may follow this agenda:

- **Heading of the meeting** - Where and when the meeting was held

- **Delegate list** - Recording who was present and who sent apologies - this may be recorded as a separate part of the notes. These may be alphabetised according to first name, last name, organisation name, job role title etc.

- **Minutes of the previous meeting** - Previous meeting minutes will be reviewed to make sure that all actions have been completed or identified as 'carry over'. Once these minutes have been accepted, record a statement to that effect, e.g. 'The minutes were accepted as a true record of the meeting - with the above corrections'

- **Agenda items** - Record the atmosphere of the discussion, noting action points and who has been assigned the responsibility of completing them. Identify any points of controversy or reasons for difficult decisions being made. This will form the body of the minutes

- **Tabled documents** - Identify documents that support agenda items and site these in the minutes, where necessary

- **Any other business** - Record any items of discussion not identified on the agenda

- **Date of next meeting** - Record the date of the next meeting and where it will be held

- **Summary of action points** - Identify all the action points captured in the minutes in one table, noting what the action point is, the person nominated to action it and the date the action is to be completed by

- **Numbering of minutes** - Minutes may be numbered in various ways. Here are some common methods:

  - Consecutively: this may be by date, by project milestone etc.

  - Successively: using an alphanumeric code system. Each set of minutes may begin with the name of project and date, e.g. HR Training and Development, HRTAD01.05.10

- **Presentation of minutes** - Minutes may be written in a free form
  or documented in a table format. They may use colour or be made
  available in hard copy, depending on the environmental practices of
  an organisation

Once the rough notes of a meeting have been transcribed into the
minutes, these should be reviewed by all members of the meeting to
make sure statements or discussion content has been attributed to
the correct person. If someone asks for a correction, either accept the
amendment as it is or, if it does not seem appropriate, negotiate an
acceptable form of words. The chairperson should be the final judge
in cases which cannot be resolved between the members
of the meeting and the minute taker. In accepting
amendments, be careful not to accept
amendments where the attendees want to
report what they 'should' have said rather
than what they 'actually' said. At the following
meeting these minutes will be discussed
and any disagreements will be resolved. The
chairperson will then sign them off as correct.
Once the minutes have been agreed they are no
longer draft minutes but final minutes.

Once the final minutes have been agreed, they should
be sent to all attendees as soon as possible, or as soon
as appropriate for the next meeting. The minutes should be stored in
accordance with good record-keeping practice, in a safe environment
and according to organisation practice.

• ACTIVITY 5

> Describe the features of taking minutes. Explain the importance of each of
> these features.

Proofreading minutes

Proofreading is an essential part of taking minutes, and it helps to
make sure the final minutes are a **quality product**. Minutes should
inform the reader, and information should be presented accurately and
well written, using appropriate language and grammar. Proofreading is
a process of revision which checks these principles have been met. If
the final draft of the minutes is produced with mistakes, the minutes are
beyond revision. Mistakes mean that the flow of reading is interrupted,

which causes the reader confusion. Mistakes also leave a bad impression of the organisation - people may think that if its employees do not care then neither does the company.

Testing your knowledge

1. What is the purpose and benefits of taking minutes?

2. What is the role of the person taking minutes?

3. How does the chairperson assist the person taking minutes?

4. Describe different ways of formatting minutes

5. What is the difference between 'rough notes' and 'final minutes'?

6. How does the person taking minutes prepare to take minutes?

7. How does the person taking minutes make sure the information they are recording accurately describes the discussion?

8. What kind of language would a person taking minutes consider using?

9. What is the purpose of proofreading minutes?

Skills

Before the meeting

This is the first stage of taking minutes. Inevitably, you will have been nominated as a minute taker to take minutes for a meeting. It is not a role that you will specifically have been employed to carry out, but it could be a function of the role you have been employed to carry out. Your aim in taking minutes is to produce an accurate reflection of the atmosphere of discussions held throughout a meeting. You will need to identify the actions that need to be taken as a result of the discussions. Your minutes should aim to be useful, meaningful and appropriate to the audience who is going to read them.

While preparing to take minutes, you may wish to **meet with the chairperson** to go over the objectives of the meeting. The chairperson may also have specific requirements that they wish to carry out which are peculiar to them. The chairperson may draw your attention to the legislation surrounding the creation of minutes. The discussion with the chairperson may involve reviewing a previous agenda, if this is a recurring meeting, or identifying the agenda items of a new meeting. Obtain the list of attendees so you will not have to worry about recording this information at the meeting. You may want to initial, e.g. Anthony Jones (AJ), each of the attendees' names to make note taking easier during the meeting.

The minute taker may or may not be the meeting organiser. The meeting organiser may also be asked to organise aspects of hospitality, such as the catering.

Either use an existing **minute template** or create a new template to record your minutes. Some organisations may require their template for recording minutes to meet legislation requirements or its articles of incorporation etc. Make sure the template has blank spaces to record your notes for each of the agenda items. You could copy the agenda from your personal computer (PC) and make spaces on it to write your notes. Include the following information in your template:

- Place, date and time of the meeting
- Purpose of the meeting
- Attendees of the meeting
- Apologies
- Name of chairperson or meeting leader
- Agreed action points
- Agreed decisions
- Any other business
- Next meeting

You will need to decide on the **resources** you use to take your minutes, e.g. pen / pencil and notepad, tape recorder or laptop if you are a fast typist. Select the resource which you are most comfortable with and find easy to use. Make sure you have a back-up or replacement to this resource, in case you run into problems. You may choose to use a combination of these resources, e.g. tape recorder as a back-up to taking notes with pen / pencil and notepad.

Review the agenda prior to the meeting and familiarise yourself with the agenda items and their running order. Obtain the minutes from the previous meeting, as either a reference or, if required, to continue the discussion with agenda items from a previous meeting. Review any background documents you think will be appropriate to assist your understanding of the agenda items to be discussed. Seek guidance from your chairperson or a previous member of the meeting if you are in doubt about any protocols of the meeting.

During the meeting

This is the **second stage** of taking minutes. You are now at the position of making notes and making judgements about the information during the meeting. This will form the basis for the minutes you create.

The first thing you need to do is make sure an **attendance list** has been circulated and signed by **meeting attendees**. To familiarise yourself with attendees you could circulate the 'sign-in' list personally, so you meet each attendee and exchange greetings. You will need to know who all the attendees are to note their contributions during discussions. Reinforce these introductions when attendees introduce themselves to the quorum, if appropriate to that type of meeting. Before the meeting is brought to order, **organise your working space**. Know where everything is in advance. Put documents in the correct order, as they appear in the agenda, so they are to hand as each agenda item is reached.

Once the meeting has been called to order or begins, make a note of the **time it started**. It is important to do this because some agenda items may have a limited time for discussion allocated to them. The chairperson will introduce each agenda item for discussion. When **taking your notes**, focus on recording general ideas of the issues discussed. You may not need to take down notes word for word - minutes are meant to give an outline of what happened in the meeting, not a record of who said what. Record the major points raised - and by whom, if that is agreed within the protocols of the meeting - the decisions / action points which were agreed and who is going to carry out the agreed activities / action points. Check occasionally to make sure you can read and understand your notes. If you cannot understand what you have written you will not be able to write anything meaningful and you will not produce a quality product. **Your role as a minute taker is as an ambassador of the skills and knowledge of your organisation**, as it is when you answer the telephone. Always make sure you are in the moment and fulfilling your responsibilities fully as a minute taker.

Make a note of who made a motion, its seconder and the result of the votes. Record the agreed decisions / action points **as they happen**. Do not wait until after the meeting to try and remember them as you may not remember them, or you may remember them incorrectly - taking minutes is not a test of memory! If you do not understand exactly what decisions / action points have been agreed or who they have been assigned to, ask the chairperson for clarification. Find an appropriate time within the discussion to ask, so as not to stop the flow of ideas. Try to limit your participation in discussions. Divided attention is liable to lead to mistakes.

Make a note of the time the meeting finished.

After the meeting

The **third and final stage** of taking minutes occurs after the meeting has ended. This is probably the most **creative time** for the minute taker. At this stage you are can be imaginative and bring your flair to the organisation and presentation of information and how the minutes are written.

Once the meeting is over, **review your notes**. Add additional comments or clarify what you did not understand. You should aim to write up your **notes into minutes as soon as possible** after the meeting to produce minutes which represent the atmosphere and the content of the discussions more accurately. The format of content should follow what you have set up in your minute template. However, although you are responsible for providing text that flows well, you do not have to write the minutes in the chronological order of the discussions - it may not work this way.

When typing up your notes:

- **Number the pages**

- **Focus on action items, not the discussions** - Define agreed decisions / action points. Record which actions are to be taken, by whom and when

- **Be objective** - Use the same tense throughout your business document. Avoid using people's names, except for motions or seconds

- **Avoid inflammatory or personal observations -** Limit the use of adjectives or adverbs. Keep to the facts
- **Create an appendix for additional documents or glossary -** You do not have to rewrite them or summarise them

When the minutes have been fully typed, they will need to be **proofread**. These are the **draft minutes**. You may like to ask a colleague to check through them before sending them to the chairperson for their review. Someone who has nothing to do with the meeting is best, as then you can be sure that what you have written is understood. Proofreading is undertaken to confirm the clarity and accuracy of the minutes, use of correct language and grammar, spelling etc. Once this stage is completed you can distribute the minutes to all members of the meeting, including those who were present and those who sent their apologies. The form of distribution will vary from organisation to organisation, e.g. electronically, hard copy, post, personal delivery.

Once you have received all of the amendments to the minutes, this will now be the final draft. At this stage, save them in the appropriate place, e.g. folder, binder or an electronic file on your PC. They may also be posted on the organisation's website.

Testing your skills

1. How do you work with your chairperson to set up the style and form of your minutes?

2. What preparation does your organisation expect you to do before you take minutes?

3. What are the legal requirements for taking minutes in your organisation?

4. What type of minute template or 'house style' does your organisation use?

5. What are your organisation's procedures for taking minutes?

6. How do you make sure that you have captured accurate and meaningful information from discussions?

7. What are the procedures for proofreading in your organisation?

8. How does your organisation store its minutes?

9. What is the time limit for storage?What is the level of confidentiality of the minutes you have produced?How much impact does the Freedom of Information Act 2000 have on the design and completion of your minutes?

Ready for assessment?
To achieve this Level 2 unit of a Business & Administration qualification, learners will need to demonstrate that they are able to perform the following activities:Made sure meeting protocols for taking minutes were agreed with the chairperson

1. Used the correct minute template

2. Recorded information accurately, and to the required depth, during the meeting

3. Recognised mistakes and corrected draft minutes prior to sending them to all attendees

4. Produced a final draft of the minutes

5. Confirmed a final draft of the minutes

6. Complied with legal requirements and organisational policies

You will need to produce evidence from a variety of sources to support the performance requirements of this unit.

If you carry out the 'ACTIVITIES' and respond to the 'NEED TO KNOW' questions, these will provide some of the evidence required.

Links to other units

While gathering evidence for this unit, evidence **may** also be used from evidence generated from other units within the Business & Administration suite of units. Below is a **sample** of applicable units; however, most units within the Business & Administration suite of units will also be applicable.

QCF NVQ
Communications
Communicate in a business environment (Level 1)
Communicate in a business environment (Level 2)
Communicate in a business environment (Level 3)
Document production
Produce text from notes using touch typing (20 wpm)
Produce text from notes using touch typing (40 wpm)
Produce text from notes using touch typing (60 wpm)
Produce documents in a business environment
Produce text from notes
Design and produce documents in a business environment

SVQ
Communications
Understand how to communicate in a business environment
Prepare to communicate in a business environment
Communicate in a business environment (Level 2)
Document production
Produce text from notes using touch typing (20 wpm)
Produce text from notes using touch typing (40 wpm)
Produce text from notes using touch typing (60 wpm)
Produce documents in a business environment
Produce text from notes
Design and produce documents in a business environment

5

Communicate in a business environment

COMMUNICATE IN A BUSINESS ENVIRONMENT

'**Communicate in a business environment**' is a <u>mandatory unit</u> which must be completed as one of a combination of units to achieve either a Qualifications and Credit Framework (QCF), National Vocational Qualification (NVQ) or Scottish Vocational Qualification (SVQ).

* The aims of this unit are to:

* Understand the purpose of planning communication

* Understand how to communicate in writing

* Know how to communicate verbally

* Understand the purpose of feedback in developing communication skills

* Be able to plan communication

* Be able to communicate in writing

* Be able to communicate verbally

* Be able to identify and agree ways of developing communication skills

To achieve the above aims of this unit, learners will be expected to provide evidence through the performance of work-based activities.

Knowledge

What is communication?

Communication is an **action**. It is the process of transmitting or transferring information from one body to another body - a body may be one person or a collection of people. The purpose of communication is to **achieve something**. The process of communication will always require a minimum of two people - one person who **sends** the **message** and one person who **receives** the message.

The action of communication may take the form of:

* **Informing -** Where information is shared, e.g. a change of address, a meeting will take place at a certain time and location. This is **one-way** communication, where a response is not generally required from the receiver

- **Calling to action** - Where someone is asked to do something, e.g. to have a report completed by a certain date. A call to action can either occur through a **direct request** or it can be **implied**, e.g. a line manager says to their employee, 'I think that could be done in ten minutes.' This is not a direct request to have it done in ten minutes. However, there is the implication to get it done within ten minutes. This is **two-way** communication, where the receiver is asked to respond to the communication

In business, these forms of communication are not always clearly separated. If a manager shares a story with their employee about a problem they are having, do they want the employee to be aware of the problem or do they want the employee to do something about it? Communication is about being **clear** about the message that is being transmitted. The sender wants to make sure that their message is **understood** without any misunderstandings.

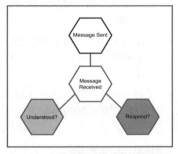

Figure 5.1. Cycle of communication

Communication is the lifeblood of a business. As a business is made up of many different parts, e.g. departments and teams that may be on many different floors of a building or geographical locations, for it to work effectively, to let each part know what is going on both within and outside of the organisation, each part of the business needs to be able to connect to other parts of the organisation to get things done.

The methods by which people communicate are:

- **Formal** - Communication delivered through 'official channels', e.g. a written memorandum from a manager to their department

- **Informal** - Communication delivered on the 'hoof', usually by word of mouth, e.g. about a director visiting the organisation

- **Diagonal** - Communication which has no obvious line of authority, e.g. team members requesting or sharing information with one another

- **Vertical** - Communication which may be top down or bottom up - from the organisation, usually via directors and managers, to its employees or from the employees to the organisation, e.g. instructions and policies sent from the Board of Directors to the employees for implementation

- **Verbal -** Communication which involves using the voice, e.g. speaking over the telephone, face to face, in a discussion, debate, interview, presentation

- **Non-verbal -** Communication where there is no use of the voice, e.g. eye contact, body language, use of sign language and signs

- **Visual -** Communication that is displayed to appeal to the eye, e.g. PowerPoint slides, public notices, advertisements

- **Written -** Communication that uses accepted symbols, e.g. the alphabet, in the written form, e.g. emails, telephone messages, letters

- **Internal -** Communication distributed to employees within an organisation, e.g. company intranet, tannoy, bulletins - email or hard copy

- **External -** Communication distributed to external customers and other stakeholders, e.g. shareholder meetings, company Internet

• ACTIVITY 7

- What is the purpose of communication?
- What forms can communications take?

Written communication

The aim of written communication is to express ideas effectively, i.e. to transmit information **appropriately** and **accurately**. To do this, the sender will need to consider all aspects of **language**. Language is a **set of rules** for facilitating the transmission of ideas. Ideas need to be meaningful and written well if the receiver is going to understand the message being sent to them. Language rules to consider when writing are:

Style

- **Words -** Use **short** words or words that are more **approachable**, e.g. 'distribute' rather than 'dissemination'. Try to avoid words that the receiver may not understand - the use of jargon, words that are specific to subject areas; acronyms, e.g. QCF and abbreviations, e.g. esp. The sender should not take it for granted that the receiver will have the same level of understanding as the sender

- **Phrases -** Try not to use a **hackneyed phrase** when a **single word** will do, e.g. the phrase 'it is the considered opinion', can be replaced by 'we / I think'. Use **short phrases** and try not to have more than **one phrase** to a sentence, as this may confuse meaning

- **Sentences** - Create sentences that are **short**. However, if an idea needs many words to make it meaningful, use them. If a sentence uses a conjunction, such as 'and', 'but' etc., could the sentence be split into two separate sentences? Use different lengths of sentences in a paragraph to interest the reader and hold their attention

- **Paragraphs** - These break up the text. Paragraphs should try to develop one idea or be a continuation of another idea. Use short paragraphs rather than long ones, but always create a paragraph that will clearly transmit its meaning to the reader

- **Layout** - To make the message more accessible and increase ease of reading, use:

Layout Style	Example
Headings	**Example**
Breaks	
	Example
Indentation	Example
Bold type	**Example**
Italics	*Example*
Underline	Example
Colour	Example

These different layout styles can be used together.

Format
There are many different forms of written communication, but for business purposes we will consider the following:

- **Letters** - Letters are a formal approach to communicating and are generally written on headed paper. An organisation may expect its employees to use a template, which will automatically prompt specific information to be written

- **Emails** - Emails are considered to be the main format for communicating within a business today. Emails are sent both internally and externally. Emails can be a less formal way of writing. They are quick to write. They elicit a quick response from the receiver and they are inexpensive to send. However, an email message is easy to delete from a personal computer (PC). Because it is such an easy form of communication, inboxes may overflow with messages, which will then need to be managed

- **Reports** - Reports may range in both the level of formality and size. Most will be prefaced with an 'executive summary', followed by various headings which will be dependent on the content of the report. An organisation may expect the content of a report to follow the organisation's '**house style**'

Spelling

When using the written form of communication, it is important to make sure that words are spelled correctly. However, this may be more difficult than it sounds, due to the influence of 'text messaging' or Americanised spelling. Protocols will be in place within an organisation for acceptable use. Spelling shows that the sender is careful about what they are writing. Incorrect spelling may confuse the reader. It may also cause the receiver to dismiss the message if there are too many spelling mistakes.

• ACTIVITY 2

Underline the correct spelling of the word.

1.	Necessary	neccessary	neccesary
2.	Beginning	bigining	begining
3.	Committment	comitment	commitment
4.	Concencus	consensus	consensis
5.	Definitely	definately	defnitely
6.	Dissapoint	disappoint	disapoint
7.	Grammer	gramar	grammar
8.	Interasting	interesting	intresting
9.	Libary	libery	library
10.	Manageable	managable	managible

The English language is more eccentric than almost any other language. It is the hardest language to learn because spelling is not consistent, i.e. there are so many different spelling rules. Some words that look the same and sound the same may have one letter that changes their meaning, e.g. 'stationery' and 'stationary', the former refers to pens and pencils, while the latter is about standing still, not moving.

• ACTIVITY 3

Underline the correct word:

1. The manager paid their team a *compliment / complement*.

2. The manager began to *marshal / martial* their team.

3. The team's thinking was not in *sink / synch* with their manager's.

4. They were the *sort / sought* of manager who *sort / sought* out confrontation.

5. It was a *bizarre / bazarr* management report.

6. The manager had taken *for / fore / four* members of staff *for / fore / four* training to get them to the *for / fore / four*.

7. The administrator took a *gambol / gamble*.

8. The presenter was *hoarse / horse* from trying to be *herd / heard* all day.

9. The team took *there / their / they're* holidays separately from each other as *there / their / they're* were so many team members.

Punctuation

Punctuation marks are a set of symbols used in writing to structure a sentence. Punctuation helps the reader to understand the message, making the written communication more meaningful and come alive from the printed page. Common symbols used in English are the following:

Capital, or upper-case, letters are used:

- To begin sentences
- Indicate proper names, e.g. 'John', 'France', 'America'
- Begin titles, e.g. 'Mr', 'Mrs', 'Sir'
- Begin days of the week, e.g. 'Wednesday', 'Saturday'
- Begin months of the year, e.g. 'June', 'August'

- Indicate acronyms, e.g. 'MoU' (Memorandum of Understanding), 'ToR' (Terms of Reference), 'NOS' (National Occupational Standard)

Commas are used:
- To separate words in a list, e.g. 'printers, photocopiers, computers and scanners'. A comma is not used before the 'and'

- Before speech, e.g. Margaret said, 'I would like the work finished before the end of the day'

- In pairs, to indicate the part of a sentence that can be removed without changing its meaning, e.g. 'Mr Jones, scratching his head, answered the question'

- To indicate pauses in sentences, e.g. 'I must finish photocopying my friend' means something different from, 'I must finish photocopying, my friend'

Semi-colons are used:
- To separate items in a list, e.g. 'the business has offices in London, England; Cardiff, Wales; Madrid, Spain and Paris, France'

- Emphasise contrasts, e.g. 'John preferred to write the presentation; Adam preferred to deliver the presentation'

- Link statements together, e.g. 'He wanted to get a job; his rent wouldn't be paid if he didn't'

- Add emphasis, e.g. 'Sandra answered the telephone; it was her boss; she knew she was in trouble'

Colons are used:
- To introduce lists, e.g. 'The supervisor asked for information on: sales, purchases, stock levels and wastage'

- Separate two parts of a sentence where the second part explains the first, e.g. 'Sales had improved during February: it was the busiest week of the month so far that year'

Hyphens are used:
- To avoid doubt, e.g. words such as 'co-respondent', 're-formed', 'coordinateinate'

- When linking two nouns, e.g. 'Southampton-Crewe train' or two adjectives, e.g. 'Austro-Hungarian fall out'
- When a noun phrase is used to qualify another noun, e.g. 'A self-closing door is self closing; a three-drawer filing cabinet has three drawers'
- For certain prefixes, e.g. 'un-British', 'anti-hunting'
- To indicate words are to be spelled out, e.g. 'C-R-E-W-E'
- To avoid difficult looking compound words, e.g. 'coattail', 'belllike', 'deice', look better as 'coat-tail', 'bell-like' and 'de-ice'

Brackets are used:
In a similar way as a pair of commas, as they separate a phrase within a sentence that could be removed without altering its meaning, e.g. 'Mrs Wentworth (the new Managing Director) will visit the office next Wednesday'

Full stops are used:
- To indicate the end of a sentence
- After initials or abbreviations, e.g. 'D. J. Campbell'

Exclamation marks are used:
- In place of a full stop to indicate an exclamation, e.g. 'The manager raced into the office shouting!'

Question marks are used:
- In place of a full stop to indicate a query, e.g. 'What time should I make the meeting for next week?'

Quotation marks or 'inverted commas' are used:
- To indicate speech, e.g. Peter said, 'I want you to work on the reception desk tomorrow'
- To indicate a quote from another source, e.g. The letter from the customer says: 'I sent the cheque on Wednesday'

• ACTIVITY 7

Punctuate the following:

1. What time will the meeting start tomorrow is it going to be a long day

2. Matthews letter to the publisher said I want you to proof read my story

3. The order included pens pencils notepaper ink notepads binders etc paper was also included the order was made for arrival on Monday

4. He was not able to get to the office in June as he was going to be in France

5. The meeting was due to start at 1000 the meeting would cover the same topics as was covered last week

6. Its going to be very difficult to finish the work on time as its going to be input by the junior whos not computer literate

7. Today of all days the computer crashed at least twice

8. The managers not able to see you today his wife has just called to say hes unwell

9. I think the computer has broken down its screen went black

10. Men are not permitted to use the ladies room

11. Information can be obtained from the citizens advice bureau between 0900 and 1700

Apostrophes are used:
- In place of missing letters, e.g:

  - 'mustn't' = must not;

  - ''til' = until;

  - ''phone' = telephone;

  - 'S'ton' = Southampton

- To indicate possession

Possessive Apostrophes are used:
- Where the noun is singular - The apostrophe comes between the noun and the 's', e.g. 'Ali's book' = the book that belongs to Ali

- Where the noun is singular but ends in 's' - The apostrophe still comes between the noun and the additional 's', e.g. 'The class's teacher' = the teacher of the class

- Where the noun is plural and ends in 's' - The apostrophe comes after the 's' and there is no additional 's', e.g. 'ladies' bags' = the bags that belong to the ladies

- Where the noun is plural and does not end in 's' - The apostrophe comes between the noun and the 's', e.g. 'men's room' = the room for men

- However, there is one exception to these rules - The word 'its'. If you mean 'it is' or 'it has', then the correct usage would be 'it's', because you are replacing the missing letters with an apostrophe. If you mean 'belonging to it', then the correct usage is 'its', without the apostrophe

• ACTIVITY 5

Correct the following sentences:

1. We need paper's, pen's, paperclips' and staples

2. Everyone involved are invited to the meeting

3. We want to get the 1000 train?

4. In case of fire use neither the lift or the escalator

5. When will the stationary order be delivered!

6. After the work is finished should, we all meet in the canteen for a coffee

7. Its been a long time since it's been this cold should, we put the heating on

8. Phillipa has mastered the new printer shes worked out how it works

9. The memo from accounts say will you forward all checks as soon as they arrive

10. If the diary is not kept up to date nobody will know were their supposed to be at any time

Each of the above symbols are used for specific purposes within a sentence to improve its meaning and make it easier for the reader to understand.

Grammar
The purpose of good grammar is to make 'meaning' clearly understood. This can be achieved by dividing up what is being communicated into paragraphs and sentences:

A sentence is a set of words which make a complete statement. Sentences must start with a capital letter and end with a full stop, exclamation mark or question mark. Sentences can be of almost any length. For clarity, they should be as short as possible - see plain English - but as a minimum they must contain a subject and a verb. Sentences are broken down into parts of speech. There are many different parts of speech in the English language. The main ones are:

- **Nouns -** A noun is the name of a person, place, thing, day of the week or month of a year, e.g. 'Jeffrey', 'Isle of Man', 'Thursday'

- **Pronouns -** A pronoun is a word used in place of a noun, e.g. 'he', 'she', 'it', 'they'

- **Verbs -** A verb is a word that shows action, e.g. 'watching', 'playing', 'worked', 'ran'

- **Adverbs -** An adverb is a word that adds to a verb, generally with an '-ly' at the end, e.g. 'slowly', 'quickly'

- **Adjectives -** An adjective is a word that describes a noun, e.g. 'big', 'small', 'hollow', 'light'

Prepositions - A preposition is a word that shows how one noun relates to another, e.g. 'towards', 'between', 'beside'

Conjunctions - A conjunction is a word that joins two other words, e.g. 'and', 'but', 'so', 'then', 'therefore'

A paragraph is a collection of sentences about a single subject which contain two or more sentences, though they may contain a single sentence in order to emphasise a point. They can be as long as it is necessary to complete the subject. When a new subject is introduced, a new paragraph starts on the line below

• ACTIVITY 6

Using emails or letters that you have written, check through them to analyse if the correct grammar has been used. Check to make sure that sentences and paragraphs are correctly formed.

Plain English

Plain English, also known as 'plain language', describes language that focuses on clarity, brevity and the avoidance of technical wording. It seeks to use a writing style that readers can understand after just one reading. It uses only as many words as are necessary. It combines forms in English that are clear, concise, direct and natural.

Plain English seeks to achieve the following principles:

- Clarity
- Simplicity
- Appropriateness to the audience - considering who they are and what relationship you want to have with them
- Directness
- Being personal
- Uses informal language, when appropriate
- Uses common, everyday language
- Accessibility to a wide audience
- Explains technical words in simple language
- Attempts to interest readers and hold their attention
- Relies heavily on simple sentence structures
- Generally avoids using the passive voice
- Is respectful of the reader

Any piece of written communication should conform to all of the above principles. It is the responsibility of the sender to make sure that the written communication will be **understood** by the receiver - there should be no misunderstandings). Any form of communication that is sent is an example of company branding and confirms how the company wishes to identify itself. Communication should be honest and open and should not distort the message. Communications are exchanged between employees within an organisation and external customers outside of the organisation. Distorted information can lead to rumour and innuendo and undermine the credibility of the sender and that of the organisation. It can also lead to uncertainty, anxiety, lowering of morale and motivation.

> Think like a wise man but communicate in the language
> of the people.
> - *William Butler Yeats*

Urgent or important communications

Lots of things are 'important', but they are not always 'urgent' - they are not the same thing. Some communication becomes 'urgent' because it has been delayed or forgotten. Some tasks can be both 'important' and 'urgent'. Many communications are not nearly as 'urgent' as the communicator believes them to be.

Sometimes what is important or urgent to the sender may not be to

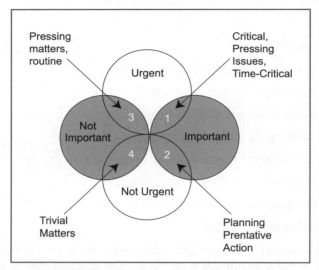

Figure 5.2. Important / urgent matrix. Stephen R. Covey, 1989, *The 7 Habits of Highly Effective People*

the receiver. Be clear about instructions when sending any form of communication, so the responder has a clear idea of when a response is required.

To help differentiate between 'urgent' and 'important', a decision needs to be made about the priority of the communication. The decision of when to complete the communication can be informed by the important / urgent matrix:

The matrix shows that not all communications will have the same level of 'urgency' or 'importance' as others.

Point 1 - Represents things that are both 'urgent' and 'important'. This box requires some time to think about the method and content of the communication, e.g. sending an email to lorry drivers about road conditions to help them meet their daily deadlines.

Point 2 - Represents things that are 'important, but not urgent'. This box is all about 'quality'. This box provides the communicator with the 'opportunity' to reflect, though still on a time schedule, to see how things can be improved. Attending to these types of communication minimises Box 1 communications.

Point 3 - Represents things that are 'urgent, but not important'. The 'urgent' creates the illusion of 'importance'. Many telephone calls, meetings and drop-in visitors fall into this box. A lot of time can be spent in this box meeting other people's priorities, overestimating them as 'urgent' and 'important'.

Point 4 - Represents communication that is 'not urgent and not important'. This is a box of activities which should be avoided if careful attention has   been given to the purpose of the communication.

Storing of written communication

It is important to keep a record of written communication. This provides proof to interested parties about when the communication was completed and sent. It also provides proof of the content of the written communication. It is also a statutory obligation under the Freedom of Information Act 2000 (FOIA) to make certain documents available to the public, if requested. There are two methods by which written communication can be filed and stored, which are:

Manual storage systems

This involves keeping copies of written communication in the following formats:

- Files

- Shelves / cupboards

- Cabinets / drawers

Each of these formats may use security devices to keep confidential information safe.

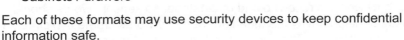

Electronic storage systems

These involve as:

- **Storing communication on a server which may use devices such as** - PCs: desktops, laptops, notebooks, palmtops etc.

- **Handsets** - 'BlackBerrys', 'iPods' etc. Handsets can be programmed to store important information. Likewise, removable memories, such as diskette, almost obsolete, compact disc (CD) and flash drives can be used as backups to store relevant information for future use

- **Microfilm** - important and confidential information can be recorded onto tapes / films

- Verbal communication

Verbal communication is composed of sound and speaking - using words and language. It is face-to-face communication. It may be formal, e.g. an appraisal meeting, or informal, e.g. a quick head-to-head. The use of spoken language can reflect class, profession and other social factors. As with written language, there will always be a purpose for

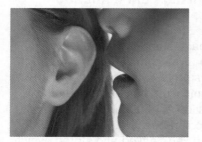

verbal communication. Speaking can either be:

Interpersonal - Most forms of verbal communication fall into this category. The speaker should avoid offending the receiver in the choice of language they use and tailor it to the receiver's needs and expectations

Public - Verbal communication that takes place in a public setting, where a speaker is aiming to persuade, inform, inspire or motivate a large body of people

> Say what you mean, and mean what you say, but don't say it mean!

When communicating verbally, the speaker needs to consider the **content** and choice of **words** they wish to use. What is being said will affect how well it is received and understood, so sensory words should be used to help convey the meaning. Sensory words create a 'picture', a 'sound' or a 'feeling'. They are particularly useful if the speaker is trying to persuade the listener to agree. There are three main types of sensory words:

- **Seeing** - 'I see what you mean', 'I can imagine'
- **Hearing** - 'I hear what you say', 'I hear you loud and clear'
- **Feeling** - 'I feel good about what I hear'

Choose words that will put the message across the way that the speaker wants. If the speaker is not sure of how their choice of words will be interpreted by the listener, use a mixture of sensory words.

The tone of voice of the speech. The tone of voice will convey the way the speaker feels about what they are saying:

- Excited
- Angry
- Distressed
- Tired
- Happy
- Positive

The **volume** of speech. The volume used - loud, quiet - will depend on the audience - size, composition etc. - and the size of the room / venue.

The **clarity** of speech. Speaking clearly helps to make sure that the message is heard accurately, particularly if speaking in a language or accent that is unfamiliar to the listener.

The **speed** of speech. The listener's level of understanding needs to be considered when choosing the speed of the speech.

Unlike written communication, during the process of verbal communication, whether actively speaking or listening, the speaker is also using their body to communicate meaning. This is also known as **body language**. Body language sends out messages whether you are speaking or not. Messages may be sent by the body on purpose or accidentally. The way people sit, stand, fold their arms, use facial expression etc. can have an affect on how verbal communication is interpreted. Body language can either add to or take away from what is being said. When speaking, positive body language involves:

- Good posture - stand or sit straight
- Looking at your audience
- Relaxing your facial muscles

- Not fidgeting
- Not tapping your feet
- Not drumming your fingers
- Not folding your arms
- Not giving the impression of being bored, nervous or disinterested

Telephone communication is similar to face-to-face communication, except that the speaker is unable to see the person they are speaking to, so they are unable to interpret the speaker's body language. The tone of voice, volume, clarity and speed are equally as important when speaking on the telephone. The way in which telephone calls are made and answered is very important. Callers will base their impression of the speaker and the organisation on what they hear. The speaker is aiming to make a friendly but efficient impression. **Smile** when answering the telephone - the listener will hear it! Avoid answering the telephone when you are eating, chewing gum or yawning. When making a call, always state why you are calling and make sure that all of the information you need to communicate and any potential questions that need to be asked are prepared in advance. Make a list of important points to communicate. Take notes of important points of the conversation that need to be acted on after the telephone conversation has ended. This will help the speaker to get the message across clearly. All telephone calls must be treated as important. Answering the telephone is not an interruption to work - it is a part of work! Callers will receive an impression of the organisation from the way the telephone is answered. Be polite, receptive and let the caller know they are being listened to. When communicating information keep it relevant and accurate. If receiving information have a pen and paper ready to make notes when necessary.

• ACTIVITY 7

Here is a list of some sensory words: harmonise, move, speak, voice, imagine, touch, search, image, sound, picture, tone, grasp, hate, tune in to, accent, appearance, celebrate, fight, blunt, colour and show.

Place them in the correct category.

Seeing	Hearing	Feeling

Listening

The purpose of verbal communication is to communicate with another person or group of people. In order to do this, the person or group of people need to **listen** to the message. If the listener does not listen to what someone is saying, the speaker is wasting their time saying it.

There is more to listening than simply being within hearing distance. There are two types of listening:

Active listening, which is making an effort to hear and understand. It is:

- Appearing involved
- Leaning towards the speaker
- Making eye contact
- Mirroring the speaker's facial expressions
- Nodding or shaking the head
- Paying attention
- Responding with 'mm', 'yes', 'okay', 'really'

Passive listening, which is hearing without taking in what is being said. It is:

- Listening but not hearing
- Switching off
- Slouching
- Not making eye contact
- Having an impassive expression
- Moving about restlessly
- Appearing disinterested
- Making no response

Actively listening gives the listener the opportunity to contribute meaningfully to the discussion or conversation. It allows the listener to contribute by asking **questions** when the meaning is not clear or they want to find out more information. There are several different types of questions:

- **Open questions** - Open questions are used if more information is needed. These are very useful for getting others to talk and share opinions, ideas and information

- **Closed questions** - Closed questions can be very specific and precise, which are used to elicit a 'yes' or 'no' answer. Closed questions would be used for getting accurate, factual information

- **Funnel questions** - Funnel questions are a combination of both open and closed questions, starting with an open question - starting wide. The response is then listened to and then further 'refined' enquiries are made, with each question getting narrower and narrower, until a closed question gives a specific and precise answer

- **Comparative questions** - These ask a person to think about two different situations and then compare them. Comparative questions are very good for revealing what matters to someone and what they value

- **Short questions** - These are used so that the speaker keeps receiving information from the other person who is doing the talking. For short questions, use **Kipling's** six friends: 'what', 'who', 'when', 'how', 'where' and 'why'. The question that is most probing is 'Why?' Handle these questions sensitively and assertively, otherwise the listener interpreting a short question may see this as a sign of aggression

- **Absence of a spoken question - pause or silence -** Sometimes the best response is no response. During the pause / silence, the speaker should maintain supportive eye contact and positive body language as they wait for a reply. This is an approach that can be used in a sensitive situation. This can sometimes be a difficult response to make, as a silence that goes on too long may be embarrassing and undermine the rapport that has been built up. However, the use of the pause / silence can also provoke the other person to speak out and reveal more information

- **Summarising questions -** These are great for checking out whether messages are being understood as you intended them to be

• ACTIVITY 8

Which of the following questions are either open or closed questions? Tick the correct box.

	OPEN	CLOSED
1. How much postage should I put on this?		
2. Do you take milk in your coffee?		
3. How many copies of this do you want?		
4. When is the computer being repaired?		
5. Are you on holiday next week?		
6. Can I take this down to engineering?		
7. Why did you not finish the input this morning?		
8. Where are the envelopes kept?		

We have two ears and one mouth so that we can listen twice as much as we speak.

- Epictetus

Evaluation of communication

Evaluation is a way of checking to see how things have been done or performed. The aim of evaluation is to learn and improve processes and performance. When evaluating the quality of communication skills, evaluation may either be carried out:

- **Subjectively** - This would be achieved through self-evaluation. Self-evaluation involves reviewing regular tasks to confirm that the most efficient methods are being used to complete them

- **Objectively** - This would be achieved through inviting an independent third party to evaluate. The independent evaluator will, generally, have had nothing to do with the person who is being evaluated. Objective evaluation involves asking people for feedback on tasks they have completed. They will be able to give feedback on whether their requirements are being satisfied and give suggestions on how to complete the task in an easier way. There are two types of objective evaluation:

  - **Formative evaluation:** looks at the way things are being done at present to judge whether the right things are being done in the right way. Formative evaluation is used to assess all of the things that are done on a day-to-day basis to see if there are any improvements that can be made

  - **Summative evaluation:** looks at a project after completion or after amendments have been put in place to judge their efficiency, effectiveness, impact and sustainability. Summative evaluation is a more formal process - the evaluation is focused on a specific project or change of process. This can be done by seeking structured feedback from everybody involved, possibly by the use of a questionnaire or feedback form, in order that the feedback is received in a manner that allows it to be analysed. This provides an evaluation that includes credible and useful information on the level of achievement and the effective use of resources

Evaluation of communication helps the communicator to move from a position of unconscious **incompetence** to unconscious **competence**. Sue Bishop[1] has identified four stages in this process:

- **Stage 1** - **Unconscious incompetence -** Where the communicator has no idea of the impact their communication is having on third parties

---

1   Sue Bishop, 1997, The Complete Guide to People Skills. Gower

- **Stage 2** - **Conscious incompetence** - Where the communicator has some idea that their communication skills are letting them down

- **Stage 3** - **Conscious competence** - Where the communicator has some idea of the effect of their communication skills, but still needs to think about how to communicate more effectively

- **Stage 4** - **Unconscious competence** - Where communication is second nature to the communicator, and they do not have to think about what they are writing or saying

While someone may have excellent communication skills, these skills are never perfect. Communication skills can always be improved. Evaluation is the means of identifying how communication skills can be improved.

As communication skills improve towards 'unconscious competence', the communicator will find they are able to build and maintain **rapport**. Rapport is about empathising with the correspondent of the communication. This will lead to a more meaningful communication by creating an environment of trust and confidence. Rapport is a natural trait which people use to a greater or lesser extent, depending on their personality. People tend to get on with each other better if they like one another, and vice versa. However, in a business environment, often there is no choice about the people being communicated with. Communication can often take place between people who have never met each other before. In this situation it is beneficial for all of the communicators to create an environment of trust and confidence by converting a stranger to the status of a friend. This can be achieved by a Neuro Linguist Programming (NLP) technique called **mirroring**. The communicators mirror, as with active listening, all behavioural elements that they have noticed in the person they are conversing with and build them into the discussion / conversation as a means of achieving a successful verbal communication, e.g. gesture; posture; use of language; voice - tone, volume.

> The most effective way to achieve right relations with any living thing is to look for the best in it, and then help that best into the fullest expression.
> - *Allen J. Boone*

In aiming to achieve successful communication, the communicators, both transmitter and receiver, should summarise the progress of their discussion as a continuing means of building and maintaining rapport. A

summary is a tool for accurately repeating back ideas and information that have been shared in a discussion or conversation. This helps to reinforce what has been discussed. A summary of the discussion can highlight areas of agreement or disagreement. If there are areas of agreement, summarising the points helps to build and maintain the rapport that is being created between the communicators. If there is disagreement, it is advisable to air any issues at the earliest opportunity, so they do not undermine the established rapport. Disagreements should be resolved to help move the discussion forward. If there is a meeting following an agenda, the agenda items will help to summarise the outcomes of each agenda point discussion. Questions may be used to summarise the content of discussions and also clarify meaning and understanding. Summarising can confirm and / or clarify key points and common ground. It will encourage all communicators to explore new information and any perceived contradictions.

A summary is not used in normal day-to-day conversation, but is a necessary tool for increasing the understanding of ideas and information in a business environment. A summary is not a statement of facts, it is a summing up of expressed ideas and information in a way that makes them come alive for the listener and corroborates what the speaker has said. It creates the opportunity to correct any misunderstanding and helps to reinforce openness and honesty in the communication process. Summarising is a valuable tool for any communicator and is a great way of testing active listening. If the communicator is unable to accurately summarise what has been said, they have probably been passively listening to what has been going on, which is an example of inappropriate behaviour.

> To effectively communicate, we must realise that we are all different in the way we perceive the world and use this understanding as a guide to our communication with others.
> - *Anthony Robbins*

Testing your knowledge

1. What are the different methods of communication?

2. When would written communication be used?

3. What are the elements of language that need to be used with written communication?

4. How does the use of language change depending on the form of written communication?

5. Why is the format of written communication important?

6. What are the principles of plain English?

7. Why is it important to check written communication before sending it?

8. What is the difference between 'urgent' and 'important' communication?

9. Why is written communication stored?

10. What elements are used by a speaker to present verbal communication successfully?

11. What is 'active listening'?

12. How does rapport improve communication?

13. Why is summarising so important in verbal communications?

14. Why should communication skills be evaluated?

Skills

Once you have agreed the purpose and methods of communication, set about writing it or contributing to verbal discussions.

Written communication

When setting out to create a piece of written communication, look for information that will support the argument you intend to write. Sift through alternative arguments and select the most appropriate information - make sure you are positive that it will hold up to scrutiny and suits the purpose of your written communication. Find some examples of what other people have written on the same subject area, you can use them as a guide to compose your written communication. Once you have assembled these, the information that you have selected must be organised, structured and formatted appropriately, i.e. it meets the intended purpose of the written communication.

Shape the communication so that it follows a logical order, building on the arguments that you want to investigate and communicate. It could just respond to a piece of written communication that has been sent to you. In the same way as composing a new written piece, answer it logically, following the layout - as you are responding to the person who wrote it, their layout is the form that they like - this method helps to build rapport and bridge understanding between you and the recipient. Mirror their style while still retaining your personality. Correct any formatting and punctuation issues etc., while not appearing obvious, you are not a schoolteacher and that is not the purpose of the communication. However, you do want it to be a fully formed and accurate written piece of communication.

Compose the written communication using the relevant forms of language - grammar, punctuation and spelling. You never know who they are going to share this with. **Remember**, all forms of communication are an opportunity to promote the values of your organisation. Make the best impression by getting it right the first time. Make sure you only use 'text' spelling if it is appropriate, i.e. casual communication with someone you know well. Use it appropriately! Check your computer to make sure your 'spell check' is in English and not American, if that is the organisation requirement.

• ACTIVITY 9

Here is a group of words which show both English and American spelling. Put either E (English) or A (American) in the column next to the word to show how it is spelled in that country.

Colour		Color	
Organization		Organisation	
Programme		Program	
Analyse		Analyze	
Center		Centre	
Equaling		Equalling	
Catalogue		Catalog	
Summarise		Summarize	
Licence		License	
Fulfill		Fulfil	

Write your communication so that it answers any questions requesting information or further information. Make sure that it is written in time to meet the request of the person to whom you will be responding to. If you are unable to make the deadline, give them a quick call to let them know. Write in a style that suits the purpose of the written communication - formal, informal or colloquial.

If writing a letter, make sure that it is printed using paper with the company letterhead on.

When you are writing, monitor your mood so that it does not overly influence the tone of your writing. If you are angry or annoyed, this may show through in your writing. If you are too upbeat, your tone of delivery may be too frivolous. **Remember** the purpose of the written communication at all times.

Remember to implement the principles of plain English. Use them to make your written communication appeal to the person to whom you are writing to - simple, simple, simple! What examples of plain English did you use? Make a final check of the written communication with your supervisor before sending it out, if and when this is necessary. Look at any corrections that have been made - what can you learn from them? Why were the corrections made? Check with someone if you do not understand why the communication had to be corrected. Once the written communication has been sent, file a copy of it in the appropriate filing system.

Verbal communication

Agree the purpose of the verbal communication you will contribute to. Research the subject matter before you contribute to the discussion, making sure you understand what is going on and can contribute meaningfully to the discussion. Check with your supervisor or work colleagues for further information before the verbal exchange takes place. Be prepared to provide the correct information to contribute meaningfully to verbal discussions. Begin to think about the contribution you are going to make and how to formulate arguments for presentation. This will help to stimulate the discussion. Aim to move the discussion forward so that it reaches a constructive, if not amicable, conclusion. While striving to achieve a positive outcome is always good practice, in some cases it may not be achieved. If things are not going the way you anticipated and you are not sure about what to do, seek assistance from colleagues who may be present, or ask to adjourn the discussion and seek advice from colleagues on how to move forward.

Throughout a discussion, actively listen to what is being discussed - do not just hear sounds being made. The correct choice of words is what will help you to contribute to a face-to-face discussion or a conversation on the telephone. Do not hesitate to ask if you are not sure about something, or make a note of it and ask for clarification after the discussion if you feel your question may distract from the theme of the discussion. If you did not hear something, ask for it to be repeated - do not leave yourself out of the discussion or lose track of what is being discussed. Hear it and actively listen to what you have heard. Keep the conversation alive for you and your fellow contributors. Give yourself time to make a response and make sure that your contribution meets your objectives. Make sure your body language is positive and interested in the discussion. Note examples of negative and positive body language that other people use in discussion or conversation. To achieve the outcomes you are looking for, use those that you think will energise a discussion and keep it alive. Summarise ideas and points of information as a means of increasing understanding and building rapport.

Evaluation of communication skills

Look at the different methods of communication that you carry out regularly, for instance - attending a team meeting, a one to one with your manager, dealing with incoming mail, dealing with making and receiving incoming telephone calls etc. Did you carry out an evaluation of your communication skills? Who carried out the evaluation? How did you evaluate your communication skills? What did you learn from the evaluation of your communication skills? How have you improved your communication skills as a result of the evaluation? How was the information of the different evaluations recorded?

Testing your skills

1. Why have you used different methods of communication?

2. How has your written communication been formatted to meet specific purposes?

3. What appropriate language has been used in your written communication?

4. What spelling mistakes did you make, if any?

5. How did you punctuate the written communication?

6. What did you have to change as a result of checking the written communication?

7. What filing system did you use to store the written communication?

8. How do you know that your verbal communication was clear?

9. What kinds of questions did you ask, and why?

10. How did your contributions move the discussion forward?

11. How did you seek feedback to improve your communication skills?

Ready for assessment?
To achieve this Level 2 unit of a Business & Administration qualification, learners will need to **demonstrate** that they are able to perform the following activities:

1. Agreed the purpose, content, style and format of the written communication

2. Agreed the final written communication before sending it

3. Agreed what is 'urgent' and 'important' before responding to written communication

4. Met deadlines for responding to written communication

5. Contributed ideas that moved the discussion forward

6. Used different kinds of questions appropriately

7. Summarised the discussion at appropriate times

8. Reflected on the outcomes of the communication

9. Learned lessons for improving communication skills

You will need to produce evidence from a variety of sources to support the performance requirements of this unit.

If you carry out the 'ACTIVITIES' and respond to the 'NEED TO KNOW' questions, these will provide some of the evidence required.

Links to other units

While gathering evidence for this unit, evidence **may** also be used from evidence generated from other units within the Business & Administration suite of units. Below is a **sample** of applicable units; however, most units within the Business & Administration suite of units will also be applicable.

QCF NVQ
Communications
Make and receive telephone calls
Use electronic message systems
Use diary systems
Take minutes
Document production
Produce documents in a business environment
Produce text from notes
Produce text from notes using touch typing (40 wpm)
Produce text from shorthand (60 wpm)
Produce text from recorded audio instruction (40 wpm)

SVQ
Make and receive telephone calls
Use electronic message systems
Use diary systems
Take minutes
Document production
Produce documents in a business environment
Produce text from notes
Produce text from notes using touch typing (40 wpm)
Produce text from shorthand (60 wpm)
Produce text from recorded audio instruction (40 wpm)
Plan how to solve business problems

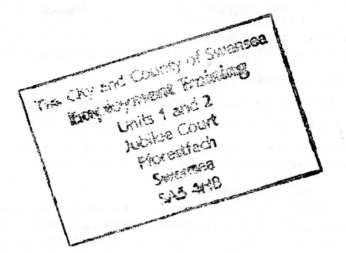

The City and County of Swansea
Employment Training
Units 1 and 2
Jubilee Court
Fforestfach
Swansea
SA5 4HB

6 **Use electronic message systems**

USE ELECTRONIC MESSAGE SYSTEMS

'**Use electronic message systems**' is an <u>optional unit</u> which may be chosen as one of a combination of units to achieve either a Qualifications and Credit Framework (QCF), National Vocational Qualification (NVQ) or Scottish Vocational Qualification (SVQ).

The aims of this unit are to:

- Understand the use of electronic message systems
- Be able to use electronic message systems

To achieve the above aims of this unit, learners will be expected to provide evidence through the performance of work-based activities.

Knowledge

Definition and types of electronic message systems
An **electronic message system (EMS)** is a message system that allows users to send or receive messages electronically using an electronic server. Messages are created, read and manipulated by servers. Servers may offer a complete voicemail, call attendant, info-line, audiotext, interactive voice response (IVR) or autodial solution. It is used like a physical postbox. The user checks for new messages every day, deletes or answers the messages and creates new messages for other users who use the EMS.

An EMS is a non-threatening addition to existing information systems. It provides an opportunity to introduce users to terminals, email, store and forward systems and electronic filing and retrieval. An EMS is also known as an **electronic mailbox** or **computer-based message system**. It may provide support for text and numeric messaging to:

- Electronic pagers
- Digital telephones
- Other portable message display devices

• ACTIVITY 1

What is an EMS?

After a message has been left, the message is stored as online media for retrieval by the **addressee**. A central computer is required to provide information control and processing functions for users of the system.

The user can switch on their EMS at any time. By leaving a message, an EMS saves time spent chasing telephone calls or when a telephone call interrupts creative writing and the time to think. It may also eliminate time wasted while another user searches for information. An EMS may help to eliminate some of the paper flow in an office. As messages are delivered to an EMS instantly, there is no expense required for intra-company mail, copying costs, delivery costs or postage. Instant delivery means no wasted effort due to the late arrival of an **important message**. It also adds to an increased feeling of teamwork between users, as all team members can be equally well informed, even if geographically separated. This benefit is increased further when a business has users in multiple time zones, or for those who travel frequently.

Communications may be either synchronous or asynchronous. **Synchronous communications** include voice telephone calls, chat or instant messaging sessions. They are live and each caller or addressee responds to each other in real time. **Asynchronous communications** include discussion forums, **electronic messaging** and email. They are not live forms of communication, as a period of time elapses before the addressee is able to read and respond to the message. Asynchronous communications promote a new form of instant global communication and collaboration. The delay in communication from discussion forums, emails and electronic messages gives addressees time to think about and consider their responses.

• ACTIVITY 2

What is the difference between 'synchronous' and 'asynchronous' communications?

Electronic messages may range in style from brief **informal messages** to extended **formal messages** containing a great deal of detailed information. Messages may either be inter-company, external to an organisation, or intra-company, internal to an organisation, communications.

Implementation of an EMS

The implementation of a successful EMS requires:

- **Input / output** - terminals for users
- A **processor** - Response time must be short as there may be many users of an EMS
- **Storage** - Sufficient online storage for several days' traffic
- A **hard copy** - Printers
- **Simplicity** - The system must be simple to operate by users
- **Remote access** - Off-site or virtual users must be able to access the system
- **Security** - Mailboxes must be protected from access by other people
- **System management tools** - The system manager must have statistics on usage and errors to effectively plan and control an EMS

An EMS can be used with network monitors, help desks, process control, plant automation and site-specific applications.

•ACTIVITY 3

What are some advantages of having an EMS?

Features of an EMS

An EMS will vary in the function for which it was designed and may provide some or all of the following features:

- Simultaneous multiple telephone line support. There could be as many as 50 telephone lines working simultaneously
- Configured and managed from an intuitive web control panel
- Caller ID logging and optional on-screen caller ID flash display
- Call key select menus and ability for the caller to enter numbers
- Call transfer
- Remote telephone access

- Save incoming messages as wav files - keep messages for legal purposes or in-house records

- Automatic hours feature - enter office hours to automatically answer after hours

- Unlimited, selectable, outgoing messages and menus

- Call simulator, to test systems off line

- Automated outbound calls and messages

- Unlimited voicemail boxes

- Text-to-speech voice synthesis as an alternative to recording or importing files

- Ability to open files or run other software to process data or report information

• ACTIVITY 4

Identify five possible features of an EMS.

Instructions for leaving messages on an EMS

When a caller leaves a message, it is imperative to make sure that instructions for leaving the message are presented clearly and concisely. This will help to maximise the caller's understanding of the instructions for leaving a message. It will also help to avoid any misunderstandings for the caller and maximise the caller's time. Instructions to encourage a caller to leave a message may include:

A **welcome greeting or auto attendant -** An auto attendant is the first voice a caller will hear when they dial through to a business telephone line. The auto attendant greets the caller and establishes trust. It is the first contact a caller may have with a business and, importantly, provides the branding or image of the business

An interactive voice response (IVR) - After the caller has heard the auto attendant, the same voice usually guides the caller through various business options, e.g. press 1 for products, press 2 for complaints, enter the extension number of the person you are calling if this is known to you, otherwise, wait for an attendant to respond to your call. These prompts direct callers to the most suitable extension. While most IVR systems use a touch-tone response system, some of the newer systems use voice recognition to allow callers to speak their answers

An **on-hold message** - This is an opportunity to market the business to potential customers. This message could inform callers of the vision of the business, etc.

A **courtesy message** - A form of on-hold message which may provide general information about the business, e.g. office opening hours. It will make callers feel that their on-hold time is not being wasted

A **voicemail message** - Record a business voicemail message to act as a generic greeting for messages that are not left on personal voicemail boxes

An **after hours message** - Thank the caller for telephoning and provide instructions to leave a message or telephone back the following business day

A **holiday message** - Customise a recorded message to cover personnel and statutory holidays

• ACTIVITY 5

What kinds of messages could be left on an EMS for callers to listen to?

Any of the above instructions allow an EMS to provide up-to-date information. This information should be altered, when required, by users who have been given access to do so, e.g. if someone is on extended sick leave and the telephone number of the person concerned needs to change within the next month. '**Information is power**' is an old adage. Empower the caller with **correct, current and critical information** required to instruct them how to make an informed response. The caller is then able to leave a meaningful message. When a caller is being asked to leave a message, the addressee of the EMS is essentially managing knowledge or a response to knowledge which the caller is being instructed to leave. **Knowledge management** is a competitive advantage for any business. Information should be provided to the caller which is specific and to the point. This will allow the caller to filter their response and leave a message in the appropriate place after following the instructions of the EMS.

Instructions for leaving a message should be designed to meet the requirements of a business and incorporate:

- **House style**
- **Grammatical accuracy**
- **Levels of formality**
- **Clarity of expression**
- **Tone of expression**
- **Volume of expression**
- **Speed of expression**
- **Comprehension** - So instructions are meaningful

Each of the above components helps to project the professional standing, image and brand of the business. Leaving a message is not a face-to-face communication; therefore, the addressee should leave instructions that persuade the caller to leave a message that is informative and positive. For example, 'Hello, you have reached the desk of John Tallis. I am sorry that I am not able to take your call. Please leave a message, along with your name and telephone number, which I will respond to as soon as I return to my desk. Thank you for your call.' There was no need to mention the time of the call in the instructions, as most EMSs will identify this.

The better the quality of the instructions - clear and succinct - left for the caller to respond to, the greater the potential is for the message left by the caller to respond to the EMS instructions. Confident instructions will help to promote a positive response from the caller. Instructions should be recorded in an environment that is quiet and free from distraction. The same environment can also be used when leaving a message. In both instances, it will help to minimise interference with the instructions being left for the caller and the message being left for the addressee.

• ACTIVITY 6

Change the text of the instructions below into a more formal and appropriate format for a professional organisation:

"Hi. Yeah, you guessed it. I'm not at my desk. Not sure when I'll be back. So do your thing, and leave me your calling card. Hope to get back to you sometime soon, but who knows. Ciao."

Describe the reasons for the changes that have been made.

Storage and organisation of electronic messages

Another purpose of an EMS is to act as a system to store messages received by the addressee. The addressee must manage the quantity of messages stored in their system and respond to them as required. Messages are information. A lost message, or a message not retrieved or responded to on time, is lost information, lost knowledge and lost power. Hopefully, the information left in a message will empower the addressee to respond in the most appropriate way. For example, increase their knowledge, allow them to make a more informed decision or resolve a business problem.

A message may have time restrictions attached to it. Messages should be checked regularly. Messages should be checked either as quickly as possible or at intervals agreed between a supervisor / manager and the employee. This could be organised as part of a 'to do list', something to be checked first thing after a computer has been switched on. A missed message or a message not checked in time could have a negative impact on a business. For example, a message left by a courier company requesting the correct address for delivering delegate presentation packs to a conference. If the message is left unchecked, the courier will be unable to deliver the delegate packs to the conference on time and the delegates may form a negative impression of the business.

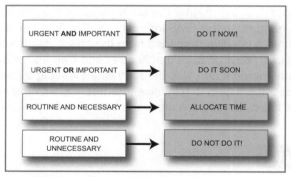

Figure 6.1. Time response to types of messages

Messages should be organised in terms of the action required by the addressee. In some cases no response is required, as the message is just imparting information, e.g. 'the team meeting due to take place this morning at 10.30 has been cancelled.' However, most messages will require some kind of prompt response. Messages may have specific timelines attached to them, which makes them easier to respond to. However, some messages may have no explicit time expectations attached to them but the caller will implicitly expect a response within a certain period of time. As a useful guide, see Figure 6.1.

The addressee will need to **organise the messages** on their system to make sure their system has sufficient space to receive incoming messages every day. Once a message has been responded to by the addressee, the addressee should:

- Delete spam messages, if a system is not set up to do this automatically
- Delete messages that do not require a response
- Delete messages that have been responded to that do not require saving
- Save messages with important or useful / critical information, for legal purposes, that can corroborate decisions taken

This will release space on the EMS and make sure it can continue to receive messages without interruption. The organisation of checking messages should be done in parallel with other aspects of daily work activities.

• ACTIVITY 7

What is the purpose of keeping an EMS up to date?

Testing your knowledge

1. What equipment can an EMS communicate with?
2. What are the main types of EMS?
3. What are the main features of an EMS?
4. What is the purpose of keeping an EMS up to date for:

   4.1 The caller?

   4.2 The addressee?
5. What is the purpose of deleting messages from an EMS?
6. What is an IVS?
7. How is an EMS organised and managed to remain current and up-to-date?
8. What type of EMS does your organisation use?

Skills

Maintain an EMS so it is up to date

To make sure an EMS works effectively for employees, it has to provide correct and up-to-date instructions for callers. Instructions should be clear about what the caller is meant to do. This may require instructions to be changed daily or weekly. For example, the addressee may want to inform the caller of their whereabouts by adding a new telephone number for the caller to use rather than leaving an electronic message.

The types of information that the addressee should provide in their instructions to the caller may include:

- A greeting, such as 'hello' or 'good morning'
- A brief reason for the addressee being unable to answer the caller, e.g. 'I am currently on annual leave and unable to answer your call'
- An invitation for the caller to leave an electronic message.

The invitation may ask the caller to leave:

- Their telephone number
- The time they rang
- A brief description explaining why the addressee needs to call back
- Additional information about whether the addressee is not in the office or has an alternative mobile phone number to call, e.g. 'If your call is urgent or important, please contact Sally Bates on 020 7513 XXX'; 'Please speak clearly after the beep'
- An indication of when the caller may expect a response, e.g. 'I shall return your call when I return to my desk'

The instructions for leaving an electronic message should be made in a quiet environment. This will make sure the instructions are clear and precise. Instructions should be brief, but make sure the caller has all of the necessary information for them to leave an electronic message. Before leaving work at the end of the day, make sure your EMS is switched on, if the system does not do this automatically.

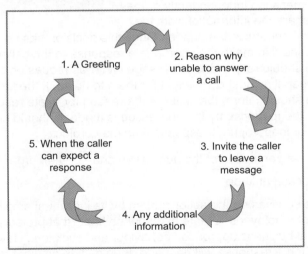

Figure 6.2. Cycle of instructions for leaving an electronic message

Organise an EMS

Once instructions have been set up to leave electronic messages on an EMS, the addressee will begin to receive electronic messages. The addressee will need to organise when and how these electronic messages should be responded to. This needs to be organised systematically. A systematic approach to responding to electronic messages will enforce a habit which will then become an automatic action that the addressee will carry out at specific times of the day.

When accessing electronic messages, the addressee should have paper and a pen to hand in order to write down the information required to respond to the caller's message. This will save time and eliminate the need to re-listen to messages. A message should be deleted once it has been listened to and all appropriate information required to contact the caller has been noted. Some EMSs may allow the addressee to delete all messages in one action, or an EMS may allow specific messages to be saved, e.g. for legal reasons. However, once all messages have been listened to, they should either be deleted or saved to free up space on the EMS and make sure that all further electronic messages can be received.

Having received an electronic message, the addressee has to decide what to do with this information. The addressee may act on the message independently or may decide to share the information with the team or their supervisor / manager. Once this decision has been made, the addressee can make the appropriate response to the caller. The addressee should respond to a message either as requested by the caller or when it is most convenient for them to do so. If the latter, the addressee should inform the caller of the reason for a late response. Whenever the response by the addressee is made, it should be 'on time'. Bad or inappropriate response time may project:

• A negative perception of the addressee and / or their organisation

• A 'don't care' attitude

A business survives on the actions taken by its individual employees or groups of employees. Create a 'response habit' that projects a professional business approach / behaviour and stick to it. Having decided when a response will be made, then decide on what form the response should take, e.g. an email, a telephone call, a personnel appearance. The form of response will be determined by any time implications. While a telephone call may build rapport with a customer, it may also eat into time. In contrast, an email may take just a few minutes. However, a telephone call may also resolve the situation more quickly, avoiding a volley of emails back and forth between the caller and the addressee.

In responding to a caller's electronic message via the telephone, the addressee, who now becomes the caller, should apply the same principles they used in setting up their instructions to leave a message, these should be:

- Brief

- Clear

- Positive

- Focused

Time and tide wait for no man.
- Geoffrey Chaucer

Testing your skills

1. How do you use an EMS?

2. What are the implications for not responding to an electronic message in time?

3. How do you organise responding to electronic messages?

4. How do you prioritise responding to electronic messages?

5. Why should you check electronic messages regularly and / or as agreed with your supervisor / manager?

6. What instructions for leaving an electronic message are most appropriate for your system?

7. How do you delete electronic messages from your EMS?

8. Who is responsible for maintaining your EMS?

Ready for assessment?

To achieve this Level 2 unit of a Business & Administration qualification, learners will need to demonstrate that they are able to perform the following activities:

1. Kept an EMS up to date

2. Left messages for an addressee

3. Received messages from a caller

4. Prioritised a response to messages from callers

5. Responded to messages from callers

6. Identified the implications of not responding to a message on time

7. Provided clear and appropriate instructions for callers to leave a message

8. Freed up EMS space by deleting relevant messages

9. Changed instructions for callers to make sure the delivery of messages was clear and appropriate, as required

You will need to produce evidence from a variety of sources to support the performance requirements of this unit.

If you carry out the 'ACTIVITIES' and respond to the 'NEED TO KNOW' questions, these will provide some of the evidence required.

Links to other units

While gathering evidence for this unit, evidence **may** also be used from evidence generated from other units within the Business & Administration suite of units. Below is a **sample** of applicable units; however, most units within the Business & Administration suite of units will also be applicable.

QCF NVQ
Communications
Communicate in a business environment (Level 1)
Communicate in a business environment (Level 2)
Communicate in a business environment (Level 3)
Make and receive telephone calls
Use a diary system
Core business & administration
Manage own performance in a business environment (Level 2)
Improve own performance in a business environment (Level 2)
Work in a business environment (Level 2)
Work with other people in a business environment (Level 2)
Solve business problems (Level 2)

SVQ
Communications
Understand how to communicate in a business environment
Prepare to communicate in a business environment
Communicate in a business environment (Level 2)
Make and receive telephone calls
Use a diary system
Core business & administration
Agree how to manage and improve own performance in a business environment
Undertake work in a business environment
Work with other people in a business environment
Plan how to solve business problems

7 Manage own performance in a business environment

MANAGE OWN PERFORMANCE IN A BUSINESS ENVIRONMENT

'**Manage own performance in a business environment**' is either a <u>mandatory</u> or <u>optional unit</u> which may be chosen as one of a combination of units to achieve a Qualifications and Credit Framework (QCF) or a National Vocational Qualification (NVQ). It is a <u>mandatory unit</u> in the Scottish Vocational Qualification (SVQ).

The aims of this unit are to:

- Understand how to plan work and be accountable to others

- Understand how to behave in a way that supports effective working

- Be able to plan and be responsible for own work, supported by others

- Be able to deliver a presentation

- Be able to evaluate a presentation

To achieve the above aims of this unit, learners will be expected to provide evidence through the performance of work-based activities.

Knowledge

Every organisation will have different expectations about how they expect their employees to work. Supervisors / managers will be trained and have the experience and expertise to manage their employees effectively. They will expect their employees to perform in ways that are productive. The culture of work has changed over the past few years because of the economic environment. Employees are being asked to work more hours for the same pay to increase productivity. In some cases this is interpreted as working longer and longer hours, which some people do. However, there is a work-life balance that needs to be struck. So instead of working longer hours, learn to work smarter.

Each employee will have specific roles and responsibilities which they will carry out on a day-to-day basis. These responsibilities will include:

- **Performing tasks / activities -** These could occur at specific appointed and agreed times throughout a day, week, month, year etc., or as they occur. As with real life, not everything goes to plan, there are times when some tasks / activities will appear to be unreasonable and cause frustration. However, a supervisor / manager will ask an employee to undertake a task / activity when they know they are able to accomplish it. This does not mean that it will be easy, as some tasks / activities are given to develop workplace skills, knowledge and confidence. It may appear to be unfair, but this feeling probably comes from not feeling confident enough to complete the task / activity

- **Being accountable -** Employees must be accountable for their own work and take responsibility for successfully completing it to the agreed requirements. Employees must keep in contact and report any problems to their supervisor / manager. They must take ownership of the task / activity they are asked to complete. This will involve working with others to plan how the task / activity will be completed. In a new task / activity, when the requirements of the task / activity may not be clear, mistakes may happen. Planning tasks / activities and making decisions with colleagues are important, as they help to minimise mistakes. Problems should be resolved with a supervisor / manager as soon as they happen. Remember, communication is important. Meeting to discuss progress or problems is an opportunity to update progress and to offer new ideas to improve the way things are done. Personal feelings may also be discussed with supervisors / managers which will help the employee to:
  - Get on better with other people
  - Get to know more people
  - Learn new skills
  - Learn to make better decisions
  - Move on to more interesting tasks

- **Working within a team or teams -** Working as part of a team can be challenging. People are working with different personalities, skills and knowledge. However, it is the responsibility of an employee to behave in a professional and courteous manner, at all times, despite their personal feelings. Working in a team opens up opportunities to develop new skills and knowledge. The team provides lots of learning opportunities, as members of the team can learn from each other and guide one another

It is the way that an employee deals with different situations that will decide how much they enjoy their time at work.

Planning work

The most successful way of completing an agreed task / activity is to **plan** what work needs to be carried out. Work should be planned so that every detail is covered. The purpose of planning is to have a clear idea of what needs to be achieved. Planning requires information: what information is required, where to get it from, whom to speak to, what are the timescales and deadlines - are they realistic? - how it is to be presented? Obtain as much detail about the work to be completed. The aim is to produce the most efficient piece of work as possible. What is the best way of planning work? Write it down. Written plans have the benefit of involving the activity of writing and thinking about the work to be completed. It is a permanent record of what has to be done and provides a blueprint of activities that need to be completed in a logical order. If it is written down, other people have access in the event of absences and it can be easily referred to. Having a plan is taking accountability for the work that has to be completed.

The key to planning work is **time management**. Time management is the art of organising and scheduling time in the most efficient ways to create more effective work and productivity. Time is a limited resource - it is not elastic and it cannot be stretched. There are techniques which can be used to make the most of the time envisaged to complete an agreed task / activity:

Prioritise tasks / activities - Make a list of things that need to be completed. This can be carried out using two methods:

- **To do list -** A 'to do list' will provide a precise list of **priorities** that can help to manage and eliminate problems that might occur. Important tasks / activities can be separated from trivial ones. Completing the 'to do list' should involve:
  - Writing down all of the tasks / activities that need to be completed
  - Breaking them down into smaller manageable tasks / activities, estimating how long each task / activity will take
  - Prioritising the tasks / activities. Create a system that categorises each task / activity, e.g. high, medium, low or important, action immediately, get more information, read, telephone. Priorities can also be described as 'must do' - be done today, 'should do' - be done sometime or 'could do' - be done when there is time
  - Listing the tasks / activities in order of priority

- Building in contingencies, as things may take longer than estimated

Using a 'to do list' should be a routine that is followed every day. It could be created at the end of the day in preparation for the next day, or the first thing that is done at the beginning of the day.

- **Diary** - A diary may be maintained using a paper or electronic system. Diary entries must be made clearly and accurately and changed as required. It should provide sufficient information about timing and the subject matter to be discussed so as to prepare for the appointment. Use the diary as a system that not only records appointments but organises how time is used in the working day. Most importantly, keep it up to date. It is no good to anyone if the diary entries bear no relationship to what is actually going to happen

Whatever system is used, avoid the temptation to concentrate on just doing the easy tasks / activities first. Always **prioritise**. Review the 'to do list' and diary to make sure time is being used and managed wisely.

> Nothing is particularly hard if you break it down into small jobs.
> *Henry Ford*

- **Plan the day's tasks / activities** - Set aside enough time to do the 'must do' tasks / activities by their deadlines. Allow time for the 'should do' tasks / activities and even the 'could do' tasks / activities if possible

- **Record the time to complete a task / activity** - It helps to keep track of time and know when an employee may be falling behind or shooting ahead of schedule

- **Deal with disruption** - If there is something important that has to be done, an employee should let colleagues know that focus and concentration needs to be applied to that task / activity for a certain length of time. Avoid needlessly disturbing the people involved in the task / activity at that time

- **Control the telephone** - List the telephone calls that need to be made and set aside a specific time to complete these. Make sure the telephone call is focused and achieves what needs to be achieved as quickly as possible

• ACTIVITY 1

Describe 'time management' and its features.

Sometimes it may feel that there is not enough time to complete tasks / activities and that there is no control over time. For example, a supervisor / manager may require a task / activity to be completed immediately. Respond with understanding and respect. Discuss what needs to be done and find out if the priority for completing the task / activity is realistic. Establish that re-routing to another task / activity will have a knock-on effect to the current task / activity. The plan will need to be updated. Always understand why a plan needs to be changed. Do not be tempted to agree to all requests without notifying a supervisor / manager of the knock-on effects of a change of plan. By agreeing to do any and everything, without any thought of the knock-on effects the change of plan requires, means that a task / activity will not be completed to the agreed time. If an employee continues to do this they will be in danger of earning the reputation of being unreliable.

If an agreed deadline cannot be met, let the supervisor / manager know as soon as possible. It may be possible to extend the deadline, or it may be necessary to get help with completing the task. If a problem is reported sooner rather than later, action can be taken. Carrying on hoping that it will sort itself out undermines the plan of work and then the plan becomes obsolete. When it is obvious that the deadline will not be met it may be too late to do anything about it. Supervisors / managers would prefer that help is asked for when something can be done about it rather than leaving it until the last minute and putting a lot of unnecessary stress and tension on the team. No one likes to be asked to take over a backlog of work which has not been completed because an employee was unwilling to admit to having a problem.

> If you have a job without any aggravations, you don't have a job.
> *- Malcolm S. Forbes*

Always make sure the authority to change something has been given by the appropriate person. Do not change the way things are done without asking first. It is quite possible things are done the way they are done 'because we have always done it that way'. On the other hand, it is also possible things are done that way for very good reasons. Changes may have consequences that an employee cannot see - these could be legal or financial. Discuss new ideas for improving the way things could be done in future with a supervisor / manager, to make sure someone is aware of this new thinking.

Realistic objectives

Planning is used to establish a baseline of the work that needs to be completed. The demands of the workplace can be fluid and demanding. Make sure the plan is linked to clear and realistic objectives, objectives which have a clear target. Objectives should be agreed to be achieved within the required time frame. Objectives have the advantage of:

- Clearly identifying what needs to be done and when
- Organising tasks / activities
- Focusing on what is essential
- Eliminating what is irrelevant
- Co-ordinating tasks / activities
- Establishing and maintaining personal discipline with which to approach work

It is important to make sure objectives remain applicable to the task / activity.

Objectives should be routinely reviewed to make sure they are realistic. If this does not happen **problems** may occur. Problems can occur in the following areas:

- **Planning**
  - Not appropriate to the tasks / activities to be completed
  - Unrealistic objectives
  - Unrealistic time frames
  - Inappropriate priorities
  - Inappropriate budget
  - Insufficient human and physical resources

- **HR**
  - People being used for the wrong tasks / activities
  - People do not have the relevant skills and knowledge
  - People do not follow instructions correctly
  - People may not report problems
  - People do not know who to report to in the event of a problem
  - Team composition
  - Motivation

- **Physical resources**
  - Either too much or too little
  - Costs
  - Logistics
- **Technical**
  - Computers or their programs breakdown
  - Machinery breaks down

A problem should be resolved at the earliest opportunity. The above list highlights the many different forms that a problem can take. However, the problem has to be resolved. Dealing with a problem can take the following stages:

- Acknowledge that there is a problem
- Look at the impact the continuation of the problem will have
- Consider the best options of how to resolve the problem
- Decide which option would be best to resolve the problem
- Implement the agreed option to solve the problem
- Review the solution

If a problem is not solved promptly it can escalate to a crisis. A problem may then become a cost to the organisation, either a financial or a reputational cost, which is to be avoided at all costs.

• ACTIVITY 2

What is an objective? How and why are objectives agreed?

Any change to the objectives of a task / activity should be reported to all who are involved in that task / activity. If an employee is not sure about the impact of a change, work with the supervisor / manager or other members of the team, if working in a team, to resolve and agree the change. There is nothing wrong with change. There is only something wrong with change if no one knows a change has happened and what the impact of that change is on the task / activity. If there is a change in plan let people know as soon as possible, so they can re-plan what needs to be done and if there is a new approach to be taken. People are not mind readers and they can only do what they have agreed to do. It is important that people are given new instructions in good time. People may be working in an organisation that uses matrix management, where employees work in different teams in different departments reporting to different supervisors / managers. They will have to let a lot of people know if there are changes to one task / activity that will affect working on other tasks / activities at the same time.

The same can be said for mistakes. Even with the best plan in the world, mistakes can happen. If a mistake is made, acknowledge it as soon as it has been discovered, and most people will be willing to help sort it out. If a mistake is covered up, when the truth is uncovered there will be little sympathy for the employee. Mistakes are easier to put right immediately than they are further down the line. Admitting to a mistake is the first step towards learning from them. One of the ways that civilisation has advanced is by learning from mistakes. Thomas Edison discovered how to make the electric light bulb from making 2,000 mistakes. However, a mistake is not always considered a virtue by an organisation.

Policy, procedures and codes of practice

An organisation will have many different **policies, procedures and processes** for completing most of its tasks / activities and for managing its people, the building and the products and services it has designed and developed. A **policy** is a document that sets out the course of actions an employee should follow. A policy will then develop procedures and processes which will identify how individual tasks / activities should be carried out. Policies, procedures and processes are developed for employees to make sure that behaviours and products are consistently completed to the same accepted standards and quality. A HR department will have created policies for managing the people within the organisation, e.g. policies and processes on the recruitment and selection of employees. They will also have policies and procedures on health and safety - most of which are designed to conform to legal requirements. The delivery of products and services will be shaped by a delivery process based on industry good practice, some of which will have codes of practice that will need to be adhered to.

A **code of practice** is a set of guidelines and regulations to be followed by members of a profession, trade, occupation, organisation etc. As with instructions, these should be respected and consulted before entering into areas of work that the employee may be unfamiliar with. A code of practice can provide guidance and lay down expected standards, conduct and practice that should be achieved within specific sectors. They may provide support by giving advice and guidance based on real-life experience. Codes of practice may include acts of parliament, e.g. the Data Protection Act 1998; however, the actual code of practice may not necessarily be binding in law.

• ACTIVITY 3

What is the difference between policies, procedures and processes and a code of practice?

Behave in a way that supports effective working
Every organisation expects to produce quality products and services. Quality products and services are designed to offer the customer consistency. An employee will work in an organisation implementing standards that will work towards achieving consistency of output. Consistency generates confidence and trust in an organisation's products and services, whether they are internal products, e.g. an organisation's employees, or external products, e.g. finished goods and services.

An organisation's appraisal system is specifically designed to measure the standard of performance its employees are achieving - this includes behaviour and attitudes. There is a wide difference between an employee doing what they are told to do and an employee who goes out of their way to achieve the highest possible standard. Aim to achieve above the set standard and achieving the required standard will be easy. By taking on a **challenge** an employee shows that they are:

*   **Adaptable** - They are not set in a routine
*   **Prepared** - To embrace change
*   **Focused** - On the needs of the business
*   **Competitive**

Nothing remains the same. The world is in a constant state of flux. This is the same for the world of business. For an organisation to remain profitable and keep up with the times, it constantly reviews what is going on around it - not only locally but internationally. An organisation has to remain competitive or it will go out of business. To remain competitive, expected standards may need to **change** within the organisation. This may have an effect on the way tasks / activities will need to be performed in the future. Most organisations will try to manage the forces of change, but sometimes changes are outside of the control of the organisation, e.g. the effects of a disaster, new technology, new products. These changes could affect the way employees work in the future. Change may also provide new challenges; challenges may be perceived as either an opportunity or a threat, depending on the employee interpreting the effects of change. Change is never easy, but the approach an employee takes to embracing change can be easy. It can be positive and provide a motivational force to help others accept the nature of change.

If an employee is struggling to cope with a new situation, a colleague can offer to help them in any way they can. Remember, it is important to be honest about how much help can be given. Focus should always remain on maintaining the agreed standard of work, so tasks / activities must continue to be completed to the agreed or new standards and timescales. As such, change may require employees to be trained in new ways of working. If there is any doubt about the expected standard that needs to be achieved, ask the supervisor / manager for their advice. Change is an opportunity to learn new things.

• ACTIVITY 4

What is the purpose of change?

The supreme accomplishment is to blur the line between work and play.
- Arnold Toynbee

Working within an organisation is like working in a beehive. Each employee has different functions to deliver; each employee will have different levels of skills and knowledge and each employee will have greater or lesser experience of working for the organisation. At some stage every employee is new. This may happen on joining an organisation or being promoted to another team within the organisation. With each introduction to new ways of working, the employee is expected to grasp the new culture. **Culture** is the 'way we do things round here', the shared values and beliefs that employees are expected to embrace and practise. These may be either:

Explicit
Clearly set out. An organisation may have specific requirements about

personal appearance - dress and personal hygiene - e.g. wearing formal attire at all times, company uniform, polished shoes, well-kept hair. Employees' personal appearance is part of the branding of an organisation and a way in which the organisation's customers view the company. Consideration must be given to how employees behave towards one another. 'Do unto others as you would have them do unto you' is a good phrase to practise. Be polite, be honest and respect others. By behaving in these ways the employee almost contracts the person with whom they are communicating with to behave in the same way, almost mirroring their behaviour. Employees should expect to be able to work in an environment that is positive and encourages growth. Employees should also have the right to be themselves within reason - the organisational requirements. If an employee disagrees with these requirements it would be best if they moved to an organisation which respected and valued their attitude and behaviours.

Implicit

Picked up from observation. For example, going out to lunch on a Friday where important bits of information are shared between employees in a relaxed atmosphere.

• ACTIVITY 5

Why do organisations have different cultures?

If an employee is behaving in a way that goes against company expectations, find out about how long they have been with the

organisation - they may not know how they are meant to behave. If an employee is new to the organisation, remember it is not always easy to fit in somewhere that is new. Make allowances for the fact that they are probably feeling nervous and uncomfortable. Do not jump to conclusions about either their abilities or their attitude. Get to know them and, until then, give them the benefit of the doubt. The support that an employee can give another employee or group of employees is important because it:

*   Increases respect from employee to employee

*   Reinforces the skills or knowledge that are being passed on in the person who is lending support

- Encourages people to reciprocate
- Creates a work environment of trust and sharing

It is a constant juggling act to achieve all these expectations, given how quickly things can change. Strive for perfection and judge imperfections as a passing weakness.

Testing your knowledge

1. What elements need to be used to make a plan?
2. What is a realistic timescale?
3. Why should a plan have realistic objectives?
4. What sort of problems can occur in the workplace?
5. What advantages are there for an employee to take on a challenge in the workplace?
6. Why is it important to keep people informed about progress?
7. Why is change important to an organisation and an employee?
8. What is 'culture' in the context of business?
9. Why is it important to treat colleagues with honesty, respect and consideration?
10. What is a work standard?
11. Why help and support others to the best of your ability?

Skills

Taking accountability for your own work involves understanding what the environment of your work is. It means finding out the expectations for achieving an agreed standard of work, whether that be in terms of behaviour or the product.

You will have been selected for your job as a result of your job interview. You should have been given a job description because that is what was used by the recruiter to make their selection. Go through the job description with your supervisor / manager. There will probably be more to your job than you will find in the job description. While the job description may have identified essential and desirable qualities that the job requires, it will not tell you exactly what that means, so find out. Go through this with your supervisor / manager. What does punctuality mean, arriving in the building at a specific time to start work or arriving at your workstation to start work? There will be lots of things that need to be expanded on for you to know how you are expected to perform.

Identify all the roles and responsibilities you will have to perform. Ask your supervisor / manager what the difference is between roles and responsibilities. Go through all of your responsibilities. Find out the tasks / activities that you will have to do to complete your responsibilities. Find out who you need to report to if you are working across teams. Find out who you will be working with who can help you - this will happen in the early stages of any new job. It is good to get a coach or a mentor for this role. Find out if some of these tasks / activities are routine and, if so, when they need to be completed each hour, day, week, month etc. Find out from your supervisor / manager who you should consult if a problem arises when they are not in attendance. Find out the timescales for completing the tasks / activities that are your responsibility. Take ownership of these responsibilities quickly, but not to the extent that they become automatic and you make mistakes.

When first performing new tasks / activities, follow instructions to the letter. Find out what the task / activity is all about and do it this way before you start thinking of ways to change it. However, people like to be on automatic pilot for some things, and this is appropriate for some tasks, e.g. the mechanics of driving a car - you do not think about changing a gear and what needs to be done, you just get on with it.

In your first few weeks in a new job, mistakes are bound to be made. Learn from them and learn from your supervisor / manager what kind of culture you work in. Is it a culture of blame, where it is difficult to make mistakes? Notice the behaviour of others towards you when you make a mistake, is it generous or not? Watch how other people behave and ask why some behaviours are favoured above others. You will want to fit in as soon as possible so you can learn more and more about your job as quickly as possible. Find out all the procedures that you have to follow. Find out why you have to follow them. Is it technological? Is it legal? Is it health and safety? Is it cultural? If appropriate, look through the codes of practice that you will need to implement.

• ACTIVITY 6

Look at some of the policies and codes of practice that your company has created.

- Why have they been created?
- What do you notice about the way they are structured?
- What codes of practice, if any, does you organisation need to comply with?

Grow with your job and take on more challenges. Make sure you have enough knowledge and skills under your belt to take on these new challenges. Do not run before you can walk! It is good to be ambitious, but make sure it does not antagonise other people you work with. Recognise that your way of working is not everyone else's way of working. If you notice something has changed, be prepared to take on board the new ways of working. Be positive about the change. Find out about why the change has come about. Add to the discussion within your group about how you can all make the change work with the minimum of fuss. It is achievable.

• ACTIVITY 7

Write a list of changes that have happened in your workplace in the past three months.

- What was the effect of these changes?
- What part did you play in these changes?
- Did the change go smoothly?

When you start a task / activity, how much planning do you need to do? Work with your supervisor / manager or other team members to agree and confirm the working plan and the working methods that will be used and fit with the agreed objectives of the task / activity. Implement work methods following either verbal or written instructions, or both. Make notes or create a checklist to remember what needs to be done and the order things need to be done in.

Stick to the plan or make changes when necessary. Set about agreeing realistic objectives which will achieve the desired target. Review these as necessary, to make sure you are still on course to meet the requirements of the plan. If objectives change because of pressure of work, make sure those you are working with know and can adapt to the agreed change. If the change is not achievable, discuss this with your supervisor / manager and agree an alternative approach. If there are any changes, make sure that these are communicated to everyone in good time.

Develop the good habit of having a 'to do list'. Write down at the beginning or the end of each day everything that you need to do that day or the next day. Use a diary to manage your time throughout the day. Subdivide these tasks / activities into smaller units of work which you can manage more easily. This will give you an idea of how long each one will take to complete. If you encounter any problems and do not know what to do, there is no shame attached to that. Ask someone to help you. It is better to get advice and fix the problem than muddle through and make the problem worse.

• ACTIVITY 8

Monitor everything that you do in a week at work to see if you can maximise more of your time. Create a diary and make a note of the start time and finish time of each task / activity you do and what you do within that time. You may find at the end of the week that you spend a lot of time on the telephone - is that appropriate or not? Review what you have done and see if there is anything that you can cut out or overhaul.

Remember who you are in all of this. Not only do you need to project the best qualities of who you are, but you must fit in with the expected behaviours that the organisation expects of you. Adopt an ethical approach to everything that you do and you will not fall foul of anything or anyone. Once you have a good feel and understanding of what it is you will be doing in your job, make sure you are performing to the required standard. Find out what the standard is and work towards achieving it. Find out from your supervisor / manager if there are National Occupational Standards (NOS) for the sector you work in and use them as a guide to managing your performance. Set yourself high standards, i.e. try to go beyond the expected standards set out in codes of practice. Finish your work so that it has clearly achieved the agreed objectives within the agreed time and to a high quality. Make sure you are able to respond unequivocally to your supervisor / manager if asked **what** you are doing, **how** you are doing it, **when** you are doing it, **why** you are doing it, **where** you are doing it and **who** you are doing it with.

Testing your skills

1. Who do you keep informed about progress?

2. Who have you agreed your work plan with?

3. How do you agree realistic timescales?

4. When do you report that deadlines may not be achievable?

5. What problems have you had to deal with and how did you resolve them?

6. What codes of practice and procedures are relevant to your work?

7. What is the importance of behaving responsibly at work?

8. What are the standards which you work by?

9. How do your standards go beyond what is expected of you?

10. How have you adapted readily to change?

Ready for assessment?

To achieve this Level 2 unit of a Business & Administration qualification, learners will need to demonstrate that they are able to perform the following activities:

1. Agreed realistic objectives and targets

2. Achieved timescales for their own work

3. Planned how to make best use of all resources to achieve the plan of work

4. Agreed and took responsibility for their own work

5. Followed the correct procedures for dealing with problems

6. Kept others informed of any changes to the work plan in time

7. Renegotiated timescales and deadlines in time

8. Followed agreed guidelines, procedures or codes of practice

9. Set a high standard and committed to achieving high standards

10. Showed a willingness to take on challenges

11. Adapted to change readily

12. Treated other people with honesty, respect and consideration

You will need to produce evidence from a variety of sources to support the performance requirements of this unit.

If you carry out the 'ACTIVITIES' and respond to the 'NEED TO KNOW' questions, these will provide some of the evidence required.

Links to other units

While gathering evidence for this unit, evidence **may** also be used from evidence generated from other units within the Business & Administration suite of units. Below is a **sample** of applicable units; however, most units within the Business & Administration suite of units will also be applicable.

QCF NVQ
Communications
Communicate in a business environment (Level 2)
Make and receive telephone calls
Core business & administration
Improve own performance in a business environment (Level 2)
Solve business problems (Level 2)
Work in a business environment (Level 2)
Work with other people in a business environment (Level 2)
Customer service
Meet and welcome visitors
Handle mail
Provide reception services

SVQ
Communications
Plan how to communicate in a business environment
Core business & administration
Plan how to solve business problems
Work with other people in a business environment
Undertake work in a business environment
Customer service
Meet and welcome visitors
Handle mail
Provide reception services

8 Improve own performance in a business environment

IMPROVE OWN PERFORMANCE IN A BUSINESS ENVIRONMENT

'**Improve own performance in a business environment**' is an <u>optional unit</u> which may be chosen as one of a combination of units to achieve either a Qualifications and Credit Framework (QCF), National Vocational Qualification (NVQ) or Scottish Vocational Qualification (SVQ).

The aims of this unit are to:

- Understand how to improve own performance
- Be able to improve own performance using feedback
- Be able to agree own development needs using a learning plan

To achieve the above aims of this unit, learners will be expected to provide evidence through the performance of work-based activities.

Knowledge

In the competitive world of business of the 21st century, continuous improvement and development is the key to survival. For a business to survive it must remain competitive and profitable. It must develop. It cannot afford to stand still. Globalisation and new working practices force businesses to evaluate where they are and make changes to maintain and improve their competitive edge, or else they will go out of business. As an integral resource of any business, this means that each of its employees will be expected to improve their performance to contribute towards sustaining the business.

From the moment an employee has been offered a position of work in an organisation they have taken their first step towards improving their performance. Once they have attended their first induction meeting they have taken their next step towards improving their performance.

Each of these steps will contribute towards an employee consolidating their skills, knowledge and attitudes. They are adding value to the business. In any business that considers itself a **learning organisation** there should be a learning strategy that encourages

its employees to embrace **lifelong learning**. This new learning can then be applied to the business and to appropriate aspects of an employee's life.

As with life, working in a business is all about continually learning: evaluating, observing, absorbing, questioning, adapting and re-evaluating.

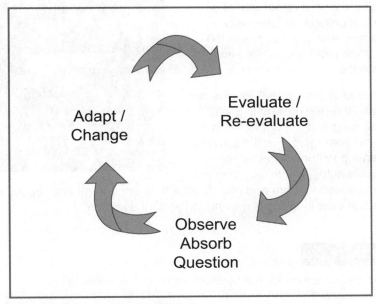

Figure 8.1. The process of continually learning

An organisation should aim to develop the full potential of its employees, who need to:

• Stay employable throughout their lifetime

• Learn methods and techniques to do specific jobs

• Extend their capabilities

• Remain motivated and attracted to a job

• Develop their career

> Success in the marketplace increasingly depends on learning, yet most people don't know how to learn.
> *- Chris Argyris*

Learning to work and working to learn is a cycle that continues throughout an employee's career. However, the opportunity to learn is influenced by two factors: the work environment - does it encourage learning by providing a time and a place to learn? and the approach the employee takes towards learning - their learning style, motivation to learn, ambition, interests, ability.

Learning can be undertaken either formally, e.g. in a classroom of a technical college, or informally, e.g. sitting with a colleague in the workplace picking up skills and knowledge.

The learning process will involve two parties - the person who is giving the learning and the person who is learning from them. For the provider of learning to know whether their learner is actually learning, they will have to question them and offer feedback to encourage and reassure them that their learning is moving in the right direction.

• ACTIVITY 1

What steps are involved in continuously improving individual performance?

Feedback
Feedback is information that is structured to be delivered to a person about the impact and implications of their performance. Good-quality feedback is an important ingredient in building constructive relation-ships and in doing a job well. It is an essential part of learning. It helps learners to maximise their potential at different stages of learning, raise awareness of and areas for improvement and identify the actions that need to be taken to improve performance. Feedback is given to confirm that learning has taken place. Feedback can come from a number of sources:

- Supervisors / managers

- Team leaders

- Colleagues / team members

- Other people working in a project
- Friends
- People the employee has met at learning events
- Customers

Feedback can be **formal**, part of an appraisal interview, or **informal**, a discussion between a supervisor / manager and their employee. Feedback is a valuable tool both for the learner and the person providing feedback. Learners may think they are doing well and have no areas that need improving; however, this is rarely the case, as there is usually always something that can be improved. If feedback is not offered to an employee it may send out a message that the employer does not care, leading to a loss of commitment and undermining of trust in the business. Feedback is offered to:

- **Influence** someone to change their approach
- **Recognise and reward** effort
- **Improve the quality** of work
- **Build and maintain** relationships
- **Clarify** expectations
- **Motivate**

• ACTIVITY 2

Why is feedback given to employees?

Feedback should be welcomed and encouraged. The important thing about feedback is that it should be constructive and be given by a credible person, a person that is respected by the employee. Encouraging feedback sends a signal to the supervisor / manager and the organisation that the employee:

- Cares about what they are doing
- Is interested in cultivating an approach to lifelong learning
- May have talent that needs to be nurtured and grown
- May be promoted within the organisation
- Could be given more demanding work to do which would stretch them

- May want to develop a career within the business

The empowered employee must determine how often and with whom they are going to encourage feedback from. It is good for an employee to hear where they have done well, but it is more constructive for them to hear about areas where they can improve their performance. This will help the employee to gain confidence and give them the will to improve. Feedback should provide the employee with a full summary of how things can be improved, explaining:

- The task

- The skills, knowledge and attitude / behaviour that were required to complete the task

- Why the task had to be done that way

- Where the employee did not meet these requirements, identifying the skills, knowledge, behavioural or attitudinal gaps in performance

Once the employee fully understands this, a learning plan can be agreed to bridge the performance gap. Feedback can improve an employee's confidence, self-awareness and enthusiasm for learning. Good feedback should be:

- Descriptive - set out expectations

- Focused on performance

- Clear and direct

- Balanced

- Specific

- Timely

- Regular

- Able to offer a solution

Barriers to feedback

Feedback is not always easy to receive. The feedback may be perceived as being based on incorrect assumptions. Both parties involved in the feedback process will need to work through negative perceptions. Receiving corrective feedback may be difficult because the employee may:

- Want to rationalise what went wrong as they may feel uncomfortable

- Feel their self-worth is undermined by suggestions for improvement

- Have had previous experiences where feedback was unhelpful or unjustified
- Be realistic about the feedback process. It is not always an easy experience for anyone. So be wary of:
- Being defensive
- Trying to prove that the person giving feedback is wrong
- Justifying the original performance
- Dismissing the feedback
- Attacking the speaker
- Feeling something has to be done to change your whole self
- Feeling helpless to do anything about what has been fed back
- Generalising the message and feeling either bad or perfect about everything
- Improve the feedback process by:
- Using questions to find out the issue behind the criticism
- Being clear about what would help
- Helping the person giving the feedback to understand what is wanted

• ACTIVITY 3

What behaviours need to be monitored when receiving feedback?

Appraisals

Appraisals are an important opportunity for supervisors / managers and staff to discuss performance. They should be seen as a joint problem-solving exercise in which opportunities to resolve any problems can be identified. The outcome of an appraisal meeting will be the development of a **learning** or **development plan** which will identify what an employee needs to do in order to achieve an acceptable level of performance and the opportunities there are for an employee to fulfil their potential.

From time to time feedback will be given formally in an appraisal meeting. An appraisal may be carried out to:

- Identify how well the job is being done

- Identify strengths and weaknesses
- Reward employee contribution in achieving objectives
- Motivate
- Identify learning and development needs
- Identify potential
- Appraisals are usually held annually.

Learning plans

A **learning plan** is a set of personal targets that have been agreed between an employee and their supervisor / manager to achieve over a specified period of time. It is also a means of recording achievement. It helps to keeps the employee on track towards achieving their work and life goals. It helps an employee to take more control of their future by reminding them what they have learned, achieved and enjoyed. It helps to increase confidence, abilities, employability and also helps them to get more out of life.

A learning plan will usually be drawn up between the employee and the employer after the appraisal interview. The learning plan will:

- Identify learning objectives that are tied to specific work
- Identify milestones, with expected outcomes that can be reviewed and amended
- Review the success / failure of a performance and include a description of why this happened

A well-written learning plan will:

- Motivate
- Build self-esteem
- Focus on what is being done well
- Recognise how to avoid time-wasting activities
- Negotiate deadlines more realistically
- Record evidence of achievements or note any qualifications the employee is working towards achieving

The content of a learning plan can be agreed using **SWOT analysis**. SWOT analysis is an analytical took which can be used in many different contexts across the life of an organisation to guide its growth and development. SWOT is a mnemonic where each letter of the mnemonic means:

S = Strengths

W = Weaknesses

O = Opportunities

T = Threats

In the context of a learning plan, an employee can work with their supervisor / manager through each of these aspects of the elements of a SWOT analysis to give them a picture of where an employee is and where they want to be, from which a learning plan can be agreed.

• ACTIVITY 4

How does a learning plan contribute to improving an employee's work?

Career progression routes

The best kind of development is self-development. Organisations may have limited resources e.g. finance, space, people etc. to focus on all the expressed and unexpressed needs of the employee. Increasingly, employees have to manage their own development beyond the resources that an organisation can offer. An employee joins a business to work. Depending on the employee, they may develop a passion for the job and want to explore it in further depth. They see themselves progressing and developing a career. The opportunity to develop a career comes mainly from the employee, who will discuss the practicality of their plans with their employer. An employee should aim to upgrade their own skills and knowledge, as the potential benefits that can come from self-development are:

• New and improved skills, knowledge and behaviours

• The ability to cope more readily with change

• Enhanced interpersonal skills

• Greater self-awareness

- Better understanding of learning
- Increased confidence
- Increased self-reliance

Opportunities to progress come from a:

- **Promotion** - Either within an organisation or moving to a new one
- **Transfer** - To another job within the organisation which may or may not have time limitations put on the transfer
- **Secondment or outplacement** - A transfer to work with another organisation for a limited period of time
- **New job** - Moving away from one organisation to work with another
- To help with progression within an organisation:
- Learn about and embrace its **culture**
- Identify and work towards achieving some **short-term objectives**
- **Network** internally and externally
- **Develop** self-reliance

Testing your knowledge

1. What is the purpose of continuously improving performance?

2. What is feedback?

3. How should negative feedback be handled?

4. Why should feedback be encouraged?

5. Why is feedback important to continuously improve work?

6. What is career progression?

7. Why should employees develop their skills and knowledge?

8. What can a learning plan be used for?

9. What are the benefits of continuous learning and development?

10. What is self-development?

11. What career progression routes are available to an employee?

Skills

The only way you will know if what you are doing is of value to both your team and the organisation, and yourself, is if someone tells you. Make it part of your work plan to improve - to do everything that you do today better tomorrow. This will be fulfilling to you and it will also be appreciated by your supervisor / manager and the organisation that you work for. So aim to improve in stages, and have a plan to work towards achieving it.

Remember the last time that you were given feedback - did you volunteer for it or was it part of a process? How often is feedback given to you? Is it enough? Do you feel like you are moving forward? Is the pace of movement too slow, too quick etc? How did you feel when you were given the feedback? If feedback is given in a positive environment it should be easy to accept, provided it is specific and clearly describes what has to be changed and the reason for the change. Everybody wants to improve their performance and add value to a business.

Look at ways of using the feedback to impact on all areas of your work. If the scope of the feedback can be applied more generally, use it. Try not to look at things in isolation but take a 'helicopter' view. Look at ways where the feedback can improve the way you work with other people and the way you support other people, the way you generally take direction from other people and how you are managed by other people. Review your behaviours and attitudes, as these are always the hardest areas to gain feedback on, both for the person giving the feedback and the person receiving the feedback. Feedback can be interpreted very personally, and sometimes that is right, but try to take an objective view and look at how the feedback is contributing to adding value to you, the job and the organisation. Once you have been given the feedback, how did you use it? Did you use it immediately or did you review it to make it work for you?

Develop a plan to encourage feedback of your work. It needs to fit organically into the management of your skills and knowledge and with the schedule of the person providing the feedback. Do not request too much feedback, as this may antagonise a busy supervisor / manager. You may also not have time to do what is required as a result of the feedback, as it may jeopardise the completion of your agreed objectives. Always be realistic about what you can and cannot handle.

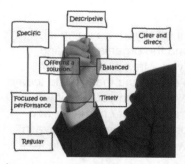

How much of the feedback that you have received has gone towards the development of your learning or development plan? Agree the learning plan with your supervisor / manager. Make sure it is realistic and achievable. There is nothing worse than having a plan which you do not or cannot achieve, as this is demoralising and can undermine your confidence. Once you have agreed your learning plan make it an organic part of your work. Use it to inform the way that you undertake your work and improve your performance. Remember, work can be a volatile environment with things changing all the time. Be prepared for the impact of change. Review your learning plan to make sure it remains relevant - change it when it needs to be changed. How often do you look at your learning plan? How often do you review your learning plan? Do you have a learning plan? Continue to update the learning plan with ideas and potential alternative routes to learning.

The best person to develop your skills and knowledge is you. If your organisation does not have a system of learning plans, create one for yourself. Set out the objectives that you want to achieve in the short, medium and long term. Look at what you need to do in each of these time spans. Once you know what you need to do, look for any gaps which will stop you from achieving your objectives. Plan to put the required learning in place to cover these gaps. Monitor your learning through discussion with your supervisor / manager. Make any changes to your learning plan as a result of these discussions. Look at ways of undertaking further learning. Remember, this does not necessarily need to take place in the workplace but could be done through studying to complete a qualification. Has your organisation helped to fund this qualification?

• ACTIVITY 5

Complete the following self-appraisal by ticking the most appropriate box against each skill. For each tick in the 'training needs' column identify an action that you can take.

	Can do	Training needs	Actions to be taken
Speak at meetings			
Join in discussions			
Answer the telephone			
Make telephone calls			
Give a talk			
Write a report			
Write a memo			
Research information			
Prioritise tasks			
Delegate			
Deal with disruption			
Say 'no' if necessary			
Admit mistakes			
Put forward ideas			
Accept feedback			
Motivate yourself			
Set high standards			
Accept new challenges			
Embrace change			

Show the completed self-appraisal to your supervisor to check that they agree with your findings.

• ACTIVITY 6

Your supervisor / manager has advised you that a new member of staff is to start work in your department next week and has asked you to carry out their induction to the whole organisation. Prepare a checklist of all the things that you will need to cover. Do not forget things like toilets, staff rooms, arrangements for lunch etc.

Develop strategies to identify further areas for your learning and development. Use your networking skills to find out what is going on in other parts of your organisation which you might be interested in pursuing. Broaden your reading to subject areas that your career could move towards. Attend meetings or conferences to open up opportunities to develop your learning. Research these new areas of work to see what you feel about them. Is shadowing someone for a few hours a viable thing to do to find out more information? Do these new areas of work fit into your overall career plan?

Testing your skills

1. How have you improved your overall performance?

2. What feedback was difficult for you to receive, and why?

3. What feedback did you receive which made you feel good, and why?

4. What changes have you made to your performance as a result of the feedback?

5. How did you agree and accept the learning plan that you used to improve your work?

6. How have you followed your learning plan?

7. What training opportunities have been available to you?

8. What have you done to find out about further learning?

Ready for assessment?

To achieve this Level 2 unit of a Business & Administration qualification, learners will need to demonstrate that they are able to perform the following activities:

1. Encouraged and accepted feedback from other people

2. Used feedback to agree ways to improve performance

3. Completed work using feedback

4. Investigated and agreed where further learning and development opportunities which could improve performance

5. Confirmed changes to your learning plan

6. Followed through a learning plan that met development needs

7. Reviewed progress against your learning plan

8. Agreed further learning

You will need to produce evidence from a variety of sources to support the performance requirements of this unit.

If you carry out the 'ACTIVITIES' and respond to the 'NEED TO KNOW' questions, these will provide some of the evidence required.

Links to other units

While gathering evidence for this unit, evidence **may** also be used from evidence generated from other units within the Business & Administration suite of units. Below is a **sample** of applicable units; however, most units within the Business & Administration suite of units will also be applicable.

QCF NVQ
Communications
Communicate in a business environment (Level 2)
Core business & administration
Manage own performance in a business environment (Level 2)
Solve business problems (Level 2)

SVQ
Communications
Prepare to communicate in a business environment
Core business & administration
Plan how to solve a business problem

9 Work in a business environment

WORK IN A BUSINESS ENVIRONMENT

'**Work in a business environment**' is an <u>optional</u> or <u>mandatory unit</u> which may be chosen as one of a combination of units to achieve either a Qualifications and Credit Framework (QCF), National Vocational Qualification (NVQ) or Scottish Vocational Qualification (SVQ).

The aims of this unit are to:

- Understand how to respect other people at work
- Understand how to maintain security and confidentiality at work and deal with concerns
- Understand the purpose and procedures for keeping waste to a minimum in a business environment
- Understand procedures for the disposal of hazardous materials
- Know how to support sustainability in an organisation
- Be able to respect and support other people at work in an organisation
- Be able to maintain security and confidentiality
- Be able to support sustainability and minimise waste in an organisation
- To achieve the above aims of this unit, learners will be expected to provide evidence through the performance of work-based activities.

Knowledge

We live in a world of finite resources. The world is coming under increasing pressure, as the earth ages, to support more people with these finite resources. Employees working in an organisation will be inducted to understand the vision and ethos of how the organisation expects them to behave and undertake the responsibilities of their job. Much of this will be covered in the legal contract an employee signs; however, there will be expectations placed on an employee which are also covered in the 'psychological contract' shared between the employee and the organisation. The 'psychological contract' has no legal standing, but is a powerful ethos of expectations built between the employee and the organisation. The mix between the 'legal contract' and the 'psychological contract' underpins how an employer and employee contribute to the values and productivity of a business. Three important areas that this covers are:

- **Supporting sustainability -** Organisations need to manage their business to sustain their future by devising policies and processes to manage an 'environmentally friendly' workplace. Organisations also seek to reduce their carbon footprint by managing waste, hazardous materials and recycling to sustain their internal economy and the rest of the world. By supporting sustainability the employee and the organisation aim to enhance their community at work

- **Supporting diversity -** Organisations need to determine how they manage the selection and organisation of their employees that takes into consideration the different cultural values that each employee brings to an organisation, which can add a new dimension to how organisations can achieve their aims and goals

- **Maintaining security and confidentiality -** Employees, the physical premises and information about all aspects held by a business should be protected at all times from threat of loss or violence

Support sustainability

Increasingly within the global economy, many organisations seek to operate in an environmentally friendly way. This has an impact on the way all employees will work to achieve, maintain and build an environmentally friendly organisation which can be achieved by aiming to:

- Reduce wasting energy, e.g. using light bulbs which are more energy efficient

- Recycle different types of resources

- Use low-emission vehicles etc.

- Increase reliance on public transport

- Use technology more efficiently in the work environment, e.g. switch off the computer and computer screen at the end of the working day

• ACTIVITY 1

How important is sustainability to the growth of an organisation?

Organisations seek to be environmentally sensitive by providing a place of work that is considerate of the environment. They will seek to do this by creating a sustainable work environment that:

- Actively seeks to minimise climate change, e.g. through energy efficiency and the use of renewable material

- Protects the environment, by minimising pollution on land, in water and in the air

- Minimises waste and disposes of it in accordance with organisational procedures

- Uses natural resources efficiently, encouraging sustainable production and consumption

- Protects and improves bio-diversity, e.g. wildlife habitats

- Enables a lifestyle that minimises negative environmental impact • and enhances positive impacts, e.g. reducing noise pollution and dependence on cars

- Creates cleaner, safer and greener neighbourhoods, e.g. by reducing litter

• ACTIVITY 2

Circle the correct answer. A sustainable work environment …

1. Disposes of waste as it wishes
2. Pollutes the air
3. Creates cleaner neighbourhoods
4. Does nothing about managing the proliferation of litter
5. Does not use renewable material

Waste can be caused in the following areas in an organisation:

- **Time** - Due to employees engaged needlessly doing personal tasks, using social networks, poor decision-making, being unproductive due to poor management direction etc.

- **Office resources and materials** - Due to theft, excessive use of printing when not required, personal use of printers and other supplies by employees etc.

- **Office technology** - Due to energy being wasted leaving lights and personal computers (PCs) turned on at night when no one is there, keeping heat or air conditioning turned too high or low, inefficient use of company vehicles etc.

• ACTIVITY 3

How is waste caused in an organisation?

The purpose of managing waste is to promote the economic use of materials / resources and methods so that waste is minimised. Any waste produced in an organisation should be reused, recycled or recovered in some other ways before disposing of any waste. Currently, it is claimed that there is a cost of £15 billion to British industry because of bad waste practices. By minimising waste in the workplace, significant financial savings can be made, as well as reducing the impact of the business on the environment. The key areas of potential physical waste are:

- Misuse
- Extravagance
- Rework
- Shrinkage

• ACTIVITY 4

What are the key areas of potential physical waste?

Waste can be reduced in the workplace by implementing the following practices:

- **Paper consumption** - Can be reduced by using double-sided photocopying, 'waste' sheets as scrap paper and email wherever possible, only printing off emails when necessary. Post visual reminders around the organisation reminding employees to consider alternatives to producing waste

- **Publications** - Try not to over-order, or consider publishing electronically

- **Amnesty Days** - The aim of which is to give up items that can be reused elsewhere and to identify wastes that can be recycled. It also raises employee awareness about how much waste is unnecessarily produced

- **Negotiate waste packaging with suppliers** - Encourage suppliers to recover and reuse packaging a number of times before disposal. Make the best use of the available recycling facilities to minimise waste. Make sure contracts are in place to recycle glass, fluorescent tubes, paper, aluminium cans, plastics, toner cartridges, batteries, I.T and electronic equipment and mobile phones

- **Recycle** - This is reprocessing used materials that would otherwise become waste. Recycling breaks down waste to reproduce new products, whereas reuse is about collecting waste to be cleaned, refilled and resold. Recycling prevents waste from being sent to landfill sites or burned by incinerators; it reduces the consumption of new raw materials and requires less energy than producing new products. Common materials that can be recycled include:

  - Glass
  - Paper
  - Aluminium
  - Asphalt
  - Steel
  - Textiles
  - Plastic

These materials can be used in either manufacturing industries, pre-consumer waste, or thrown away by consumers, post-consumer waste. The recycling of waste requires a system to sort the waste. Recycling leads to reducing the amount of new materials required for production, or to change the way manufacturers use resources, the amount of waste going to landfill sites or incinerators, and it saves money, e.g. recycling of aluminium saves 95% of the carbon dioxide emissions compared to refining new metal. The purpose of recycling is to change the way industrial societies behave to maintain the planet's resources for posterity.

There are some materials that cannot be recycled or, as waste, need to follow special procedures for disposing of them. These are called hazardous materials. Hazardous materials should be disposed of safely following these procedures:

• ACTIVITY 5

What is the difference between pre-consumer and post-consumer waste?

Identify the hazardous substances in the workplace and the potential risks they pose to people's health or the environment

- Decide what precautions are needed to eliminate the risks
- Eliminate the hazardous substances wherever possible or control exposure to protect the health of the environment
- Implement control measures or procedures which employees use consistently to avoid any risks to health
- Monitor exposure
- Implement health surveillance, e.g. medical checks for employees
- Prepare plans and procedures to deal with accidents, incidents and emergencies

- Train and supervise employees to make sure that their health is not damaged when using or when coming into contact with hazardous substances

Examples of hazardous wastes include:

- Asbestos
- Lead-acid batteries
- Used engine oils and oil filters
- Solvents and solvent-based substances
- Chemical waste
- Pesticides
- Fluorescent light tubes
- Computers
- Medicines

• ACTIVITY 6

When do waste materials become 'hazardous'?

When do waste materials become 'hazardous'?

Legislation that covers the management of waste and hazardous materials are:

- The Environmental Protection Act

- Hazardous Waste (England and Wales) Regulations 2005

Managers are duty bound to make sure hazardous waste is correctly identified at each stage of production. They must implement procedures to protect the health of employees and contractors who transport or dispose of waste. This is covered by the **Health and Safety at Work Act 1974** and the **Control of Substances Hazardous to Health Regulations (COSHH) 1999 (SI 1999 No. 437)**.

Office equipment and technology is the fastest-growing energy consumer. However, it can be reduced using energy-saving measures, e.g. turning on power-saving modes on PCs and laptops, switching equipment off overnight, attaching timers to light switches, making sure windows are closed in winter, using different lighting bulbs. The Carbon Trust estimates that most businesses can make vast savings, e.g. in the service sector it could reduce energy bills by an estimated 20-30%.

Most businesses waste energy through unnecessary use of equipment and technology. This can be overcome by:

- Training employees to use equipment correctly or retrain them to do so, e.g. cutting or drilling into raw materials using accurate measurements or double-sided printing and low toner setting on office printers

- Installing low-cost equipment, e.g. motion-sensor controlled lighting, replacing current equipment with equipment which has a lower consumption of energy, making equipment more energy efficient

- Maintaining equipment regularly

- Changing processes to reduce waste

- Effectively storing and handling finished goods

- Minimising the packaging used on finished goods

Support diversity

As the EU expands or as the world contracts, more and more people from different backgrounds and different countries will enter the British employment market. Many organisations conduct their business globally, with different offices located throughout the world. This offers their employees the opportunity to be transferred to different countries. Employment no longer caters for a clearly defined single group of people. It is a mix of people from different races, nationalities and religions. When people from diverse backgrounds enter an organisation they bring with them their experience of different cultures and values. Diversity refers to the different human qualities exhibited from different groups of people. Diversity in the workforce means employing people without discrimination on the basis of gender, age and ethnic or racial background. Diversity also relates to issues of:

- Disability

- Religion

- Job title

- Physical appearance

- Sexual orientation

- Nationality

- Multiculturism

- Competency

- Training

- Experience

- Personal habits

Diversity is to be valued because it adds richness to an organisation. However, it also adds challenges. Policies and procedures in organisations should focus on developing effective working relationships with a diverse workforce. To achieve effective working relationships in a diverse community of people, an organisation needs to focus on similarities rather than differences. Building relationships from within a diverse community of people is critical for the success of any organisation in the 21st century. Different points of view can be invaluable to an organisation as they can provide opportunities that a business may not have considered in the past. An organisation with a diverse workforce has a greater pool of experiences to work with to produce ideas for products that cater to different cultures.

• ACTIVITY 7

What are the issues that are covered in diversity?

Organisations, irrespective of size, that employ a diverse workforce are in a better position to understand the demographics of its customers. This gives them the advantage of being able to increase market share by reaching out to new markets and new customers. An organisation that supports a diverse workforce is also better able to address employee satisfaction and retention issues. It also has a larger pool of potential employees from which it can select to join the organisation. Organisations should seek to promote inclusion so the organisation can take advantage of the wide range of experiences within the organisation.

Valuing diversity means creating a workplace that respects and includes differences. It recognises the unique contributions that employees with many types of differences can make, and creates a work environment that strives to maximise the potential of all employees. Employees working in an organisation should respect, honour and appreciate the differences that a diverse workforce can add to help achieve the goals and ambitions of any organisation of any size. It is important to acknowledge similarities and likenesses to foster an understanding and appreciation of diversity in the workplace.

There are a number of strategies that can be used to increase sensitivity towards the needs of others in an environment which encourages diversity:

- **Increase awareness of what others might be experiencing** - Be careful not only about the words used, but also about not saying anything at all. Be thoughtful and tactful about expressing awareness of another employee's actions and reactions or of others' actions or reactions

- **Do not** assume - It makes an ass of 'u' and 'me'. Assumptions are often mistaken because we rarely understand the complexities of another's life. Avoid labelling a person, but imagine why they act the way they do or say the things they do

- **Respect others -** Our status - marital, financial or social - does not define us, so it should not determine the way we treat others. If you start to feel irritated, stop yourself from saying anything. Think to yourself that there is a reason this person is acting the way they are acting, and that you should respect how they feel at the moment, even if it bothers you

Show understanding and avoid gossip

- **Resist taking offence -** Everyone deals with something difficult and we all have weaknesses. Some deficits are more obvious than others, but everyone must overcome some obstacles. Help to build each other up

- **Empathise -** Do not let one encounter ruin the perception of that person, e.g. just because someone seemed to be in a bad mood when spoken to, that does not mean they are constantly angry and depressed

- **Do not let your insecurities or beliefs get in the way** – e.g. It is common to meet people with different beliefs, likes and dislikes than you, so do not be put off if the person you are talking to does not like something you do, or likes something you do not

Organisations should aim to be an '**inclusive**' organisation. An 'inclusive' organisation seeks to reflect the needs and aspirations of all employees by respecting and valuing difference and promoting '**equal opportunity**' for all. 'Equal opportunity' is a commitment to minimise and eliminate barriers to participation in an organisation's activities. An organisation provides a culture of 'equal opportunities' to offer equal treatment to its internal and external customers, where everyone has the right to be treated with respect and dignity.

• ACTIVITY 8

What do employees need to consider to act more sensitively towards people in an organisation that encourages diversity?

Organisations will usually have policies and procedures that cover 'equal opportunities' in the workplace, where all types of customers are expected to:

- Treat others fairly. Appreciate that first impressions can be misleading. Give people the opportunity to be discovered

- Learn from others
- Not support people who treat others unfairly
- Support equal-opportunity programmes

For example, people with disabilities or the elderly may require help with access to the building; visitors, of either gender, may require crèche facilities for their babies or small children; hearing-impaired colleagues may need more visual aids.

• ACTIVITY 9

What does an 'equal-opportunities' programme aim to achieve?

Organisations have 'equal-opportunity' programmes designed to:

- Improve team success through respect and dignity for all by making sure employees are judged on their abilities and past performance. This is covered by an organisation's policies on recruitment, promotion training, benefits and dismissal
- Reduce stress levels and absenteeism
- Improve safety performance
- Reduce the costs of recruiting new staff
- Increase sales by making staff more committed
- Widen the customer base
- Homogenise behaviour in the workplace

For an organisation, 'equal opportunities' is about good business practice and can:

- Reduce costs
- Improve efficiency
- Lower staff turnover
- Improve customer relations

An organisation will aim to make their 'equal opportunity' policies more successful by:

- Managing **discrimination** and **harassment** in the workplace
- Treating all employees equally

- Providing appropriate advice and training
- Offering flexible working time
- Handling complaints promptly

It does not necessarily matter if an employer intended to discriminate. It is the effect of the discrimination which is important. There are two types of discrimination:

- **Direct** - Direct discrimination happens when people are treated less favourable because of their gender, ethnicity, sexual orientation etc. For example, selecting a male for the supervisor's position ahead of a better qualified female because the majority of the staff are male and the supervisor has always been a male

- **Indirect** - Discrimination which takes a more subtle form where a provision or condition that appears neutral actually disadvantages a person or group of people, e.g. when a rule states that everyone applying for a job must have attended a public school when there is no good reason for this

• ACTIVITY 10

What is discrimination?

Harassment - On the other hand, is an unwelcome or offensive remark, request or other act that discriminates against a person by harming their job performance or satisfaction. Sexual harassment is a criminal offence. Other types of harassment that may be judged as criminal include:

- Offensive jokes, remarks or insults based on ethnicity, nationality or other characteristics
- Bullying
- Threats, verbal or physical abuse
- Threatening or discriminating against someone for reporting a breach of the law

Victimisation - May occur in many different ways, e.g. when an employee:

- Has made a complaint about being discriminated against or harassed

- Has made a complaint about discrimination or harassment
- Intends to act as a witness or give evidence in support of another employee that relates to a complaint about discrimination or harassment
- May have been refused requests for time off
- May have been denied promotion or training
- May have been ignored by their manager or colleagues
- May have been criticized continually for their work
- Is gay and has been treated less favourably, having previously made a complaint of discrimination

Employees can be compensated for cases of victimisation. An organisation should have a clear process for complaint or grievance where discrimination has occurred. If an employee is being discriminated against or harassed they should approach either their manager or the organisation's diversity and inclusion manager. Any behaviour that discriminates against an employee in any form is unacceptable behaviour.

There used to be many parliamentary acts that covered discrimination in its many forms. However, from October 2010 all of these acts will be subsumed into one act, called the **Equality Act 2010**. The Equality Act aims to:

- Provide a new cross-cutting legislative framework to protect the rights of individuals and advance equality of opportunity for all
- Update, simplify and strengthen previous legislation
- Deliver a simple, modern and accessible framework of discrimination law which protects individuals from unfair treatment and promotes a fair and more equal society

The provisions in the Equality Act will come into force at different times to allow time for the people and organisations affected by the new laws to prepare for them. The Equality Act will introduce new laws to help narrow the gender pay gap and strengthen anti-discrimination legislation. It will also consolidate the numerous pieces of existing discrimination legislation into one act. The Equality Act is the most far-reaching discrimination legislation for years which:

- Will allow employers to take further positive action in favour of women and minorities at the recruitment and promotion stage
- Gives wider powers to employment tribunals
- Bans 'gagging clauses' on pay
- Will require some organisations to publish diversity and gender pay statistics

• ACTIVITY 11

What does the Equality Act 2010 do?

The Equality Act has 16 parts:

- Part 1 Socio-economic inequalities
- Part 2 Equality: key concepts
- Part 3 Services and public functions
- Part 4 Premises
- Part 5 Work
- Part 6 Education
- Part 7 Associations
- Part 8 Prohibited conduct: ancillary
- Part 9 Enforcement
- Part 10 Contracts etc.
- Part 11 Advancement of equality
- Part 12 Disabled persons: transport
- Part 13 Disability: miscellaneous
- Part 14 General exceptions
- Part 15 Family property
- Part 16 General and miscellaneous

The Equality Act replaces previous legislation which covered age, race, gender, disability etc. In such acts as:

- **The Sex Discrimination Acts 1975 & 1986**

- **Race Relations Act 1976**
- **Disability Discrimination Act 1995**
- **Employment Rights Act 1996**
- **Employment Equality Regulations 2003**
- **Employment Equality (Age) Regulations 2006**
- **Health and Safety at Work Act 1974**

'Equal opportunities' at work involves the attitude of people about colleagues who are different from themselves. This makes the best use of the organisation's HR. 'Equal opportunities' policies have the potential to bring out the best in people and transform an organisation.

Maintain security and confidentiality

Organisations need to make sure that their employees, buildings and facilities, and the intellectual property that they create, are free from risk or danger. An organisation needs to make sure that these dimensions of its business are kept safe. An organisation needs to minimise the threat to these areas by devising policies and procedures that cover:

- **Security and security risk management** – e.g. To cover buildings and their external perimeter, the design of an office space. Also to recognise signs of drug and alcohol abuse in the workplace and the dangers that this can represent

- **Intruder detection** – e.g. An alarm system for the building or control of access to the premises by visitors, defining where visitors can and cannot go. This may involve employing the services of security personnel or installing closed-circuit television (CCTV) cameras, alarms etc., or having locked access doors for certain staff members to access only. An organisation may also carry out regular security checks

- **Conference security** – e.g. Work with an external event provider to make sure its delegates are kept safe

- **CCTV**

- **Company hospitality** – e.g. Prevent overlooking or overhearing of confidential and important information

- **Bomb threats**

- **Fire and flood** - A major risk to premises is fire. The priority must be to prevent fire and to reduce the damage if one starts. To prevent fire:

- Report any faulty equipment or wiring
- Switch off any faulty equipment until it has been repaired
- Do not put papers, clothing etc., near heaters or equipment that gets hot
- Switch off all equipment at the end of the day
- To minimise the effect of fire:
- Do not block fire doors or fire exits
- Do not prop fire doors open
- Know where the fire exits are
- Take fire drills seriously
- Know where fire fighting equipment is and how to use it
- Know how to raise the alarm
- Know where employee assembly points are to facilitate completion of the roll call

- Leave the building immediately by the nearest fire exit
    - Do not stop to pick up personal possessions
    - Re-enter the premises when given the all clear by the fire officer
- **IT -** Keeping confidential information safe or destroying confidential information
- **Contingency planning**

• ACTIVITY 12

Why is it important for an organisation to have policies about security in place?

Security procedures should be in place to protect the employees of an organisation. The procedures should be followed by both internal and external customers, e.g. contractor and maintenance people, clients, visitors. Anything suspicious should be reported immediately to the appropriate person.

The development of these policies and procedures and the physical protection afforded by the physical resources of an organisation's building will equip the organisation and its employees with the physical and psychological defences to reduce the likelihood of these threats. By maintaining security and confidentiality an organisation:

- Reduces and eliminates threats to its reputation
- Manages and minimises costs to the business of systems upgrades
- Remains responsive to emerging risks
- Increases confidence in the business by internal and external customers
- Provides a safe organisation and a culture that looks after the community of people it interacts with

This will vary from organisation to organisation and their scale of implementation will depend on the size of an organisation. Most crimes are directed towards employees or offices that have little or no security in place.

Organisations should aim to reduce threats to its business by assessing its security needs to prevent the many forms of crime by asking the following questions:

- Do the available security resources, policies and procedures meet the potential threat?
- What is the prevailing attitude toward security?
- Who is responsible for the overall security programme?
- How are security policies enforced?
- What are the possible targets?
- When was the current emergency preparedness plan developed, including fire, power failure, bomb threat and other types of physical disaster?
- What resources are available locally?
- How rapid are the response times for fire, police and ambulance?
- What kind of physical security systems and controls are presently used?
- Are employees sufficiently trained to understand the threats to security and confidentiality, e.g. are telephone numbers publicised, contact persons identified and employees drilled in the event of threats?

There are various procedures that can increase an organisation's security. An organisation may:

- Install key-card access systems

- Issue access control badges

- Upgrade perimeter control systems with intercoms and closed-circuit monitoring devices

- Keep master and extra keys locked in a security office. There should be a system in place to record who has access to keys, which will cover access to a keyholder if a problem happens outside of working hours. A list of keyholders should be held by the police or a private security company. Keys to internal doors, cabinets, safes etc., should be removed from a building at night

- Develop crisis communication among key personnel and security office

- Have a back-up communication system, e.g. a two-way radio

- Design executive offices near the inner core of the building to provide maximum protection and to avoid external surveillance

- Organise office space so visitors who are not escorted can be easily noticed

- Have staff follow strict access control procedures without exception

- Keep important papers locked in secure cabinets or password protected

- Keep offices neat and orderly to identify strange objects or unauthorised people more easily. Rearrange office furniture etc., so that employees in daily contact with external customers are surrounded by natural barriers, e.g. desks, countertops, partitions, to separate employees from external customers

- Empty rubbish bins often

- Open packages and large envelopes in executive offices only if the source or sender is positively identified

- Keep all types of cupboards locked at all times

- Protect crucial communications equipment and utility areas with an alarm system

- Avoid stairwells and other isolated areas during an emergency

- Close and unlock, unless the contents of a room are valuable, internal doors to prevent the spread of fire

- Do not work late alone or on a routine basis

- Keep publicly accessible washroom doors locked and set up a key control system. If there is a combination lock, only office personnel should open the lock for visitors

- Post a security guard at the main building entrance

- Install a metal detector or CCTV camera to monitor people entering all building entrances

- Brief employees on steps to take if a threatening or violent incident occurs

- Establish code words to alert co-workers and supervisors that immediate help is needed

- Provide an under-the-counter duress alarm system to signal a supervisor or security officer if a customer becomes threatening or violent

• ACTIVITY 13

What procedures might increase an organisation's security?

Prevent burglary and theft by:

- Locking external doors and windows

- Removing vulnerable items from view

- Using any security devices available

- Making sure that safes are left open at the end of business to minimise damage by burglars

In the event that a burglary has happened:

- Telephone the police by dialling 999

- Contact the appropriate manager or the security officer

- Do not disturb any evidence

If an employee observes a theft taking place, or is suspicious of one taking place, they should:

- Watch until they are sure a theft has taken place

- Ask a colleague to alert security or a manager
- Try to keep the thief under constant observation
- Do not give the thief the opportunity to pass on the stolen items to anyone else
- Avoid confronting the thief, as this may lead to violence
- Take a detailed description of the thief
- Keep a safe distance from the thief
- Avoid any risks

• ACTIVITY 14

What should an employee do if they suspect a theft if taking place?

There is no such thing as a typical criminal. They come from all walks of life, cultures and ages. People who are intent on stealing from others will be creative. They may steal from offices, hotels, leisure centres etc. Some criminals may be employees working in the organisation who may feel that stealing from a large organisation is not really theft, as nobody suffers. However, the cost of theft is passed on to the customer of the organisation through higher prices or higher charges. It also increases insurance premiums. A further effect of theft is that there is less profit available in the organisation to pay wages and salaries. An organisation can reduce the risk to property being stolen by:

- Marking expensive equipment with the organisation's name
- Keeping a record of serial numbers of equipment
- Changing the codes used to access areas regularly
- Employees can assist in this process by:
- Not leaving valuable equipment unattended
- Not assuming things will not be stolen if they are not considered valuable
- Signing in and out portable equipment

Under the **Police and Criminal Evidence Act 1984** an employee has the power of arrest; however, this does not give the employee the authority to search people, cars or premises - only the police have this authority. If an employee searches someone without their permission they could be accused of assault. An employee can ask the suspected thief to empty their pockets, handbag, briefcase etc., but they cannot insist the suspect complies with this request. Always make sure there is a third person present to act as a witness.

Remember: most thieves are opportunists. Get rid of the opportunity; get rid of the stealing! So:

- Do not take valuables to work unless absolutely necessary, when at work they should be locked away safely
- Keep handbags, wallets, mobile phones in a safe place and out of sight
- Challenge visitors found in an area of the building where they are not permitted

A major risk to employees is violence which may be perpetrated against them by an intruder, or external customers that they may be serving who become violent, who has been identified on the premises. In this situation:

- Remain calm and polite
- Ask them their business
- Walk away if threatened
- Be vigilant and alert
- **DO NOT** put anyone at risk
- **DO NOT** argue with them
- **DO NOT** be confrontational
- **DO NOT** chase after them

An organisation should consider different means of safeguarding its employees against violence by providing, as appropriate:

- Panic buttons
- Glass screens
- Two-way radios
- Improved training so employees know in advance what to do if they feel threatened
- Work schedules that avoid employees working alone

Confidentiality is about keeping customer, internal and external, and business information private. Many employees will work with information that is confidential. It is their responsibility to protect this information, to keep confidential any information concerning their customers and the business. What is seen and heard in the workplace remains in the workplace. No confidential information can be told to anyone outside the workplace. Confidential issues should only be discussed in areas where visitors or the public may not be able to overhear. No information should be given to customers without permission from the appropriate person. If confidential information is to be released, employees should make sure they follow organisational procedures before releasing information on request. Employees can only access files if given permission. No confidential material or files should leave a business.

• ACTIVITY 15

What could happen if confidential information was given to unauthorised people?

One of the fastest growing types of theft is the theft of information, e.g. through industrial espionage. This may be commercial information or personal information. If confidential information is held on a computer it should be encrypted and protected by passwords. Hard copies of confidential information should not be left in plain sight on desks. Confidential information should be shredded before being disposed of or disposed of in the appropriate recycling bins. Personal information about living individuals, including customers, employees, suppliers etc., should be held on computers or hardcopy covered by the organisation's policies and procedures that are governed by the **Data Protection Act 1998**.

If, at any time, an employee identifies a risk that is being imposed by lack of adherence to security or confidentiality, it should be reported to the appropriate person in line with organisational procedures. A breach of confidentiality will affect a business's reputation and cause financial loss. An employee can be dismissed if information is given out, either on purpose or by accident. Legal action may be taken against an employee or the organisation that reveals customer and business information.

Testing your knowledge

1. Why should an organisation implement environmentally friendly policies?

2. Why should waste be reduced?

3. What are the key areas of potential waste in an organisation?

4. Why should equipment be maintained regularly?

5. What is energy efficiency?

6. What legislation covers hazardous materials?

7. Why do organisations bother about 'inclusivity'?

8. What is the difference between 'discrimination' and 'harassment'?

9. What is the difference between 'harassment' and 'victimisation'?

10. How many parts are there in the Equality Act 2010?

11. What should an employee do if they confront an intruder in an organisation?

12. What should an employee do in the event of a bomb threat?

13. What should an employee do in the event of a fire?

14. What does the Police and Criminal Evidence Act 1984 empower an employee to do?

15. What legislation covers personal information?

Skills

Supporting sustainability

As part of your induction to an organisation you should have been shown what the organisation's policies were about supporting sustainability and maintaining an environment which minimise the production of waste. This will vary in depth and breadth from organisation to organisation, depending on the sector that the organisation works in. At a minimum, you should be aware of how your organisation handles the disposal of waste, what waste it recycles, how it deals with hazardous materials and the signage it has to remind employees of their responsibilities around the organisation.

You should be aware of how to use equipment and technology effectively and efficiently so as to minimise the production of waste, e.g. not printing documents when it is not necessary, and saving on paper, or using colour when printing documents. Check equipment to make sure that it has been maintained regularly. If it has missed a maintenance check discuss this with your supervisor / manager. If the organisation recycles waste be aware of where the recycle bins are kept. Make sure that you follow the correct procedures for recycling.

• ACTIVITY 16

Look around your workplace and identify areas of waste. Write about these and recommend how things could be changed to minimise waste. Discuss your findings with your supervisor.

Supporting diversity

You will be working in an environment where you will be working with many different types of people. This not only covers people from different cultures, but also different gender, sexuality, intelligence etc. You will be surrounded by people who are different from you but who are as equally important to you in your work life as you are to them. Look at what makes you similar rather than what separates you by differences. Build on the similarities to bring you closer to your fellow team members and focus on the ambitions the team has for achieving its aims and goals. As you work with other people be aware of how they interact with you. Is it different from how they interact with other members of the team? Look at why you think there is a difference. Is this different way of being treated acceptable? What could you do to improve the way you get on with other people in your team and how they get on with you?

Question what you do not understand. Do not jump to conclusions when your opinions are based on observations which are not backed up by evidence. Look at the different backgrounds and cultures people come from to gain an understanding of what makes them tick. How are their values, customs and beliefs different from what you believe? Is there something that you can learn from any difference that you have identified? Get to know what your organisational policies are on working with others, e.g. its 'equal-opportunity' programme.

Rather than criticise, look to ways of conforming to the expectations of these policies. Ask for feedback from you supervisor / manager if you are having problems. Seek out their guidance. Employ other behavioural strategies that increase your sensitivity towards the differences that other people you work with might have.

• ACTIVITY 17

You have been asked to write a short piece for the newsletter on 'Diversity in the Workplace'. The editor is looking for about 200 words written from your point of view. Include any real-life situations, but also your views on the subject as a whole. Show your piece to your supervisor and ask for feedback.

Maintaining security and confidentiality

As an employee of an organisation you have a responsibility to make sure that the premises you work in are safe and protected. Make sure exits are not blocked, waste bins are not over filled etc. This will help to make sure that the exit from the building is not blocked, making it a safer environment to work in. Follow all organisational procedures for identifying suspicious material or behaviour and report your findings to the appropriate person. Make sure all doors are closed as they should be and locked appropriately. Make sure that you are aware of all the people who work in your work area, particularly in large organisation, so you can identify any strangers walking around which should be reported.

• ACTIVITY 18

Find out about the security procedures in place your building. Suggest improvements that could be made to offer better protection to the premises, people and property. Show these suggestions to your line manager and ask them to give you feedback.

When working with confidential information make sure you follow organisational procedures for making sure that it is only given to or discussed by those with the appropriate security clearance. Avoid taking confidential documents from the building unless you have prior permission to do so. Be careful not to discuss confidential information outside the organisations - 'loose lips sink ships'! Make sure if you have any concerns about security and confidentially that you share these concerns with the appropriate authority within the organisation.

Testing your skills

1. How can you make sure that you and other employees follow sustainability policies?

2. What policies does your organisation have to cover the use and maintenance of equipment and other technology?

3. What are your organisation's policies on recycling?

4. What are your organisation's policies on hazardous materials?

5. What do you do if you observe someone being discriminated against?

6. How can a disabled person be discriminated against?

7. What do the security policies cover in your organisation?

8. What should you do if you discover a burglary?

9. What process do you have to follow in the event of a fire in your organisation?

10. How do you maintain the security of property in your organisation?

11. What would you do if you found someone walking around your building without the appropriate identification badge?

12. How do you deal with confidential information in your organisation?

Ready for assessment?

To achieve this Level 2 unit of a Business & Administration qualification, learners will need to demonstrate that they are able to perform the following activities:

1. Completed work tasks alongside other people in a way that showed respect for:

    1.1 Backgrounds

    1.2 Abilities

    1.3 Values, customs and beliefs

2. Completed work tasks with other people in a way that is sensitive to their needs

3. Used feedback and guidance from other people to improve own way of working

4. Followed organisational procedures and legal requirements in relation to discrimination legislation, as required

5. Kept property secure, having followed organisational procedures and legal requirements, as required

6. Kept information secure and confidential, having followed organisational procedures and legal requirements

7. Followed organisational procedures to report concerns about security / confidentiality, as required

8. Completed work tasks, having kept waste to a minimum

9. Used technology in a work task (s) in a way that minimised waste

10. Followed procedures for recycling and disposing of hazardous items, as required

11. Followed procedures for the maintenance of equipment in own work?

You will need to produce evidence from a variety of sources to support the performance requirements of this unit.

If you carry out the 'ACTIVITIES' and respond to the 'NEED TO KNOW' questions, these will provide some of the evidence required.

Links to other units

While gathering evidence for this unit, evidence **may** also be used from evidence generated from other units within the Business & Administration suite of units. Below is a **sample** of applicable units; however, most units within the Business & Administration suite of units will also be applicable.

QCF NVQ
Communications
Communicate in a business environment (Level 2)
Make and receive telephone calls
Use electronic message systems
Use a diary system
Take minutes
Core business & administration
Manage own performance in a business environment (Level 2)
Improve own performance in a business environment (Level 2)
Solve business problems (Level 2)
Work with other people in a business environment (Level 2)
Customer service
Handle mail
Meet and welcome visitors
Provide reception services

SVQ
Communications
Prepare to communicate in a business environment
Make and receive telephone calls
Use electronic message systems
Use a diary system
Take minutes
Core business & administration
Agree how to manage and improve own performance in a business environment
Plan how to solve business problems
Work with other people in a business environment
Customer service
Handle mail
Meet and welcome visitors
Provide reception services

10 Work in a business environment

SOLVE BUSINESS PROBLEMS

'Solve business problems' is an <u>optional unit</u> which may be chosen as one of a combination of units to achieve either a Qualifications and Credit Framework (QCF), National Vocational Qualification (NVQ) or Scottish Vocational Qualification (SVQ).

The aims of this unit are to:

- Know how to recognise business problems and their causes
- Understand techniques for solving business problems
- Know how to review approaches and solutions to business problems
- Be able to recognise business problems
- Be able to plan and carry out a solution to the business problem
- Be able to review a solution to the business problem

To achieve the above aims of this unit, learners will be expected to provide evidence through the performance of work-based activities.

Knowledge
Causes of business problems

A business problem occurs when there is an obstacle to achieving a desired objective. A business problem occurs when something that has been planned for has not happened as expected. Essentially, a business problem is about managing the effects of change. The result of a business problem could have a positive or negative effect on a business. For example, a business problem resulting in a negative effect would be if a delivery is going to be late due to a van breaking down. The customer tells the provider that they will take their business to another provider if they do not get the delivery on time. So the provider has various options to consider regarding how to solve the business problem: get another driver to drive to the broken-down van, collect the parcel and deliver it to the customer; do nothing and lose the customer, which is not the best option; deliver the parcel late but agree with the customer to give them a full credit for the cost of the delivery or reimburse all costs as a result of the later delivery. Something, a van breaking down, has got in the way of a planned situation - the delivery of a parcel - and this problem needs to be resolved. If the business problem is not resolved as soon as possible, it may become an even greater problem, a catastrophic business problem, e.g. the Enron scandal of 2001 in America, which resulted in Enron, and many other companies, closing down.

A supervisor / manager may develop possible problem scenarios to help them develop a business plan. This would lead to a clearer picture of a business situation in order to minimise business problems from happening. Such **business forecasting** tries to minimise the level of disruption to a business.

> A problem understood is half solved.
> *- Albert Einstein*

Business is built around the **routinisation** of jobs. When business problems upset a routine they have a cost implication to a business, which all business strives to avoid. The cause of business problems are varied and many. To highlight just a few:

- **Uncontrolled change -** This occurs outside the control of the business. The business takes a reactive role in identifying what the business problem is and how best to solve it. These changes could come about through changes in government impacting on policy; legislation; environment; social upheaval; technology etc.

- **Controlled change -** This occurs as a result of a business re-evaluating an existing strategy or work plan etc. These changes could come either from within the organisation, e.g. the effects of change to other parts of a business that are looking at ways of becoming leaner, or from outside the organisation, e.g. deciding to launch a new product ahead of schedule when it hears that a competitor is about to launch a similar product

Figure 10.1. Causes of business problems: the winds of change

Each of these changes will upset the established routine for a plan of work. The plan of work, which would have included all tasks / activities that fell under the project, will have already been signed off, so an evaluation will have to take place to determine the effect of this change and see how much of a problem it may cause the business, so the business can resolve the business problem accordingly. When a business problem is found it is best to resolve it as soon as possible, so it does not increase costs to the business. A business problem will tend to maximise waste. One of the aims of business is to minimise waste through effective routinisation of work.

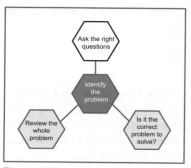

Figure 10.2. Identifying a business problem

• ACTIVITY 1

What causes business problems?

Identify a problem

Take a positive approach when solving a business problem. Approach the business problem with confidence and a desire to spend time and effort to find an appropriate solution to the business problem. To overcome or resolve a business problem, the business problem needs to be identified. Identifying or defining a business problem requires describing the business problem in detail. To identify the business problem, ask the following questions:

- What is the business problem?
- What happened?
- When did it happen?

- Where did it happen?

- How did it happen?

- Who was involved?

Write down what the business problem is. By writing the business problem down, it forces the problem-solver to think about the issues that need to be resolved. This could be achieved through a brainstorming session, which aims to promote a free flow of ideas. At this stage there should be no judgements about whether the idea (s) are good or bad, will work or will not work etc. It is important to create a relaxed environment to identify what the business problem is and collect lots of ideas. Analyse the current situation to understand why the business problem occurred:

- Check to make sure that the right questions to identify the business problem have been asked

- Make sure that there are no detours which only identify parts of the business problem

- Make sure that the business problem that has been identified is the correct one to solve

The business problem needs to be explored in detail to identify what it is. This will help to determine which solution will be the most effective in resolving the business problem. Understand where the problem is coming from, how it came about, how it fits in with current developments and how it needs to be resolved - then solve it.

• ACTIVITY 2

How can possible business problems be identified?

Have a set of criteria to evaluate the proposed solution to see whether it is workable or not. Spend time analysing the business problem by reviewing the current situation and consider what needs to be changed. Continue to reassess the business problem so that it is still valid. People often discover that the business problem they really wanted to answer is very different from their original interpretation of it.

Ways of solving business problems
As a result of identifying a business problem a number of solutions will

have presented themselves. There may be a number of different ways of solving a particular business problem. When looking at different ways of solving a business problem, there is no fixed route to solving a business problem. Each business problem will be defined differently.

> Identify your problems, but give your power and energy to solutions.
> - *Anthony Robbins*

Create a number of solutions. Do not censor any of the possible solutions as they appear. Write them all down or, if brainstorming, use post-it notes and put these on a wall. If working in a group this should generate a number of possible solutions. Every solution is worthy of consideration. When making a decision about which way to solve a business problem, think about the following elements, as they will each have an impact on the way the business problem will be solved:

- **Time -** How long will it take? This will need to take into consideration the decision-making process to sign off the agreed way of solving the business problem

- **Resources -** How much resource - physical, human, technological - will be required?

- **Costs -** How cheap or expensive will it be?

- **Size of the solution -** What minimal solution will solve the business problem? How much of a compromise is the business willing to make?

- **Reputation -** What will be the impact on the business, both positive and negative?

- **Risks -** What will happen to the business if the business problem is not resolved?

Think about when a solution has to be signed off. Review the priorities about what must be done first to agree which solution should be adopted. If this is a solution that requires many parts to it, prioritise when each part needs to be accomplished. Use experience gained from other business problems to help shape thinking and see if past solutions or an adaptation of a past solution may solve the current business problem. Once all these elements have been agreed, plan how and when the business problem needs to be resolved.

Planning to resolve the business plan will require updating the original work plan, if it existed, depending on how large a piece of work is required as a result of solving the business problem. As with any business plan, agree what the purpose of the solution is aiming to achieve. Prioritise each stage of this work. Monitor each stage of the work to make sure it is achieving targets and objectives as agreed. Evaluate the success of the implementation of the solution to see if it has been effective in minimising a cost to the business.

Knowing when a business problem has been solved

The solution that resolves the business problem is often a compromise between conflicting needs. The successful solution to a business problem is the one that fits the ideal solution most closely. The successful solution will have optimised the required resources to resolve the business problem. The successful solution will have minimised any risks attached to the delivery of the solution. A business problem will be solved when it:

- Delivers the results that the solution promised to deliver
- Is able to deliver the benefits that the solution promised to deliver
- Has overcome all barriers to achieving the delivery of the solution
- Has been accepted by all the people involved in resolving the business problem, if more than one person was involved
- Has used available resources productively
- Has minimised the risks that the delivery of the business problem is aiming to achieve
- Meets legal and / or organisation policy
- Delivers the maximum acceptable result

> When is a problem not a problem?
> When it becomes a challenge!

Not all of the above may be appropriate in deciding when a business problem has been solved, as solutions will vary with the complexity of the business problem. A successful solution will be the one which will have maximised the advantages and minimised the disadvantages attached to the delivery of that solution, from all available solutions, e.g. a successful solution may not impact on or be influenced by legal requirements.

• ACTIVITY 3

How is a business problem solved?

A successful solution will be one that is methodical; is committed to solving the business problem; has used information accurately to solve the business problem, using analytical and creative thinking, and has made sure that it was effectively implemented.

> We can't solve problems by using the same kind of thinking we used when we created them.
> - *Albert Einstein*

Work with others to solve a business problem

Solving business problems can either take place individually or with a group of colleagues. In the latter context, this may happen **formally**, e.g. a meeting arranged to resolve a problem, or **informally**, e.g. a group of colleagues who meet when a problem comes up. At both formal and informal meetings, people share points of view until a consensus is agreed. Each member of the group will contribute towards resolving the business problem. When aiming to resolve a business problem it is best to use a group setting, as:

- A problem can be defined in many different ways

- Information about the problem is diverse

- It may be a specialised problem and a diverse approach may help to identify a solution

The problem may impact on many different people.

- There may be many different possible solutions to the business problem

- It may be a complex business problem

- A solution can only be implemented when it has been agreed to by others

The most suitable and relevant people should be involved in this process of sharing ideas.

Advantages of working with others:

- **Increased output -** The more people there are the more skills, knowledge and experience can be pooled to find a solution

- **Exchange of ideas -** Ideas are explored that may not have been considered by one person

- **Reduced bias -** A group can explore unrealistic ideas that personal prejudice may not have considered

- **Risk taking -** As more people are involved in the discussion, individuals are more willing to take risks in sharing their ideas

- **Commitment -** In a group, commitment is improved as a result of sharing a common purpose

- **Communication -** In a group, communication is improved due to the involvement and expertise this brings to the project

- **Better solutions -** A stimulating environment is created which encourages the discussion of diverse ideas which lead to more solutions and better solutions

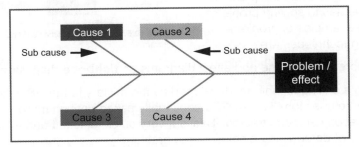

Figure 10.3. Example of a fishbone diagram

Disadvantages of working with others:

- **Competition** - In a group, competition may undermine the problem-solving process because the perception of behaviours encourages negative behaviour

- **Conformity** - People will reduce their thinking to the agreed decisions, they will not want to upset the group or be seen as different

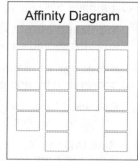

Figure 10.4. Example of an Affinity diagram

- **Lack of direction** - Where a meeting has been arranged with no effective direction in place to solve the business problem

- **Time** - Arranging a meeting can be a slow process. Having lots of different people adding lots of different ideas during the meeting can also take up valuable time

Problem-solving techniques

There are a number of well-known problem-solving techniques that are used within organisations. These techniques have established formal procedures for interrogating a problem and for solving it. They are planned approaches to solving problems. Some examples of problem-solving techniques are:

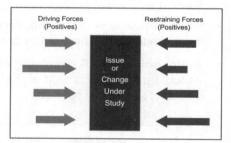

Figure 10.5. Example of a force field analysis diagram

- Appreciation cause and effect diagrams or '**fishbone diagrams**'

This is a drilling technique, developed by the military in the US, where the same question, 'so what?' is continually asked until no more information can be extracted. This is a very quick, efficient and reliable method of determining a solution to a problem.

- Cause and effect diagrams or '**fishbone diagrams**'

Used to focus on identifying the **cause** of a problem, these allow a deep exploration of every cause rather than the most obvious causes. An example of a 'cause and effect diagram' is an Ishikawa diagram. This technique uses **brainstorming** to gather information. This is done in four steps:

1. **Identify the problem** - Write down the exact problem in a box on the left-hand side of a page. Draw a line from it across the page. This creates the spine of the fish and space to develop ideas either side of it

2. **Identify major factors** - Identify all the factors that added to the problem. Draw lines off the 'spine' for each factor and label them. Each factor looks like the bones of a fish

3. **Identify possible causes** - Identify possible causes that relate to each factor

4. **Analyse the diagram** - The diagram is complete, showing all possible causes of a problem. Investigate the most likely causes further. Use various tests to see if the assessments that have been made about the causes are valid

Affinity diagrams
Used to organise and make sense of a large amount of information as a result of interrogating a problem. An 'affinity diagram' is also known as the **'KJ method'**, after Kawakita Jiro, the Japanese anthropologist who developed it. This method looks at finding the relationships that exist between ideas.

Force field analysis
Used to analyse all the positive and negative forces acting on making a decision about a problem. This strengthens the forces supporting the decision and minimises the forces opposing the decision.

Edward de Bono, thinking tools
These tools have been developed by Edward de Bono, one of the world leaders on teaching thinking as a skill. Some tools he has promoted include:

- **The APC tool** - This technique forces the mind to think about alternatives. Where A = Alternatives, P = Possibilities and C = Choices

- **The Ideal Solution method** - This technique lists the alternatives and then ignores them. This then identifies an 'ideal solution' and the 'alternatives' can be compared with the 'ideal solution'

- **The TEC framework** - A technique with strict time limits, e.g. five minutes. Where T = Target, E = Expand and Explore and C = Contract and Conclude. Using this technique focuses the mind to produce results

The reason for selecting any of the above problem-solving techniques will depend on either the type of problem that needs to be solved or the stage at which the business problem has had an effect on the plan of work. Most work within a business will be planned to achieve objectives. Once a business problem has been identified, and processes agreed to solve it, the problem-solvers must continue to review what has been resolved at each stage to solve the business problem.

- What has been agreed is correct and still targets the identified business problem

- The alternative solutions address the identified business problem

- The chosen solution addresses the identified business problem

- The result of solving the business problem does actually solve the identified business problem

Any of the above problem-solving techniques can be used to review the approach taken to solve the business problem.

> OPEN your mind up to things that have no connection with the problem you're trying to solve: subscribe to an unusual magazine; spend a morning at an elementary school; go to work two hours early; test drive an exotic car; attend a city council meeting; try an Indonesian recipe.
>
> *- Roger von Oech*

• ACTIVITY 4

A can of soft drink has fallen into the photocopying machine. As a result, the printing that had been completed is ruined. It will have to be redone. It has to be completed within the next hour for an urgent delivery. If this print batch is not printed and delivered on time, the customer will go to another supplier. The photocopying machine has also stopped working. The office technician is not available to repair or replace the photocopying machine for 24 hours.

Use the scenario outlined above to answer the following questions:

1. What are the explicit business problems raised in the above scenario?

2. What is the most important business problem that has to be solved first?

3. Why has this business problem been given the highest priority to be solved?

4. What problem-solving techniques could be used to solve the business problems?

5. Who would need to be involved to resolve the most important business problem? Why?

6. What problem-solving techniques could be used to analyse the business problems?

Testing your knowledge

1. How is a business problem recognised?

2. How are the potential causes of business problems identified?

3. What problem-solving techniques could be used to analyse a business problem?

4. Why would other people be consulted when solving a business problem?

5. What are the advantages and disadvantages of working with other people to solve a business problem?

6. What effects could business problems have on business plans?

7. Why is it important to check the progress of solving a business problem?

8. What indicates when a business problem has been solved?

9. How is the approach taken to solving a business problem reviewed?

Skills

Something has gone wrong, or things have not gone entirely to plan. It is at this time when you might think there is a business problem. If the plan is to reach certain objectives at an agreed time, something needs to be done. However, nothing can be done until you understand that there is a problem and the nature of the problem - then you can begin to solve it.

You have reviewed the situation and confirmed that there is indeed a business problem. If something is not done to overcome the business problem, there will be even bigger business problems. You will now have to deal with the business problem. Determine, from an initial review of the business problem, if it is something that you can handle on your own or if you will need the help of other people, including your supervisor / manager. Either option will have an impact on the way you go about identifying what the problem is. The more people involved in the process the more ideas are generated to help solve the business problem.

Your initial investigation is to discover what went wrong, why it went wrong and if there was anything that you could have done to prevent it from going wrong. Gather together as much information as you can about the problem - there can never be too much information. When did it happen? Who did it happen to? What happened exactly? How did it happen? Why did it happen? A business problem could be caused by technology, because of absences in the workplace or because the plan of work was not appropriate in the first place. There are lots of reasons why business problems happen. The trick is to minimise them by good work planning; however, things do happen over which no one has any control, e.g. a natural disaster.

If you are not sure how to approach solving the problem, ask colleagues or your supervisor / manager for advice. They may have the experience to help you. Use this help. If there is an opportunity to work with others, take it. Learn from the experience and see how other people approach solving the business problem differently from you. Learn from this. Adopt and adapt what you find is most relevant to enhance your thinking in the future.

There are many different problem-solving techniques which can be used to solve business problems. Review possible choices of problem-solving techniques. If you are not sure of the value of using one technique rather than another, seek advice from your supervisor / manager. Work through the advantages and disadvantages of different problem-solving techniques. Once you have decided the problem-solving technique to use, begin your thinking from a very open position. Eliminate any preconceptions you may think of. If you have not fully identified what the problem is, preconceptions are only likely to send you down the wrong path and solve the wrong problem. There are many different ways of solving a business problem, which each business problem should help you to identify. Keep returning to what the business problem is to make sure your thinking is focused on resolving it and not some other business problem.

Plan how many people will be involved in the problem-solving working group. If having a brainstorming session, use post-it notes to jot down ideas. Collect the notes and start to categorise them. How will you categorise them? Which problem-solving techniques would be helpful for you to do this? It is important that no one makes any value statements about ideas; otherwise people will be reluctant to share their ideas. Judging ideas should not happen at the beginning of a thinking session. This is a time for letting all ideas to come to the surface. You still do not know what the solution is, so it would be premature to discount anyone else's ideas at this stage. After you have gathered a number of ideas you can select which ones you think will be most effective in solving the business problem. Get rid of the solutions that obviously will not work. With the remaining solutions, analyse each one to see what the costs for implementing them will be to you, the team, the organisation etc. You will rarely work in isolation. You will need to consider the impact the solution you have chosen will have. It has to meet the requirements of the plan of work and be of value to the organisation.

Implement an action plan for resolving the business problem. Look at the knock-on effects of what this new plan will have to work practices. Agree these with your supervisor / manager and, as appropriate, inform people of their new roles and responsibilities. Make sure people know why their roles / responsibilities are changing and make sure they review their new roles / responsibilities to make sure this is the correct course of action. If these people are unaware of the issues get them to review the new course of action, they might have a different perspective to add which has not been thought of before.

Always be disciplined and methodical in how you approach identifying and recognising when you think a problem has been solved. Solving a business problem is about minimising waste, which is a costly factor. Waste can take different forms in terms of cost, resources, time etc. If working with a group of people, decisions that will be made will need to be agreed with by everyone or the majority view within the group. Be generous about this decision if it is not one that you agree with. There will be other business problems which will not only be solved by you, but which you will influence in a group situation. Decide, with those you are working with to solve the business problem, how you think you will know when the business problem has been solved. Identify criteria appropriate to the specific business problem, use it as a checklist and keep returning to it to make sure you are still on the right course to solving the business problem appropriately. These criteria will vary from business problem to business problem.

Once the business problem has been resolved and the business plan is back on course, review the whole process of solving the business problem. Of the problem-solving techniques used, were they the best way of solving the business problem? If not, what ones would have been better? Why would they have been better? Were enough people involved in the brainstorming activities to solve the business problem?

Do not see what you want to see or expect to see, see what is there, in context.

Testing your skills

1. How did you recognise when a business problem existed?

2. How did you identify it as a business problem?

3. What kind of information did you gather to help you identify what the business problem was?

4. How many other people did you discuss the business problem with?

5. Why did you work with the people you worked with when trying to resolve the business problem?

6. What contributions did you make to solve the business problem?

7. How did you agree the approach to take to solve the business problem?

8. Why did you use the problem-solving techniques that you used?

9. What criteria did you agree with others to recognise when a business problem was solved?

10. Did you have to agree your plan with someone or did you work alone?

11. Why did you work with the number of people you worked with to solve the business problem?

12. How effective was the support and feedback you got from others to help you solve the business problems?

13. What checks did you have in place to make sure progress was being made towards solving the business problem?

14. How did you review the approach to solving the business problem?

15. What lessons did you learn?

Ready for assessment?

To achieve this Level 2 unit of a Business & Administration qualification, learners will need to demonstrate that they are able to perform the following activities:

1. Recognised when a business problem exists
2. Confirmed they understood the business problem
3. Discussed the business problem with others
4. Agreed an approach to solve the business problem
5. Planned the agreed approach to solving the business problem
6. Decided how to recognise when the business problem has been solved
7. Agreed the plan of approach with the appropriate authority
8. Put the plan into action
9. Used support and feedback from others, when appropriate
10. Checked progress towards solving the business problem, adjusting plans as necessary
11. Reviewed the approach taken to solving the business problem, having identified any other approaches which may have been more productive

You will need to produce evidence from a variety of sources to support the performance requirements of this unit.

If you carry out the 'ACTIVITIES' and respond to the 'NEED TO KNOW' questions, these will provide some of the evidence required.

Links to other units

While gathering evidence for this unit, evidence **may** also be used from evidence generated from other units within the Business & Administration suite of units. Below is a **sample** of applicable units; however, most units within the Business & Administration suite of units will also be applicable.

QCF NVQ
Communications
Communicate in a business environment (Level 2)
Core business & administration
Manage own performance in a business environment (Level 2)
Improve own performance in a business environment (Level 2)
Work in a business environment (Level 2)
Work with other people in a business environment (Level 2)

SVQ
Communications
Prepare to communicate in a business environment
Core business & administration
Agree how to manage and improve own performance in a business environment
Undertake work in a business environment
Contribute to working with others in a business environment

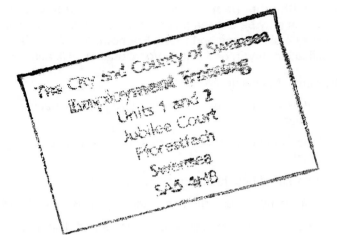

11

Work with other people in a business environment

WORK WITH OTHER PEOPLE IN A BUSINESS ENVIRONMENT

'**Work with other people in a business environment**' is an <u>optional</u> unit which may be chosen as one of a combination of units to achieve either a Qualifications and Credit Framework (QCF), National Vocational Qualification (NVQ) or Scottish Vocational Qualification (SVQ).

The aims of this unit are to:

- Understand how your role fits with organisational values and practices

- Understand how to work as part of a team to achieve goals and objectives

- Understand how to communicate as part of a team

- Understand the contribution of individuals within a team

- Understand how to deal with problems and disagreements

- Understand the purpose of feedback when working as a team

- Be able to work in a way that fits with organisational values and practices

- Be able to work in a team to achieve goals and objectives

- Be able to deal with or refer problems in a team

- Be able to use feedback on objectives in a team

To achieve the above aims of this unit, learners will be expected to provide evidence through the performance of work-based activities.

Knowledge
The most essential ingredient that any organisation must have to succeed is to have a clear purpose for its existence. There are various purposes an organisation may have, e.g. a profit, to offer products and services to achieve financial returns, or not-for-profit, to organise and deliver social reforms; however, the purpose or an organisation will vary depending on the nature of the organisation.

 An organisation is energised by its purpose when it is aligned to achieving specific goals. An effectively run organisation needs to have the following tools in place to identify how it will achieve its purpose:

- **Mission statement** - So its customers understand why it is delivering its business in a particular sector. A mission statement should address concepts such as the moral / ethical position of the business, its public image, its target market, its products / services, its geographic sphere and its expectations of growth and profitability

- **Vision statement** - So its customers understand where the organisation wants to be within certain timescales

- **Values statement** - Which sets out the behaviours that it will need to achieve its purpose

- **Strategies and business plans** - Which will set out how the organisation aims to achieve its purpose

- **Financial plans** - Which will set out the targets the organisations is aiming to achieve

• ACTIVITY 1

Circle the correct answer. A mission statement tells people …
- Where the organisation wants to be
- How an organisation will achieve its purpose
- Why it is delivering its business in a particular sector
- What its targets are
- What behaviours it will need to achieve its purpose

These tools will identify for people whether they want to be a part of the business of a particular organisation, either as internal or external customers. They will also be motivated by an organisation's size, e.g. a multi-national company or a small business. An organisation's internal customers, their employees, will use these tools to decide if they want to work for this type of organisation. An organisation's most important resource is its employees. How an organisation organises it employees is integral to achieving its purpose.

At an **individual level**, employees will need to be aware of what it is they have been specifically selected and employed by the organisation to do. They will need to know how their role fits into the structure of the organisation, e.g. what department they work in and how this contributes to achieving the organisation's goals. An employee will need to establish what it is they need to do on a day-to-day basis, what they are responsible for and the limits of authority they have for achieving their responsibilities. There will be specific **policies and procedures** that an employee will need to follow, e.g. human resource policies covering diversity and 'equal opportunities' in the workplace. Policies and procedures are an employee's compass for navigating the behaviours that they will need to adapt to or adopt as they work within the culture of the organisation.

At a **collective level**, no employee works independently. Most employees will be organised into teams to achieve specific objectives. An employee may be a member of more than one team at any one time, which is increasingly the case as organisations opt to work within the principles of **matrix-management**, e.g. a member of the production team carrying out stocktaking while working with the management team to arrange for additional staff to help. There are many different types of teams which can be established within a business, which may have two different timescales:

Temporary
- **Task Force - functional teams** - Formed to investigate a specific issue or problem. Usually from the same hierarchical level within the organisation

- **Problem-solving Team** - Formed to solve a specific problem. Usually five - twelve employees who meet to improve quality, efficiency and the work environment, e.g. an HR group

- **Product Design Team** - Formed to design a new product or service

- **Committee** - Formed to act on some matter

Permanent
- **Work Group** - A group that receives direction from a specific leader

- **Work Team or Self-Directed Work Team / Self-Managed Work Team** - Which is an ongoing group who share a common mission, collectively managing their own affairs within agreed parameters. Usually 10–15 employees who are usually self-selected and evaluate each other's work

- **Quality Circle** - Which is a group from the same functional area who meet regularly to uncover and solve work-related problems and seek work improvement opportunities

What is the difference between 'temporary' and 'permanent' teams?

All of these different types of teams may also be organised into **virtual teams**. Virtual teams allow members of a team to function online without the hindrance of geography or time constraints. However, they have the disadvantage of not allowing team members to observe non-verbal communication.

Employees come together and are organised to work in teams to achieve something much bigger and work more effectively than would be achieved by working independently as an individual. Working in a team provides the opportunity to bring together different strengths, which can compensate for different weaknesses. Strengths and weaknesses present a strong 'synergy' of individual contributions from each team member: experience, expertise, knowledge, skills, personalities etc., which are focused towards achieving the same short, clear team aims and objectives.

A team's aims and objectives should be managed so that they:

- Clearly identify who is doing what, by when, and avoid the conflict of overlapping authority
- Build trust within the team by creating an atmosphere of honesty and openness
- Involve the whole team in the decision-making process, which will promote a sense of ownership from within the team. Ownership will lead to commitment to the team's aims and objectives
- Identify clear lines of communication so all members of the team are kept fully informed

What should a team's aims and objectives be managed to achieve?

There are many rewards to be achieved from working as a team; however, it also presents many challenges. There are many opportunities for problems, e.g. different personalities may cause problems or similar personalities may start vying to dominate the team. Even if aims and objectives are clear, there may be lack of agreement on how they will be achieved; there may be little trust within the team which blocks communication and can lead to loss of coordination by individual team members etc. For a team to work effectively and achieve positive results it needs to have a good leader who can bring the above elements together.

As teams are a collective of individuals, it is important that each member of the team recognises how they can support the achievement of the team's aims and objectives. This can be done through:

Communication
Communicate, communicate and communicate! A team member can never communicate enough. A team member should not isolate themselves by bottling up unexpressed emotions / ideas / problems, as this will undermine both themselves and what the team is aiming to achieve. Make points by being assertive rather than aggressive. Effective teams are those where all team members feel able to talk to each other openly whenever they have anything to say, and in a positive environment of mutual trust. Team members will communicate using a combination of:

- **Written communication** - Written forms of communication will be used to set out ideas about how the team is going to achieve its goals, agree plans, set up milestones so team members know what is expected of them etc.

- **Verbal communication** - Verbal communication uses the spoken word; however, team members will also take cues from non-verbal communication – what the body is saying when speaking, e.g. gesturing, posture. Team members should be aware of how they use their voice, e.g. volume, pitch, tone. Communication is a two-way process. It is important to actively listen to what other team members are saying. Clarify meaning by asking questions, either closed, usually receive a 'yes' or 'no' response, or open, usually do not receive a 'yes' or 'no' response, questions depending on what the team member is aiming to understand

•ACTIVITY 4

What is 'active listening'?

Working effectively with people is a skill that team members will need to do all the time. This is true not only of working in a team but also working with anybody else inside or outside of the organisation. Co-operating with others creates a harmonious work environment which enables team members to achieve more, which makes work more enjoyable.

> Speak up, speak out, but do not speak down!
> Write up, write out, but do not write off!

•ACTIVITY 5

Why is communication so important for the success of a team? Give an example of effective communication.

- **Taking responsibility** - Eliminate 'blame' from a team's vocabulary. Identify a delay or assist a team member who might be delayed so it becomes a shared responsibility of the team to overcome

- **Supporting team members' ideas** - Take account of other team members' ideas rather than discount them out of hand, as this shows interest not only in individual members of the team but in the team ideal

- **Framing the context of how the team will work** - Team members should recognise that they are not working alone. They are working interdependently with other members of the team. Team members should show respect to other members by attending team meetings on time – implement the principles of good time management – and always be prepared to contribute positively to the aims of the meeting. If a team member is going to be late they will need to let another member of the team know. Team members should behave positively, as being in a team creates a new culture of working. Team members will have different attitudes, behaviours which need to be appreciated, understood and worked with. All members of a team will modify their behaviour appropriately towards other members of the team. Agree to offer criticism in a positive fashion by being polite

- **Humility** - Team members should be discrete rather than conceited about the success of their contribution to the team's achievements. Avoid creating tension in the team by recognising that other team members will know when individual team members are doing well
- **Active involvement** - Share suggestions, ideas, solutions and proposals with team members. Take the time to help fellow teammates, no matter what the request

• ACTIVITY 6

What is the value of exercising humility as a team member? Give an example of when this behaviour would be appropriate.

There is no employee working in any organisation who has not at some time in their life been a member of a team, e.g. they will have been a member of a family or played sports where they were a team member. The whole organisation is one big team that should override any internal divisions between departments. When people work effectively together the business will thrive. If people are working against each other it will cause friction and nothing effective will be achieved. If passing a telephone that is ringing and there is nobody else free to answer it, pick it up and take a message. The truly great teams are those that are committed to excellence in everything they do. The goal is to achieve at the highest level; a commitment which is sustained by all members of the team and at every level of the team.

From the outset of the formation of a team, the level of quality the team is aiming to achieve should be agreed by all members of the team. The team should know how they work with one another and take care of each other. Team members need to be perceptive, empowering and innovative by setting achievable goals for each member of the team and agree ways of getting there so the whole team has the same expectations. A team should aim to link what needs to be achieved by their team to the overall goals of what the organisation is aiming to achieve. Celebrate the diversity that the members of a team bring to the composition of a team and use those different skills and knowledge to help team growth and support one another. Above all, keep the communication channels open at all times. As expressed previously, team members can never communicate too much or listen too much.

Successful teams are made up of diverse people with complementary abilities. In all teams there will be a leader, although they may not have been appointed as such. In fact, the leadership role may change from member to member depending on the situation. Leadership depends on power, which can be found in different people in different situations and at different times. Other roles within the team will involve:

- **The innovator** - Who comes up with new ideas
- **The peacemaker** - Who mediates between people
- **The co-ordinator** - Who takes the ideas and gets on with achieving the team's goals
- **The analyst** - Who keeps the team on track and sees the overall picture
- **The dissenter** - Who disagrees with the majority view and keeps the team open-minded

• ACTIVITY 7

Circle the correct answer. The role of a co-ordinator in a team is someone who …

- Keeps the team on track
- Sees the overall picture
- Always disagrees with the majority view
- Gets on with achieving the team's goals
- Mediates between people

A team member may take on more than one role while working in a team. A team member may also change roles as the team grows. It is important for team members to recognise what their specific abilities  are, and the abilities of other team members so they can be used where they are most effective to achieve the team's goals. Team members must be supportive of the diversity that the team is composed of. Differences can bind a team together, with each team member contributing positively with their skills to achieving the team's goals. Team members can empower one another to succeed by recognising other team members' skills and celebrating them as a team when milestones are achieved. In some organisations teams are organised competitively to motivate the team members to achieve goals. This needs careful handling as it can have a negative effect. Team members can become demotivated if their team is consistently unsuccessful, or if teams do not co-operate with each other in an attempt to 'win'. However, regardless of why teams are formed, they will all focus on achieving team goals.

> A team with a star player is a good team, but a team without one is a great team.
> - *Author unknown*

Teams will be organised to achieve specific purposes; however, despite how well they may be organised and constituted, problems will arise. If there is a clear plan of how the team is going to achieve its goals, it should be able to anticipate difficulties before they happen and work out a solution so that the difficulty does not become a problem. Approach problem-solving by identifying what the problem is, why it happened, what should be done to resolve it, implement the problem-solving initiative and then evaluate the outcome of the implementation. Team members may approach problems to do with:

- Clash of team members' **personalities**
- **Goals not clearly defined**
- Team **responsibilities not clearly defined**
- **Changing circumstances** of the organisation
- **Poor leadership**
- Team members having **insufficient skills and knowledge** to do what they have been tasked to achieve
- **Insufficient time** to complete tasks
- **Poor communication** as a result of misunderstandings. These problems should be tackled by direct communication with the team member involved. If the problem is too difficult, a supervisor / manager should be consulted
- **Lack of motivation** - Team members should keep focused on what they need to achieve and contribute positively to the team going forward. Seek assistance when required and offer assistance if fellow team members require help
- **Poor feedback** - It is important that all members of the team know whether they are meeting those objectives or not. Team members should be aware of how well they are performing within the team and meeting expectations. Feedback encourages team members to give of their best by making sure of mutual satisfaction and improvement.

Feedback should provide the team members with information on their strengths and weakness which is fair and offered without bias or favouritism. Feedback is given to reward team members with praise and identify any development opportunities which a team member should do. Areas of feedback to team members may cover their approach to how they have:

- Achieved team goals
- Taken ownership of their responsibilities
- Worked collaboratively with others
- Added value to the achievement of the team's goals
- Managed their time to achieve team goals
- Communicated with others, within and outside the team
- Been committed to achieving the team goals

• ACTIVITY 8

What kinds of problems may arise when working within a team?

To overcome problems always look to what it is the team is aiming to achieve. A team is never static; a team will evolve and build on itself as a result of the normal elements of change that are experienced in an organisation.

Team building is a never-ending process which builds on the success of a team and recognises its weaknesses and overcomes them by taking action. As a team, always focus on producing work to the required standard and by the agreed deadlines.

Testing your knowledge

1. What is the purpose of an organisation?

2. What is a 'mission' statement?

3. Why do organisations share their 'values' with their customers?

4. What is meant by the word 'synergy'?

5. Why is it important to have a positive attitude?

6. When should a team member offer advice?

7. What are the important factors involved in building a successful team?

8. Why are the best teams made up of a diverse group of people?

9. What is the difference between an 'open' and 'closed' question?

10. What are the different roles in a team?

11. What is the purpose of giving 'feedback' to team members?

Skills

You should be aware of the purpose of your organisation. Your team goals should be aligned in some way to the overall organisation purpose. Gather together information about your organisation's mission statement, value statement and any other business plans that you may have access to. Discuss these with team members as well as your supervisor / manager if you need to clarify your understanding. The mission and values of the organisation should be developed as part of your behaviour – there will be some changes that you will need to consider to work effectively in the culture of whatever organisation you work in. Every organisation will have a different culture – the way they do things differently from other organisations. Some will be explicit, like the expectations that will come from the policies and procedures you need to implement, but others will be implicit, which you will observe as you work with colleagues and different team members. These behaviours should not only be exercised within the organisation but also to external customers. If you are not sure about organisational policies and procedures, check with your supervisor / manager.

• ACTIVITY9

Identify an improvement that could be achieved in your workplace if members of your team were to co-operate in changing the status quo. List the stages that you would go through to achieve the desired result, stating what the necessary change is; how it would improve the workplace; who would be affected; what actions would need to be taken, and who by; whose approval would be needed; whose co-operation would be needed; how you would obtain their commitment and how you would monitor the result.

The most important function a team should accomplish is the agreement to what it is aiming to do and how you as a team member will contribute towards achieving the goal (s). Once you have been assigned your role within the team, check:

- Who the leader of the team is and the chain of command
- The programme of meetings
- What exactly you have to do
- When you need to achieve the allotted tasks
- How you need to complete tasks – the standard and level of excellence you should be working towards achieving
- Who you will be working with specifically on your tasks, if anyone
- Who to report to in the event of problems, if you cannot resolve them yourself
- The budget you will work with, if appropriate

Your first task should be to consider how you can contribute positively to achieving the goals for which the team has been assembled. Continue to work collaboratively – find opportunities to support others, not only to be of help but to increase your learning of the team's project – clearly, concisely and to add value to the tasks you have been asked to complete. Being in a team is an opportunity to do a stocktake of your skills and knowledge. Are you equipped to complete the tasks for the team that you have been asked to complete? Find learning opportunities to advance your skills and knowledge when in a team.

Being a member of a team means that you will no longer be working alone. You will be working with different people, with different skills and knowledge, personalities, behaviours, attitudes etc. It will be a diverse environment which you will need to be a part of. Rather than consider the differences that may separate members of a team, consider the differences that may pull the team together. Diversity in a team is something to be celebrated. It is an opportunity to learn different ways of thinking and approaching your work which may be more effective that what you have normally done in the past. If problems occur when working in a team, communicate what the problems are and aim to resolve them. If you cannot resolve problems work them out within the team, or if the problem is of a sensitive nature, discuss the problem with either your team leader or your supervisor / manager.

Working as a member of a team is a great learning opportunity, as you will be working with lots of different people who will do things differently from you. Learn from differences. Make sure you are receiving feedback on the quality of your performance. This should form part of your appraisal process, if your organisation carries out this function. Always try to find ways of improving how you work in an organisation so as to be meaningful and add value.

• ACTIVITY 10

You have been asked to join a team to market a new product which is a completely new avenue for the organisation. Prepare your notes for the first meeting listing the questions you think need to be answered.

Testing your skills

1. What are the organisational policies and procedures that you must work with to achieve the goals of your team?

2. How many teams have you been a member of and what was your role?

3. How do you contribute to the agreement of your team's goals?

4. How do you work with other team members?

5. What skills and knowledge have you used to achieve the tasks you have been given in your team?

6. What must you do if you realise you are going to be late for a team meeting?

7. How do you deal with problems you have working in a team?

8. What has empowered you working in a team?

9. How do you accept constructive feedback?

10. How do you communicate with colleagues in your team?

11. How do you agree quality measures with your colleagues?

12. How do you tell if someone is 'actively' listening?

Ready for assessment?

To achieve this Level 2 unit of a Business & Administration qualification, learners will need to demonstrate that they are able to perform the following activities:

1. Followed organisational policies, systems and procedures relevant to their role

2. Applied relevant organisational values across all aspects of their work

3. Worked with outside organisations and individuals in a way that protected the image of their organisation, when relevant

4. Sought guidance when unsure about organisational policies, systems, procedures and values

5. Communicated effectively with other people in a team

6. Contributed to the agreement of work objectives and quality measures with a team, to achieve a positive outcome

7. Made sure work goals and objectives were achieved in a way that made best use of own abilities in a team

8. Provided support to members of a team, when required

9. Showed respect for individuals in a team

10. Made sure own work met agreed quality standards and was on time

11. Identified problem (s) or disagreement (s) in a team

12. Resolve problem (s) or disagreement (s) within limit of own authority and experience

13. Referred problems, as required

14. Contributed to providing constructive feedback on the achievement of objectives to a team

15. Received constructive feedback on own work

16. Used feedback on the achievement of objectives to identify improvements in own work

You will need to produce evidence from a variety of sources to support the performance requirements of this unit.

If you carry out the 'ACTIVITIES' and respond to the 'NEED TO KNOW' questions, these will provide some of the evidence required.

Links to other units

While gathering evidence for this unit, evidence may also be used from evidence generated from other units within the Business & Administration suite of units. Below is a sample of applicable units; however, most units within the Business & Administration suite of units will also be applicable.

QCF NVQ
Communications
Communicate in a business environment (Level 2)
Make and receive telephone calls
Use electronic message systems
Use a diary system
Take minutes
Core business & administration
Manage own performance in a business environment (Level 2)
Improve own performance in a business environment (Level 2)
Solve business problems (Level 2)
Work with other people in a business environment (Level 2)
Customer service
Handle mail
Meet and welcome visitors
Provide reception services

SVQ
Communications
Prepare to communicate in a business environment
Make and receive telephone calls
Use electronic message systems
Use a diary system
Take minutes
Core business & administration
Agree how to manage and improve own performance in a business environment
Plan how to solve business problems
Work with other people in a business environment
Customer service
Handle mail
Meet and welcome visitors
Provide reception services

12 Meet and welcome visitors

MEET AND WELCOME VISITORS

'**Meet and welcome visitors**' is an <u>optional unit</u> which may be chosen as one of a combination of units to achieve either a Qualifications and Credit Framework (QCF), National Vocational Qualification (NVQ) or Scottish Vocational Qualification (SVQ).

The aims of this unit are to:

- Understand the procedures for meeting and welcoming visitors
- Be able to meet and welcome visitors

To achieve the above aims of this unit, learners will be expected to provide evidence through the performance of work-based activities.

Knowledge

To conduct face to face business, an organisation will play host to visitors. Visitors can either be internal customers who will attend a meeting within their own organisation or they will be external customers who attend a meeting at another organisation they do not belong to. In both cases, an organisation meets and greets visitors. In a large organisation, people who work for the organisation will be requested to attend meetings in other parts of the building or with teams they do not work with. In most situations, people will be visiting an organisation, more or less, as strangers.

The visitor, whether internal or external to the organisation, will have a very good reason and purpose for attending the organisation. They will wish to conduct some form of business. The business will always involve some form of a partnership, where issues are discussed and

resolved to agree a clear way forward. To do this effectively visitors should be able to work in a professional environment relaxed enough for them to freely express themselves and where a positive relationship can be built and sustained between working colleagues.

First impressions

The first stage of building a positive relationship between working colleagues is to project a positive impression of the organisation. This begins with how a visitor is met and greeted at the point of entry to the organisation. Every organisation has a first point of contact for any visitor, regardless of how big or small it is. The visitor will immediately make a judgement about the organisation based on the physical appearance of the building. This first impression will be strengthened or diminished by how they are met and greeted by the host's representative. The visitor will expect to be made to feel welcome. They will want to feel relaxed and ready to do what they are there to do. Behaviour towards visitors should be courteous, respectful and pleasant, projecting a friendly tone. These behaviour traits will begin to build a positive relationship between the visitor and their host, which will contribute towards achieving a successful relationship and outcome of the visit. A visitor will have made a judgement about the host organisation within thirty seconds.

The way that visitors are greeted will vary depending on the purpose of the visit, e.g. a Chief Executive visiting a business will be greeted differently from a person who is visiting for a job interview. While everyone will be met with the same level of courtesy, there will be slight variations, depending on who the visitor is and how important they are to the business, e.g. the Chief Executive and the job applicant will both want to be assured that they are in a professional organisation, but the behaviour shown towards them will vary.

• ACTIVITY 1

Which of the following behaviours would not be appropriate towards a visitor enquiring about their appointment:

1. Continue eating lunch
2. Check how long they have been waiting
3. Read a book
4. Chat to the security guard
5. Welcome them on arrival

On meeting a visitor, the first host representative should establish:

- Who they are
- Who they are meeting
- The time of their meeting

Depending on the size of an organisation, there may be a string of host people that the visitor meets before they are eventually introduced to the person they are there to meet. Each one of these intermediary hosts should act with the same level of courtesy, respect and friendliness. Be professional. Behave purposefully. Be positive, vocally and physically, and polite. Make sure the visitor leaves the building with a good impression of the organisation because of how they have been treated by all host representatives.

• ACTIVITY 2

Match the sentences 1-6 to the responses A-F.

1. Nice to meet you.
2. Hello, I'm Sonja Blum.
3. Thank you for coming today.
4. How are you?
5. Would you like a coffee?
6. Hello, it's nice to see you again

A. Not at all. Thank you for seeing me.
B. Hello, it's nice to see you too.
C. Very well, thank you.
D. Yes please, that would be nice.
E. Hi, Adam Wright.
F. Nice to meet you, too.

Which pairs of sentences would be used by people meeting for the first time? Which would be used by people who have met before? Which could be used by both?

If the visitor is external to the organisation, they will need to be made aware of any specific **health and safety regulations** which they will need to implement. This could include:

- Wearing appropriate dress, e.g. hard hats, fluorescent tabards
- Being made aware of restricted access to certain areas or parts of the building
- Fire procedures to follow, in the event of a fire
- Emergency drill, e.g. What to do in the event of a bomb threat
- Using the sign-in book to keep track of their presence in the building. They may be requested to sign out when leaving the building as well

Visitors may also be asked to use the **sign-in book**. They will be asked to do this for a number of reasons:

- **Health and safety procedures** - Once a visitor enters a building, that organisation becomes responsible for their welfare. The receptionist will carry out all the necessary procedures to protect their visitors, e.g. supplying a hard hat if the building is being refurbished in some way that may pose a threat to the visitor

- **Entry and security procedures** - Access may be limited to certain areas of an organisation which only allows certain people to visit. There may be restrictions on how people can visit, e.g. they must be accompanied by specific people from specific departments. They must be wearing appropriate access badges etc., at all times

- **Emergency procedures** - These are the procedures for handling visitors to an organisation in the event of fire, bomb threat or any other emergency situation. A receptionist may tell visitors that there is an expected fire warning to go off at a particular time. They will only be responsible for those visitors who are still in their working area. They will take charge and direct visitors as required by the emergency procedures

Visitors may also be given a pass to wear at all times when they are in the building. If the visitor has any accessibility requirements, make sure these are complied with according to the requirements of health and safety and organisational procedures, e.g. a person visiting in a wheelchair. Whatever a visitor may be asked to do or **comply with** should be explained to them clearly and carefully, so they gain a good understanding of how and why they are being looked after. If possible, visitors should have the opportunity to be offered some form of refreshment. Also, they should be made aware of the washroom facilities in case they want to freshen up before their meeting.

A visitor should have the full attention of the host representative. The host representative should minimise distractions, e.g. stop talking to work colleagues about what they did last night. It cannot be stressed enough how important it is to communicate well with visitors. **Positive communication skills** will add to the impression of the organisation that the visitor is forming about the organisation they are visiting. Use all the elements of communication skills that go towards building a positive relationship with the visitor:

- **Face** - Open and expressive
- **Eyes** - Make eye contact to build confidence and trust
- **Posture** - A professional appearance - not slouching, hands in pockets, arms crossed etc.
- **Gestures** - Be natural and culturally sensitive
- **Voice** - Use appropriate volume, tone, speed etc.
- **Movement** - Keep movements subtle, assertive but not aggressive
- **Touch** - Do not touch the visitor, unless in an emergency
- **Appearance** - Appropriate to the requirements of the culture of the organisation

Some **greeting tips** include:

- Smile first
- Shake hands
- Do not rush
- Remember the visitor's name and use it
- Eye contact
- Confident and positive body language
- Be ready to converse. Have three sure-fire topics of conversation prepared
- Avoid personal questions

Once the visitor has completed all the '**housekeeping**' activities they have been asked to comply with, contact the person with whom they are there to meet and tell them their visitor has arrived. If the host has any special instructions from this conversation, let the visitor know. For example, apologies that, due to unforeseen circumstances, they will be delayed for fifteen minutes. Let the visitor know that their host will be with them shortly. Offer the visitor a seat, if available. Monitor how long the visitor has been waiting for their host to pick them up, if this is the appropriate procedure. If the visitor has been waiting too long, follow up with the host and let the visitor know that they have not been forgotten, and apologise for the delay, if necessary. If the organisation's instructions insist on chaperoning visitors to their hosts, organise for the appropriate person to do this.

• ACTIVITY 3

What aspects of communications skills can be used with visitors to build a positive image of the organisation?

Most visitors to an organisation will have been **expected and planned for**. The host representative will generally have a list of visitors expected to visit the organisation each day. Beyond those visitors that are invited to an organisation, other types of visitors who will be **unexpected** and not planned for will include:

- People delivering post
- Couriers
- Delivery drivers
- Maintenance people
- Contractors
- Sales people
- Charity workers

As some of these visitors may be regular customers, a routine will have been established. For example, couriers may be expected to go to the back of a building to the post room and take off their helmets. However, for some, e.g. sales people who turn up on the off chance of securing a meeting with an office manager, there will be organisation procedures that need to be followed regarding how to deal with them.

Most organisations would rather not have **unsolicited visitors**. The organisation will expect unsolicited visitors to speak to specific people in the organisation to organise a formal meeting. Have a list of all names and telephone numbers of the people who work in the organisation if manning a central visitor access centre. There will be other people who visit because they want information. An employee whose main function it to meet and greet visitors should aim to gain as much knowledge as possible about the organisation, so that all types of enquiries from visitors can be handled effectively. If an appropriate response cannot be offered to a visitor make sure there is access to someone who will be able to help. Do not give the impression that unexpected visitors are an unnecessary intrusion.

Deal with challenging behaviour from visitors

Every visitor that walks through the doors of an organisation is different, e.g. they may be young / old, male / female. They also feel they are different and want to be treated as individuals. Maintaining a personal approach to dealing with visitors and using the three Ps of professional behaviour is a way of making sure visitors receive a service that will meet their personal needs. The three Ps are:

- **Purpose** - Behave with intention to meet the needs of a visitor

- **Positive** - Address visitors with a smile, physically and in the voice

- **Polite** - There is nothing that is difficult to do for a visitor

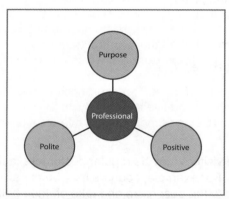

Figure 12.1 The three Ps of professional behaviour when greeting visitors

Visitors do not go out of their way to be difficult. However, they do go out of their way to get what they want, which may appear unreasonable. As a result, they may end up behaving badly.

Relate to visitors as individuals. Remain calm and:

- **Communicate** - Do not ignore a visitor, but actively listen to what they have to say. Use 'open' questions to resolve visitor enquires

- **Communicate confidence** - Both physical, including body language, and verbal

- **Be prepared** - Anything can happen in a day, so know the procedures to be followed to deal with most scenarios. Offer alternative approaches to resolving issues. Be part of the solution rather than part of the problem

- **Be a font of knowledge** - Know the kinds of information that visitors will need to be reassured of. Make sure you know information about the local area, transport systems etc.

- **Take the initiative** - Make it work for the visitor visiting the organisation for the first time. Keep their impression of the organisation positive

Some visitors will be in a hurry, may have dealt with the organisation before or know exactly what they want. Personalise the way you approach their difficulty and be **precise** in the response you make to them, e.g. if they are in a hurry, pick up on this and address it specifically. Other visitors may be overly sensitive, e.g. they may think that they are very important so they should not have to wait for anything. The best thing to do in this situation is to **pacify** them. Get it right the first time by being very polite, and do not feel annoyed by their behaviour. Try not to let them repeat themselves. There may be other visitors who **demand attention**, which can result in the host representative being deflected away from other visitors, e.g. a visitor may be especially shy and need reassurance on their visit, and so engage the host representative exclusively. In this situation minimise attention to them by being friendly but not overly involved, and take the personal approach.

Take a natural approach to every situation. Avoid acting in a biased manner to any visitor. Be **personable** and personalise the service each visitor receives. Meet every customer's needs as required. The organisation that 'goes the extra mile' is the one that will still be in business in the future. There is never an excuse to be rude or shout at a visitor. If a host representative feels they are unable to deal with the situation, they should seek advice or find out what the organisational procedures are for dealing with difficult visitors.

• ACTIVITY 4

Describe different types of difficult behaviour demonstrated by some visitors.

All visitors must be treated with the same standard of courtesy. The host representative is the public face of the organisation. The way a visitor is received will make a lasting impression on the visitor. Business can be lost before the meeting even takes place if the visitor is given a poor impression of the organisation. Always take a personal and individual approach to each visitor who walks through the doors of the organisation. Know and follow the organisation's procedures for dealing with visitors and the wide range of circumstances that can arise when greeting them.

> **Every visitor is a guest, treat them as such and you won't go far wrong.**

Testing your knowledge

1. Why should visitors be treated politely?

2. What is the difference between expected and unexpected visitors?

3. How differently would expected and unexpected visitors be treated?

4. What is the difference between internal and external visitors?

5. How is a positive image of the organisation projected to visitors?

6. What are the three Ps?

7. Why are communication skills so important when meeting and greeting visitors?

8. What is the importance of positive body language when greeting visitors?

9. What is the difference between making eye contact and staring?

Skills

Within an organisation there are many different situations where you might be expected to meet and greet visitors. This could be part of your job role as a receptionist, help desk representative, security office etc. Alternatively, you could be asked by your manager to go and pick up a visitor from a location and bring them to your manager's office for a meeting, particularly in very large organisations. Whether they are external or internal visitors, you should meet and greet them politely, making them feel welcome. Every visitor should have your full attention. Nothing should distract you from making a visitor feel welcome.

Guide the visitor to use the sign-in book or a visitors' book. Follow your organisation's procedures for doing this. If your organisation has specific requirements for doing this, help the visitor to fill in the sign-in book. Clarify with the visitor that they must return to the sign-in area to return their badge and sign out. If it is appropriate, explain why it is necessary for them to do this. Depending on the reason for the visit, guide the visitor to the correct area. Some organisations organise many meetings during a day and have special procedures in place, especially if visitors are attending a conference. They may have set up separate procedures and staff to oversee this. The remaining visitors would go to the appropriate host representative and follow through with the same sign-in process. Make sure that the visitor has the appropriate security badge. Check with them if they would like to visit the toilets. If there are any particular special needs that the visitor has, address these. This is part of making the visitor feel welcome.

•ACTIVITY 5

Where are meetings held?
- In the reception area
- In a meeting room
- At someone's desk

What do you offer visitors to drink?
- A cold drink before the meeting
- A hot drink
- A choice of hot or cold drinks

At the same time as these expected visitors appear, you may have unexpected visitors during the day, e.g. post, courier services. Follow any relevant organisational needs when dealing with these types of visitors, e.g. some couriers will be asked to visit the post room of the organisation to make their deliveries and some may not. Be respectful of the courier's job, as they too are meeting customer's expectations and have deadlines to meet. If a contractor is visiting your organisation, ask them who they need to see. Contact this person and then organise for the contractor to be collected or sent to the appropriate department. Are you familiar with the layout of your organisation so you know how long it may take a visitor to get to where they need to be?

• ACTIVITY 6

If your company has an internal telephone directory find a copy and reorganise it so that it is easy for you to find extensions when you need them.

If the visitor's host is not ready to meet the visitor, make sure they are aware of any delay. Explain why there has been a delay. Ask them if they would like some form of refreshment and supply this if requested. Guide them to wait in the seating area. Make sure they are not forgotten. Check with the visitor's host if there has been any change and communicate this with the visitor. This assumes that you are dealing with one visitor in a nice orderly way. However, visitors attend in no particular order: early, late, in a hurry, stressed etc. There may be times when you have four or five, if not more, visitors at any one time. Make sure you let them know that you will get to them as quickly as possible. Attend to the needs of each visitor on an individual basis. Do not feel you have to rush, but behave in a professional manner. Do not dismiss the other visitors who are waiting. Acknowledge them, but concentrate on the visitor you are dealing with. Remember, they can see you are dealing with another person and will be with them as soon as possible. The situation could become difficult if a visitor saw that you were talking with colleagues and treating them very casually.

• ACTIVITY 7

Keep a work diary over the period of a month, recording all of the visitors you deal with, their requirements and how you met them, indicating any security procedures involved.

Always behave in a professional manner and make sure each visitor's needs are being satisfied.

If you are late for a meeting or collecting a visitor, apologise. Give them a reason for the delay, if it seems appropriate. Engage in conversation if you feel the visitor would be comfortable to do so. However, do not allow them to become a distraction, as you will have other visitors to attend to.

• ACTIVITY 8

You are working as a receptionist in a doctor's surgery. The doctor is running behind with their appointments, so there are a number of patients in the waiting room. At 10.30 the patient due to see the doctor at 10.00 has still not been seen. The doctor indicates that they are ready to see the next patient and you call Amanda Patel, whose appointment was for 10.00. Matthew Graham, who has just arrived for his 10.30 appointment, comes to the desk and protests loudly that he should be seen now as it is time for his appointment and he has urgent work to return to. How do you deal with this situation?

Testing your skills

1. How are you expected to address visitors?

2. When is it appropriate to call visitors by their first name?

3. What reasons are there for being unable to meet visitors' needs?

4. How do you explain to visitors that you cannot help them?

5. What alternatives could you offer a visitor?

6. What do you do if you are unable to offer a positive solution to a visitor?

7. Do you know how to politely pass on the information to an unexpected visitor that they cannot be seen today?

8. What is your organisation's policy towards engaging visitors in small talk - do you discuss their journey, last night's episode of TV viewing or do you simply invite them to take a seat?

9. Can you tell from a visitor's body language if they want to chat or not?

10. What information is needed in a visitors' book?

11. Do contractors have to sign in a visitors' book?

12. Do you know where to keep the keys, visitors' book etc., when they are not in use?

13. Could you tell from the entries in the visitors' book which visitors are currently in the building?

14. Do you know why vehicle registration numbers are recorded in the visitors' book?

15. Do visitors to your organisation need any form of identification - if so, what is acceptable?

16. How do you deal with different types of visitors, e.g. post, couriers, contractors?

17. How do you deal with different types of deliveries?

18. Do you know what types of post need to be signed for?

19. Do you know where the assembly point is in the event of an evacuation?

20. How do you deal with difficult visitors?

21. Have you had training on dealing with problems that you might encounter with visitors?

22. Who do you refer to if you need further assistance when dealing with visitors?

23. What are the limits of your authority when meeting a visitor's needs?

24. Where do you find the extension number of everybody in your organisation?

25. Do you know where every department is in your organisation?

26. What transport systems lead to or away from your organisation?

27. If a visitor needs to freshen up before their appointment, where would you direct them?

28. What is the difference in the way you treat external visitors and internal visitors?

Ready for assessment?
To achieve this Level 2 unit of a Business & Administration qualification, learners will need to demonstrate that they are able to perform the following activities:

1. Met and greeted visitors promptly

2. Treated visitors politely and made them feel welcome

3. Identified visitors and the reason for their visit

4. Used organisation systems to receive and record visitors, if appropriate

5. Made sure a visitor's needs were met

6. Explained to visitors the reasons for any delay in dealing with them

7. Kept visitors informed of developments

8. Presented a positive image of themselves and the organisation

9. Followed organisational, health, safety and security procedures

10. Promptly informed relevant people about a visitor's arrival

11. Dealt with any problems that may have occurred or referred them on to an appropriate colleague

You will need to produce evidence from a variety of sources to support the performance requirements of this unit.

If you carry out the 'ACTIVITIES' and respond to the 'NEED TO KNOW' questions, these will provide some of the evidence required.

Links to other units

While gathering evidence for this unit, evidence may also be used from evidence generated from other units within the Business & Administration suite of units. Below is a sample of applicable units; however, most units within the Business & Administration suite of units will also be applicable.

QCF NVQ
Communications
Communicate in a business environment (Level 2)
Core business & administration
Manage own performance in a business environment (Level 2)
Improve own performance in a business environment (Level 2)
Work in a business environment (Level 2)
Work with other people in a business environment (Level 2)
Customer service
Assist in handling mail
Handle mail
Provide reception services

SVQ
Communications
Prepare to communicate in a business environment
Core business & administration
Agree how to manage and improve own performance in a business environment
Undertake work in a business environment
Contribute to working with others in a business environment
Customer service
Assist in handling mail
Handle mail
Provide reception services

13 Handle mail

HANDLE MAIL

'**Handle mail**' is an <u>optional unit</u> which may be chosen as one of a combination of units to achieve either a Qualifications and Credit Framework (QCF), National Vocational Qualification (NVQ) or Scottish Vocational Qualification (SVQ).

The aims of this unit are to:

- Understand security procedures when handling mail or packages
- Understand the range of available internal and external mail services
- Be able to receive, distribute and collect internal mail or packages
- Be able to follow procedures for despatching mail or packages
- Be able to resolve, report or refer problems that may occur in handling mail or packages
- To achieve the above aims of this unit, learners will be expected to provide evidence through the performance of work-based activities.

Knowledge
Mail or post is a method of distributing and despatching letters or packages from a sender to a recipient. This is generally carried out by a postal service, which may be operated publicly, e.g. the Royal Mail, or privately, e.g. DHL. There are two main types of mail:

- **External mail** - Incoming or outgoing mail. Mail that is managed by an external service
- **Internal Mail** - Incoming or outgoing mail. Mail that is managed by an organisation itself

Mail may be sent or received in the following ways:

- **Post**
- **Fax**
- **Email**

Handling mail will be managed differently depending on the size of an organisation, but the functions that will be carried out will be the same. Most large organisations will generally have a separate mail or post room where staff will deal with the mail / post coming into and leaving the organisation.

Organisations with mail rooms or post rooms may employ staff specifically to look after the smooth running of these functions. Small to medium size organisations may not have mail-room or post-room facilities. In this case, employees within the organisation will have a specific responsibility to look after these functions. Despite the increased use of email, there is still the need to send some mail physically:

- Documents that need signing
- Cheques
- Advertising
- Parcels
- Contracts
- Stock
- Samples

All mail that is processed within an organisation will need to be checked. Once it has been checked it will need to be sorted. Anything that is identified as damaged or suspicious should be dealt with separately. Working in a mail or post room will require some or all of the following:

- A letter opener or automatic mail opening equipment
- A date stamp, to record when the mail arrived
- Electronic scales
- An up-to-date copy of Royal Mail Guidance
- Stamps or a franking machine
- Access to a computer
- A mail record book

The person who looks after the distribution and despatch of mail / post will aim to make sure that all mail / post is delivered or picked up from the correct person at the required time. Large organisations will have a map of every floor, with the relevant staff names for that floor, to assist with the speedy delivery and pick up of mail / post. Organisations will also focus on minimising the cost of using any postal service.

Incoming mail

Mail / post will be delivered to an organisation by either postmen / postwomen at set times during the working day or couriers who may arrive at any time during the day. Some organisations may collect mail / post from the Post Office themselves. Some mail / post will need to be signed for, which may include:

- **Special Delivery**
- **Recorded Delivery**
- **Couriered** items

All will need dealing with as quickly as possible. If the delivery of incoming mail is held up, problems may occur:

- Deadlines may be missed
- Appointments may be missed
- Banking of cheques may be delayed

In some organisations incoming mail is left in the sealed envelopes, unless it has to be opened to find out who it is for. In others it will all be opened unless marked 'personal' or 'confidential'. It is important to open mailbags carefully, so as not to damage any mail / post. Mail opening equipment may be available, but this should only be used with the correct training. If a letter opener is being used to open mail / post, be careful not to damage the contents of the envelope.

Once all mail / post has been received into an organisation it will need to be **checked**. It is checked to make sure it is for the organisation. Any mail / post incorrectly delivered should be put into the outgoing mail to be picked up later that day. Checks are also made for suspicious or damaged items. Staff handling mail / post may decide to categorise mail as 'familiar' or 'unfamiliar', to speed up the checking process.

Since 9/11, every organisation has increased their vigilance when dealing with suspicious packages. Packages that match any of the following should be treated as suspicious:

- Restrictive endorsements, such as 'personal' or 'confidential'
- An address to title only or incorrect title
- A strange odour
- A powdery, granular or sand-like substance, residue or liquid that is visible on the cover of the packet or leaking from it
- Badly typed / written address
- Oily stains, discolorations or crystallisation on wrapper
- Excessive wrapping tape or string
- Signs of wiring or tinfoil

Once a package has been identified as suspicious, the correct authority within the organisation should be notified. Specific instructions, such as those listed below, should be followed in the event that an item must be opened by the correct authority:

- The addressee or supervisor should decide whether or not to open the piece of mail
- If the mail need not be opened, consideration should be given regarding how to dispose of this mail, which may include throwing it away
- Open the mail as far away from the face as is comfortably possible
- Open the mail over a clean table or countertop
- Use gloves and a mask if available
- The envelope should be opened carefully, e.g. with a letter opener, and the contents removed carefully to avoid dispersing any unusual substance that might be present
- After opening the envelope or package, inspect the inside for any unusual substance before removing the contents

• ACTIVITY 1

Keep a work diary over the period of a month, recording any suspicious / damaged / junk mail that is received. Explain what was done with the items.

If an item is damaged, note this and record it in the appropriate book, if the mail or post room has one. Make a note of the fact that it is damaged on the receipt. Any item that is damaged, whether signed for or not, needs to be recorded.

Record on the exterior of the item when it was received. Some organisations use a stamp to help sort the mail, which could show the various departments within the organisation. The person opening the mail will tick the department it is intended for, e.g.

Department	Date received
Accounts	
Sales	
Purchase	16.08.2010
Engineering	
Despatch	
HR	

In some organisations all incoming mail / post will be recorded in a **post book**. In others, it is only mail / post that needs to be signed for that is recorded. Separate mail that needs a signature, as this will need to be delivered and a signature obtained, or the person will need to be contacted to collect or be given the item. Mail that does not need to be signed for will be sorted in one of a number of ways: by department, by floor or by individual. This will require a thorough knowledge of everyone who works at an organisation: their name, their role, their department and their location in the building.

• ACTIVITY 2

Look at the two lists of departments shown below. Each department in the first list matches a department in the second list - they are just called by different names. Match each department in list 1 with the equivalent department in list 2.

List 1	List 2
Personnel	Purchasing
Accounts	Visual Merchandising
Buying	Finance
Display	Catering
Hospitality	HR

Most organisations will be set up to manage certain types of mail / post using a very strict procedure, which should be adhered to and will vary depending on the size of the organisation. For example, in

large organisations they will have a dedicated post / mail room. An organisation may insist that after mail / post has been sorted into various departments it is delivered to departments in a strict order based on the priority of the business, e.g. all mail to the finance department is delivered first. This may be more of a requirement at a certain time of the month, depending on the business. Staff in a mail / post room may receive special requests to look out for incoming mail which they will have been asked to deliver to a person or department by a specific time, e.g. the receipt of tender documents. Some mail or post rooms may not deliver the post to the individual, but instead have a pigeonhole system. The procedures here are exactly the same as when physically delivering to employees around an organisation. Items must be placed in the correct pigeonholes. Any mail that goes into the wrong pigeonhole will be delayed, and this could have serious consequences. There is also the possibility of 'confidential' information falling into the wrong hands.

Outgoing mail
Mail may be despatched from an organisation by using either a postal system or courier service. If a mail or post room has been set up within an organisation, there will probably be a timetable of collection times from around the building where employees will know where to place their mail / post. The mail will then need to be collected from this area at the specific time. Note any special requests that have been put on the post item. If unsure of what the instruction means, check with the sender. In small organisations there will probably be 'in mail' and 'out mail' trays, or 'mail trays' identifying the type of mail service the sender wants to use.

If outgoing mail is delayed:

• Sales could be lost

• Deliveries could be late

• Customers' confidence could be lost

Once all the mail has been collected, decisions will need to be made about the **type of service** to use, e.g. first or second class. Organisations usually have a system in place so the sender can inform whoever is organising the despatch of mail the type of service they want to use, usually with a post-it note attached to the mail item. Once these decisions have been made, mail items should be sorted into different types. Some organisations keep a record of the mail it sends. Some organisations record the cost of outgoing mail so it can be charged to the department that sent it. Mail may also be brought to the mail / post room.

Why should the mail / post room have a list of people / departments that the mail handling staff need to collect mail from?

When all the mail / post has been sorted, identify any items that have been nominated to use a courier service. Complete the courier's documentation according to their requirements. Put the items with the documentation for the courier to collect at the required time and in the required place. Most couriers will check the documentation, sign it and give a receipt to the mail / post room staff.

The following options are available from Royal Mail. For domestic post in the UK:

- **First Class letters** - Royal Mail aims to deliver these the next working day

- **Second Class letters** - Royal Mail aims to deliver these by the third working day

- **Special Delivery** - An express service for urgent or valuable items. Delivery is guaranteed to most parts of the UK the next day

- **Recorded Delivery** - A signature is required when delivered. This gives the sender proof of posting and of delivery

- **Packet** - These can be sent first or second class - up to a certain weight

- **Standard Parcel** - Royal Mail aims to deliver these within five days

- **Enhanced Compensation Parcel** - Extra compensation is available if the parcel is lost or damaged

For post overseas:

- **Airmail** - Letters sent to Europe should be delivered within three days. To the rest of the world they should arrive within five days

- **Surface Mail** - Non-urgent mail is sent by sea and land. No guarantees are given on the time it takes

- **Airsure** - The fastest way to send important letters overseas. Mail leaves on the earliest possible flight and its progress can be tracked electronically

- **International Signed For** - Mail is electronically tracked until it leaves the UK. It is then sent on the first available flight and signed for on delivery

	URGENT	NON-URGENT	PROOF OF DELIVERY REQUIRED	COMPENSATION REQUIRED IF LOST
First Class	YES			
Second Class		YES		
Special Delivery	YES		YES	YES
First Class Recorded	YES		YES	
Second Class Recorded		YES	YES	
Packet	YES			
Standard Parcel		YES		
Enhanced Compensation parcel		YES		YES
Airmail	YES			
Surface Mail		YES		
Airsure	YES			YES
International Signed For	YES		YES	YES

Table 13.1. Postage options for different items

There are size and weight limits for both domestic and international mail / post. Weigh and measure the mail to work out the cost. Many franking machines have scales in them.

When using a **franking machine**, once the franking is printed, the credit has been used, so:

- Check that the correct amount of postage is used

- Make sure there is sufficient credit available

- Use adhesive labels on packages that will not fit into the machine

- Return the machine to the minimum amount after use

Check when using the franking machine that everything has been done correctly, as mistakes cannot be rectified. If placing stamps on the mail / post make sure they:

- Are placed in the top right-hand corner
- Are for the right value
- Do not cover up any part of the address

• ACTIVITY 4

Find out the cost of the following mail items.

Item	Option	Destination	Weight (g)	Size (mm)
Letter	First	Southampton	60	240 x 165 x 5
Letter	Second	Cardiff	127	240 x 165 x 5
Letter	First	Sheffield	60	260 x 360 x 5
Parcel	Standard	Dundee	550	210 x 297 x 248
Letter	Airmail	Australia	40	240 x 165 x 5
Letter	Airsure	New Zealand	65	240 x 165 x 5

If sending **large quantities of mail**, Printed Postage Impressions (PPIs) may be used. These are a simple, pre-printed alternative to postage stamps or franking machines. The Royal Mail supply First Class and Second Class pre-printed envelopes.

Some days of the week or month there will be more outgoing mail than others. This may be because invoices or 'mailshots' are being sent. Plan these in a diary so they are not missed. Make sure there is enough time to meet the collection deadline. There will be occasions when more mail appears than expected. This may cause a problem in getting it all ready before the deadline. If this happens a supervisor should be informed, so they can organise what to do.

Some organisations keep an outgoing post book. This may record the number of letters or full details of the mail being despatched. Make sure the necessary details are filled in every day.

Handling mail is an integral function of any size of organisation. All employees within an organisation trust that their mail / post will be delivered to them and collected from them at specific times of the day. This is the service that the mail- or post-room staff will provide. In small organisations this may be carried out by an individual who has been given this role. Mail / post items will be expected to be delivered or collected by the person responsible for delivering this function. Employees within an organisation should always let the person know who is responsible for looking after the mail / post how important a mail item is that they are either expecting or sending, so it can be processed appropriately.

Testing your knowledge

Incoming mail
1. When is a post book used, if there is one?
2. Which items of mail might need signing for?
3. Why should mail be distributed as quickly as possible?
4. What are the characteristics of mail that might identify it as 'suspicious'?
5. Why is 'junk' mail discarded?

Outgoing mail
1. What is the difference between Special Delivery and Recorded Delivery?
2. What are the advantages of Airmail over Surface Mail?
3. Why is it important to put the franking machine back to the minimum amount after use?
4. Why is a 'courier' service used?
5. What type of problems might happen with incoming and outgoing mail?

Skills
Find out from your supervisor / manager what you will be expected to do with the incoming and outgoing mail each day. Once you are aware of the limits of your responsibility start thinking about how you will organise your working day around these activities.

Familiarise yourself with the space you will be working in. Make a note of the different types of equipment you will be working with. If you are not familiar with all the different types of equipment you will be using make sure you get the training you need to use it properly. Do not use equipment that you are not familiar with. If you are not familiar with the building that you will be delivering and collecting mail in, do a tour of the building, so that you become familiar with all of the locations. If you are in a small office make sure you know who everyone is and what their procedures are for handling mail. If you are new to the organisation, go with someone so they can point out any difficulties or security issues that you will need to be aware of. Always get to know the building you will be working in or people that you will be working with.

Work through all the requirements your organisation expects you to perform. Your first priority will probably be incoming mail, as this usually happens for the first time at the beginning of the day. You may have to service a few deliveries of mail throughout your working day depending on the size and arrangements of an organisation. Identify what time the mail arrives in the building and if there are any special arrangements for where it is left. Are there separate bags for letters and packages? Are you expected to sort the bags on the floor or work from a table? Once all the mail has been emptied out of the bags, start looking at all the names. Are the names associated with any departments? How do your mail room staff or business like to distribute mail, by name, by department, by floor etc? Confirm with your supervisor / manager how this is done. Make any notes about the best way to do things. There may be some special circumstances or employee requirements that you will need to know about. Make sure that mail which is labelled 'private' or 'confidential' is not opened but delivered as it was received to the recipient.

When sorting the mail, you should look out for 'junk' and 'damaged' mail, as these will be easy to identify. Follow through with your organisation's procedures for dealing with junk / damaged mail. Record what has been damaged in a damage book, if this is what your organisation expects you to do. Make any notes on the package for the person it will be delivered to so they are aware of the condition it was received in. Mail which may be less obvious to recognise is 'suspicious' mail. Check with your organisation's procedures for sorting 'suspicious' mail. Follow this through carefully, as it may affect your life and the lives of others. In the first instance, report anything 'suspicious' to your supervisor and follow their lead.

Be aware of what is going on around you. As you are checking and putting mail in designated places, couriers and special deliveries may be arriving. Couriers will probably expect you to sign for these parcels. Do so in a professional manner. Do not lose track of your sorting. You have targets to achieve. As with ordinary mail and packages, check the parcel from the courier to make sure that it has not been damaged. Make a note of who the courier is and see if they regularly deliver to the post room over the next few weeks. Establish relationships with these people.

• ACTIVITY 5

Write a short account of what you would do if you opened and read, by mistake, a letter marked 'private and confidential'.

Once all the mail has been sorted, you will probably go out and do your 'rounds', making deliveries throughout the building or business. Let someone know that you are about to do this so they are aware of where you are. If new to a large organisation, you will be accompanied with a colleague the first few times this happens, until you are familiar with where to go and how to get there. Observe where you go first and check to see if this is always the route taken. If necessary, make notes of how this is done. Make a note of any special arrangements that you need to be aware of, e.g. you may have to start with the Chief Executive's office first each day. Check to see how many times you deliver throughout the day. You may have to deliver mail items received from couriers immediately, depending on your organisation's procedures. Make a note of these. Plan your breaks and lunch around these events.

Most of the mail that is being sent from an organisation will be collected in the afternoon, unless there is a special delivery which has been ordered for a courier to collect. You should have been alerted to this and collected the item so there is enough time for it to be in the mail / post room or your desk when the courier arrives. When collecting mail to be sent, check to see if there are any special requests, usually written on the envelopes, about which service to use. There may be policies in place which have already identified this to all employees, so you will follow through with the correct procedures. Make sure that when you are collecting mail being sent from the building you are not too early, as people may plan their day so they get their correspondence completed just before the mail collection time.

Once all the mail has been collected, return to the mail or post room and start sorting out the service that will be charged for each piece of mail. You may either use stamps or a franking machine. If you use a franking machine, make sure that it has been set up correctly. Make sure each piece of mail is charged correctly. If this has to be recorded for each department, set this up and follow through what needs to be done. You may want to separate mail into domestic and international piles, as they will be charged differently. Check to see if there are any special deliveries that need to be made. Carry out the correct documentation for these. Log charges, as required, in line with your organisation's procedures.

If your organisation uses courier services regularly, familiarise yourself with their documentation, as they will expect to have them completed in full and correctly. You want to make sure that you will be billed for the correct service. You will need to make sure that if an invoice is required that it has been filled out correctly. If not, this may hold up the delivery of the item at the point of delivery. This may have a cost implication for the organisation as well as setting a bad impression. Get it right first time. If in doubt, check with the original sender or your supervisor, as it may be a regular item that is sent and they will be familiar with the sender's requirements. At the end of the day, prepare your workspace so that it is ready for the next day's activities.

• ACTIVITY 6

Spend one week dealing with incoming and outgoing mail at work. Write a brief account of your activities. Check to make sure you have been following your organisation's procedures correctly.

Throughout your working day you will comes across problems. Deal with those that you are able to deal with; however, if you are not sure of what to do, check with your supervisor / manager, as they will guide you.

Testing your skills

Incoming mail

1. What are the different services provided by the staff in the mail / post room in your organisation?

2. How and when do you distribute mail in your organisation?

3. Who signs for the receipt of incoming mail in your organisation?

4. How do you recognise a 'suspicious' package in your organisation?

5. What are the procedures for dealing with 'damaged' mail items in your organisation?

6. Who manages your organisation's post book?

Outgoing mail

1. In your organisation, which Royal Mail services are used and in what different circumstances are they used?

2. Which 'courier' service does your organisation use, and why?

3. What is the deadline for outgoing mail in your organisation?

4. What is the process for completing Royal Mail Recorded Delivery?

5. How do you find out the correct postage for various weights and sizes of mail?

' does mail have to be collected at the correct time?

Ready for assessment?

To achieve this Level 2 unit of a Business & Administration qualification, learners will need to demonstrate that they are able to perform the following activities:

1. Received and checked incoming mail or packages

2. Sorted incoming mail or packages

3. Disposed of unwanted 'junk' mail

4. Followed the correct procedures for 'suspicious' or 'damaged' items

5. Distributed incoming mail or packages

6. Followed the correct procedure when there were problems with incoming mail

7. Collected outgoing mail or packages

8. Sorted outgoing mail or packages

9. Identified best options for despatching mail

10. Arranged for a courier service to collect outgoing mail or packages, where requested

11. Prepared items for urgent or special delivery

12. Calculated the correct postage charges for outgoing mail or packages

13. Recorded postage costs in line with agreed procedures

14. Despatched outgoing mail or packages on time

15. Followed the correct procedures when there were problems with outgoing mail

You will need to produce evidence from a variety of sources to support the performance requirements of this unit.

If you carry out the 'ACTIVITIES' and respond to the 'NEED TO KNOW' ıese will provide some of the evidence required.

Links to other units

While gathering evidence for this unit, evidence may also be used from evidence generated from other units within the Business & Administration suite of units. Below is a sample of applicable units; however, most units within the Business & Administration suite of units will also be applicable.

QCF NVQ
Communications
Communicate in a business environment (Level 2)
Core business & administration
Manage own performance in a business environment (Level 2)
Improve own performance in a business environment (Level 2)
Work in a business environment (Level 2)
Work with other people in a business environment (Level 2)
Customer service
Meet and welcome visitors
Provide reception services

SVQ
Communications
Prepare to communicate in a business environment
Core business & administration
Agree how to manage and improve own performance in a business environment
Undertake work in a business environment
Contribute to working with others in a business environment
Customer service
Meet and welcome visitors
Provide reception services

14

Provide reception services

PROVIDE RECEPTION SERVICES

'**Provide reception services**' is an <u>optional unit</u> which may be chosen as one of a combination of units to achieve either a Qualifications and Credit Framework (QCF), National Vocational Qualification (NVQ) or Scottish Vocational Qualification (SVQ).

The aims of this unit are to:

- Understand the purpose of reception services in a business environment
- Understand the procedures to be followed when providing reception services
- Understand ways of improving reception services and developing own role
- Provide a reception service

To achieve the above aims of this unit, learners will be expected to provide evidence through the performance of work-based activities.

Knowledge
A receptionist is generally the first point of contact that a customer will have with an organisation. The receptionist is therefore the representative of the organisation. Receptionists must behave in a professional, courteous and efficient manner. They are 'image makers'. Their behaviour is often considered the most important quality they can bring to their work, as it is often a lasting one, the one the customer will walk away with. Receptionists spend much of their time behind a reception desk. They need to look smart. In some organisations they will be issued with a uniform.

Alternative titles used to describe receptionists include:

- Customer Services Assistant
- Secretary
- Clerk
- Telephonist
- Switchboard Operator
- Administrator

Receptionists answer telephones, often using telephone systems with multiple lines. They may manage email and often answer general questions submitted through the organisation's website. Receptionists also greet visitors to the organisation. Sometimes receptionists must screen access or alert security to suspicious people entering a building.

However, the role of a receptionist will be determined by the type of organisation they work in and the sector that they work in:

- Hotel receptionist
- Dental receptionist
- Medical receptionist
- Bank receptionist
- Beauty Salon receptionist
- Leisure Centre receptionist
- Legal secretary
- Office receptionist
- School receptionist

Some receptionists will work alone. Others may work in large organisations where they are part of a team. Sometimes the role is combined with other tasks, such as handling cash payments etc.

• ACTIVITY 1

Why is it important for a receptionist to project a positive image of themselves and the organisation?

The receptionist needs to project a positive image not only of themselves but also of the organisation they work for. This will involve building a positive relationship with a customer to project a positive impression of the organisation. This is done through the way the visitor is met and greeted at the point of entry to the organisation. A visitor will expect to feel welcome. They will want to feel relaxed and ready to do what they are there

to do. Behaviour towards visitors should be courteous, respectful and pleasant, projecting a friendly tone. These behaviour traits will begin to build a positive relationship. Most visitors will have made a judgement about the host organisation within thirty seconds.

On meeting a visitor / caller, establish:

- Who they are
- Who they are meeting
- The time of their meeting

Be professional. Behave purposefully. Be positive, both vocally and physically, and polite. Make sure the visitor leaves the building with a good impression of the organisation because of how they have been treated by all host representatives.

• ACTIVITY 2

What should a receptionist do on meeting a visitor?

Dealing with visitors
A visitor should have the full attention of the receptionist. They should feel that they are at the centre of the attention of the receptionist who is looking after them. Minimise distractions, e.g. stop talking to work colleagues about what you did last night. It cannot be stressed enough how important it is to communicate well to visitors. Positive communication skills will add to the impression of the organisation that the visitor is forming in their head. Use all the elements of communication skills that go towards building a positive relationship with the visitor:

- **Face** - Open and expressive
- **Eyes** - Make eye contact to build confidence and trust
- **Posture** - A professional appearance: not slouching, hands in pockets, arms crossed etc.
- **Gestures** - Be natural and culturally sensitive
- **Voice** - Use appropriate volume, tone, speed etc.
- **Movement** - Keep movements subtle, assertive but not aggressive
- **Touch** - Do not touch the visitor, unless in an emergency

- **Appearance** - Appropriate to the requirements of the culture of the organisation

A receptionist may also provide badges that their visitors will need to wear at all times in the building. If the visitor has any accessibility requirements they will need to comply with these within the requirements of health and safety and organisational procedures, e.g. a person that visits a building who uses a wheelchair.

• ACTIVITY 3

What is the value of good communication skills to a receptionist?

Visitors may also be asked to use the sign-in book. They will be asked to do this for a number of reasons:

- Health and safety procedures - Once a visitor enters a building, that organisation becomes responsible for their safety and welfare. The receptionist will carry out all the necessary procedures to protect their visitors, e.g. supplying a hard hat if the building is being refurbished in some way that may pose a threat to the visitor

- Entry and security procedures - Access may be limited to certain areas of an organisation which only allows certain people to visit. There may be restrictions on how people can visit, e.g. they must be accompanied by specific people from specific departments. They must be wearing appropriate access badges etc., at all times

- Emergency procedures - These are the procedures for handling visitors to an organisation in the event of fire, bomb threat or any other emergency situation. A receptionist ma visitors that there is an expected fire warning to go at a particular time. They will only be responsible for those visitors who are still in their working area. They will take charge and direct visitors as required by the emergency procedures

SECURITY BADGE

• ACTIVITY 4

Why does a receptionist need to make sure that their visitors comply with health and safety regulations?

A receptionist should explain clearly what they may ask their visitor to do, so the visitor understands that they are meeting organisational requirements. If relevant, the receptionist could also offer their visitor refreshments or access to the washroom facilities, in case they want to freshen up before a meeting etc. Once the visitor has completed all the 'housekeeping' activities they have been asked to comply with, the receptionist should contact the person with whom the visitor is there to meet and tell them their visitor has arrived. If the host has any special instructions from this conversation, let the visitor know. For example, apologies that, due to unforeseen circumstances, they will be delayed for 15 minutes. Let the visitor know that their host will be with them shortly. Offer the visitor a seat, if available. Monitor how long the visitor has been waiting for their host to pick them up, if this is the appropriate procedure. If the visitor has been waiting too long, follow up with the host and let the visitor know that they have not been forgotten, and apologise for the delay, if necessary. If the organisation's instructions insist on chaperoning visitors to their host, organise for the appropriate person to do this.

Some tips for meting and greeting visitors include:

- Smile first
- Shake hands
- Do not rush
- Remember to use the visitor's name
- Eye contact
- Confident and positive body language
- Be ready to converse. Have three sure-fire topics of conversation
- Avoid personal questions

• ACTIVITY 5

What aspects of communications skills can be used with visitors to build a positive image of the receptionist and their organisation?

Receptionists will have to attend to many different types of visitors to the organisation. For example:

- Postmen / Postwomen
- Couriers
- Delivery drivers

- Maintenance people
- Contractors
- Sales people

Some of these people will be regular customers, where a relationship will have been established with them, e.g. collecting the post from the postman / postwoman each morning. Most organisations will have procedures in place to facilitate unexpected and unsolicited visitors / callers. A receptionist should gain as much knowledge about the organisation they work in so they are able to respond to any visitor's / caller's requests for information. Do not give the impression that unexpected visitors / callers are an unnecessary intrusion.

Dealing with telephone calls

Telephone communication is similar to face-to-face communication with visitors, except that the speaker is unable to see the person they are speaking to, so they are unable to interpret the speaker's body language. The tone of voice, volume, clarity and speed are equally as important when speaking on the telephone. The way in which telephone calls are made and answered is very important. Some organisations have a very specific technique for answering telephone calls. Callers will base their impression of the speaker and the organisation on what they hear.

The receptionist should be aiming to make a friendly but efficient impression. Smile when answering the telephone - the listener will hear it! Avoid answering the telephone when eating, chewing gum, yawning etc., in fact, at any time where it may sound like the receptionist is being distracted. When making a telephone call, always state who is calling and why the telephone call is being made - it may be to connect with a manager in a department. Prepare in advance all information to ask any potential questions that need to be asked. Make a list of important points to communicate. Take notes of important points made during the telephone conversation that need to be acted on after the telephone conversation has ended. This will help the receptionist to get the message across clearly. Answering the telephone is not an interruption to work - it is a part of work! Callers will receive an impression of the organisation from the way the telephone is answered. Be polite, receptive and let the caller know they are being listened to. When communicating information keep it relevant and accurate. When receiving information during the telephone call have a pen and paper ready to make notes when necessary.

Transferring telephone calls

If transferring telephone calls a receptionist should make sure the transfer is to the correct person. Do not leave the telephone caller unattended to if searching for the person with whom they are to be connected with. Always keep them updated with what is going on. If the transfer of a telephone call is not possible, let the caller know. Take a message from them or ask them to call back later - let them know when would be a good time to do this. When taking a message, make sure that all the information for the person who has been asked to return the call has been taken correctly. When leaving the message, make sure it is placed on the person's desk where it will not be missed or lost. As part of a receptionist's job, depending on how important the message is, they could follow up to make sure that the telephone call has been returned at the agreed time, if that is necessary.

Private and confidential

Receptionists will often be privy to lots of 'private' and 'confidential' information that is either shared with them or they will pick up in the course of their work. A skilled receptionist will develop techniques for protecting this information so that it is only shared with appropriate people, if at all. They will need to be careful about what is said, making sure that, with highly 'private' and 'confidential' information, they cannot be overheard, either physically or on the telephone. There should be organisational procedures and guidance in place to follow, depending on the type of reception work being done. For example, in a doctor's surgery a receptionist will need to be very careful how they deal with patients so that very personal information remains private between the patient and the receptionist.

What may be considered to be normal social conversation or friendly gossip may be quite unacceptable and unethical behaviour. Always consider the risks of what information is shared and with whom it is shared. The people that the receptionist is working with need to be confident that the information they share with the receptionist remains 'private' and 'confidential'. This relationship is very important to building trust in the way a receptionist works with the people that they support in an organisation.

• ACTIVITY 6

Why is it important to behave in an ethical manner when dealing with matters of a 'private' and 'confidential' nature?

The receptionist needs to be equally vigilant with leaving documents on their desk, whether incomplete documents or complete documents. A receptionist should have some means of putting these documents away when they are not working on them. This could be done by having a private drawer where they put documents or leaving them with the person whom they are working with on the documents. While maintaining 'confidentiality' is important in any organisation, in some organisations it may be paramount, especially if they are open to industrial espionage, e.g. where products are being developed which have not been released to the market which a competitor would find invaluable to know.

The same vigilance needs to be applied to computer screens. These should not be left unattended if they are showing information of a 'private' and 'confidential' nature, e.g. financial records or records about absences in an organisation.

Difficult customers

Every visitor that walks into the reception area is different, e.g. they may be young / old, male / female. They also feel that they are different and want to be treated as individuals. People do not go out of their way to be difficult. However, they do go out of their way to get what they want, which may appear unreasonable. As a result, they may be perceived as behaving badly.

Relate to them as an individual. Remain calm and:

- **Communicate** - Do not ignore them, but 'actively listen' to what they have to say. Use 'open' questions to resolve visitor enquires

- **Communicate confidence** - Both physical, body language, and verbal

- **Be prepared** - Anything can happen in a day, but know what it is that has to be done in most scenarios. Offer alternative approaches to resolving issues. Be part of the solution rather than part of the problem

- **Be a font of knowledge** - Know the kinds of information that visitors will need to be reassured of. Make sure information is known to assist visitors about the local area, transport systems etc.

- **Take the initiative** - Make it work for the customer visiting the organisation for the first time. Keep their impression positive

Some visitors will be in a hurry, have dealt with the organisation before or know exactly what they want. Personalise the behaviour used to approach their difficulty and be precise in the response made to them, e.g. if they are in a hurry, pick up on this and address it specifically. Other visitors may be overly sensitive, e.g. they may think that they are very important so they should not have to wait for anything. The best thing to do in this situation is to pacify them. Get it right first time by being very polite, and do not feel angry or annoyed by the visitor's behaviour. Try not to let them repeat themselves. There may be other visitors who demand attention, which can result in the receptionist being deflected away from other visitors, e.g. a visitor may be especially shy and need reassurance on their visit, and so engage the receptionist exclusively. In this situation, minimise attention to them by being friendly but not overly involved, and take the personal approach.

Take a natural approach to every situation. Avoid acting in a biased manner to any visitor. Be personal and personalise the service each visitor receives. Meet every customer's needs as required. The organisation that 'goes the extra mile' is the one that will still be in business in the future. There is never an excuse to be rude or shout at a visitor. If you feel that you are unable to deal with the situation, you should seek advice or find out what the organisational procedures are for dealing with difficult visitors.

• ACTIVITY 7

Describe different types of difficult behaviour demonstrated by some visitors.

All visitors must be treated with the same courtesy. The receptionist is the public face of the organisation. The way a visitor is received will make a lasting impression on the visitor. Business can be lost before the meeting even takes place if the visitor is given a poor impression of the organisation. Always take a personal and individual approach to each visitor who walks into the reception area. Know and follow the organisation's procedures for dealing with visitors and the wide range of circumstances that can arise when greeting them.

Other responsibilities
A receptionist may be called upon to do many different duties:

- Collect and send mail - This could include setting up a courier to come and collect a parcel
- Fill and seal envelopes
- Organise travel arrangements
- Organise refreshments and meals for meetings
- Organise meeting rooms or conference halls
- Run personal or professional errands
- Organise documents

A receptionist should also look at how they can improve their working conditions. This does not include just the amount of hours that they are devoted to the job, but how they can improve their working area, e.g. through reorganisation of the space, the equipment that they work with, the people they work with and, finally, themselves. There are always ways that a receptionist can become better at their role.

If there are times when the receptionist has little or nothing to do they should always enquire about any additional duties that they can take on when it is quiet. This will help out others in their department and also add some skills or knowledge to their portfolio.

It is clear from the above that a receptionist will need to have good organisational skills. They will need to plan a full and changing programme of activities, always be prepared to tackle new tasks and learn new skills or knowledge. They must also have the ability to prioritise. If there are conflicting demands and the receptionist is not sure of which one to tackle first, they should approach their supervisor / manager for advice and guidance.

Testing your knowledge

1. What is the role of a receptionist?

2. Why is the role of a receptionist so important to an organisation?

3. Why is it important to make sure visitors abide by 'health and safety' regulations?

4. Why should an organisation have 'security' procedures?

5. How and why should a reception area be improved?

6. How should a 'private and confidential' situation be handled?

Skills

As a receptionist responsible for presenting a positive image of the organisation you work for, your first priority will be to make sure that your working area is presentable - clean and tidy - and to make sure that this is the case throughout your working day. As the first point of contact for visitors coming into the organisation, this is a continuing priority. You will need to make sure that your personal appearance also reflects the appearance of the office space you work in, so that you present a consistent picture of professionalism.

Aside from your normal routine throughout the day you will want to check your diary to see what meetings have been set and make a list of visitors that you are expecting. Prepare for known events as much as you can, and be aware that you will be continually called on to help with unexpected activities. As a receptionist, one of your functions is to multitask. While multitasking, you will need to make sure that you are in control of all of the different tasks. As a visitor enters the reception area and you prepare for their arrival, making sure they sign in, handing out a security badge, offering refreshments etc., anything else that you were doing before the visitor's arrival will need to be taken up when they have left. You may have promised to complete these other tasks at agreed times, so watch to make sure that you keep to these deadlines. Let someone know that their visitor has arrived and check to make sure that they are going to be collected, or give the visitor directions - at the appropriate time - to make their way to the venue of their meeting. If the visitor needs directions to the washroom, give them this information too. Some visits may occur on the spot, with people tuning up on the off chance. Check with the person with whom these visitors would like to speak to see if this is possible. If not, check the diary and make an appointment for them to return at a later date. If any relevant health and safety requirements need to be taken, make sure that these are addressed. As a receptionist in your organisation, you are responsible for a visitor's initial welfare.

You will also answer the telephone throughout the day. Answering the telephone is not an interruption to your work, but a part of your work. You are representing your organisation when you answer the telephone, so be polite and use the appropriate greeting required by organisational guidelines. Use the correct tone when speaking over the telephone, one that is warm and inviting. Transfer telephone calls or take telephone messages. If taking a telephone message, make sure you have all the correct information before saying goodbye to the caller. Do not keep any caller holding on the telephone line for long without keeping them updated about what is going on.

As someone who is responsible for the welfare of visitors etc., check with your manager about whether you should be trained in 'first aid', as this is something you may have to administer to people whom you are looking after.

Deal with any difficult customers in the appropriate way. Above all, 'actively listen' to them and treat them as individuals who have an individual voice. Most visitors are not setting out to be difficult, but they have demands which are higher than usual.

• ACTIVITY 8

Keep a 'time' diary of each day, recording everything that you do for a week. Review the 'time' diary to see if there are any areas where you can make improvements to the way you carry out your receptionist responsibilities.

Continue to make sure that the reception area remains clean and tidy. If you think there are some ways that it could be improved, tell your supervisor / manager. Discuss the reasons for your suggestions.

Respond throughout the day to any additional duties that your supervisor / manager may ask you to take on board. If extra duties do not come via your supervisor / manager and it is a particularly complex task, check with your supervisor / manager to make sure it is okay to take this task on board.

Continue to present a positive image of your organisation to both external customers and to those that you work with.

Testing your skills

1. How do you present a positive image of your organisation?
2. How do you present a positive image of yourself?
3. How do you greet a visitor to your organisation?
4. What steps do you take a visitor through when they visit your organisation?
5. What 'health and safety' regulations are important in your organisation?
6. What are the emergency procedures in your organisation for a:
     6.1 Fire?
     6.2 Bomb threat?
     6.3 Lift breakdown?
     6.4 Accident?
7. How and when do you maintain the reception area?
8. What improvements have you made to your role as a receptionist?
9. What are the 'privacy and confidentiality' guidelines in your organisation?
10. How do you implement guidelines on 'privacy and confidentiality'?

Ready for assessment?
To achieve this Level 2 unit of a Business & Administration qualification, learners will need to demonstrate that they are able to perform the following activities:

1. Presented a positive image of themselves and the organisation

2. Provided individuals with requested information and other information which may have been useful to them, within guidelines on confidentiality

3. Implemented the correct entry and security procedures

4. Followed the relevant health and safety procedures

5. Referred any issues that could not be dealt with personally to the appropriate person

6. Maintained the reception area to give a positive impression of the organisation

7. Suggested ideas for improving the reception area

8. Followed organisational procedures in the event of an accident or emergency

9. Carried out additional duties during quiet periods, if they arose

You will need to produce evidence from a variety of sources to support the performance requirements of this unit.

If you carry out the 'ACTIVITIES' and respond to the 'NEED TO KNOW' questions, these will provide some of the evidence required.

Links to other units

While gathering evidence for this unit, evidence may also be used from evidence generated from other units within the Business & Administration suite of units. Below is a sample of applicable units; however, most units within the Business & Administration suite of units will also be applicable.

QCF NVQ
Communications
Communicate in a business environment (Level 2)
Use electronic message systems (Level 2)
Use a diary system (Level 2)
Core business & administration
Manage own performance in a business environment (Level 2)
Improve own performance in a business environment (Level 2)
Work in a business environment (Level 2)
Work with other people in a business environment (Level 2)
Customer service
Handle mail
Meet and welcome visitors
Document production
Produce documents in a business environment
Prepare text from notes
Events and meetings
Support the organisation of an event
Support the organisation of business travel or accommodation
Support the organisation of meetings
Innovation and change
Respond to change in a business environment

SVQ
Communications
Prepare to communicate in a business environment
Use electronic message systems
Use a diary system
Core business & administration
Agree how to manage and improve own performance in a business environment
Undertake work in a business environment
Contribute to working with others in a business environment
Customer service
Handle mail
Meet and welcome visitors
Document production
Produce documents in a business environment
Prepare text from notes
Events and meetings
Support the organisation of an event
Support the organisation of business travel or accommodation
Support the organisation of meetings
Innovation and change
Respond to change in a business environment

15

Produce documents in a business environment

PRODUCE DOCUMENTS IN A BUSINESS ENVIRONMENT

'**Produce documents in a business environment**' is an <u>optional unit</u> which may be chosen as one of a combination of units to achieve either a Qualifications and Credit Framework (QCF), National Vocational Qualification (NVQ) or Scottish Vocational Qualification (SVQ).

The aims of this unit are to:

- Understand the purpose of producing high-quality and attractive documents in a business environment

- Know what resources and technology are available and how to use them when producing documents in a business environment

- Understand the purpose of following procedures when producing documents in a business environment

- Be able to prepare for tasks

- Be able to produce documents to agreed specifications

To achieve the above aims of this unit, learners will be expected to provide evidence through the performance of work-based activities.

Knowledge
The production of documents in a business environment should look professional and attractive. The document projects the image, branding and professionalism of an organisation, i.e. a professionally produced document shows the expertise and care an organisation will invest in its employees to deliver. This could have a vital effect on a customer's decision to do business with an organisation. When a document lands in front of a customer it needs to make an impact, it needs to grab the reader's attention. The effective production of documents is about helping important information to stand out. The document should be attractive enough to invite the audience for whom the document has been designed to want to read it, assimilate it and respond to it, if necessary. The document should be easy to read and look inviting.

• ACTIVITY 1

Why should documents look professional and attractive?

The features that can be used to create and produce quality, professional and attractive documents are:

- **Preparation** - Before starting to produce any document, make sure that there is a rationale for the development of the document, including any resources that will be needed to complete the document, e.g. the addition of images or diagrams. Every document must have a clearly defined purpose and objectives it is aiming to achieve for its audience. This should create a document that is meaningful and of value to the recipient, clear, concise and delivered by a set deadline. A deadline is when a document is due by a certain time, in a certain format and containing the required information. If a document is not delivered against these requirements it will appear unprofessional, particularly if lateness has not been discussed with the recipient, which could lead to loss of business. Having an agreed deadline will help to plan and prioritise tasks / activities

- **Information and Content** - Organise information in the document so that it does not overwhelm the recipient. Make choices and give important content sufficient space within the document to be understood by the reader, e.g. placing content in a box or surrounding it with white space. Be selective about what information is included in a document. Create a theme using the appropriate software, that is, a co-ordinated set of fonts, colours and graphic effects that can be applied with one click. Use graphics to illustrate key points - which can be done using SmartArt

- **Style** - Many organisations have an agreed policy about the way their documents should look so they are presented consistently and to the same quality, e.g. do not use abbreviations. This is often referred to as the 'house style'

- **Accuracy** - A well-presented, correctly spelled, grammatical and accurately punctuated document will create a positive impression which will last. After producing a document it should be checked carefully, as errors in spelling or grammar could have a potentially disastrous effect. If in doubt about the intended meaning, refer back to the original author

- **Layout** - A document should have a layout with features that present the finished document in the agreed format, e.g. type of paper, margins, line spacing, type of font

The above features can be remembered using the pneumonic PICSAL. If documents are produced using PICSAL it will aid the process of communication between the senders and receivers of messages.

• ACTIVITY 2

Circle the correct answer. A letter should contain as many images as possible to improve the effect of the document?

True   False

There is a wide range of software available that will help to produce the highest-quality documents possible. Each piece of software will have a number of different features that can be added to a document, e.g. images, graphs, tables, diagrams. During the production of the document, name it according to the organisation's policy on naming files. Regularly save the document throughout its creation so no work is lost in the event of software or electrical breakdown.

If the document being created is 'private and confidential', make sure it is identified as such and follows the organisation's policy on 'private and confidential' documents, e.g. the contents of the document should not be discussed publicly so unauthorised people can hear. Confidential information is information that has great value, is considered to be of a private nature and is only permitted to be seen by designated people within an organisation. 'Confidential information' can embrace commercial secrets as well as general information, e.g. medical records. An organisation can be damaged if its privacy of information is not upheld and respected, which could result in the organisation being devalued.

There is no single Act of Parliament defining 'confidential information' or governing how it is protected, or setting out rights and obligations in respect of it. However, the law on 'confidential information' is currently undergoing radical change as a result of developing European and UK legislation and decisions of the courts. Place 'confidentiality' warnings on standard communications, e.g. faxes or emails, to make sure if an individual receives the information by accident they are notified of its 'confidential' nature.

'Private and confidential' documents also includes commercially sensitive information, which needs to be protected from being read by an organisation's competitors. If the content of a document covers personal information it must conform to the requirements of the Data Protection Act 1998.

All documents should be stored safely and securely according to the storage system being used within an organisation, e.g. a manual paper-based system, an electronic-based system or both. Documents should be stored in accordance with the organisation's policy on storing documents, so they are easily accessible when required. Organisations may have different means of codifying their documents. However, as a rule, the following will need to be in place to access documents:

• ACTIVITY 3

Which of the following documents are likely to be confidential?

1. Letter of dismissal
2. Report on fraud within the organisation
3. Memo stating date and time of a meeting
4. Fax copy of an invoice
5. Minutes of staff meeting
6. Study on potential redundancies

- **Title or subject** - Category or reference number

- **Dated** - Note should be taken of how a 'date' is written. In the UK, the 7th September 2010 is written as 07.09.10. In America, it would be written as 09.07.10

- **Author** - Hard copies of documents can be stored manually using different methods:

  - **Alphabetical** - Information is stored in order from A-Z. Files starting with the same letter are filed in order of the second letter: Aa, Ab, Ac etc. People's names are filed by their surnames, and if more than one has the same surname, by their first names. Names starting with 'The' are filed by ignoring the 'The'. Names beginning with 'Mac' or 'Mc' come before 'Ma', 'Mb' etc.

  - **Numerical** - Information is coded using a numbering system, e.g. purchase orders, invoice

  - **Alpha-numerical** - Information is stored using a combination of letters and numbers, e.g. National Insurance numbers. Usually large databases hold this type of coded information, as they hold more information than numerical systems and are more flexible than alphabetical systems. The order of filing depends on the sequence of the file name. If file names start with letters followed by numbers, they are filed in alphabetical order first and numerical order within each letter

- **Chronological** - This method is often used within one of the other methods, e.g. customers' records are filed alphabetically, but the information within the file is stored chronologically, usually with the latest at the front. This provides a history of all activities undertaken for a particular file of information. It can also be based on dates of birth or start dates

- **Geographical** - This is a method of sorting by areas, e.g. North West England, East Anglia or counties, towns, cities

- **By subject or category** - Some organisations need to sort their filing under topics rather than names, e.g. a shoe manufacturer may keep files under product names such as Ladies, Gentlemen and Children

Whichever method is adopted documents must be stored **accurately**, to allow people to find information easily and quickly. People should find what they are looking for in the place that they expect to find it. Documents should be stored as quickly as possible to allow access to users within an organisation. When amending information held electronically, saving the file will automatically update the previous version.

Types and styles of documents

There are several types of documents that may be produced in an organisation, which include:

Memos

These are used for internal communication within an organisation. They may vary in the level of formality in which they are written. They:

- May be addressed to more than one recipient

- Will usually not include addresses

- Will have a subject line, similar to 'emails'

- Will state the date, name of the recipient (s), the name of the sender and the content

- May have the recipient and sender's job titles and departments

- Will usually be produced on a template which reflects the organisation's 'house style'

Most organisations still use memos for important internal messages, if they have not been replaced by the use of 'emails'.

MEMORANDUM

To: All selling staff

From: Sales Manager

Date: 27th August 2010

Subject: Sales targets

Last week saw total sales of £127,436, an increase of 3.1% on last year. This week we have a challenging target of £148,000, or 3.7% on last year. This will require 100% effort from all of us, but I am confident we can do it.

REMEMBER: PROMOTE DISPOSABLE BARBECUES.

Faxes

A fax is any document that is sent using a telephone line, e.g. a memo, letter, invoice. Organisations may use a cover sheet to precede the document, which may include the name and fax numbers of the sender and recipient and the number of pages being sent

---

FACSIMILE COVER SHEET

To: Peter Robinson
               Motor Vehicle Repairs

Fax No: 02274 55369

From: Ronald R. Barker
               Paving Co. Ltd.

Fax No: 02564 33465

No of Pages: 1 plus this cover sheet

Letters

Letters will usually be written on paper headed with the organisation's address. Letters may also need to follow the design and style set out in an organisation's 'house style'.

Letters will normally:

- Be addressed to one person, e.g. 'Dear Sir' or 'Dear Madam'

- Be dated
- Contain a salutation, e.g. 'Dear ...'
- Have a reference number / title / heading - these are optional
- Contain the body of text for writing the letter
- End with a closing statement that summarises the main points for writing the letter
- Include a compliment - e.g. 'Yours sincerely'
- Include a signature

Matthew and Son Builders
Allington Place
West Billington
WW1 1AD
Tel: 01632 566854

Our ref: GM / RA / 124
Your ref: VH / AK

13 August 2010

Mr V Harmison
Oval Walk
West Billington
WW2 1AX

Dear Mr Harmison

Thank you for your letter dated 6th August 2010 accepting our quotation to extend your office building.

The work will commence on 6th September 2010 and will be completed within 6 working weeks.

If you have any queries, please do not hesitate to contact me.

Yours sincerely

Graham Matthew
Director

Business letters are usually produced:

- **Fully blocked** - All parts of the document start at the left-hand margin

- **With open punctuation** - Punctuation used only in the body of the letter, where it is essential for grammatical accuracy and understanding

• ACTIVITY 4

Circle the correct answer. A letter with the salutation, 'Dear Sir or Madam' should have which compliment?

1. Yours faithfully
2. Yours sincerely
3. Yours truly
4. Best regards

Reports

These are produced in response to a request for information. They may be formal or informal, depending on the audience they are being written for. For example, a report written to a Board of an organisation will generally be more formal than a report to the members of a club. A report is written to inform the reader of facts about a subject. The depth of information contained in a report will depend on the purpose of the report and its intended audience. All reports will follow a similar structure, however detailed they may be:

- **Front page** - This contains the title of the report, the name of the author and the date

- **Contents** - This will list all the subjects covered in the report

- **Executive summary** - This gives a brief outline of the report

- **Background information** - This gives the reasons why the report was produced

- **Methodology** - This outlines the methods used to produce the data in the report, e.g. surveys, questionnaires

- **Findings** - These are the results of the methods used to explore the purpose of the report. Findings may be presented by:

  - Importance: where the central ideas are presented

- Chronology: where ideas are presented in the order of events, starting either with the latest or the first

- Sequence: where one idea follows from another

- Comparison: where two ideas are compared in alternate paragraphs

- **Conclusion** - This outlines the conclusions that can be drawn from the findings of the research

- **Recommendations** - This outlines the actions that are recommended to be taken as a result of the conclusion

- **Acknowledgements** - This records the contribution others have made to the report

- **Bibliography** - This outlines the source material used in the research. There are a number of different ways that a bibliography can be drawn up

- **Appendices** - This sets out all the information referred to in the report which is too detailed to be given in full without distracting from the purpose of the report

The content of a written report will vary in how it is organised, using the above headings depending on the purpose of the written report. For example, a short report may only include the 'main content' and 'recommendations'.

There are a number of ways of ordering the contents of a report. These include, by:

- **Importance** - Beginning with the central idea

- **Chronology** - In order of events, starting either with the latest or the first

- **Sequence** - Where one idea follows from another

- **Comparison** - Where two ideas are compared in alternate paragraphs

You may be able to set up templates for standard documents on your computer, this will save time when you are asked to produce the same type of document at a later date.

• ACTIVITY 5

Circle the correct answer. Which document would be used to advise colleagues of the date and location of an internal meeting?

1. A report
2. A letter
3. A memo
4. A fax

Resources

The resources required to finish a document will depend on the purpose for which the document has been designed. Everyone in an organisation will have a workstation equipped with a computer. To produce a finished document in hard copy the following will be required:

- **Paper** - Headed, letter quality or copy quality. If there is more than one page, consideration needs to be given to how these will be held together, if at all

- **Printer** - Gives choice of paper; quality settings: best, normal or draft and colour or black and white

- **Envelopes** - Letters to external addresses will need good-quality envelopes, while internal memos may be sent using internal envelopes which can be used a number of times. Consideration should be given to the size of envelope needed and if using a transparent window. In the latter case, the document should be typed using the organisation's template. Documents with several pages should be placed unfolded in an envelope

- **Attachments** - Consideration needs to be given to how these will be held together: paper clip or staple

Formatting the document

Gather together all the information that needs to be included in a document. This may come from any number of sources, including the letter being replied to, previous reports, databases, the Internet etc. Having decided the content, it will need to be organised so that it can be found when required. It may be useful to produce a first draft to see where the content fits into the whole. For long or complex documents, plan a draft of the document using topics or headings

to organise the content before writing the detail. Consideration will then need to be given to:

- **The size of paper to use** - Most documents are printed on A4 paper, 210mm x 297mm. However, A5, half of A4, could be used for memos, leaflets and brochures. A3, twice the size of A4, can be used for providing large spreadsheets of information or posters

- **Whether to present a document in portrait or landscape form** - Most standard documents are presented in portrait form. Landscape is generally used for tables and spreadsheets, where it is helpful to be able to see the full row of information at a glance

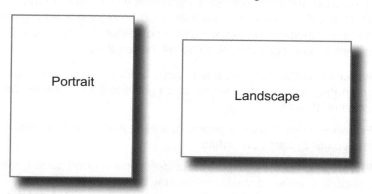

- **Any diagrams or tables** to be inserted into the document. Diagrams will usually be imported from elsewhere. Tables may be produced in a document or imported from elsewhere. Tables are produced from the 'table' menu

• ACTIVITY 6

What is the rough outline of a long and complex document called?

The computer provides a lot of functions that allow a document to be easily edited, for example:

- **Delete** - Ctrl+delete - This allows a single letter, group of letters or whole parts of a document to be deleted

- **Paste** - Ctrl+v - This is used in combination with either the 'cut' or 'copy', see below, instruction. Paste will add the last data selected to the document 'copied' or stored on the 'clipboard', which will provide other recently 'copied' information

- **Cut** - Ctrl+x - This is used to highlight a piece of text and remove it from the document. It can then be 'pasted', see above, to another part of the document or a new document

- **Copy** - Ctrl+c - This is used to highlight a piece of text and copied. It can then be 'pasted', see above, to another part of the document or a new document

- **Find and replace** - Ctrl+f - This function is used to change all the examples of a particular word to another word. For example, replace the word 'company' with the word 'organisation', there is no need to retype every example, use 'find' and / or 'replace' to make all the changes

- **Inserting special characters and symbols** - This function enables the use of other alphabets, e.g. Arabic شةكةق, and other signs / symbols, e.g. o, û, ©, %

- **Mail merge** - This function is useful if the same letter is going to several recipients, as it can just change the name and address of each recipient

- **Track changes** - This function allows the originator of a document to share it with other colleagues, inviting them to make changes which can be tracked by name and highlighted

At any stage during the production of a document the format of the text can be changed. There are various options available in the format menu, e.g. font, which allows the font to be changed to different styles, sizes, colour. It is possible to format characters, pages or whole sections of a document. A part of a document can be formatted and used again later in the document by selecting 'styles and formatting', and the software will show what formatting has been used previously in the document.

If text is being produced which will have more than one page, it is advisable to use a **'header and footer'**, with required information and / or **'page numbers'**. Using both functions will allow the title to be put onto each page with a page number. It is also possible to **'number paragraphs'** and include an **'index'** or **'table of contents'** to help the reader find their way around the text.

• ACTIVITY 7

What are the following abbreviations of?

NB		cm	
adj.		e.g.	
Ltd.		i.e.	
cent.		cm	
mm		NOS	
RSVP		sq.	
plc.			

Any '**picture**', '**diagram**' or '**table**' already held on your hard drive or on a disk can be imported. 'Tables' are excellent way to organise information. They look great and they are simple to manage. They can hold text, graphics or other tables. They can simplify even the most complex layouts. 'Tables' are a powerful and flexible function.

'**Footnotes**' or '**endnotes**' can be used to support information. **Objects** can also be imported from other software on a computer, through a connected scanner or digital camera or from the Internet. Care will need to be taken when importing non-text objects. In a letter, 'less is more' where 'pictures' and 'diagrams' are concerned. In a report, 'pictures' and 'diagrams' can certainly add to the impact. 'Pictures' and 'diagrams' should be used wisely, and only when they are relevant and make the content more meaningful. Their positioning and size must also be carefully considered.

Some **tips when using a software programme**:

- Use '**styles**' - Avoid direct formatting
- Use '**templates**'
- **Do not** use line feeds to make space between paragraphs
- **Do not** use the 'spacebar' to make spaces or align text
- Use only one '**space**' after a full stop
- **Do not** manually number pages
- Minimise the use of '**sections**'
- Avoid manual '**page breaks**'

Checking the document

Once a document has been completed it is essential that it is checked for accuracy. On completing the check make any changes as necessary. Most software programmes contain spell checking and grammar checking facilities. Use these first to correct the more obvious errors; however, they must not be relied on entirely as some will be programmed with the default to use American spelling and grammar, e.g. the computer will accept 'color' and reject 'colour'. When the automatic checking is complete, read the document carefully to look for missed errors, and also for correct use of paragraphs, headings and subheadings, style and formatting. Remember the 'Five Cs' when checking documents:

- **Conciseness** - Have the amount of words been minimised to clearly express points of information?
- **Completeness** - Is everything the recipient needs there?
- **Courtesy** - Is the tone of the document polite?
- **Clarity** - Will the recipient understand the points being made?
- **Correctness** - Are all statements accurate and true?

Be particularly careful to proofread numbers, dates, times and amounts. Check for errors between similar words, such as 'affect' and 'effect' or 'less' and 'fewer'.

• ACTIVITY 8

You have been given the following handwritten notice and asked to type it up and place it on the notice board. Correct the errors in spelling, punctuation and grammar and produce a finished notice. Underneath, list the spelling errors which would not be picked up by the computer using the spell check function.

Mr. Wilson will not be avalaible to give the lecture on Friday 15th she is sick he wil be replaiced by Mr, Jefferson who will now be giving the lecture on Adminastration in the motor industry. The thyme of the lectur has also changed it will knot be at 11.00 am butt at 14.00 pm. The locasion has not changed it'll still be held on the 5th flaw in the charity room.

If the document has been completed for another person, make sure that they check for the accuracy of statements and details. For example, if the author has dictated 'we will sell petrol only to people in a metal container', you should suggest rewording this to clarify that it is not necessary for the purchasers of petrol to be inside a metal container at the time of purchase.

• ACTIVITY 9

Which of the following are correct?

1. Would we have less problems if we had fewer departments?
2. Neither Edinburgh or Glasgow is in England
3. The customers are always right
4. The customer's always right
5. The ship's crew was up to its full complement
6. The customer's are always right

The completed document will need to be presented either for despatch or for the original author by the agreed deadline and in the style agreed. If unforeseen circumstances mean that the style or content has been changed, or if unable to meet the agreed deadline, it is important that this is reported as soon as the situation arises. It is too late to be told that a deadline will not be met when the deadline arrives. It is not acceptable to lower the agreed quality standards in order to meet the deadline.

Whatever type of document is produced, always confirm the purpose, content, style, quality standards and deadline.

Testing your knowledge

1. What does PICSAL stand for?
2. How are tasks prioritised?
3. How is a database accessed?
4. What is the layout for a formal letter?
5. What is meant by 'house style'?
6. Which function is used to replace words on a computer?
7. When would it be appropriate to use images?
8. How are images integrated into a report?
9. What is the difference between the layout of memos, letters and   reports?
10. What are the five Cs?
11. What are the benefits of placing electronic files in folders?
12. What is the difference between 'there', 'they're' and 'their'?

Skills
Before starting work on the creation and / or production of any document in a business environment, make sure you are clear about:

- The purpose of the document
- The content of the document
- The style of the content
- The deadlines within which the document needs to be completed

Each of these aspects of preparing to create or produce a document will help inform the planning of the work you will need to do for either yourself or, if you are producing the document on behalf of someone else, its original author. Organise your work around all the tasks that you have to complete so you finish the document at the agreed time.

Once you are clear about what has to be done, gather together all the resources you will require to complete the task. If the stationery has run out, report it to the appropriate colleague so it can be replenished.

Think about the content of the document. Is it in response to another piece of correspondence? If so, be guided by the form and content of that communication in your response. If it is an original piece of communication be very clear about what you are aiming to achieve with the production of this document in whatever style it will be presented. Remember to implement the five Cs.

• ACTIVITY 10

Write a report to your supervisor suggesting ways in which your current filing systems can be improved. Consider the best way to order the contents of the report.

When producing the document on your PC, make sure you are fully up to date with the functions of your software so you can add images, tables etc., effectively and efficiently. Chat to someone who is very confident in this area, or your supervisor / manager, to check that you are fully conversant with the functionality of the technology you are using. This will not only save you time but make your document look more professional. Be judicious about the images etc. that you include in your document. You do not want to overwhelm the recipient of the document with too much inappropriate information. Remember to produce a document which will give sufficient information to the recipient. That alone will impress them. Adding too much information will not impress them and they may not finish reading your document.

Make sure that you are clear about the style, layout and format that you wish, or the original author wishes, the document to take. Clarify all these components of your document. Integrate the non-text objects so that they make the information that you are presenting very clear. Make sure, when importing or integrating non-text objects, you use the technology effectively so that they objects are in line with the appropriate text in the document and do not jump about to different places when you are working on the document.

If you are working on a large document, check through what you will include in the content of the document. If necessary, produce a draft document and check through this with the original author to make sure it meets all the requirements that they are aiming to achieve. Check through the document to make sure that it accurately presents information, i.e. there are no spelling mistakes. Make sure your computer is set to the correct defaults, the grammar has been correctly used and edit the text for conciseness. Check against the five Cs.

• ACTIVITY 11

Select a number of documents that you have produced which you feel demonstrate your competence in using correct layout, spelling, punctuation and grammar. Consider the question of confidentiality in making your selection.

Once you have checked the document, check the aims of the document with the original author, to make sure that they have been achieved. When working on the production of the document, if you are not sure, at any stage of its development, that it is progressing along the right track, pause and reflect on what the document is aiming to achieve. Check with the original author - if it is not you. If anything changes with the development of the document check with the original author that they are happy with the change of direction that the document may have to take.

Testing your skills

1. Where would you look to find the relevant content of a document?

2. Do you know how to select options on your printer?

3. What types of documents do you produce?

4. How do you access databases?

5. How do you layout a formal letter?

6. Does your organisation have its own 'house style'?

7. How do you use your word processing package?

8. Could you find appropriate images for a report on the London Olympics 2012?

9. How do you manipulate images to fit the purpose of the document?

10. How and when do you use spell check and grammar check?

11. How do you check that your spelling, punctuation and grammar have been used correctly?

12. If you were filing vehicle records by registration number, which filing method would you use?

13. What is your organisation's convention for naming electronic files?

14. What are the filing methods used in your organisation?

Ready for assessment?

To achieve this Level 2 unit of a Business & Administration qualification, learners will need to demonstrate they can perform the following activities:

1. Confirmed the purpose, content, styles and deadlines for the document

2. Prepared the required resources

3. Organised the required content

4. Used available technology appropriate for producing the document

5. Produced the document in the agreed style

6. Integrated non-text objects in the agreed layout, where required

7. Checked for accuracy, editing and correcting text, as necessary

8. Clarified the document's requirements, when necessary

9. Stored the document safely and securely in approved locations

You will need to produce evidence from a variety of sources to support the performance requirements of this unit.

If you carry out the 'ACTIVITIES' and respond to the 'NEED TO KNOW' questions, these will provide some of the evidence required.

Links to other units
While gathering evidence for this unit, evidence may also be used from evidence generated from other units within the Business & Administration suite of units. Below is a sample of applicable units; however, most units within the Business & Administration suite of units will also be applicable.

QCF NVQ
Communications
Communicate in a business environment (Level 2)
Make and receive telephone calls
Use electronic message systems
Core business & administration
Manage own performance in a business environment (Level 2)
Improve own performance in a business environment (Level 2)
Work in a business environment (Level 2)
Work with other people in a business environment (Level 2)
Customer service
Handle mail
Document production
Prepare text from notes
Prepare text from notes using touch typing (40 wpm)
Prepare text from shorthand (60 wpm)
Prepare text from recorded audio instruction (40 wpm)
Mange information and data
Store and retrieve information

SVQ
Communications
Prepare to communicate in a business environment
Make and receive telephone calls
Use electronic message systems
Core business & administration
Agree how to manage and improve own performance in a business environment
Undertake work in a business environment
Work with other people in a business environment
Customer service
Handle mail
Document production
Prepare text from notes
Prepare text from notes using touch typing (40 wpm)
Prepare text from shorthand (60 wpm)
Prepare text from recorded audio instruction (40 wpm)
Mange information and data
Store and retrieve information

16

**Prepare text
from notes**

PREPARE TEXT FROM NOTES

'**Prepare text from notes**' is an <u>optional unit</u> which may be chosen as one of a combination of units to achieve either a Qualifications and Credit Framework (QCF), National Vocational Qualification (NVQ) or Scottish Vocational Qualification (SVQ).

The aims of this unit are to:

- Understand preparing text from notes
- Understand the purpose and benefits of following procedures when preparing text from notes
- Be able to prepare text from notes
- Be able to prepare text from notes

To achieve the above aims of this unit, learners will be expected to provide evidence through the performance of work-based activities.

Knowledge
Different types of documents that can be produced from notes
Different types of organisations working in many different sectors will have the need to produce text from notes. These will include emails, memos, letters, reports and minutes of meetings. Notes will have been produced from a variety of sources, e.g. shorthand, audio recordings.

Many text documents will be prepared from handwritten notes which can be made by an author who will:

Prepare the text - This should be relatively easy to transcribe as the person preparing the text is translating handwritten notes which they have made, so legibility and shortcuts should not be a problem

Not prepare the text - This may be a little more difficult to transcribe as the person preparing the text is not translating their own handwritten notes. They may not understand the handwriting or the shortcuts that the author has made. If this occurs, the person transcribing the text should clarify from the author any script that is not legible

Before preparing the transcription of any notes into text make sure that the purpose, format and deadline of the text has been agreed. A deadline is when a document is due by a certain time, in a certain format and containing the required information. It is important that all parties involved in the production of text are all agreed on what the finished product will look like and when it can be expected. Before starting to produce any text from notes, include resources that will be needed to complete the text, e.g. the addition of images or diagrams. The text should be clear. If a document is not delivered against these requirements it will appear unprofessional, particularly if lateness has not been discussed with the recipient, and this could lead to loss of business. Having an agreed deadline will help to plan and prioritise tasks / activities.

• ACTIVITY 1

Choose a piece of text that contains at least 1,000 words. Switch off the spell check function on the computer. Type the text for 10 minutes. Calculate the typing speed using the following method:

- Count the total number of characters typed, including spaces.
- Divide the answer by 5 - the average length of a word.
- This gives the gross number of words typed.
- Divide the answer by 10 - 10 minutes spent typing - to give the gross number of words per minute (wpm).
- Count the number of mistyped words.
- Deduct the number of mistyped words from the gross wpm.
- This gives the net wpm.
- If the computer has a word count facility, make sure that the 'characters with spaces' figure is used.

Whatever source material is going to be used, documents will be produced from the following formats:

Memos
These are used for internal communication within an organisation. They may vary in the level of formality in which they are written. They:

- May be addressed to more than one recipient
- Will usually not include addresses

- Will have a subject line, similar to 'emails'
- Will state the date, name of the recipient (s), the name of the sender and the content
- May have the recipient and sender's job titles and departments
- Will usually be produced on a template which reflects the organisation's 'house style'

Most organisations still use memos for important internal messages, if they have not been replaced by the use of emails.

MEMORANDUM

To: All selling staff

From: Sales Manager

Date: 27th August 2010

Subject: Sales targets

Last week saw total sales of £127,436, an increase of 3.1% on last year. This week we have a challenging target of £148,000, or 3.7% on last year. This will require 100% effort from all of us, but I am confident we can do it.

REMEMBER: PROMOTE DISPOSABLE BARBECUES.

Business letters

These are usually printed on paper headed with the organisation's address and business details. There is a recognised format to letter writing; however, an organisation may choose to adopt its own 'house style'. Letters will normally:

- Be **addressed to one person** - e.g. 'Dear <u>Sir</u>' or 'Dear <u>Madam</u>'
- Be dated
- Contain a **salutation** - e.g. 'Dear ...'
- Have a reference number / title / heading - These are optional
- Contain the body of text for writing the letter
- End with a **closing statement** that summarises the main points for writing the letter
- Include a **compliment** - e.g. 'Yours sincerely'
- Include a **signature**

Business letters are usually produced:

- **Fully blocked -** All parts of the document start at the left-hand margin

- **With open punctuation -** Punctuation used only in the body of the letter, where it is essential for grammatical accuracy and understanding

---

Matthew and Son Builders
Allington Place
West Billington
WW1 1AD
Tel: 01632 566854

Our ref: GM / RA / 124
Your ref: VH / AK

13 August 2010

Mr V Harmison
Oval Walk
West Billington
WW2 1AX

Dear Mr Harmison

Thank you for your letter dated 6th August 2010 accepting our quotation to extend your office building.

The work will commence on 6th September 2010 and will be completed within 6 working weeks.

If you have any queries, please do not hesitate to contact me.

Yours sincerely

Graham Matthew
Director

A letter addressed to Mrs Jayne Wilcox, 12 Manvers Street, London SW19 7ER can be sent using the following salutations and complimentary phrases:

SALUTATION	Dear Jayne	Dear Mrs Wilcox	Dear Madam
COMPLIMENT	Kind regards	Yours sincerely	Yours faithfully

If someone knows Jayne Wilcox well they will probably use Jayne. If a sender does not know Jayne well they may feel more comfortable addressing her as Mrs Wilcox. If they do not know Mrs Wilcox at all, they will probably usually the formal term 'Madam'. As the salutation becomes more formal so does the complimentary close.

With the advent of electronic means of communication the number of letters written and received by organisations has declined. Letters will probably be written if there is no access to an email address on an organisation's website, for legal reasons or the sender may want a formal record of the communication.

• ACTIVITY 2

What is the difference between a 'salutation' and a 'compliment'?

Reports

These are produced in response to a request for information. They may be formal or informal, depending on the audience they are being written for. For example, a report written to a Board of an organisation will generally be more formal than a report to the members of a club. A report is written to inform the reader of facts about a subject. The depth of information contained in a report will depend on the purpose of the report and its intended audience. All reports will follow a similar structure, however detailed they may be:

- **Front page -** This contains the title of the report, the name of the author and the date

- **Contents -** This will list all the subjects covered in the report

- **Executive summary -** This gives a brief outline of the report

- **Background information -** This gives the reasons why the report was produced

- **Methodology -** This outlines the methods used to produce the data in the report, e.g. surveys, questionnaires

- **Findings -** These are the results of the methods used to explore the purpose of the report. Findings may be presented by:

- **Importance**: where the central ideas are presented

- **Chronology -** where ideas are presented in the order of events, starting either with the latest or the first

- **Sequence**: where one idea follows from another

- **Comparison**: where two ideas are compared in alternate paragraphs

- **Conclusion** - This outlines the conclusions that can be drawn from the findings of the research

- **Recommendations** - This outlines the actions that are recommended to be taken as a result of the conclusion

- **Acknowledgements** - This records the contribution others have made to the report

- **Bibliography** - This outlines the source material used in the research. There are a number of different ways that a bibliography can be drawn up

- **Appendices** - This sets out all the information referred to in the report which is too detailed to be given in full without distracting from the purpose of the report

Minutes

These are a record of the discussions and agreed actions that will need to be followed up as a result of a meeting. Minutes can be recorded in a number of different forms:

- **Verbatim** - Where everything is recorded word for word

- **Narrative** - Where a summary of the meeting is recorded. Formal resolutions will be recorded verbatim

- **Resolution** - Where a motion which has been voted on and passed gives details of the proposer and seconder of the motion, with a verbatim recording of the resolution

- **Action** - Where only the action and the name of the person or persons responsible for carrying out the action are recorded

• ACTIVITY 3

Someone working in an estate agent's office has left a note for you to type up the following information:

A new house has just come onto the market can you type the details? 112 Bestonic Street semi situated in a pop. and est. res. location convenient for local schools and shops and town centre, vestibule, entrance hall, lounge, dining room, three bedrooms CH gas garage, upvc DG throughout fully fitted kitchen cloakroom on ground family bath on 1st gardens front and rear.

Lounge 8.1x3.48

Dining room 4.72x4.22

Kitchen 2.39x4.5

Bed 1 3.12x4.62

Bed 2 3.61x2.95

Bed 3 3.42x4.56

Make sure you point out that the house has a large, well looked after garden, is in council tax band B and the photo is to follow.

Accuracy of text prepared from notes

Any piece of text produced from notes should be a quality piece of work. It should be executed with the correct spelling, the use of grammatical rules and the correct application of punctuation to produce a product that both gives a good impression of the organisation and, more importantly, conveys the intended message of the text.

Spelling

A computer will automatically check the spelling of words and highlight them in the document being worked on. However, spell check cannot:

- Differentiate between American and English spelling of words, so make sure that the spell check default is aligned to the correct country

• ACTIVITY 4

Circle the correct spelling in the following list of words:

Adjoin	adjoin	adjoine
Purtain	pertain	purrtain
Arange	arrang	arrange
Pleasure	pleajure	pleasur
Decieve	deceive	deseive
Plackate	playcate	placate
Shean	sheen	shein
Posible	possible	possable
Lovelly	lovly	lovely
Burial	buriel	burrial

- Differentiate between words that are spelled correctly but used incorrectly, e.g. using 'through' when it should be 'threw'. Some of the most commonly confused words are:

  - We are pleased to <u>accept</u> your donation - Everyone made a donation <u>except</u> Mr Jones

  - Never listen to <u>advice</u> from your parents - I would <u>advise</u> you always to listen to your parents

  - The increase in interest rates will <u>affect</u> everyone - The <u>effect</u> of the increase was felt by everyone

  - She thought she was <u>eligible</u> for a grant - The letter she received was <u>illegible</u>

  - You must <u>ensure</u> that your car is <u>insured</u>

  - Lowestoft is <u>farther</u> east than Birmingham - I need <u>further</u> information on the location of Hull

  - There are <u>fewer</u> days in February than in June - It is <u>less</u> likely to rain today than it was yesterday

  - My <u>personal</u> opinion is that it will rain today - The HR Department deals with <u>personnel</u>

  - I visited the local doctors' <u>practice</u> this morning - I need to <u>practise</u> my spelling more often

  - The <u>principal</u> cause of heart disease is overeating - The minister resigned over a matter of <u>principle</u>

- The traffic on the M6 was <u>stationary</u> for two hours - We need to order some more <u>stationery</u> this week

- This week's sales were better <u>than</u> last week's - We will look at this week's plan, <u>then</u> next week's

- The girls picked up <u>their</u> handbags - The boys will be over <u>there</u> tomorrow - <u>They're</u> planning to visit next week

Grammar

Grammar can loosely be defined at the 'rules of language'. However, in English, the 'rules' are not consistent, which makes it complicated to learn and apply. Grammar is important to make sure that the intended meaning of a sentence is communicated to the recipients of the communication. For example, 'Use both lanes when turning right' actually requires drivers to straddle the two lanes, which is a highly dangerous manoeuvre to carry out. The correct sentence construction should be: 'Use either lane when turning right'.

There are five parts of speech which are commonly used:

- **Nouns -** These are the names of a person, place or thing, e.g. 'book', 'television', 'Sunday', 'Norfolk'

- **Pronouns -** These are used instead of a noun, e.g. instead of saying 'John' in a paragraph that refers only to him, use 'he' or 'him'

- **Verbs -** These are words that express doing things, e.g. 'ran', 'run' or 'running'

- **Adverbs -** These words give information about how a verb was executed, e.g. 'he ran <u>quickly</u>' or 'he ran <u>fast</u>'. Note that while most adverbs will be formed by the addition of '-ly' to the end of a verb, it is not always the case, as can be seen by the second example in this paragraph

• ACTIVITY 5

Proofread and correct the following and produce a corrected version.
Switch off the spell check function on the computer.

Our ref: DT / GY / 1256

Mr G Willims
Apart 21
The shore
Manchster
M6 7yu

23.06.023

Dear nr Williams

Account number 45678956 -Flat 24 tge maltings, Manchester

Thankyou for you're recent enqiry regarding your mortgage, and the
interst rates available to you. I am enclosing a quotition showing what
yur new payments would be at a new rate of interst. Yhjis has been
calculated on and Interest only Basis.

At the moment you're monthly payments is ^189.23 vased ib a rate if
6.75%. Should you decide to except our offer (details) attached, your
new repayments would be approx $206.93. The admin fee of £120.00
gas veeb added ti tyour balance for quotation's pyrposes only.

This offer is valid for 14 day's from the date of the enclosed quotation.
you should of receved further details yesterday.

Transferring yourmortgage onto the new rate couldnt be easier,
Simply return the Deed of Variation enclosed, signed by all partied to
the mortgage.

We will charge you the aministration fee of £120.00. This sum can be
added to the loan or may be paid by check if you wish.

If you have any questions, plesse contact me on 02356 56998 Monday
to Friday between 9.00pm and 5.00pm.

Yours faithfyully

W Gaines
Consultant Mortgage Provider

- **Adjectives** - These describe nouns, e.g. 'an <u>interesting</u> book', '<u>reality</u> television'

Sentences are formed by linking parts of speech together. Simple sentences contain a subject and a verb, e.g. 'I am', where 'I' is the subject and 'am' is the verb. More complicated sentences will have a subject, verb and object, e.g. 'I am going to London', where the object of the sentence is London. Sentences must start with a capital letter and end with some form of punctuation, e.g. a full stop, question mark. Capital letters are also used to indicate **proper names**, e.g. America, Anthony; **titles**, e.g. Mr, Mrs, Lord; **days of the week or months of the year** and **acronyms** (RAF, CIA, FBI, MI5, RAC).

• ACTIVITY 6

What is the difference between a 'noun' and a 'pronoun'?

A paragraph is formed by linking two or more sentences together. If the subject of a paragraph changes, it is advisable to start a new paragraph.

Punctuation

As with grammar, the correct use of punctuation will make it easier for people to understand the content of a piece of communication. For example, if someone said 'Fred, the dog is ill', they would be telling someone called Fred that the dog is unwell. If they said 'Fred the dog is ill', they would be telling someone that the dog called Fred is unwell. Three of the most common punctuation marks in use are:

- **Full stops** - These are used to mark the end of a sentence or after abbreviations

- **Commas** - These are used to separate words in a list or phrases in a sentence, or to make sentences easier to read

- **Apostrophes** - There are two uses of the apostrophe: to replace a missing letter, e.g. 'I'm, he's, don't' or to indicate something belongs to someone, the possessive case, e.g. 'Jim's book, Pauline's shoes, women's clothing, babies' bottles'

Whatever text is produced, it is important that it is checked for accuracy before being distributed.

Formatting the text

At any stage during the production of text, formatting will be necessary.

This can be as simple as changing the type of font used in the text to using text effects, e.g. 'strikethrough'.

It is possible to format:

- **Characters -** By selecting 'font' it allows the following functions to be carried out: style, colour and size of letters, **embolden**, *italicise*, <u>underline</u>, change the s p a c i n g

- **Paragraphs -** Align text using the 'centre' or 'justify' options, or by selecting 'bullets and numbering' add bullet points or numbers. Other amendments can be made by selecting 'borders and shading', or by altering the line spacing, tabs and indent

- **Pages -** Changes can be made to the 'size', 'orientation' and 'margins' of pages. 'Page numbers' can be inserted as well as 'headers and footers' or the 'date and time'. 'Insert page breaks' can be made to indicate where a new page should begin, or 'columns' can divide the page vertically

- **Sections -** It is not necessary for the whole text to be in the same format. Different sections of text can use different formats

If part of the text is formatted in a certain way and this style is to be used later in the text, select 'styles and formatting' and the software will show what has been used previously in the document. This will help to give consistency to the design of the text.

Checking and editing text

As identified previously, text from notes can be accomplished in two ways. If the transcription of notes is being undertaken on behalf of someone else who has made the notes, check with them to clarify any meanings or phrases which are not clear. Make sure the correct interpretation of words and phrases is agreed as early on in the process as possible, so to minimise the amount of changes that have to be made to a document. To help with the process of transcribing the notes, produce a 'draft' copy, so that the originator can check what has been produced matches with what was intended. Make sure that the draft is free from errors.

Most word processing packages contain spell checking and grammar checking facilities. Use these first to correct the obvious errors, but do not rely on them entirely. Check to make sure that the spell check default is not using American spelling and grammar, as the document will accept 'color' and reject 'colour' etc. When the automatic checking is complete, read the document carefully to look for missed errors, and also for correct use of paragraphs, headings and subheadings, style and formatting. Be particularly careful to proofread numbers, dates, times and amounts. Check for errors between similar words, such as 'affect' and 'effect' or 'less' and 'fewer'.

Look for errors of context and content. The draft text will be returned by the originator indicating where any changes need to be made to the document. Changes may come about as a result of:

- Input errors
- Errors in the source material
- Amendments to the content

Changes may have been agreed not necessarily because of poor transcription skills but because the originator of the notes wants to make changes to the document to improve the tone and meaning.

A computer provides a lot of functions that allow text to be easily edited:

- **Delete** - Ctrl+delete - This allows a single letter, group of letters or whole parts of a document to be deleted

- **Paste** - Ctrl+v - This is used in combination with either the 'cut' or 'copy', see below, instruction. Paste will add the last data selected to the document 'copied' or stored on the 'clipboard', which will provide other recently 'copied' information

- **Cut** - Ctrl+x - This is used to highlight a piece of text and remove it from the document. It can then be 'pasted', see above, to another part of the document or a new document

- **Copy** - Ctrl+c - This is used to highlight a piece of text and copied. It can then be 'pasted', see above, to another part of the document or a new document

- **Find and replace** - Ctrl+f - This function is used to change all the examples of a particular word to another word, e.g. replace the word 'company' with the word 'organisation', there is no need to retype every example, use 'find' and / or 'replace' to make all the changes

- **Inserting special characters and symbols** - This function enables the use of other alphabets, e.g. Arabic شءةكق, and other signs / symbols, e.g. o, û, ©, %

- **Mail merge** - This function is useful if the same letter is going to several recipients, as it can change the name and address of each recipient

- **Track changes** - This function allows the originator of a document to share it with other colleagues, inviting them to make changes which can be tracked by name and highlighted

At any stage during the transcription of text from notes the format of the text can be changed. There are various options available in the format menu, e.g. font, which allows the font to be changed to different styles, sizes, colour etc. It is possible to format characters, pages or whole sections of a document. A part of the text can be formatted and used again later in the document by selecting 'styles and formatting', and the software will show what formatting has been used previously in the text.

If text is being produced which will have more than one page, it is advisable to use a 'header and footer', with required information and / or 'page numbers'. Using both functions will allow the title to be put onto each page with a page number. It is also possible to 'number paragraphs' and include an 'index' or 'table of contents' to help the reader find their way around the text.

• ACTIVITY 7

Correct the following piece of text:

Minutes of sales and marketing team held on 20th August 2010, Imperial Hotel, Russell Sq, London WC1, 9.30

Present

John Towers - Chair
Peter Benson
Jill Harper
Steve Lilley
Keith Barnett
Michael Hope
Terry Johnson

Apologies were received from:
Michelle Peterson
Andrew Carr

minutes of the last meeting were approved

None matters arising.

It was suggested that a farther meeting be held in sept to agree the final steppes of th sales plan for the new year. All 7 present agreed.

Christmas is fast approaching and it will be very busy. As Peter will be leave it will effect the way the team will work.

New stationary to be ordered for the team.

Next meeting on Tues, 24 Sept 2010.

Having made all the requested alterations, produce a final draft and pass that to the originator. Hopefully there will be no further amendments at this stage. Once this has been signed off it can be printed to the quality standard requested, not forgetting that a copy of the text should be stored in the appropriate storage system.

Storing text

Every piece of text will probably need to be stored in some way. This can be done using a manual paper-based system, an electronic-based system or both. A computer will have its own in-built sorting and storing mechanisms. Text should be stored accurately in the approved locations so anyone can find it quickly and easily. Folders should be used that can be held within the main directory of the computer system. Folders should be used to group files together to speed up their retrieval. Paper copies will be stored manually using one of the following methods:

- **Alphabetical** - Information is stored in order, from A-Z. Files starting with the same letter are filed in order of the second letter: Aa, Ab, Ac etc. People's names are filed by their surnames, and if more than one has the same surname, by their first names. Names starting with 'The' are filed by ignoring the 'The'. Names beginning with 'Mac' or 'Mc' come before 'Ma', 'Mb' etc.

- **Numerical** - Information is coded using a numbering system, e.g. purchase orders, invoices

- **Alpha-numerical** - Information is stored using a combination of letters and numbers, e.g. National Insurance numbers. Usually large databases hold this type of coded information, as they hold more information than numerical systems and are more flexible than alphabetical systems. The order of filing depends on the sequence of the file name. If file names start with letters followed by numbers, they are filed in alphabetical order first and numerical order within each letter

- **Chronological** - This is often used within one of the other methods, e.g. customers' records are filed alphabetically, but the information within the file is stored chronologically, usually with the latest at the front. This provides a history of all activities undertaken for a particular file of information. It can also be based on dates of birth or start dates

- **Geographical** - This is a method of sorting by areas, e.g. North West England, East Anglia or counties, towns, cities

- **By subject or category** - Some organisations need to sort their filing under topics rather than names, e.g. a shoe manufacturer may keep files under product names such as Ladies, Gentlemen and Children

• ACTIVITY 8

What methods can be used to store texts?

The original source material from which the text has been produced will also need to be filed and stored if it needs to be referred to at a later date. An organisation may have its own system of referencing documents which should be followed. If using a system to reference documents, make sure that the original source material is referenced with the same reference number as the completed text. The source material should be stored in a logical manner:

- Handwritten notes can be attached to the file copy of the completed document

- Shorthand notebooks should be stored chronologically, with the start and end date written on the front

- Audio tapes should be stored chronologically and labelled with the date

If the document being created is 'private and confidential', make sure it is identified as such and follows the organisation's policy on 'private and confidential' documents, e.g. the contents of the document should not be discussed publicly so unauthorised people can hear. Confidential information is information that has great value, is considered to be of a private nature and is only permitted to be seen by designated people within an organisation. 'Confidential information' can embrace commercial secrets as well as general information, e.g. medical records. An organisation can be damaged if its privacy of information is not upheld and respected, which could result in the organisation being devalued.

There is no single Act of Parliament defining 'confidential information' or governing how it is protected, or setting out rights and obligations in respect of it. However, the law on 'confidential information' is currently undergoing radical change as a result of developing European and UK legislation and decisions of the courts. Place 'confidentiality' warnings on standard communications, e.g. faxes or emails, to make sure if an individual receives the information by accident they are notified of its 'confidential' nature.

'Private and confidential' documents also includes commercially sensitive information, which needs to be protected from being read by an organisation's competitors. If the content of a document covers personal information it must conform to the requirements of the Data Protection Act 1998.

Testing your knowledge

1. What are the different uses of memos, reports, minutes and letters?

2. What is meant by 'fully blocked'?

3. Why is it necessary to meet deadlines?

4. What type of document will always have a signature?

5. What forms can minutes take?

6. What is the sequence of content that can be presented in a report?

7. What do you understand by an 'appendix'?

8. What punctuation is used in a letter using 'open' punctuation?

9. What is meant by proofreading?

10. What types of amendments might be made to a draft?

11. Why is the source material filed as well as the completed document?

12. Why it is important to be able to locate the source material if requested?

13. What does 'confidential' mean in terms of text storage?

Skills

Before starting work on the transcription of any piece of text, make sure you are clear about:

- The purpose of the text
- The format of the text
- The deadlines within which the text needs to be completed

• ACTIVITY 9

Attend a meeting - this could be a team meeting at work, a social club meeting, a meeting at college - and take longhand notes of what is said OR obtain notes that need to be transcribed into text. Produce a short typed report from the notes. Time yourself inputting the text and count the number of words. Proofread the document and calculate the net words per minute.

Each of these aspects of preparing to transcribe a piece of text will inform the planning of the work you will need to do for either yourself or if you are producing the text from original source material. Organise your work around all the tasks that you have to complete so you finish the transcription of the text at the agreed time. Once you are clear about what has to be done, gather together all the resources you will require to complete the task.

• ACTIVITY 10

Write a report to your supervisor suggesting ways in which your current filing systems can be improved. Consider the best way to order the contents of the report.

When transcribing text from notes make sure you are fully up to date with the functions of your software so you can edit the text effectively and efficiently. Chat to someone who is very confident in this area, or your supervisor / manager, to check that you are fully conversant with functionality of the technology you are using. This will not only save you time but make your text look more professional.

Make sure that you are clear about the style, layout and format that you wish, or the original author wishes, the text to take. Clarify all these components of your text.

• ACTIVITY 11

Select a number of texts that you have produced which you feel demonstrate your competence in using correct layout, spelling, punctuation and grammar. Share these with your supervisor / manager to get their feedback on the quality of your work.

Produce a draft document and check through this with the original author to make sure it meets all the requirements that they are aiming to achieve. Check through the document to make sure that it accurately presents information, that is, there are no spelling mistakes. Make sure your computer is set to the correct defaults and that grammar and punctuation have been used correctly.

Once you have checked the text, check the aims of the text with the original author, to make sure that they have been achieved. When working on the production of the text, if you are not sure, at any stage of its development, that the text is progressing along the right track, pause and reflect on what the text is aiming to achieve. Check with the original author - if it is not you. If anything changes with the development of the text check with the original author that they are happy with the change of direction that the text may have to take. Complete the final draft of the text and present this to the author of the original source material if it is not yourself.

Make sure the text has been referenced in line with your organisation's procedures. Then file it using whatever storage system your organisation uses.

Testing your skills

1. How do you make sure that spelling, punctuation and grammar has been used correctly?

2. How is the content of a business letter laid out?

3. How and when would you use the format menu?

4. If you were asked to emphasise a sentence in a report how would you do it?

5. How do you proofread your own work?

6. When would you use printers' correction symbols?

7. What functions would you use to edit text, and why?

8. Why should you produce a final draft of your text?

9. Why is it important to raise any queries with the originator of the original source material before producing the draft?

10. How does your organisation reference text documents?

11. What system (s) of storing text documents does your organisation use?

Ready for assessment?

To achieve this Level 2 unit of a Business & Administration qualification, learners will need to demonstrate that they are able to perform the following activities:

1. Agreed the purpose, format and deadlines for the transcription

2. Inputted the text using keyboarding skills

3. Formatted the text, making efficient use of available technology

4. Checked content for accuracy

5. Edited and corrected the text

6. Clarified text requirements, when necessary

7. Stored the text and original notes safely and securely in approved locations

8. Presented the text in the required format within agreed deadlines

You will need to produce evidence from a variety of sources to support the performance requirements of this unit.

If you carry out the 'ACTIVITIES' and respond to the 'NEED TO KNOW' questions, these will provide some of the evidence required.

Links to other units

While gathering evidence for this unit, evidence **may** also be used from evidence generated from other units within the Business & Administration suite of units. Below is a **sample** of applicable units; however, most units within the Business & Administration suite of units will also be applicable.

QCF NVQ
Communications
Communicate in a business environment (Q206)
Make and receive telephone calls
Use electronic message systems
Core business & administration
Manage own performance in a business environment (Q201)
Improve own performance in a business environment (Q202)
Work in a business environment (Q203)
Work with other people in a business environment (Q205)
Customer service
Handle mail
Document production
Produce documents in a business environment
Prepare text from notes using touch typing (40 wpm)
Prepare text from shorthand (60 wpm)
Prepare text from recorded audio instruction (40 wpm)
Mange information and data
Store and retrieve information

SVQ

Communications

Prepare to communicate in a business environment

Make and receive telephone calls

Use electronic message systems

Core business & administration

Agree how to manage and improve own performance in a business environment

Undertake work in a business environment

Work with other people in a business environment

Customer service

Handle mail

Document production

Produce documents in a business environment

Prepare text from notes using touch typing (40 wpm)

Prepare text from shorthand (60 wpm)

Prepare text from recorded audio instruction (40 wpm)

Mange information and data

Store and retrieve information

17

Prepare text from notes using touch typing (40 wpm)

PREPARE TEXT FROM NOTES USING TOUCH TYPING (40 WPM)

'**Prepare text from notes using touch typing (40 wpm)**' is an <u>optional unit</u> which may be chosen as one of a combination of units to achieve either a Qualifications and Credit Framework (QCF), National Vocational Qualification (NVQ) or Scottish Vocational Qualification (SVQ).

The aims of this unit are to:

- Understand the preparing of text from notes using touch typing

- Understand the purpose and benefits of following procedures when preparing text using touch typing

- Be able to prepare for tasks

- Be able to prepare text using touch typing at 40 wpm

To achieve the above aims of this unit, learners will be expected to provide evidence through the performance of work-based activities.

Knowledge

Touch typing

Before starting to use the keyboard always make sure that the workstation is ergonomically prepared to meet the individual requirements of the keyboard user - sit up straight, feet flat on the floor, elbows close to the body, wrists straight and forearms parallel to the work surface. And remember to take regular breaks from touch typing.

The attraction of touch typing is to increase typing speed, which will ultimately increase productivity. While speed may be a major aim of touch typing, the main aim is accurate touch typing. The benefits derived from touch typing come from no requirement of conscious thought or visual confirmation. For example, when typing a letter there is no need to interrupt the thought pattern by having to look at the keyboard. Or the touch typist can copy text directly from the source text without having to divide their attention between the source material, the computer screen and the keyboard.

When learning to touch type the learner should always rest their fingers lightly on the 'home row' of the keyboard. The **F** and **J** keys usually have small raised bumps on the two keys so the fingers can feel that they are resting on the correct keys of the home row.

THE HOME ROW									
LEFT HAND					RIGHT HAND				
LLF	LRF	LMF	LIF	LIF	RIF	RIF	RMF	RRF	RLF
A	S	D	F	G	H	J	K	L	;

- The **left index finger (LIF)** will control the **F** and **G** keys, and the **right index finger (RIF)** will control the **J** and **H** keys
- The **left middle finger (LMF)** will control the **D** key, and the **right middle finger (RMF)** will control the **K** key
- The **left ring finger (LRF)** will control the **S** key, and the **right ring finger (RRF)** will control the **L** key
- The **left little finger (LLF)** will control the **A** key, and the **right little finger (RLF)** will control the **;** key
- The **spacebar** is controlled by the **right thumb**

The locations of all the other keys on the keyboard are learned in relation to the **home keys**. Touch typing relies finding the home keys and working from them to type in the other keys on the keyboard. When learning to touch type, get used to finding the home keys without looking at the keyboard. Try not to look at the keyboard when learning each of the keys on the keyboard. Focus should be on the text that is being typed, which can be seen on the computer screen. Take time to relax and just feel where the fingers are resting on the **F** and **J** keys in relation to the rest of the keyboard.

THE QWERTY ROW									
LEFT HAND					RIGHT HAND				
LLF	LRF	LMF	LIF	LIF	RIF	RIF	RMF	RRF	RLF
Q	W	E	R	T	Y	U	I	O	P
A	S	D	F	G	H	J	K	L	;

- The **LIF** will control the **R** and **T** keys, and the **RIF** will control the **U** and **Y** keys
- The **LMF** will control the **E** key, and the **RMF** will control the **I** key

- The **LRF** will control the **W** key, and the **RRF** will control the **O** key
- The **LLF** will control the **Q** key, and the **RLF** will control the **P** key
- The **QWERTY row** is perhaps the hardest-working row on the keyboard, because it has four vowels: **E, I, O** and **U**

THE FIRST ROW									
LEFT HAND					RIGHT HAND				
LLF	LRF	LMF	LIF	LIF	RIF	RIF	RMF	RRF	RLF
Q	W	E	R	T	Y	U	I	O	P
A	S	D	F	G	H	J	K	L	;
Z	X	C	V	B	N	M	,	.	/

- The **LIF** will control the **V** and **B** keys, and the **RIF** will control the **M** and **N** keys
- The **LMF** will control the **C** key, and the **RMF** will control the **,** key
- The **LRF** will control the **X** key, and the **RRF** will control the **.** key

The **LLF** will control the **Z** key, and the **RLF** will control the **/** key

Once the first row on the keyboard is learned, all the alpha keys on the keyboard will have been learned.

THE NUMBER ROW									
LEFT HAND					RIGHT HAND				
LLF	LRF	LMF	LIF	LIF	RIF	RIF	RMF	RRF	RLF
1	2	3	4	5	6	7	8	9	0
Q	W	E	R	T	Y	U	I	O	P
A	S	D	F	G	H	J	K	L	;
Z	X	C	V	B	N	M	,	.	/

- The **LIF** will control the **4** and **5** keys, and the **RIF** will control the **7** and **6** keys
- The **LMF** will control the **3** key, and the **RMF** will control the **8** key
- The **LRF** will control the **2** key, and the **RRF** will control the **9** key
- The **LLF** will control the **1** key, and the **RLF** will control the **0** key

The number row is the furthest row from the typist's fingers' resting position, the **home row**.

THE NUMBER ROW - UPPERCASE									
LEFT HAND					RIGHT HAND				
LLF	LRF	LMF	LIF	LIF	RIF	RIF	RMF	RRF	RLF
!	"	£	$	%	^	&	*	(	)
Q	W	E	R	T	Y	U	I	O	P
A	S	D	F	G	H	J	K	L	;
Z	X	C	V	B	N	M	,	.	/

The number row has two sets of symbols on it: numbers and symbols. To access the symbols use the appropriate shift key.

Capitals. The keyboard should have two shift keys, one to the left and one to the right. Use the little finger of the inactive hand to work one of the shift keys when capitals are needed. For example, if typing a capital **A**, strike the **A** key with the index finger of the left hand while depressing the shift key with the little finger of the right hand. This can feel a little awkward in the beginning, but it will feel natural after sufficient repetition of use.

Some tips when first starting out to learn how to touch type:

- **Never look at the keyboard!** Check the computer for accuracy
- Always check for the starting position of the fingers on the **F** and **J** keys in the **home row**, and feel the bumps on the keys
- Do not worry about typing non-words at first, as this is to gain familiarity with the keys of the keyboard

- Measure your **typing speed periodically**, to see when you have achieved 40 wpm. The speed being typed should avoid any mistakes, and this is what you are aiming to achieve - **accuracy**. Aim always to reduce the number of mistakes while increasing your touch typing speed

- Speed is measured in **words per minute (wpm)**, where a word is represented by five key strokes, including using the space bar and the shift bar

- Both your accuracy and speed will improve with practice

- A good phrase to use when practicing is, '**The quick brown fox jumped over the lazy dog**', as this uses all the letters of the alphabet

- Practice! Practice! Practice!

•ACTIVITY 1

Type the following passages aiming to reach a speed of 40 wpm. Aim to eliminate any mistakes. Type the whole passage in each exercise, including the brackets containing the number of words and character spaces:

Exercise 1
In one dimension the ease with which a man can move to another dimension is amazing. There are thousands of people who strive to do this but they are stopped at the first hurdle – their fear! So what can they do to get over their fear? It is tricky but achievable. Don't be lazy and put mind over matter. The cosmos is continually expanding in size so there will always be more dimensions out there for us to discover. How many years will that take? 1, 2, 3, 5, 10 or infinity? (98 words, 509 character spaces)

Exercise 2
We expect 50 tonnes of vegetables in 3 months, which should represent 50% of the stock that we will need over the next 12 months. In the first quarter this will cost £300,000.00 or $450,00.00; second quarter £354,126.00 or $538,938.00; third quarter £236,971.00 or $376,928.00; and the final quarter, £90,318.00 or $135,201.00. The total cost will be £981,415.00 or $1,501,067.00. This represents an increase of 23% for each quarter compared with last year. (78 words, 490 character spaces)

Exercise 3

George, John, Paul and Ringo had been booked to travel from London on a world tour in 1965 (their first tour). They would take in 3 continents in their travels, which were Europe, Asia and Australia. The cities they travelled to included: Paris, Rome, Venice, Istanbul, Singapore, Hong Kong, Vladivostok, Sydney, Melbourne and Madrid. John enjoyed Paris most, then Hong Kong and Sydney; Ringo did not like Venice or Vladivostok; Paul was not well for most of the tour so did not really enjoy many of the cities that he went to and George though the best cities were Melbourne and Madrid. (107 words, 621 character spaces)

Different types of documents that can be produced from notes

Different types of organisations working in many different sectors will have the need to produce text from notes. These will include emails, memos, letters, reports and minutes of meetings. Notes will have been produced from a variety of sources, e.g. shorthand, audio recordings.

Many text documents will be prepared from handwritten notes which can be made by an author who will:

- **Prepare the text** - This should be relatively easy to transcribe as the person preparing the text is translating handwritten notes which they have made, so legibility and shortcuts should not be a problem

- **Not prepare the text** - This may be a little more difficult to transcribe as the person preparing the text is not translating their own handwritten notes. They may not understand the handwriting or the shortcuts that the author has made. If this occurs, the person transcribing the text should clarify from the author any script that is not legible

Before preparing the transcription of any notes into text make sure that the purpose, format and deadline of the text has been agreed. A deadline is when a document is due by a certain time, in a certain format and containing the required information. It is important that all parties involved in the production of text are all agreed on what the finished product will look like and when it can be expected. Before starting to produce any text from notes, include resources that will be needed to complete the text, e.g. the addition of images or diagrams. The text should be clear. If a document is not delivered against these requirements it will appear unprofessional, particularly if lateness has not been discussed with the recipient, and this could lead to loss of business. Having an agreed deadline will help to plan and prioritise tasks / activities. Whatever source material is going to be used, documents will be produced from the following formats:

Memos

These are used for internal communication within an organisation. They may vary in the level of formality in which they are written. They:

- May be addressed to more than one recipient
- Will usually not include addresses
- Will have a subject line, similar to emails
- Will state the date, name of the recipient (s), the name of the sender and the content
- May have the recipient and sender's job titles and departments
- Will usually be produced on a template which reflects the organisation's 'house style'

MEMORANDUM

To: All selling staff

From: Sales Manager

Date: 27th August 2010

Subject: Sales targets

Last week saw total sales of £127,436, an increase of 3.1% on last year. This week we have a challenging target of £148,000, or 3.7% on last year. This will require 100% effort from all of us, but I am confident we can do it.

REMEMBER: PROMOTE DISPOSABLE BARBECUES.

Most organisations still use memos for important internal messages, if they have not been replaced by the use of 'emails'.

Business letters

These are usually printed on paper headed with the organisation's address and business details. There is a recognised format to letter writing; however, an organisation may choose to adopt its own 'house style'. Letters will normally:

- Be **addressed to one person** - e.g. 'Dear <u>Sir</u>' or 'Dear <u>Madam</u>'
- Be dated
- Contain a **salutation** - e.g. 'Dear ...'

- Have a reference number / title / heading - These are optional
- Contain the body of text for writing the letter
- End with a **closing statement** that summarises the main points for writing the letter

---

Matthew and Son Builders
Allington Place
West Billington
WW1 1AD
Tel: 01632 566854

Our ref: GM / RA / 124
Your ref: VH / AK

13 August 2010

Mr V Harmison
Oval Walk
West Billington
WW2 1AX

Dear Mr Harmison

Thank you for your letter dated 6th August 2010 accepting our quotation to extend your office building.

The work will commence on 6th September 2010 and will be completed within 6 working weeks.

If you have any queries, please do not hesitate to contact me.

Yours sincerely

Graham Matthew
Director

- Include a **compliment** - e.g. 'Yours sincerely'
- Include a **signature**

Business letters are usually produced:

- **Fully blocked -** All parts of the document start at the left-hand margin
- With **open punctuation -** Punctuation used only in the body

of the letter, where it is essential for grammatical accuracy and understanding

A letter addressed to Mrs Jayne Wilcox, 12 Manvers Street, London SW19 7ER can be sent using the following salutations and complimentary phrases:

SALUTATION	Dear Jayne	Dear Mrs Wilcox	Dear Madam
COMPLIMENT	Kind regards	Yours sincerely	Yours faithfully

If someone knows Jayne Wilcox well they will probably use Jayne. If a sender does not know Jayne well they may feel more comfortable addressing her as Mrs Wilcox. If they do not know Mrs Wilcox at all, they will probably usually the formal term 'Madam'. As the salutation becomes more formal so does the complimentary close.

With the advent of electronic means of communication the number of letters written and received by organisations has declined. Letters will probably be written if there is no access to an email address on an organisation's website, for legal reasons or the sender may want a formal record of the communication.

• ACTIVITY 2

What is the difference between a 'salutation' and a 'compliment'?

Reports

These are produced in response to a request for information. They may be formal or informal, depending on the audience they are being written for. For example, a report written to a Board of an organisation will generally be more formal than a report to the members of a club. A report is written to inform the reader of facts about a subject. The depth of information contained in a report will depend on the purpose of the report and its intended audience.

All reports will follow a similar structure, however detailed they may be:

- **Front page -** This contains the title of the report, the name of the author and the date

- **Contents -** This will list all the subjects covered in the report

- **Executive summary -** This gives a brief outline of the report

- **Background information** - This gives the reasons why the report was produced

- **Methodology** - This outlines the methods used to produce the data in the report, e.g. surveys, questionnaires

- **Findings** - These are the results of the methods used to explore the purpose of the report. Findings may be presented by:

  - Importance: where the central ideas are presented

  - Chronology: where ideas are presented in the order of events, starting either with the latest or the first

  - Sequence: where one idea follows from another

  - Comparison: where two ideas are compared in alternate paragraphs

- **Conclusion** - This outlines the conclusions that can be drawn from the findings of the research

- **Recommendations** - This outlines the actions that are recommended to be taken as a result of the conclusion

- **Acknowledgements** - This records the contribution others have made to the report

- **Bibliography** - This outlines the source material used in the research. There are a number of different ways that a bibliography can be drawn up

- **Appendices** - This sets out all the information referred to in the report which is too detailed to be given in full without distracting from the purpose of the report

Minutes

These are a record of the discussions and agreed actions that will need to be followed up as a result of a meeting. Minutes can be recorded in a number of different forms:

- **Verbatim** - Where everything is recorded word for word

- **Narrative** - Where a summary of the meeting is recorded. Formal resolutions will be recorded verbatim

- **Resolution** - Where a motion which has been voted on and passed gives details of the proposer and seconder of the motion, with a verbatim recording of the resolution

- **Action** - Where only the action and the name of the person or persons responsible for carrying out the action are recorded

• ACTIVITY 3

Someone working in an estate agent's office has left a note for you to type up the following information.

A new house has just come onto the market can you type the details? 112 Bestonic Street semi situated in a pop. and est. res. location convenient for local schools and shops and town centre, vestibule, entrance hall, lounge, dining room, three bedrooms CH gas garage, upvc DG throughout fully fitted kitchen cloakroom on ground family bath on 1st gardens front and rear.

Lounge 8.1x3.48

Dining room 4.72x4.22

Kitchen 2.39x4.5

Bed 1 3.12x4.62

Bed 2 3.61x2.95

Bed 3 3.42x4.56

Make sure you point out that the house has a large, well looked after garden, is in council tax band B and the photo is to follow.

Accuracy of text prepared from notes

Any piece of text produced from notes should be a quality piece of work. It should be executed with the correct spelling, the use of grammatical rules and the correct application of punctuation to produce a product that both gives a good impression of the organisation and, more importantly, conveys the intended message of the text.

Spelling

A computer will automatically check the spelling of words and highlight them in the document being worked on. However, spell check cannot:

- Differentiate between American and English spelling of words, so make sure that the spell check default is aligned to the correct country

- Differentiate between words that are spelled correctly but used incorrectly, e.g. using 'through' when it should be 'threw'. Some of the most commonly confused words are:

  - We are pleased to <u>accept</u> your donation

- Everyone made a donation except Mr Jones
- Never listen to advice from your parents
- I would advise you always to listen to your parents
- The increase in interest rates will affect everyone
- The effect of the increase was felt by everyone
- She thought she was eligible for a grant
- The letter she received was illegible
- You must ensure that your car is insured
- Lowestoft is farther east than Birmingham
- I need further information on the location of Hull
- There are fewer days in February than in June
- It is less likely to rain today than it was yesterday
- My personal opinion is that it will rain today
- The HR Department deals with personnel
- I visited the local doctors' practice this morning
- I need to practise my spelling more often
- The principal cause of heart disease is overeating
- The minister resigned over a matter of principle
- The traffic on the M6 was stationary for two hours
- We need to order some more stationery this week
- This week's sales were better than last week's
- We will look at this week's plan, then next week's
- The girls picked up their handbags
- The boys will be over there tomorrow
- They're planning to visit next week

• ACTIVITY 4

Circle the correct spelling in the following list of words:

Adjoin	Addjoin	Adjoine
Purtain	Pertain	Purrtain
Arange	Arrang	Arrange
Pleasure	Pleajure	Pleasur
Decieve	Deceive	Deseive
Plackate	Playcate	Placate
Shean	Sheen	Shein
Posible	Possible	Possable
Lovelly	Lovly	Lovely
Burial	Buriel	Burrial

Grammar

Grammar can loosely be defined at the 'rules of language'. However, in English, the 'rules' are not consistent, which makes it complicated to learn and apply. Grammar is important to make sure that the intended meaning of a sentence is communicated to the recipients of the communication. For example, 'Use both lanes when turning right' actually requires drivers to straddle the two lanes, which is a highly dangerous manoeuvre to carry out. The correct sentence construction should be: 'Use either lane when turning right'.

There are five parts of speech which are commonly used:

- **Nouns** - These are the names of a person, place or thing, e.g. 'book', 'television', 'Sunday', 'Norfolk'

- **Pronouns** - These are used instead of a noun, e.g. instead of saying 'John' in a paragraph that refers only to him, use 'he' or 'him'

- **Verbs** - These are words that express doing things, e.g. 'ran', 'run' or 'running'

- **Adverbs** - These words give information about how a verb was executed, e.g. 'he ran quickly' or 'he ran fast'. Note that while most adverbs will be formed by the addition of '-ly' to the end of a verb, it is not always the case, as can be seen by the second example in this paragraph

- **Adjectives** - These describe nouns, e.g. 'an interesting book', 'reality television'

• ACTIVITY 5

What is the difference between a 'noun' and a 'pronoun'?

Sentences are formed by linking parts of speech together. Simple sentences contain a subject and a verb, e.g. 'I am', where 'I' is the subject and 'am' is the verb. More complicated sentences will have a subject, verb and object, e.g. 'I am going to London', where the object of the sentence is London. Sentences must start with a capital letter and end with some form of punctuation, e.g. a full stop, question mark. Capital letters are also used to indicate **proper names**, e.g. America, Anthony; **titles**, e.g. Mr, Mrs, Lord; **days of the week or months of the year** and **acronyms** (RAF, CIA, FBI, MI5, RAC).

A paragraph is formed by linking two or more sentences together. If the subject of a paragraph changes, it is advisable to start a new paragraph.

• ACTIVITY 6

Proofread and correct the following and produce a corrected version. Switch off the spell check function on the computer.

Our ref: DT / GY / 1256

Mr G Willims
Apart 21
The shore
Manchster
M6 7yu

23.06.023

Dear nr Williams

Account number 45678956 -Flat 24 tge maltings, Manchester

Thankyou for you're recent enqiry regarding your mortgage, and the interst rates available to you. I am enclosing a quotition showing what yur new payments would be at a new rate of interst. Yhjis has been calculated on and Interest only Basis.

At the moment you're monthly payments is ^189.23 vased ib a rate if 6.75%. Should you decide to except our offer (details) attached, your new repayments would be approx $206.93. The admin fee of £120.00 gas veeb added ti tyour balance for quotation's pyrposes only.

This offer is valid for 14 day's from the date of the enclosed quotation. you should of receved further details yesterday.

Transferring yourmortgage onto the new rate couldnt be easier, Simply return the Deed of Variation enclosed, signed by all partied to the mortgage.

We will charge you the aministration fee of £120.00. This sum can be added to the loan or may be paid by check if you wish.

If you have any questions, plesse contact me on 02356 56998 Monday to Friday between 9.00pm and 5.00pm.

Yours faithfyully

W Gaines
Consultant Mortgage Provider

Punctuation

As with grammar, the correct use of punctuation will make it easier for people to understand the content of a piece of communication. For example, if someone said 'Fred, the dog is ill', they would be telling someone called Fred that the dog is unwell. If they said 'Fred the dog is ill', they would be telling someone that the dog called Fred is unwell. Three of the most common punctuation marks in use are:

- **Full stops** - These are used to mark the end of a sentence or after abbreviations

- **Commas** - These are used to separate words in a list or phrases in a sentence, or to make sentences easier to read

- **Apostrophes** - There are two uses of the apostrophe: to replace a missing letter, e.g. 'I'm, he's, don't' or to indicate something belongs to someone, the possessive case, e.g. 'Jim's book, Pauline's shoes, women's clothing, babies' bottles'

Whatever text is produced, it is important that it is checked for accuracy before being distributed.

Formatting the text

At any stage during the production of text, formatting will be necessary. This can be as simple as changing the type of font used in the text to using text effects, e.g. 'strikethrough'.

It is possible to format:

- **Characters** - By selecting 'font' it allows the following functions to be carried out: style, colour and size of letters, **embolden**, *italicise*, <u>underline</u>, change the s p a c i n g

- **Paragraphs** - Align text using the 'centre' or 'justify' options, or by selecting 'bullets and numbering' add bullet points or numbers. Other amendments can be made by selecting borders and shading, or by altering the line spacing, tabs and indent

- **Pages** - Changes can be made to the 'size', 'orientation' and 'margins' of pages. 'Page numbers' can be inserted as well as 'headers and footers' or the 'date and time'. 'Insert page breaks' can be made to indicate where a new page should begin, or 'columns' can divide the page vertically

- **Sections** - It is not necessary for the whole text to be in the same format. Different sections of text can use different formats

If part of the text is formatted in a certain way and this style is to be used later in the text, select 'styles and formatting' and the software will show what has been used previously in the document. This will help to give consistency to the design of the text.

Checking and editing text

As identified previously, text from notes can be accomplished in two ways. If the transcription of notes is being undertaken on behalf of someone else who has made the notes, check with them to clarify any meanings or phrases which are not clear. Make sure the correct interpretation of words and phrases is agreed as early on in the process as possible, so to minimise the amount of changes that have to be made to a document. To help with the process of transcribing the notes, produce a 'draft' copy, so that the originator can check what has been produced matches with what was intended. Make sure that the draft is free from errors.

Most word processing packages contain spell checking and grammar checking facilities. Use these first to correct the obvious errors, but do not rely on them entirely. Check to make sure that the spell check default is not using American spelling and grammar, as the document will accept 'color' and reject 'colour' etc. When the automatic checking is complete, read the document carefully to look for missed errors, and also for correct use of paragraphs, headings and subheadings, style and formatting. Be particularly careful to proofread numbers, dates, times and amounts. Check for errors between similar words, such as 'affect' and 'effect' or 'less' and 'fewer'.

Look for errors of context and content. The draft text will be returned by the originator indicating where any changes need to be made to the document. Changes may come about as a result of:

- Input errors
- Errors in the source material
- Amendments to the content

Changes may have been agreed not necessarily because of poor transcription skills but because the originator of the notes wants to make changes to the document to improve the tone and meaning.

A computer provides a lot of functions that allow text to be easily edited:

- **Delete** - Ctrl+delete - This allows a single letter, group of letters or whole parts of a document to be deleted

- **Paste -** Ctrl+v - This is used in combination with either the 'cut' or 'copy', see below, instruction. Paste will add the last data selected to the document 'copied' or stored on the 'clipboard', which will provide other recently 'copied' information

- **Cut -** Ctrl+x - This is used to highlight a piece of text and remove it from the document. It can then be 'pasted', see above, to another part of the document or a new document

- **Copy -** Ctrl+c - This is used to highlight a piece of text and copied. It can then be 'pasted', see above, to another part of the document or a new document

- **Find and replace -** Ctrl+f - This function is used to change all the examples of a particular word to another word. For example, replace the word 'company' with the word 'organisation', there is no need to retype every example, use 'find' and / or 'replace' to make all the changes

- **Inserting special characters and symbols -** This function enables the use of other alphabets, e.g. Arabic, ﺵﺀﺓﻚﻗ, and other signs / symbols, e.g. o, û, ©, %

- **Mail merge -** This function is useful if the same letter is going to several recipients, as it can change the name and address of each recipient

- **Track changes -** This function allows the originator of a document to share it with other colleagues inviting them to make changes which can be tracked by name and highlighted

At any stage during the transcription of text from notes the format of the text can be changed. There are various options available in the format menu, e.g. font, which allows the font to be changed to different styles, sizes, colour. It is possible to format characters, pages or whole sections of a document. A part of the text can be formatted and used again later in the document by selecting '**styles and formatting**', and the software will show what formatting has been used previously in the text.

If text is being produced which will have more than one page, it is advisable to use a '**header and footer**', with required information and / or '**page numbers**'. Using both functions will allow the title to be put onto each page with a page number. It is also possible to 'number paragraphs' and include an '**index**' or '**table of contents**' to help the reader find their way around the text.

• ACTIVITY 7

Correct the following piece of text:

Minutes of sales and marketing team held on 20th August 2010, Imperial Hotel, Russell Sq, London WC1, 9.30

Present

John Towers - Chair
Peter Benson
Jill Harper
Steve Lilley
Keith Barnett
Michael Hope
Terry Johnson

Apologies were received from:
Michelle Peterson
Andrew Carr

minutes of the last meeting were approved

None matters arising.

It was suggested that a farther meeting be held in sept to agree the final steppes of th sales plan for the new year. All 7 present agreed.

Christmas is fast approaching and it will be very busy. As Peter will be leave it will effect the way the team will work.

New stationary to be ordered for the team.

Next meeting on Tues, 24 Sept 2010.

Having made all the requested alterations, produce a final draft and pass that to the originator. Hopefully there will be no further amendments at this stage. Once this has been signed off it can be printed to the quality standard requested, not forgetting that a copy of the text should be stored in the appropriate storage system.

Storing text

Every piece of text will probably need to be stored in some way. This can be done using a manual paper-based system, an electronic-based system or both. A computer will have its own in-built sorting and storing mechanisms. Text should be stored accurately in the approved locations so anyone can find it quickly and easily. Folders should be used that can be held within the main directory of the computer system. Folders should be used to group files together to speed up their retrieval. Paper copies will be stored manually using one of the following methods:

- **Alphabetical** - Information is stored in order, from A-Z. Files starting with the same letter are filed in order of the second letter: Aa, Ab, Ac etc. People's names are filed by their surnames, and if more than one has the same surname, by their first names. Names starting with 'The' are filed by ignoring the 'The'. Names beginning with 'Mac' or 'Mc' come before 'Ma', 'Mb' etc.

- **Numerical** - Information is coded using a numbering system, e.g. purchase orders, invoices

- **Alphanumerical** - Information is stored using a combination of letters and numbers, e.g. National Insurance numbers. Usually large databases hold this type of coded information, as they hold more information than numerical systems and are more flexible than alphabetical systems. The order of filing depends on the sequence of the file name. If file names start with letters followed by numbers, they are filed in alphabetical order first and numerical order within each letter

- **Chronological** - This method is often used within one of the other methods. For example, customers' records are filed alphabetically, but the information within the file is stored chronologically, usually with the latest at the front. This provides a history of all activities undertaken for a particular file of information. It can also be based on dates of birth or start dates

- **Geographical** - This is a method of sorting by areas, e.g. North West England, East Anglia or counties, towns, cities

- **By subject or category** - Some organisations need to sort their filing under topics rather than names. For example, a shoe manufacturer may keep files under product names such as Ladies, Gentlemen and Children

• ACTIVITY 8

What methods can be used to store texts?

The original source material from which the text has been typed will also need to be filed and stored if it needs to be referred to at a later date. An organisation may have its own system of referencing documents which should be followed. If using a system to reference documents, make sure that the original source material is referenced with the same reference number as the completed text. The source material should be stored in a logical manner:

- Handwritten notes can be attached to the file copy of the typed document

- Shorthand notebooks should be stored chronologically, with the start and end date written on the front

- Audio tapes should be stored chronologically and labelled with the date

If the document being created is 'private and confidential', make sure it is identified as such and follows the organisation's policy on 'private and confidential' documents, e.g. the contents of the document should not be discussed publicly so unauthorised people can hear. Confidential information is information that has great value, is considered to be of a private nature and is only permitted to be seen by designated people within an organisation. 'Confidential information' can embrace commercial secrets as well as general information, e.g. medical records. An organisation can be damaged if its privacy of information is not upheld and respected, which could result in the organisation being devalued.

There is no single Act of Parliament defining 'confidential information' or governing how it is protected, or setting out rights and obligations in respect of it. However, the law on 'confidential information' is currently undergoing radical change as a result of developing European and UK legislation and decisions of the courts. Place 'confidentiality' warnings on standard communications, e.g. faxes or emails, to make sure if an individual receives the information by accident they are notified of its 'confidential' nature.

'Private and confidential' documents also includes commercially sensitive information, which needs to be protected from being read by an organisation's competitors. If the content of a document covers personal information it must conform to the requirements of the Data Protection Act 1998.

Testing your knowledge

1. What are the different uses of memos, reports, minutes and letters?

2. What is meant by 'fully blocked'?

3. Why is it necessary to meet deadlines?

4. What type of document will always have a signature?

5. What forms can minutes take?

6. What is the sequence of content that can be presented in a report?

7. What do you understand by an 'appendix'?

8. What punctuation is used in a letter using 'open' punctuation?

9. What is meant by proofreading?

10. What types of amendments might be made to a draft?

11. Why is the source material filed as well as the completed document?

12. Why it is important to be able to locate the source material if requested?

13. What does 'confidential' mean in terms of text storage?

Skills

Make sure that you have organised your workstation so that your posture is fully supported when you are touch typing. Follow your organisation's policy for good ergonomic practice in the work environment. Place your keyboard so that your arms are parallel to your work surface and your elbows are close to your body.

Before starting work of the transcription of any piece of text using touch typing, make sure you are clear about:

- The purpose of the text
- The format of the text
- The deadlines within which the text needs to be completed

• ACTIVITY 9

Attend a meeting – this could be a team meeting at work, a social club meeting, a meeting at college – and take longhand notes of what is said OR obtain notes that need to be typed into text. Produce a short typed report from the notes. Time yourself inputting the text and count the number of words. Proofread the document and calculate the net words per minute.

Each of these aspects will inform the planning of the work you will need to do for either yourself or if you are typing the text from original source material. Organise your work around all the tasks that you have to complete so you finish the touch typing transcription of the text at the agreed time. Once you are clear about what has to be done, gather together all the resources you will require to complete the task.

• ACTIVITY 10

Write a report to your supervisor suggesting ways in which your current filing systems can be improved. Consider the best way to order the contents of the report.

When touch typing text from notes make sure you are fully up to date with the functions of your software so you can edit the text effectively and efficiently. Chat to someone who is very confident in this area, or your supervisor / manager, to check that you are fully conversant with functionality of the technology you are using. This will not only save you time but make your text look more professional.

Make sure that you are clear about the style, layout and format that you wish, or the original author wishes, the text to take. Clarify all these components of your text.

• ACTIVITY 11

Select a number of texts that you have produced which you feel demonstrate your competence in using correct layout, spelling, punctuation and grammar. Share these with your supervisor / manager to get their feedback on the quality of your work.

Type up a draft document and check through this with the original author to make sure it meets all the requirements that they are aiming to achieve. Check through the document to make sure that it accurately presents information, that is, there are no spelling mistakes. Make sure your computer is set to the correct defaults and that grammar and punctuation have been used correctly.

Once you have checked the typed text, check with the original author to make sure that the aims of the typed text have been achieved. When working on the typing of text, if you are not sure, at any stage of its development, that the text is progressing along the right track, pause and reflect on what the text is aiming to achieve. Check with the original author - if it is not you. If anything changes with the development of the text check with the original author that they are happy with the change of direction that the text may have to take. Complete the final draft of the typed text and present this to the author of the original source material if it is not yourself.

Make sure the text has been referenced in line with your organisation's procedures. Then file it using whatever storage system your organisation uses.

Testing your skills

1. How do you make sure that spelling, punctuation and grammar have been used correctly?

2. How is the content of a business letter laid out?

3. How and when would you use the format menu?

4. If you were asked to emphasise a sentence in a report, how would you do it?

5. How do you proofread your own work?

6. When would you use printers' correction symbols?

7. What functions would you use to edit text, and why?

8. Why should you produce a final draft of your text?

9. Why is it important to raise any queries with the originator of the original source material before producing the draft?

10. How does your organisation reference text documents?

11. What system (s) of storing text documents does your organisation use?

Ready for assessment?

To achieve this Level 2 unit of a Business & Administration qualification, learners will need to demonstrate that they are able to perform the following activities:

1. Agreed the purpose, format and deadlines for typing of texts

2. Inputted texts using touch typing at a minimum speed of 40 wpm

3. Formatted texts to an agreed style and layout, making efficient use of available technology

4. Clarified text requirements, when necessary

5. Read and checked texts, as required

6. Edited and corrected texts, as required

7. Stored texts and the original notes safely and securely following organisational procedures

8. Presented texts in the required format within agreed deadlines

You will need to produce evidence from a variety of sources to support the performance requirements of this unit.

If you carry out the 'ACTIVITIES' and respond to the 'NEED TO KNOW' questions, these will provide some of the evidence required.

Links to other units

While gathering evidence for this unit, evidence **may** also be used from evidence generated from other units within the Business & Administration suite of units. Below is a **sample** of applicable units; however, most units within the Business & Administration suite of units will also be applicable.

QCF NVQ
Communications
Communicate in a business environment (Level 2)
Make and receive telephone calls
Use electronic message systems
Core business & administration
Manage own performance in a business environment (Level 2)
Improve own performance in a business environment (Level 2)
Work in a business environment (Level 2)
Work with other people in a business environment (Level 2)
Document production
Produce documents in a business environment
Prepare text from notes using touch typing (40 wpm)
Prepare text from shorthand (60 wpm)
Prepare text from recorded audio instruction (40 wpm)
Mange information and data
Store and retrieve information

SVQ
Communications
Prepare to communicate in a business environment
Make and receive telephone calls
Use electronic message systems
Core business & administration
Agree how to manage and improve own performance in a business environment
Undertake work in a business environment
Work with other people in a business environment
Document production
Produce documents in a business environment
Prepare text from notes using touch typing (40 wpm)
Prepare text from shorthand (60 wpm)
Prepare text from recorded audio instruction (40 wpm)
Mange information and data
Store and retrieve information

18

Prepare text from shorthand (60 wpm)

TEXT FROM SHORTHAND (60 WPM)

'**Prepare text from shorthand (60 wpm)**' is an <u>optional unit</u> which may be chosen as one of a combination of units to achieve either a Qualifications and Credit Framework (QCF), National Vocational Qualification (NVQ) or Scottish Vocational Qualification (SVQ).

The aims of this unit are to:

- Understand the task of preparing text from shorthand

- Understand the purpose and value of following procedures when preparing text from shorthand

- Be able to prepare for tasks and use shorthand to take dictation

- Be able to produce texts from shorthand

To achieve the above aims of this unit, learners will be expected to provide evidence through the performance of work-based activities.

Knowledge
Prepare text from shorthand
Shorthand is a system of taking notes of the spoken word quickly and efficiently using handwriting, using different symbols for the sound of words. There are different systems of shorthand which use a variety of techniques, including simplifying existing letters or characters and using special symbols to represent phonemes, the sound units of a word, words and phrases of words.

Stenography alphabet

	A	B	C	D	E	F	G	H	I	J	K	L	M	N	O	P	Q	R	S	T	U	V	W	X	Y	Z
Antiquity																										
M.Ages																										
J.Willis																										
Mason																										
Macaulay																										
Byrom																										
Nash																										
Cossard																										
Roe																										
Fayet																										
Taylor																										
Pitman																										
Gabelsberger																										

Two of the most popular shorthand systems include:

Pitman Shorthand
Devised by Sir Isaac Pitman, 1813 -1897, it was first published in 1837. Since then it has been improved upon and adapted for 15 different languages. The notable features of the Pitman system are:

- **It is phonetic** - It records the sounds of speech rather than the spelling, e.g. the sound F in 'form', 'elephant' and 'rough' is written the same for each word

- **Vowel sounds are optional** - They are written with small dots, dashes or other shapes next to the main strokes, which helps to increase writing speed because most words can be identified from their consonants only

- The thickness, length and position of strokes are all significant

- **There are many special abbreviations** - And other tricks to increase writing speed

The record speed for Pitman shorthand is 350 wpm, tested in 1922.

Gregg Shorthand
Invented by John Robert Gregg, 1867-1948, it was first published in 1888. Since then many different versions have appeared. Gregg's shorthand is still used in the USA. Some of the notable features of the Gregg system are:

- It is phonetic, as with Pitman

- Vowels are written as 'hooks'

- Consonants are written as 'circles'

• ACTIVITY 1

Ask a colleague to read a document containing at least 600 words to you at dictation speed; this should take no more than 10 minutes. Take notes in shorthand. Type the document from the notes. Proofread the typed version against the original shorthand notes.

When taking shorthand notes make sure that the workstation being worked from has been modified to the ergonomic requirements of the user. The shorthand notebook should be held in a convenient position, e.g. on a lap or on a desk. Have a sharp pencil to use to take shorthand notes, and spares. Listen very carefully to what is being said. If a word is missed or not fully understood, ask for clarification immediately. If someone is dictating too quickly, particularly if they are a person new to dictation, ask them to slow down a little until you are used to their delivery. It is better to clarify this as the dictation goes along rather than to wait until the end of the dictation session. Building a rapport with the person giving dictation makes it easier to understand what they mean and enables you to record it efficiently.

Different types of documents that can be produced from notes
Different types of organisations working in many different sectors will have the need to produce text from notes. These will include emails, memos, letters, reports and minutes of meetings. Notes will have been produced from a variety of sources, e.g. shorthand, audio recordings.

Many text documents will be prepared from handwritten notes which can be made by an author who will:

- **Prepare the text -** This should be relatively easy to transcribe as the person preparing the text is translating handwritten notes which they have made, so legibility and shortcuts should not be a problem

- **Not prepare the text -** This may be a little more difficult to transcribe as the person preparing the text is not translating their own handwritten notes. They may not understand the handwriting or the shortcuts that the author has made. If this occurs, the person transcribing the text should clarify from the author any script that is not legible

Before preparing the transcription of any notes into text make sure that the purpose, format and deadline of the text has been agreed. A deadline is when a document is due by a certain time, in a certain format and containing the required information. It is important that all parties involved in the production of text are all agreed on what the finished product will look like and when it can be expected. Before starting to produce any text from notes, include resources that will be needed to complete the text, e.g. the addition of images or diagrams. The text should be clear. If a document is not delivered against these requirements it will appear unprofessional, particularly if lateness has not been discussed with the recipient, and this could lead to loss of business. Having an agreed deadline will help to plan and prioritise tasks / activities.

• ACTIVITY 2

Choose a piece of text that contains at least 1,000 words. Switch off the spell check function on the computer. Type the text for 10 minutes. Calculate the typing speed using the following method:

- Count the total number of characters typed, including spaces.
- Divide the answer by 5 - the average length of a word.
- This gives the gross number of words typed.
- Divide the answer by 10 - 10 minutes spent typing - to give the gross number of words per minute (wpm).
- Count the number of mistyped words.
- Deduct the number of mistyped words from the gross wpm.
- This gives the net wpm.
- If the computer has a word count facility, make sure that the 'characters with spaces' figure is used.

Whatever source material is going to be used, documents will be produced from the following formats:

Memos

These are used for internal communication within an organisation. They may vary in the level of formality in which they are written. They:

- May be addressed to more than one recipient
- Will usually not include addresses
- Will have a subject line, similar to emails
- Will state the date, name of the recipient (s), the name of the sender and the content
- May have the recipient and sender's job titles and departments
- Will usually be produced on a template which reflects the organisation's 'house style'
- Most organisations still use memos for important internal messages, if they have not been replaced by the use of emails.

MEMORANDUM

To: All selling staff

From: Sales Manager

Date: 27th August 2010

Subject: Sales targets

Last week saw total sales of £127,436, an increase of 3.1% on last year. This week we have a challenging target of £148,000, or 3.7% on last year. This will require 100% effort from all of us, but I am confident we can do it.

REMEMBER: PROMOTE DISPOSABLE BARBECUES.

Business letters

These are usually printed on paper headed with the organisation's address and business details. There is a recognised format to letter writing; however, an organisation may choose to adopt its own 'house style'. Letters will normally:

- Be **addressed to one person** - e.g. 'Dear Sir' or 'Dear Madam'

- Be dated

- Contain a **salutation** - e.g. 'Dear ...'

- Have a reference number / title / heading - These are optional

- Contain the body of text for writing the letter

- End with a **closing statement** that summarises the main points for writing the letter

- Include a **compliment** - e.g. 'Yours sincerely'

- Include a **signature**

Business letters are usually produced:

- **Fully blocked** - All parts of the document start at the left-hand margin

- **With open punctuation** - Punctuation used only in the body of the letter, where it is essential for grammatical accuracy and understanding

Matthew and Son Builders
Allington Place
West Billington
WW1 1AD
Tel: 01632 566854

Our ref: GM / RA / 124
Your ref: VH / AK

13 August 2010

Mr V Harmison
Oval Walk
West Billington
WW2 1AX

Dear Mr Harmison

Thank you for your letter dated 6th August 2010 accepting our quotation to extend your office building.

The work will commence on 6th September 2010 and will be completed within 6 working weeks.

If you have any queries, please do not hesitate to contact me.

Yours sincerely

Graham Matthew
Director

A letter addressed to Mrs Jayne Wilcox, 12 Manvers Street, London SW19 7ER can be sent using the following salutations and complimentary phrases:

SALUTATION	Dear Jayne	Dear Mrs Wilcox	Dear Madam
COMPLIMENT	Kind regards	Yours sincerely	Yours faithfully

If someone knows Jayne Wilcox well they will probably use Jayne. If a sender does not know Jayne well they may feel more comfortable addressing her as Mrs Wilcox. If they do not know Mrs Wilcox at all, they will probably usually the formal term 'Madam'. As the salutation becomes more formal so does the complimentary close.

With the advent of electronic means of communication the number of letters written and received by organisations has declined. Letters will probably be written if there is no access to an email address on an organisation's website, for legal reasons or the sender may want a formal record of the communication.

• ACTIVITY 3

What is the difference between a 'salutation' and a 'compliment'?

Reports

These are produced in response to a request for information. They may be formal or informal, depending on the audience they are being written for. For example, a report written to a Board of an organisation will generally be more formal than a report to the members of a club. A report is written to inform the reader of facts about a subject. The depth of information contained in a report will depend on the purpose of the report and its intended audience. All reports will follow a similar structure, however detailed they may be:

- **Front page** - This contains the title of the report, the name of the author and the date

- **Contents** - This will list all the subjects covered in the report

- **Executive summary** - This gives a brief outline of the report

- **Background information** - This gives the reasons why the report was produced

- **Methodology** - This outlines the methods used to produce the data in the report, e.g. surveys, questionnaires

- **Findings** - These are the results of the methods used to explore the purpose of the report. Findings may be presented by:

  - Importance: where the central ideas are presented

  - Chronology: where ideas are presented in the order of events, starting either with the latest or the first

  - Sequence: where one idea follows from another

  - Comparison: where two ideas are compared in alternate paragraphs

- **Conclusion** - This outlines the conclusions that can be drawn from the findings of the research

- **Recommendations** - This outlines the actions that are recommended to be taken as a result of the conclusion

- **Acknowledgements** - This records the contribution others have made to the report

- **Bibliography** - This outlines the source material used in the research. There are a number of different ways that a bibliography can be drawn up

- **Appendices** - This sets out all the information referred to in the report which is too detailed to be given in full without distracting from the purpose of the report

Minutes

These are a record of the discussions and agreed actions that will need to be followed up as a result of a meeting. Minutes can be recorded in a number of different forms:

- **Verbatim** - Where everything is recorded word for word

- **Narrative** - Where a summary of the meeting is recorded. Formal resolutions will be recorded verbatim

- **Resolution** - Where a motion which has been voted on and passed gives details of the proposer and seconder of the motion, with a verbatim recording of the resolution

- **Action** - Where only the action and the name of the person or persons responsible for carrying out the action are recorded

• ACTIVITY 4

Someone working in an estate agent's office has left a note for you to type up the following information.

A new house has just come onto the market can you type the details? 112 Bestonic Street semi situated in a pop. and est. res. location convenient for local schools and shops and town centre, vestibule, entrance hall, lounge, dining room, three bedrooms CH gas garage, upvc DG throughout fully fitted kitchen cloakroom on ground family bath on 1st gardens front and rear.

Lounge 8.1x3.48

Dining room 4.72x4.22

Kitchen 2.39x4.5

Bed 1 3.12x4.62

Bed 2 3.61x2.95

Bed 3 3.42x4.56

Make sure you point out that the house has a large, well looked after garden, is in council tax band B and the photo is to follow.

Accuracy of text prepared from notes

Any piece of text produced from notes should be a quality piece of work. It should be executed with the correct spelling, the use of grammatical rules and the correct application of punctuation to produce a product that both gives a good impression of the organisation and, more importantly, conveys the intended message of the text.

Spelling

A computer will automatically check the spelling of words and highlight them in the document being worked on. However, spell check cannot:

*   Differentiate between American and English spelling of words, so make sure that the spell check default is aligned to the correct country

• ACTIVITY 5

Circle the correct spelling in the following list of words:

Adjoin	adjoin	adjoine
Purtain	pertain	purrtain
Arange	arrang	arrange
Pleasure	pleajure	pleasur
Decieve	deceive	deseive
Plackate	playcate	placate
Shean	sheen	shein
Posible	possible	possable
Lovelly	lovly	lovely
Burial	buriel	burrial

- Differentiate between words that are spelled correctly but used incorrectly, e.g. using 'through' when it should be 'threw'. Some of the most commonly confused words are:

    - We are pleased to accept your donation - Everyone made a donation except Mr Jones

    - Never listen to advice from your parents - I would advise you always to listen to your parents

    - The increase in interest rates will affect everyone - The effect of the increase was felt by everyone

    - She thought she was eligible for a grant - The letter she received was illegible

    - You must ensure that your car is insured

    - Lowestoft is farther east than Birmingham - I need further information on the location of Hull

    - There are fewer days in February than in June - It is less likely to rain today than it was yesterday

    - My personal opinion is that it will rain today - The HR Department deals with personnel

    - I visited the local doctors' practice this morning - I need to practise my spelling more often

    - The principal cause of heart disease is overeating - The minister resigned over a matter of principle

- The traffic on the M6 was <u>stationary</u> for two hours - We need to order some more <u>stationery</u> this week

- This week's sales were better <u>than</u> last week's - We will look at this week's plan, <u>then</u> next week's

- The girls picked up <u>their</u> handbags - The boys will be over <u>there</u> tomorrow - <u>They're</u> planning to visit next week

Grammar

Grammar can loosely be defined at the 'rules of language'. However, in English, the 'rules' are not consistent, which makes it complicated to learn and apply. Grammar is important to make sure that the intended meaning of a sentence is communicated to the recipients of the communication. For example, 'Use both lanes when turning right' actually requires drivers to straddle the two lanes, which is a highly dangerous manoeuvre to carry out. The correct sentence construction should be: 'Use either lane when turning right'. There are five parts of speech which are commonly used:

- **Nouns -** These are the names of a person, place or thing, e.g. 'book', 'television', 'Sunday', 'Norfolk'

- **Pronouns -** These are used instead of a noun, e.g. instead of saying 'John' in a paragraph that refers only to him, use 'he' or 'him'

- **Verbs -** These are words that express doing things, e.g. 'ran', 'run' or 'running'

- **Adverbs -** These words give information about how a verb was executed, e.g. 'he ran <u>quickly</u>' or 'he ran <u>fast</u>'. Note that while most adverbs will be formed by the addition of '-ly' to the end of a verb, it is not always the case, as can be seen by the second example in this paragraph

- **Adjectives -** These describe nouns, e.g. 'an <u>interesting</u> book', '<u>reality</u> television'

• ACTIVITY 6

What is the difference between a 'noun' and a 'pronoun'?

Sentences are formed by linking parts of speech together. Simple sentences contain a subject and a verb, e.g. 'I am', where 'I' is the subject and 'am' is the verb. More complicated sentences will have a subject, verb and object, e.g. 'I am going to London', where the object of the sentence is London. Sentences must start with a capital letter and end with some form of punctuation, e.g. a full stop, question mark. Capital letters are also used to indicate **proper names**, e.g. America, Anthony; **titles**, e.g. Mr, Mrs, Lord; **days of the week or months of the year** and **acronyms** (RAF, CIA, FBI, MI5, RAC).

A paragraph is formed by linking two or more sentences together. If the subject of a paragraph changes, it is advisable to start a new paragraph.

• ACTIVITY 7

Proofread and correct the following and produce a corrected version. Switch off the spell check function on the computer.

Our ref: DT / GY / 1256

Mr G Willims
Apart 21
The shore
Manchster
M6 7yu

23.06.023

Dear nr Williams

Account number 45678956 -Flat 24 tge maltings, Manchester

Thankyou for you're recent enqiry regarding your mortgage, and the interst rates available to you. I am enclosing a quotition showing what yur new payments would be at a new rate of interst. Yhjis has been calculated on and Interest only Basis.

At the moment you're monthly payments is ^189.23 vased ib a rate if 6.75%. Should you decide to except our offer (details) attached, your new repayments would be approx $206.93. The admin fee of £120.00 gas veeb added ti tyour balance for quotation's pyrposes only.

This offer is valid for 14 day's from the date of the enclosed quotation. you should of receved further details yesterday.

Transferring yourmortgage onto the new rate couldnt be easier, Simply return the Deed of Variation enclosed, signed by all partied to the mortgage.

We will charge you the aministration fee of £120.00. This sum can be added to the loan or may be paid by check if you wish.

If you have any questions, plesse contact me on 02356 56998 Monday to Friday between 9.00pm and 5.00pm.

Yours faithfyully

W Gaines
Consultant Mortgage Provider

Punctuation

As with grammar, the correct use of punctuation will make it easier for people to understand the content of a piece of communication. For example, if someone said 'Fred, the dog is ill', they would be telling someone called Fred that the dog is unwell. If they said 'Fred the dog is ill', they would be telling someone that the dog called Fred is unwell. Three of the most common punctuation marks in use are:

- **Full stops** - These are used to mark the end of a sentence or after abbreviations

- **Commas** - These are used to separate words in a list or phrases in a sentence, or to make sentences easier to read

- **Apostrophes** - There are two uses of the apostrophe: to replace a missing letter, e.g. 'I'm, he's, don't' or to indicate something belongs to someone, the possessive case, e.g. 'Jim's book, Pauline's shoes, women's clothing, babies' bottles'

Whatever text is produced, it is important that it is checked for accuracy before being distributed.

Formatting the text

At any stage during the production of text, formatting will be necessary. This can be as simple as changing the type of font used in the text to using text effects, e.g. 'strikethrough'.

It is possible to format:

- **Characters** - By selecting 'font' it allows the following functions to be carried out: style, colour and size of letters, **embolden**, *italicise*, underline, change the s p a c i n g

- **Paragraphs** - Align text using the 'centre' or 'justify' options, or by selecting 'bullets and numbering' add bullet points or numbers. Other amendments can be made by selecting 'borders and shading', or by altering the line spacing, tabs and indent

- **Pages** - Changes can be made to the 'size', 'orientation' and 'margins' of pages. 'Page numbers' can be inserted as well as 'headers and footers' or the 'date and time'. 'Insert page breaks' can be made to indicate where a new page should begin, or 'columns' can divide the page vertically

- **Sections -** It is not necessary for the whole text to be in the same format. Different sections of text can use different formats

If part of the text is formatted in a certain way and this style is to be used later in the text, select 'styles and formatting' and the software will show what has been used previously in the document. This will help to give consistency to the design of the text.

Checking and editing text

As identified previously, text from notes can be accomplished in two ways. If the transcription of notes is being undertaken on behalf of someone else who has made the notes, check with them to clarify any meanings or phrases which are not clear. Make sure the correct interpretation of words and phrases is agreed as early on in the process as possible, so to minimise the amount of changes that have to be made to a document. To help with the process of transcribing the notes, produce a 'draft' copy, so that the originator can check what has been produced matches with what was intended. Make sure that the draft is free from errors.

Most word processing packages contain spell checking and grammar checking facilities. Use these first to correct the obvious errors, but do not rely on them entirely. Check to make sure that the spell check default is not using American spelling and grammar, as the document will accept 'color' and reject 'colour' etc. When the automatic checking is complete, read the document carefully to look for missed errors, and also for correct use of paragraphs, headings and subheadings, style and formatting. Be particularly careful to proofread numbers, dates, times and amounts. Check for errors between similar words, such as 'affect' and 'effect' or 'less' and 'fewer'.

Look for errors of context and content. The draft text will be returned by the originator indicating where any changes need to be made to the document. Changes may come about as a result of:

- Input errors
- Errors in the source material
- Amendments to the content

Changes may have been agreed not necessarily because of poor transcription skills but because the originator of the notes wants to make changes to the document to improve the tone and meaning.

A computer provides a lot of functions that allow text to be easily edited:

- **Delete -** Ctrl+delete - This allows a single letter, group of letters or whole parts of a document to be deleted

- **Paste -** Ctrl+v - This is used in combination with either the 'cut' or 'copy', see below, instruction. Paste will add the last data selected to the document 'copied' or stored on the 'clipboard', which will provide other recently 'copied' information

- **Cut -** Ctrl+x - This is used to highlight a piece of text and remove it from the document. It can then be 'pasted', see above, to another part of the document or a new document

- **Copy -** Ctrl+c - This is used to highlight a piece of text and copied. It can then be 'pasted', see above, to another part of the document or a new document

- **Find and replace -** Ctrl+f - This function is used to change all the examples of a particular word to another word, e.g. replace the word 'company' with the word 'organisation', there is no need to retype every example, use 'find' and / or 'replace' to make all the changes

- **Inserting special characters and symbols -** This function enables the use of other alphabets, e.g. Arabic ش،ءةكق, and other signs / symbols, e.g. o, û, ©, %

- **Mail merge -** This function is useful if the same letter is going to several recipients, as it can change the name and address of each recipient

- **Track changes -** This function allows the originator of a document to share it with other colleagues, inviting them to make changes which can be tracked by name and highlighted

At any stage during the transcription of text from notes the format of the text can be changed. There are various options available in the format menu, e.g. font, which allows the font to be changed to different styles, sizes, colour etc. It is possible to format characters, pages or whole sections of a document. A part of the text can be formatted and used again later in the document by selecting 'styles and formatting', and the software will show what formatting has been used previously in the text.

If text is being produced which will have more than one page, it is advisable to use a 'header and footer', with required information and / or 'page numbers'. Using both functions will allow the title to be put onto each page with a page number. It is also possible to 'number paragraphs' and include an 'index' or 'table of contents' to help the reader find their way around the text.

• ACTIVITY 8

Correct the following piece of text:

Minutes of sales and marketing team held on 20th August 2010, Imperial Hotel, Russell Sq, London WC1, 9.30

Present

John Towers - Chair
Peter Benson
Jill Harper
Steve Lilley
Keith Barnett
Michael Hope
Terry Johnson

Apologies were received from:
Michelle Peterson
Andrew Carr

minutes of the last meeting were approved

None matters arising.

It was suggested that a farther meeting be held in sept to agree the final steppes of th sales plan for the new year. All 7 present agreed.

Christmas is fast approaching and it will be very busy. As Peter will be leave it will effect the way the team will work.

New stationary to be ordered for the team.

Next meeting on Tues, 24 Sept 2010.

Having made all the requested alterations, produce a final draft and pass that to the originator. Hopefully there will be no further amendments at this stage. Once this has been signed off it can be printed to the quality standard requested, not forgetting that a copy of the text should be stored in the appropriate storage system.

Storing text
Every piece of text will probably need to be stored in some way. This can be done using a manual paper-based system, an electronic-based system or both. A computer will have its own in-built sorting and storing

mechanisms. Text should be stored accurately in the approved locations so anyone can find it quickly and easily. Folders should be used that can be held within the main directory of the computer system. Folders should be used to group files together to speed up their retrieval. Paper copies will be stored manually using one of the following methods:

- **Alphabetical** - Information is stored in order, from A-Z. Files starting with the same letter are filed in order of the second letter: Aa, Ab, Ac etc. People's names are filed by their surnames, and if more than one has the same surname, by their first names. Names starting with 'The' are filed by ignoring the 'The'. Names beginning with 'Mac' or 'Mc' come before 'Ma', 'Mb' etc.

- **Numerical** - Information is coded using a numbering system, e.g. purchase orders, invoices

- **Alpha-numerical** - Information is stored using a combination of letters and numbers, e.g. National Insurance numbers. Usually large databases hold this type of coded information, as they hold more information than numerical systems and are more flexible than alphabetical systems. The order of filing depends on the sequence of the file name. If file names start with letters followed by numbers, they are filed in alphabetical order first and numerical order within each letter

- **Chronological** - This is often used within one of the other methods, e.g. customers' records are filed alphabetically, but the information within the file is stored chronologically, usually with the latest at the front. This provides a history of all activities undertaken for a particular file of information. It can also be based on dates of birth or start dates

- **Geographical** - This is a method of sorting by areas, e.g. North West England, East Anglia or counties, towns, cities

- **By subject or category** - Some organisations need to sort their filing under topics rather than names, e.g. a shoe manufacturer may keep files under product names such as Ladies, Gentlemen and Children

• ACTIVITY 9

What methods can be used to store texts?

The original source material from which the text has been produced will also need to be filed and stored if it needs to be referred to at a later date. An organisation may have its own system of referencing documents which should be followed. If using a system to reference documents, make sure that the original source material is referenced with the same reference number as the completed text. The source material should be stored in a logical manner:

- Handwritten notes can be attached to the file copy of the completed document

- Shorthand notebooks should be stored chronologically, with the start and end date written on the front

- Audio tapes should be stored chronologically and labelled with the date

If the document being created is 'private and confidential', make sure it is identified as such and follows the organisation's policy on 'private and confidential' documents, e.g. the contents of the document should not be discussed publicly so unauthorised people can hear. Confidential information is information that has great value, is considered to be of a private nature and is only permitted to be seen by designated people within an organisation. 'Confidential information' can embrace commercial secrets as well as general information, e.g. medical records. An organisation can be damaged if its privacy of information is not upheld and respected, which could result in the organisation being devalued.

There is no single Act of Parliament defining 'confidential information' or governing how it is protected, or setting out rights and obligations in respect of it. However, the law on 'confidential information' is currently undergoing radical change as a result of developing European and UK legislation and decisions of the courts. Place 'confidentiality' warnings on standard communications, e.g. faxes or emails, to make sure if an individual receives the information by accident they are notified of its 'confidential' nature.

'Private and confidential' documents also includes commercially sensitive information, which needs to be protected from being read by an organisation's competitors. If the content of a document covers personal information it must conform to the requirements of the Data Protection Act 1998.

Testing your knowledge

1. What are the different uses of memos, reports, minutes and letters?

2. What is meant by 'fully blocked'?

3. Why is it necessary to meet deadlines?

4. What type of document will always have a signature?

5. What forms can minutes take?

6. What is the sequence of content that can be presented in a report?

7. What do you understand by an 'appendix'?

8. What punctuation is used in a letter using 'open' punctuation?

9. What is meant by proofreading?

10. What types of amendments might be made to a draft?

11. Why is the source material filed as well as the completed document?

12. Why it is important to be able to locate the source material if requested?

13. What does 'confidential' mean in terms of text storage?

Skills

Before starting work on the transcription of any piece of text from shorthand notes, make sure you are clear about:

- The purpose of the text
- The format of the text
- The deadlines within which the text needs to be completed

• ACTIVITY 10

Attend a meeting - this could be a team meeting at work, a social club meeting, a meeting at college - and take longhand notes of what is said OR obtain notes that need to be transcribed into text. Produce a short typed report from the notes. Time yourself inputting the text and count the number of words. Proofread the document and calculate the net words per minute.

Each of these aspects of preparing to transcribe a piece of text will inform the planning of the work you will need to do for either yourself or if you are producing the text from original source material. Organise your work around all the tasks that you have to complete so you finish the transcription of the text at the agreed time. Once you are clear about what has to be done, gather together all the resources you will require to complete the task.

• ACTIVITY 11

Write a report to your supervisor suggesting ways in which your current filing systems can be improved. Consider the best way to order the contents of the report.

When transcribing text from shorthand notes make sure you are fully up to date with the functions of your software so you can edit the text effectively and efficiently. Chat to someone who is very confident in this area, or your supervisor / manager, to check that you are fully conversant with functionality of the technology you are using. This will not only save you time but make your text look more professional.

Make sure that you are clear about the style, layout and format that you wish, or the original author wishes, the text to take. Clarify all these components of your text.

• ACTIVITY 12

Select a number of texts that you have produced which you feel demonstrate your competence in using correct layout, spelling, punctuation and grammar. Share these with your supervisor / manager to get their feedback on the quality of your work.

Produce a draft document and check through this with the original author to make sure it meets all the requirements that they are aiming to achieve. Check through the document to make sure that it accurately presents information, that is, there are no spelling mistakes. Make sure your computer is set to the correct defaults and that grammar and punctuation have been used correctly.

Once you have checked the text, check the aims of the text with the original author, to make sure that they have been achieved. When working on the production of the text, if you are not sure, at any stage of its development, that the text is progressing along the right track, pause and reflect on what the text is aiming to achieve. Check with the original author - if it is not you. If anything changes with the development of the text check with the original author that they are happy with the change of direction that the text may have to take. Complete the final draft of the text and present this to the author of the original source material if it is not yourself.

Make sure the text has been referenced in line with your organisation's procedures. Then file it using whatever storage system your organisation uses.

Testing your skills

1. How do you make sure that spelling, punctuation and grammar has been used correctly?

2. How is the content of a business letter laid out?

3. How and when would you use the format menu?

4. If you were asked to emphasise a sentence in a report how would you do it?

5. How do you proofread your own work?

6. When would you use printers' correction symbols?

7. What functions would you use to edit text, and why?

8. Why should you produce a final draft of your text?

9. Why is it important to raise any queries with the originator of the original source material before producing the draft?

10. How does your organisation reference text documents?

11. What system (s) of storing text documents does your organisation use?

Ready for assessment?

To achieve this Level 2 unit of a Business & Administration qualification, learners will need to demonstrate that they are able to perform the following activities:

1. Agreed the purpose, format and deadlines for preparing text from shorthand

2. Took dictation using shorthand at a minimum speed of 60 wpm

3. Clarified text requirements, when necessary

4. Inputted and formatted texts to an agreed format from shorthand notes

5. Made efficient use of technology, as required

6. Read and checked texts for accuracy

7. Edited and corrected the text, as required

8. Stored texts and original shorthand notes safely and securely following organisational procedures

9. Presented texts to the required format and within the agreed deadlines

You will need to produce evidence from a variety of sources to support the performance requirements of this unit.

If you carry out the 'ACTIVITIES' and respond to the 'NEED TO KNOW' questions, these will provide some of the evidence required.

Links to other units

While gathering evidence for this unit, evidence **may** also be used from evidence generated from other units within the Business & Administration suite of units. Below is a **sample** of applicable units; however, most units within the Business & Administration suite of units will also be applicable.

QCF NVQ
Communications
Communicate in a business environment (Level 2)
Make and receive telephone calls
Use electronic message systems
Core business & administration
Manage own performance in a business environment (Level 2)
Improve own performance in a business environment (Level 2)
Work in a business environment (Level 2)
Work with other people in a business environment (Level 2)
Customer service
Handle mail
Document production
Produce documents in a business environment
Prepare text from notes using touch typing (40 wpm)
Prepare text from shorthand (60 wpm)
Prepare text from recorded audio instruction (40 wpm)
Mange information and data
Store and retrieve information

SVQ
Communications
Prepare to communicate in a business environment
Make and receive telephone calls
Use electronic message systems
Core business & administration
Agree how to manage and improve own performance in a business environment
Undertake work in a business environment
Work with other people in a business environment
Customer service
Handle mail
Document production
Produce documents in a business environment
Prepare text from notes using touch typing (40 wpm)
Prepare text from shorthand (60 wpm)
Prepare text from recorded audio instruction (40 wpm)
Mange information and data
Store and retrieve information

19 Prepare text from recorded audio instruction (40 wpm)

PREPARE TEXT FROM RECORDED AUDIO INSTRUCTION (40 WPM)

'**Prepare text from recorded audio instruction (40 wpm)**' is an optional unit which may be chosen as one of a combination of units to achieve either a Qualifications and Credit Framework (QCF), National Vocational Qualification (NVQ) or Scottish Vocational Qualification (SVQ).

The aims of this unit are to:

*   Understand the task of preparing text from recorded audio instruction

*   Understand the purpose and value of following procedures when preparing text from recorded audio instruction

*   Be able to produce texts from audio recordings

To achieve the above aims of this unit, learners will be expected to provide evidence through the performance of work-based activities.

Knowledge
Before starting to use the keyboard always make sure that the workstation is ergonomically prepared to meet the individual requirements of the keyboard user - sit up straight, feet flat on the floor, elbows close to the body, wrists straight and forearms parallel to the work surface. And remember to take regular breaks from typing.

The equipment and skills required to type up notes from a recorded audio machine includes:

*   **A computer** - And all its associated equipment

*   **A headset**

*   **A foot pedal** - Preferably the USB kind

*   Depending on the format used, e.g. DVD, mp3, cassette, microcassette, **additional equipment** may be required for audio playback

*   **A good typing speed** and **good listening skills**

Audio recordings are used greatly in the legal and medical profession, which may impose some compliance issues to content with, e.g. if creating a medical transcription, will HIPPA compliance issues be involved?

Some issues that need to be considered when typing from an audio recording:

- **Sound quality**
- **Multiple speakers**
- **Accents**
- **People talking over each other** and audience interaction, as this can slow down the transcription process causing frustration and reducing productivity
- Use of **'templates'** within organisations
- **Focus to exclude other functions**, e.g. no telephone calls or tweets
- If **'real-time' transcription** is required, the client will need to be available at the same time of transcription, which does not allow much time for editing or breaks
- **Verbatim transcription** or an edited version, deleting 'umms' and other unfinished thoughts

• ACTIVITY 1

Using any pre-recorded text, e.g. a talking book, type for 10 minutes. Ask a colleague to proofread your version against the recording. Count the number of words you have typed and calculate the net words per minute.

Different types of documents that can be produced from recorded audio instructions

Different types of organisations working in many different sectors will have the need to produce text from audio recordings. Many text documents will be prepared from audio recordings which can be made by a speaker(s) who will:

- **Prepare the text** - This should be relatively easy to transcribe as the person preparing the text is translating audio recordings which they have made, so the quality of the voice and vocal shortcuts should not be a problem to transcribe

- **Not prepare the text** - This may be a little more difficult to transcribe as the person preparing the text is not translating their own audio recording. They may not understand the vocal landscape or the vocal shortcuts of the audio recording. Clarify any vocal idiosyncrasies

Before preparing the transcription of any audio recording into text, make sure that the purpose, format and deadline of the text has been agreed. A deadline is when a document is due by a certain time, in a certain format and containing the required information. It is important that all parties involved in the production of text are all agreed on what the finished product will look like and when it can be expected. Before starting to produce any text from the audio recording, include resources that will be needed to complete the text, e.g. the addition of images or diagrams. The text should be clear. If a document is not delivered against these requirements it will appear unprofessional, particularly if lateness has not been discussed with the recipient, which could lead to loss of business. Having an agreed deadline will help to plan and prioritise tasks / activities.

Whatever source material is going to be used, documents will be produced from the following formats:

Memos

These are used for internal communication within an organisation. They may vary in the level of formality in which they are written. They:

- May be addressed to more than one recipient

- Will usually not include addresses

- Will have a subject line, similar to 'emails'

- Will state the date, name of the recipient (s), the name of the sender and the content

- May have the recipient and sender's job titles and departments

- Will usually be produced on a template which reflects the organisation's 'house style'

Most organisations still use memos for important internal messages, if they have not been replaced by the use of emails.

MEMORANDUM

To: All selling staff

From: Sales Manager

Date: 27th August 2010

Subject: Sales targets

Last week saw total sales of £127,436, an increase of 3.1% on last year. This week we have a challenging target of £148,000, or 3.7% on last year. This will require 100% effort from all of us, but I am confident we can do it.

REMEMBER: PROMOTE DISPOSABLE BARBECUES.

Business letters

These are usually printed on paper headed with the organisation's address and business details. There is a recognised format to letter writing; however, an organisation may choose to adopt its own 'house style'. Letters will normally:

- Be **addressed to one person** - e.g. 'Dear Sir' or 'Dear Madam'
- Be dated
- Contain a **salutation** - e.g. 'Dear ...'
- Have a reference number / title / heading - These are optional
- Contain the body of text for writing the letter
- End with a **closing statement** that summarises the main points for writing the letter
- Include a **compliment** - e.g. 'Yours sincerely'
- Include a **signature**

Business letters are usually produced:

- **Fully blocked -** All parts of the document start at the left-hand margin
- **With open punctuation -** Punctuation used only in the body of the letter, where it is essential for grammatical accuracy and understanding

Matthew and Son Builders
Allington Place
West Billington
WW1 1AD
Tel: 01632 566854

Our ref: GM / RA / 124
Your ref: VH / AK

13 August 2010

Mr V Harmison
Oval Walk
West Billington
WW2 1AX

Dear Mr Harmison

Thank you for your letter dated 6th August 2010 accepting our quotation to extend your office building.

The work will commence on 6th September 2010 and will be completed within 6 working weeks.

If you have any queries, please do not hesitate to contact me.

Yours sincerely

Graham Matthew
Director

A letter addressed to Mrs Jayne Wilcox, 12 Manvers Street, London SW19 7ER can be sent using the following salutations and complimentary phrases:

SALUTATION	Dear Jayne	Dear Mrs Wilcox	Dear Madam
COMPLIMENT	Kind regards	Yours sincerely	Yours faithfully

If someone knows Jayne Wilcox well they will probably use Jayne. If a sender does not know Jayne well they may feel more comfortable addressing her as Mrs Wilcox. If they do not know Mrs Wilcox at all, they will probably usually the formal term 'Madam'. As the salutation becomes more formal so does the complimentary close.

• ACTIVITY 2

What is the difference between a 'salutation' and a 'compliment'?

With the advent of electronic means of communication the number of letters written and received by organisations has declined. Letters will probably be written if there is no access to an email address on an organisation's website, for legal reasons or the sender may want a formal record of the communication.

Reports

These are produced in response to a request for information. They may be formal or informal, depending on the audience they are being written for. For example, a report written to a Board of an organisation will generally be more formal than a report to the members of a club. A report is written to inform the reader of facts about a subject. The depth of information contained in a report will depend on the purpose of the report and its intended audience. All reports will follow a similar structure, however detailed they may be:

- **Front page** - This contains the title of the report, the name of the author and the date

- **Contents** - This will list all the subjects covered in the report

- **Executive summary** - This gives a brief outline of the report

- **Background information** - This gives the reasons why the report was produced

- **Methodology** - This outlines the methods used to produce the data in the report, e.g. surveys, questionnaires

- **Findings** - These are the results of the methods used to explore the purpose of the report. Findings may be presented by:

  - Importance: where the central ideas are presented

  - Chronology: where ideas are presented in the order of events, starting either with the latest or the first

  - Sequence: where one idea follows from another

  - Comparison: where two ideas are compared in alternate paragraphs

- **Conclusion** - This outlines the conclusions that can be drawn from the findings of the research

- **Recommendations** - This outlines the actions that are recommended to be taken as a result of the conclusion

- **Acknowledgements** - This records the contribution others have made to the report

- **Bibliography** - This outlines the source material used in the research. There are a number of different ways that a bibliography can be drawn up

- **Appendices** - This sets out all the information referred to in the report which is too detailed to be given in full without distracting from the purpose of the report

Minutes

These are a record of the discussions and agreed actions that will need to be followed up as a result of a meeting. Minutes can be recorded in a number of different forms:

- **Verbatim** - Where everything is recorded word for word

- **Narrative** - Where a summary of the meeting is recorded. Formal resolutions will be recorded verbatim

- **Resolution** - Where a motion which has been voted on and passed gives details of the proposer and seconder of the motion, with a verbatim recording of the resolution

- **Action** - Where only the action and the name of the person or persons responsible for carrying out the action are recorded

• ACTIVITY 3

Someone working in an estate agent's office has left a note for you to type up the following information.

A new house has just come onto the market can you type the details? 112 Bestonic Street semi situated in a pop. and est. res. location convenient for local schools and shops and town centre, vestibule, entrance hall, lounge, dining room, three bedrooms CH gas garage, upvc DG throughout fully fitted kitchen cloakroom on ground family bath on 1st gardens front and rear.

Lounge 8.1x3.48

Dining room 4.72x4.22

Kitchen 2.39x4.5

Bed 1 3.12x4.62

Bed 2 3.61x2.95

Bed 3 3.42x4.56

Make sure you point out that the house has a large, well looked after garden, is in council tax band B and the photo is to follow.

Accuracy of text prepared from notes

Any piece of text produced from notes should be a quality piece of work. It should be executed with the correct spelling, the use of grammatical rules and the correct application of punctuation to produce a product that both gives a good impression of the organisation and, more importantly, conveys the intended message of the text.

Spelling

A computer will automatically check the spelling of words and highlight them in the document being worked on. However, spell check cannot:

- Differentiate between American and English spelling of words, so make sure that the spell check default is aligned to the correct country

• ACTIVITY 4

Circle the correct spelling in the following list of words:

Adjoin	adjoin	adjoine
Purtain	pertain	purrtain
Arange	arrang	arrange
Pleasure	pleajure	pleasur
Decieve	deceive	deseive
Plackate	playcate	placate
Shean	sheen	shein
Posible	possible	possable
Lovelly	lovly	lovely
Burial	buriel	burrial

- Differentiate between words that are spelled correctly but used incorrectly, e.g. using 'through' when it should be 'threw'. Some of the most commonly confused words are:

  - We are pleased to <u>accept</u> your donation - Everyone made a donation <u>except</u> Mr Jones

  - Never listen to <u>advice</u> from your parents - I would <u>advise</u> you always to listen to your parents

  - The increase in interest rates will <u>affect</u> everyone - The <u>effect</u> of the increase was felt by everyone

  - You must <u>ensure</u> that your car is <u>insured</u>

  - Lowestoft is <u>farther</u> east than Birmingham - I need <u>further</u> information on the location of Hull

  - There are <u>fewer</u> days in February than in June - It is <u>less</u> likely to rain today than it was yesterday

  - My <u>personal</u> opinion is that it will rain today - The HR Department deals with <u>personnel</u>

  - I visited the local doctors' <u>practice</u> this morning - I need to <u>practise</u> my spelling more often

  - The <u>principal</u> cause of heart disease is overeating - The minister resigned over a matter of <u>principle</u>

  - The traffic on the M6 was <u>stationary</u> for two hours - We need to order some more <u>stationery</u> this week

- This week's sales were better <u>than</u> last week's - We will look at this week's plan, <u>then</u> next week's
- The girls picked up <u>their</u> handbags - The boys will be over <u>there</u> tomorrow - <u>They're</u> planning to visit next week

Grammar

Grammar can loosely be defined at the 'rules of language'. However, in English, the 'rules' are not consistent, which makes it complicated to learn and apply. Grammar is important to make sure that the intended meaning of a sentence is communicated to the recipients of the communication. For example, 'Use both lanes when turning right' actually requires drivers to straddle the two lanes, which is a highly dangerous manoeuvre to carry out. The correct sentence construction should be: 'Use either lane when turning right'.

There are five parts of speech which are commonly used:

- **Nouns -** These are the names of a person, place or thing, e.g. 'book', 'television', 'Sunday', 'Norfolk'

- **Pronouns -** These are used instead of a noun, e.g. instead of saying 'John' in a paragraph that refers only to him, use 'he' or 'him'

- **Verbs -** These are words that express doing things, e.g. 'ran', 'run' or 'running'

- **Adverbs -** These words give information about how a verb was executed, e.g. 'he ran <u>quickly</u>' or 'he ran <u>fast</u>'. Note that while most adverbs will be formed by the addition of '-ly' to the end of a verb, it is not always the case, as can be seen by the second example in this paragraph

- **Adjectives -** These describe nouns, e.g. 'an <u>interesting</u> book', '<u>reality</u> television'

> **• ACTIVITY 5**
>
> What is the difference between a 'noun' and a 'pronoun'?

Sentences are formed by linking parts of speech together. Simple sentences contain a subject and a verb, e.g. 'I am', where 'I' is the subject and 'am' is the verb. More complicated sentences will have a subject, verb and object, e.g. 'I am going to London', where the object of the sentence is London. Sentences must start with a capital letter and end with some form of punctuation, e.g. a full stop, question mark. Capital letters are also used to indicate **proper names**, e.g. America, Anthony; **titles**, e.g. Mr, Mrs, Lord; **days of the week or months of the year** and **acronyms** (RAF, CIA, FBI, MI5, RAC).

A paragraph is formed by linking two or more sentences together. If the subject of a paragraph changes, it is advisable to start a new paragraph.

• ACTIVITY 6

Proofread and correct the following and produce a corrected version. Switch off the spell check function on the computer.

Our ref: DT / GY / 1256

Mr G Willims
Apart 21
The shore
Manchster
M6 7yu

23.06.023

Dear nr Williams

Account number 45678956 -Flat 24 tge maltings, Manchester

Thankyou for you're recent enqiry regarding your mortgage, and the interst rates available to you. I am enclosing a quotition showing what yur new payments would be at a new rate of interst. Yhjis has been calculated on and Interest only Basis.

At the moment you're monthly payments is ^189.23 vased ib a rate if 6.75%. Should you decide to except our offer (details) attached, your new repayments would be approx $206.93. The admin fee of £120.00 gas veeb added ti tyour balance for quotation's pyrposes only.

This offer is valid for 14 day's from the date of the enclosed quotation. you should of receved further details yesterday.

Transferring yourmortgage onto the new rate couldnt be easier, Simply return the Deed of Variation enclosed, signed by all partied to the mortgage.

We will charge you the aministration fee of £120.00. This sum can be added to the loan or may be paid by check if you wish.

If you have any questions, plesse contact me on 02356 56998 Monday to Friday between 9.00pm and 5.00pm.

Yours faithfyully

W Gaines
Consultant Mortgage Provider

Punctuation

As with grammar, the correct use of punctuation will make it easier for people to understand the content of a piece of communication. For example, if someone said 'Fred, the dog is ill', they would be telling someone called Fred that the dog is unwell. If they said 'Fred the dog is ill', they would be telling someone that the dog called Fred is unwell. Three of the most common punctuation marks in use are:

- **Full stops** - These are used to mark the end of a sentence or after abbreviations

- **Commas** - These are used to separate words in a list or phrases in a sentence, or to make sentences easier to read

- **Apostrophes** - There are two uses of the apostrophe: to replace a missing letter, e.g. 'I'm, he's, don't' or to indicate something belongs to someone, the possessive case, e.g. 'Jim's book, Pauline's shoes, women's clothing, babies' bottles'

Whatever text is produced, it is important that it is checked for accuracy before being distributed.

Formatting the text

At any stage during the production of text, formatting will be necessary. This can be as simple as changing the type of font used in the text to using text effects, e.g. 'strikethrough'.

It is possible to format:

- **Characters** - By selecting 'font' it allows the following functions to be carried out: style, colour and size of letters, **embolden**, *italicise*, <u>underline</u>, change the s p a c i n g

- **Paragraphs** - Align text using the 'centre' or 'justify' options, or by selecting 'bullets and numbering' add bullet points or numbers. Other amendments can be made by selecting 'borders and shading', or by altering the line spacing, tabs and indent

- **Pages** - Changes can be made to the 'size', 'orientation' and 'margins' of pages. 'Page numbers' can be inserted as well as 'headers and footers' or the 'date and time'. 'Insert page breaks' can be made to indicate where a new page should begin, or 'columns' can divide the page vertically

- **Sections -** It is not necessary for the whole text to be in the same format. Different sections of text can use different formats

If part of the text is formatted in a certain way and this style is to be used later in the text, select 'styles and formatting' and the software will show what has been used previously in the document. This will help to give consistency to the design of the text.

Checking and editing text

As identified previously, text from notes can be accomplished in two ways. If the transcription of notes is being undertaken on behalf of someone else who has made the notes, check with them to clarify any meanings or phrases which are not clear. Make sure the correct interpretation of words and phrases is agreed as early on in the process as possible, so to minimise the amount of changes that have to be made to a document. To help with the process of transcribing the notes, produce a 'draft' copy, so that the originator can check what has been produced matches with what was intended. Make sure that the draft is free from errors.

Most word processing packages contain spell checking and grammar checking facilities. Use these first to correct the obvious errors, but do not rely on them entirely. Check to make sure that the spell check default is not using American spelling and grammar, as the document will accept 'color' and reject 'colour' etc. When the automatic checking is complete, read the document carefully to look for missed errors, and also for correct use of paragraphs, headings and subheadings, style and formatting. Be particularly careful to proofread numbers, dates, times and amounts. Check for errors between similar words, such as 'affect' and 'effect' or 'less' and 'fewer'.

Look for errors of context and content. The draft text will be returned by the originator indicating where any changes need to be made to the document. Changes may come about as a result of:

- Input errors
- Errors in the source material
- Amendments to the content

Changes may have been agreed not necessarily because of poor transcription skills but because the originator of the notes wants to make changes to the document to improve the tone and meaning.

A computer provides a lot of functions that allow text to be easily edited:

- **Delete** - Ctrl+delete - This allows a single letter, group of letters or whole parts of a document to be deleted

- **Paste** - Ctrl+v - This is used in combination with either the 'cut' or 'copy', see below, instruction. Paste will add the last data selected to the document 'copied' or stored on the 'clipboard', which will provide other recently 'copied' information

- **Cut** - Ctrl+x - This is used to highlight a piece of text and remove it from the document. It can then be 'pasted', see above, to another part of the document or a new document

- **Copy** - Ctrl+c - This is used to highlight a piece of text and copied. It can then be 'pasted', see above, to another part of the document or a new document

- **Find and replace** - Ctrl+f - This function is used to change all the examples of a particular word to another word. For example, replace the word 'company' with the word 'organisation', there is no need to retype every example, use 'find' and / or 'replace' to make all the changes

- **Inserting special characters and symbols** - This function enables the use of other alphabets, e.g. Arabic شءةكق, and other signs / symbols, e.g. o, û, ©, %

- **Mail merge** - This function is useful if the same letter is going to several recipients, as it can change the name and address of each recipient

- **Track changes** - This function allows the originator of a document to share it with other colleagues, inviting them to make changes which can be tracked by name and highlighted

At any stage during the transcription of text from notes, the format of the text can be changed. There are various options available in the format menu, e.g. font, which allows the font to be changed to different styles, sizes, colour etc. It is possible to format characters, pages or whole sections of a document. A part of the text can be formatted and used again later in the document by selecting 'styles and formatting', and the software will show what formatting has been used previously in the text.

If text is being produced which will have more than one page, it is advisable to use a 'header and footer', with required information and / or 'page numbers'. Using both functions will allow the title to be put onto each page with a page number. It is also possible to 'number paragraphs' and include an 'index' or 'table of contents' to help the reader find their way around the text.

Having made all the requested alterations, produce a final draft and pass that to the originator. Hopefully there will be no further amendments at this stage. Once this has been signed off it can be printed to the quality standard requested, not forgetting that a copy of the text should be stored in the appropriate storage system.

• ACTIVITY 7

Correct the following piece of text:

Minutes of sales and marketing team held on 20th August 2010, Imperial Hotel, Russell Sq, London WC1, 9.30

Present

John Towers - Chair
Peter Benson
Jill Harper
Steve Lilley
Keith Barnett
Michael Hope
Terry Johnson

Apologies were received from:
Michelle Peterson
Andrew Carr

minutes of the last meeting were approved

None matters arising.

It was suggested that a farther meeting be held in sept to agree the final steppes of th sales plan for the new year. All 7 present agreed.

Christmas is fast approaching and it will be very busy. As Peter will be leave it will effect the way the team will work.

New stationary to be ordered for the team.

Next meeting on Tues, 24 Sept 2010.

Storing text

Every piece of text will probably need to be stored in some way. This can be done using a manual paper-based system, an electronic-based system or both. A computer will have its own in-built sorting and storing mechanisms. Text should be stored accurately in the approved locations so anyone can find it quickly and easily. Folders should be used that can be held within the main directory of the computer system. Folders should be used to group files together to speed up their retrieval. Paper copies will be stored manually using one of the following methods:

- **Alphabetical** - Information is stored in order, from A-Z. Files starting with the same letter are filed in order of the second letter: Aa, Ab, Ac etc. People's names are filed by their surnames, and if more than one has the same surname, by their first names. Names starting with 'The' are filed by ignoring the 'The'. Names beginning with 'Mac' or 'Mc' come before 'Ma', 'Mb' etc.

- **Numerical** - Information is coded using a numbering system, e.g. purchase orders, invoices

- **Alpha-numerical** - Information is stored using a combination of letters and numbers, e.g. National Insurance numbers. Usually large databases hold this type of coded information, as they hold more information than numerical systems and are more flexible than alphabetical systems. The order of filing depends on the sequence of the file name. If file names start with letters followed by numbers, they are filed in alphabetical order first and numerical order within each letter

- **Chronological** - This is often used within one of the other methods, e.g. customers' records are filed alphabetically, but the information within the file is stored chronologically, usually with the latest at the front. This provides a history of all activities undertaken for a particular file of information. It can also be based on dates of birth or start dates

- **Geographical** - This is a method of sorting by areas, e.g. North West England, East Anglia or counties, towns, cities

- **By subject or category** - Some organisations need to sort their filing under topics rather than names, e.g. a shoe manufacturer may keep files under product names such as Ladies, Gentlemen and Children

• ACTIVITY 8

What methods can be used to store texts?

The original source material from which the text has been produced will also need to be filed and stored if it needs to be referred to at a later date. An organisation may have its own system of referencing documents which should be followed. If using a system to reference documents, make sure that the original source material is referenced with the same reference number as the completed text. The source material should be stored in a logical manner:

- Handwritten notes can be attached to the file copy of the completed document

- Shorthand notebooks should be stored chronologically, with the start and end date written on the front

- Audio tapes should be stored chronologically and labelled with the date

If the document being created is 'private and confidential', make sure it is identified as such and follows the organisation's policy on 'private and confidential' documents, e.g. the contents of the document should not be discussed publicly so unauthorised people can hear. Confidential information is information that has great value, is considered to be of a private nature and is only permitted to be seen by designated people within an organisation. 'Confidential information' can embrace commercial secrets as well as general information, e.g. medical records. An organisation can be damaged if its privacy of information is not upheld and respected, which could result in the organisation being devalued.

There is no single Act of Parliament defining 'confidential information' or governing how it is protected, or setting out rights and obligations in respect of it. However, the law on 'confidential information' is currently undergoing radical change as a result of developing European and UK legislation and decisions of the courts. Place 'confidentiality' warnings on standard communications, e.g. faxes or emails, to make sure if an individual receives the information by accident they are notified of its 'confidential' nature.

'Private and confidential' documents also includes commercially sensitive information, which needs to be protected from being read by an organisation's competitors. If the content of a document covers personal information it must conform to the requirements of the Data Protection Act 1998.

Testing your knowledge

1. What are the different uses of memos, reports, minutes and letters?

2. What is meant by 'fully blocked'?

3. Why is it necessary to meet deadlines?

4. What type of document will always have a signature?

5. What forms can minutes take?

6. What is the sequence of content that can be presented in a report?

7. What do you understand by an 'appendix'?

8. What punctuation is used in a letter using 'open' punctuation?

9. What is meant by proofreading?

10. What types of amendments might be made to a draft?

11. Why is the source material filed as well as the completed document?

12. Why it is important to be able to locate the source material if requested?

13. What does 'confidential' mean in terms of text storage?

Skills
Before starting work on the transcription of any piece of text, make sure you are clear about:

- The purpose of the text

- The format of the text

- The deadlines within which the text needs to be completed

• ACTIVITY 9

Attend a meeting - this could be a team meeting at work, a social club meeting, a meeting at college - and take longhand notes of what is said OR obtain notes that need to be transcribed into text. Produce a short typed report from the notes. Time yourself inputting the text and count the number of words. Proofread the document and calculate the net words per minute.

Each of these aspects of preparing to transcribe a piece of text will inform the planning of the work you will need to do for either yourself or if you are producing the text from original source material. Organise your work around all the tasks that you have to complete so you finish the transcription of the text at the agreed time. Once you are clear about what has to be done, gather together all the resources you will require to complete the task.

• ACTIVITY 10

Write a report to your supervisor suggesting ways in which your current filing systems can be improved. Consider the best way to order the contents of the report.

When transcribing text from notes make sure you are fully up to date with the functions of your software so you can edit the text effectively and efficiently. Chat to someone who is very confident in this area, or your supervisor / manager, to check that you are fully conversant with functionality of the technology you are using. This will not only save you time but make your text look more professional.

Make sure that you are clear about the style, layout and format that you wish, or the original author wishes, the text to take. Clarify all these components of your text.

• ACTIVITY 11

Select a number of texts that you have produced which you feel demonstrate your competence in using correct layout, spelling, punctuation and grammar. Share these with your supervisor / manager to get their feedback on the quality of your work.

Produce a draft document and check through this with the original author to make sure it meets all the requirements that they are aiming to achieve. Check through the document to make sure that it accurately presents information, that is, there are no spelling mistakes. Make sure your computer is set to the correct defaults and that grammar and punctuation have been used correctly.

Once you have checked the text, check the aims of the text with the original author, to make sure that they have been achieved. When working on the production of the text, if you are not sure, at any stage of its development, that the text is progressing along the right track, pause and reflect on what the text is aiming to achieve. Check with the original author - if it is not you. If anything changes with the development of the text check with the original author that they are happy with the change of direction that the text may have to take. Complete the final draft of the text and present this to the author of the original source material if it is not yourself.

Make sure the text has been referenced in line with your organisation's procedures. Then file it using whatever storage system your organisation uses.

Testing your skills

1. How do you make sure that spelling, punctuation and grammar has been used correctly?

2. How is the content of a business letter laid out?

3. How and when would you use the format menu?

4. If you were asked to emphasise a sentence in a report how would you do it?

5. How do you proofread your own work?

6. When would you use printers' correction symbols?

7. What functions would you use to edit text, and why?

8. Why should you produce a final draft of your text?

9. Why is it important to raise any queries with the originator of the original source material before producing the draft?

10. How does your organisation reference text documents?

11. What system (s) of storing text documents does your organisation use?

Ready for assessment?

To achieve this Level 2 unit of a Business & Administration qualification, learners will need to demonstrate that they are able to perform the following activities:

1. Agreed the purpose, format and deadlines for the transcription

2. Inputted the text using keyboarding skills

3. Formatted the text, making efficient use of available technology

4. Checked content for accuracy

5. Edited and corrected the text

6. Clarified text requirements, when necessary

7. Stored the text and original notes safely and securely in approved locations

8. Presented the text in the required format within agreed deadlines

You will need to produce evidence from a variety of sources to support the performance requirements of this unit.

If you carry out the 'ACTIVITIES' and respond to the 'NEED TO KNOW' questions, these will provide some of the evidence required.

Links to other units
While gathering evidence for this unit, evidence **may** also be used from evidence generated from other units within the Business & Administration suite of units. Below is a **sample** of applicable units; however, most units within the Business & Administration suite of units will also be applicable.

QCF NVQ
Communications
Communicate in a business environment (Level 2)
Make and receive telephone calls
Use electronic message systems
Core business & administration
Manage own performance in a business environment (Level 2)
Improve own performance in a business environment (Level 2)
Work in a business environment (Level 2)
Work with other people in a business environment (Level 2)
Document production
Produce documents in a business environment
Prepare text from notes using touch typing (40 wpm)
Prepare text from shorthand (60 wpm)
Prepare text from recorded audio instruction (40 wpm)
Manage information and data
Store and retrieve information

SVQ
Communications
Prepare to communicate in a business environment
Make and receive telephone calls
Use electronic message systems
Core business & administration
Agree how to manage and improve own performance in a business environment
Undertake work in a business environment
Work with other people in a business environment
Document production
Produce documents in a business environment
Prepare text from notes using touch typing (40 wpm)
Prepare text from shorthand (60 wpm)
Prepare text from recorded audio instruction (40 wpm)
Manage information and data
Store and retrieve information

20 Support the organisation of an event

SUPPORT THE ORGANISATION OF AN EVENT

'**Support the organisation of an event**' is an <u>optional unit</u> which may be chosen as one of a combination of units to achieve either a Qualifications and Credit Framework (QCF), National Vocational Qualification (NVQ) or Scottish Vocational Qualification (SVQ).

The aims of this unit are to:

* Understand the role and purpose of providing support with the organisation of an event

* Be able to support the organisation of an event

To achieve the above aims of this unit, learners will be expected to provide evidence through the performance of work-based activities.

Knowledge
What is an event?

An event can be defined as a very large meeting which can be organised for a business, a social occasion or a combination of both. An event will be organised to bring together a group of people for a common purpose, usually to present new or re-formed information, at a specific time and location. Planning an event is time consuming and can be a stressful affair; it can also be costly to undertake. Events can be planned to take place for small or large groups of people. Events can be planned and organised by teams within an organisation or by 'event management' organisations who have specialised skills and knowledge to undertake this function. The event will be planned and organised to engage with its audience, its stakeholders, so they walk away buying in to what has been presented to them. As with meetings, events will focus on some form of change.

Events may be either:

- **Major** - A more complex combination of elements that will require detailed organisation. This will take many months to plan. This may also involve a number of different organisations
- **Minor** - Less complex than a major event and will have less elements to organise. This will take less time to plan. This will probably be limited to being offered by one organisation

Events will vary in:

- **Size** - This may refer to the physical size of the venue being used or to the number of delegates that will be invited to the event
- **Duration** - This may last one day or for more than a week, e.g. the Ideal Home Exhibition, which runs for nearly two weeks
- **Purpose**
- **Planning**
- **Cost**

The organisation of an event will vary from event to event, depending on the purpose of holding the event:

- **Conference** - Events arranged to last at least one day which will be based around a specific theme, e.g. an annual conference based on new policies that an organisation is about to launch
- **Exhibition** - Events arranged to display an organisation's products or services
- **Product launch** - Events arranged to launch a new product or service
- **Prize / award presentation** - Events arranged to award employees or customers with honours for their efforts on behalf of the organisation
- **Seminar** - Similar to conferences but smaller and of a shorter duration
- **Briefing session** - Events arranged to provide information to delegates on a topic
- **Party** - Events arranged to celebrate specific themes, e.g. a staff Christmas party
- **Development day** - Events arranged as part of a 'learning and

development' plan to gather employees together to share and discuss changes within the organisation

Whatever the size or purpose of the event it will require some degree of planning.

• ACTIVITY 1

Describe the different features events may have.

Planning an event

Most events will have an event planner or event organiser. They will be dedicated to organising a successful event. They will aim to organise all relevant resources to be in place and available for the delegates who will be invited to the event. The event planner may have a team to support the implementation of the event plan. However, the level of support that the event planner will need will vary depending on the complexity of the event being planned. The event support team will contribute to the implementation of the plan. They may be asked to take responsibility for specific elements of the event plan, e.g. to search for the venue. They  may be given specific tasks to complete which cover different elements of the event plan. Their level of responsibility will vary from task to task, where they may take a lead role or a subordinate role. Whatever their role, the support team will be dedicated to implementing an event plan that will lead to a successful event. The event planner will organise meetings to feedback on the completion of tasks to make sure the plan is being delivered to the agreed timetable. The event plan will be a document with some or all of the following features:

- Management arrangement for the event - Details of everything, e.g. security arrangements, access arrangements, parking

- Site plan - Details of the venue, e.g. entrances and exits, toilets, information booths

- Risk assessment plan - This should identify hazards or potential hazards, e.g. contractors have been trained to the required level of expertise required for the event, who might be affected by them and what will be done to eliminate or minimise the hazards. The plan should also identify control systems

- Contingency arrangements - Details of dealing with emergencies etc., e.g. an evacuation plan, communication arrangements, medical responses

- Any other relevant documents - Any other relevant documentation, e.g. copies of qualification certificates of people working at the venue

• ACTIVITY 2

Design the components that could appear on a risk assessment plan. Why have these components been identified?

An event planner will:

- Agree the event brief - Agree with the client what they are aiming to achieve at their event, how they are aiming to achieve it, when it will occur etc. The event planner will work with their client, who may be internal or external to the organisation. The client will be able to advise what kind of event they require, when it is to take place and approximately how many people will attend. This information will form the basis of an event brief. The event planner will need to get this brief agreed in writing with as much detail as possible

- Agree an agenda for the event - This should set out each agenda item that will be presented throughout the event, how it will be presented, how much time it will take to present the item, the type of layout required etc.

- Negotiate a budget - There may be a fixed sum or specific criteria that needs to be met. The event planner will agree the budget with the client and identify any potential overspends. The budget may be agreed when the client has identified either:

- A maximum sum of money available to pay for the whole event. The event planner will provide the best event within that budget

- Specific requirements for the location, standard of accommodation, levels of equipment, duration and season for the event etc. The event planner will agree the best price to meet the client's requirements

- Locate suitable venues - Consider size, location, resources and facilities for delegates with special requirements, price etc. The decision on the venue will depend on factors such as:

- The purpose of the event
- The budget of the event
- The number of delegates to be invited
- The standard of venue required to suit the delegates
- The geographic location of the delegates
- Using the organisation's in-house facilities or contracting externally from the organisation
- The potential disruption to the business

Selecting a venue space in-house or near to the host organisation has the advantage of saving on travelling time and costs for people based on the premises. If the venue is external to the organisation obtain quotes from suitable suppliers. There are many organisations that conduct venue searches free of charge. This service could be

used to select suitable venues that match the requirements of an event. Venues that have been used in the past could also be used or search for a new venue by carrying out a search on the Internet.

When searching for the right venue for an event make sure the standard of hospitality and catering is appropriate. Make sure the menu chosen meets the expectations of the delegates. Make sure it is clear exactly what is being provided. Have alternative menus agreed for vegetarians, halal, gluten free etc. Many venues will offer a choice of different delegate tariffs:

- A daily delegate rate which includes a meeting room and refreshments, at a price per delegate, but does not include equipment and other resources, e.g. use of an audio-visual technician
- A daily delegate rate which includes a meeting room, equipment, lunch and refreshments, at a price per delegate

- A 24-hour delegate rate which includes a meeting room, equipment, lunch and refreshments, dinner, accommodation and breakfast, at a price per delegate

- An executive rate which includes all of the above plus superior accommodation and meals, at a price per delegate

• ACTIVITY 3

What needs to be taken into consideration when making the right venue choice for events?

Once all the information about costs, size etc., have been collected from potential venues, the event planner will make a shortlist. The event planner should visit as many shortlisted venues as possible to make sure descriptions are accurate. If the event planner knows of someone who has used the venue in the past, they could ask for their feedback on venue standards. There will also be a choice of room layout to be decided. This will be determined by the various purposes of the agreed agenda items. The event may require different types of set up throughout its duration.

• ACTIVITY 4

Why would the following layouts be used?

1. Theatre
2. U-shape
3. Cabaret
4. Banquet

Arrange the hire of the venue
Discuss with the venue the plans for the event, e.g. provisional numbers of delegates, which will be confirmed as agreed. The venue coordinator will require a purchase order from the event planner confirming an agreement to their booking terms and conditions. This will form the basis of a contract between the organisation, or the event planner, and the venue, which will be subject to contract law. This will cover charges for cancellations or changes to arrangements subsequent to confirmation. There will usually be a sliding scale of charges depending on changes to the event plan. The event planner will need to check through the contract to make sure it is correct and as agreed.

Organise the necessary resources

Discuss with the venue the resources they can provide and those which will have to be outsourced. Design a brand motif if appropriate, organise and confirm speakers / demonstrators / layout of the venue etc.

Speakers will need to be agreed with the client. Some speakers may be booked up in advance, so it is best to agree these speakers as soon as possible, e.g. motivational speakers or Master of Ceremonies for the event. The event planner will organise with each speaker when the final copy of their presentation needs to be agreed and signed off. This will need to be done before material for the delegate pack is printed. The presentations will need to make sure they have the right tone and do not present anything controversial or oppose anything being presented in other parts of the event.

Organise with the client what resources they will need on the day of the event. This may include:

- Laptop and multimedia projector
- Overhead projector and screen
- Video and monitor
- Microphones for the head tables and for delegates asking questions - make sure the speaker system has been organised so it does not deafen delegates
- Flip chart and easel
- Free-standing lectern
- Public address system
- Post-it notes
- Pencils / pens / paper for delegates
- Bowl of sweets for delegate tables to help keep the throat lubricated

Different types of events will require different resources, depending on the purpose of the event. These may also include accommodation, car parking facilities etc.

Arrange the attendance of delegates

Agree on the delegates to be invited, design the invitation, send it out and collate the responses from the delegates. Delegates should be invited to the event as soon as possible. This will give enough time for the delegates to record the event in their diary and advise whether or not they are able to attend. They can also advise if they have a replacement. At this stage they will be asked if they have any special requests - these are additional arrangements that will need to be made, e.g. access to the venue or dietary needs. Delegates may also be asked to nominate attendance at seminars that will be held throughout the event.

Prepare a delegate list and delegate sign-in list once all the responses have been received from delegates invited to attend the event. Make a note of any special requirements, e.g. dietary, mobility, hearing or vision impairment, travel and accommodation. These will need to be discussed with the venue management team to make sure they can all be catered for. Confirm each delegate's attendance via a letter and, at the same time, also send out relevant information about the event to each delegate, e.g. a map showing directions and the location of the event, car parks and the nearest railway station

Organise delegate materials. Once the agenda has been agreed for the event, decisions will need to be made about the materials that will be given out to delegates. These will vary depending on the type of event, however, a normal template of documents would be:

Pre-event:

- Delegate invitation
- Draft agenda
- Directions to the event venue
- Dietary requirements
- Any accessibility issues, e.g. if a person is blind

Event: The delegate pack, which will normally include:

- Event agenda
- Agenda item documents
- Seminar materials, if appropriate
- Expenses claim form, if necessary
- Feedback form

Coordinating the event

- Help to coordinate the event - Attend the event and offer any services as required

- Help to vacate the venue at the end of the event - Remove all equipment and other resources that do not belong to the venue

- **Evaluate the event** - Design a feedback form which is given to delegates with their delegate pack. At some stage throughout the day, ask delegates to complete the feedback form. This may need to be repeated a few times throughout the event to get delegates to co-operate. Collate and analyse the feedback from delegates

- **Prepare accounts comparing actual cost with the budget** - Keep track of how the budget was spent

- **Provide delegates with any follow-up material** - Either provide electronic or hard-copy versions of handouts, sales brochures, order acknowledgements or appointments etc., to delegates

- **Agree promotional material and public relations (PR)** - Sign off the advertising campaign for the event and agree which exhibitors want to set up a booth at the event

The event planner will also need to cover health, safety and security during the event, legislation surrounding any contracts with the venue or suppliers of hired equipment, insurance, if appropriate, and coping with problems that arise prior to, during and after the event.

The event organiser will delegate the above tasks to members of their support team. The event planner will delegate tasks / activities according to a person's strengths and weaknesses. This may be an opportunity for someone to develop new skills and knowledge. The support team will take responsibility for the tasks they have been asked to complete. This is an integral part of the event planning. The event planner will come to rely on their support team and build relationships between all the members of the support team to execute all aspects of the event plan. The support team will keep the event planner informed of progress and any problems through the organisation and planning of the event. As with most things in a business, the strength of an event's success will depend on the quality of its communication. As a member of the support team, make sure work is delivered to a high quality, with meaning and, above all, meets the requirements of the event planner.

Testing knowledge

1. What activities could someone supporting the organisation of an event be asked to do?

2. What are the different types of events?

3. What risks and contingencies need to be considered when planning an event?

4. What kinds of information do delegates need on an event invitation to make an informed choice regarding whether or not to attend?

5. What is the most important element that needs to be considered when making a choice regarding the venue of the event?

6. What needs to be considered when making a choice of room layout for an event?

7. What are all the delegates' special requirements that need to be considered in planning an event?

8. What health and safety requirements need to be considered when selecting a venue for an event?

Skills

As a member of the support team you will contribute to the organisation and planning of an event as required by the event planner. The tasks that you will be asked to contribute to will vary in the depth and breadth of commitment depending on the level of your skills and knowledge. These tasks will also need to be balanced against other plans of work that you have been assigned by your supervisor / manager. Your commitment to carrying out any task to do with the organisation and planning of an event may include leading on a small aspect of the event plan or contributing to a number of tasks of the event plan.

While the event plan will probably be agreed with the client before you are asked to support the event project, there is nothing to stop you from adding any comments that you think will improve the event plan. You will probably be given a budget, where appropriate, that you will need to stick to in the task (s) that you have been assigned. Always work within this budget. If you find from the work that you are doing that you are not able to fulfil the task (s) within budget, you will need to discuss this with the event planner. The plans may need to be amended and the budget changed to accommodate an increase in the budget for particular tasks. The areas of work in the planning of an event that you will most likely be asked to contribute towards will be, though not exclusively:

- Locating suitable venues
- Arranging the hire of the venue
- Organising the necessary resources
- Arranging the attendance of delegates
- Organising delegate materials
- Providing delegates with any follow-up material
- Agreeing promotional material and PR

• ACTIVITY 5

You have been asked to source the venue for an event. You have been given the following information:
- Budget: £10,000
- Length of the event: 1 - 2 days
- Space requirements: main hall for initial presentation and plenary; six additional seminar rooms; sufficient space for exhibitors to display their booths
- Task to be completed by: 1 working day from when you have been assigned the task

1. What further pieces of information do you need to complete this task?
2. Explain if there is sufficient time to complete the task. If there is not sufficient time, what do you need to do?
3. How do you plan to complete this task?
4. What will you do?
5. Design a checklist to work with.

As you go about your work in any of these areas, you will always be guided by the event plan. The event planner will have worked with you to agree:

- When you need to complete the task
- The amount of budget you have
- The supervisor you will report to
- The team you will be working with
- What to do in the event of any problems
- Attendance at planning meetings
- The amount of time you will spend on the assigned task (s) for the event project

For any tasks that you have been assigned make sure you design a checklist to keep track of what you need to do, if necessary. Tick off each stage of your mini plan as each sub-task is completed. This will help your work and build confidence with the team you are working with. Work with other members of your team to resolve any issues that you are not sure about. A last resort for clarification will be to report to the event planner for their feedback.

Use this opportunity to learn something new about your organisation. Make sure you have identified the new skills and knowledge that you have acquired as a result of this task in your learning / development plan.

• ACTIVITY 6

You have been asked to prepare the materials for a delegate pack. You have been told the following about the event:

Budget: £2,500

- Delegate pack layout: bound booklet
- Task to be completed by: one week prior to the event
- Contributions: there will be slide presentations from six speakers and materials for the six seminars that are being offered

1. What further material (s) do you need to complete this task?
2. How do you plan to complete this task?
3. What will you do?
4. Design a checklist to work with.

You have been told by your event planner that the Director, who is giving the opening speech, has changed their presentation slides after the delegate pack has gone to print. What do you do?

Testing your skills

1. What did you do to support the implementation of the event plan?

2. How did your tasks / activities meet the agreed objectives of the event plan?

3. How did you work with other people on the event team to complete the objectives of the event plan?

4. How did you contribute to achieving the budget objectives in the tasks / activities you were asked to do?

5. How did you support the selection of the venue?

6. What responsibilities did you have when organising the invitations and responses to delegates?

7. Which delegate materials were you involved in organising? How did you do this?

8. How did you use the event plan to complete your tasks / activities?

9. What legislation did you apply / consider appropriate to the tasks / activities you were asked to do?

Ready for assessment?

To achieve this Level 2 unit of a Business & Administration qualification, learners will need to demonstrate that they are able to perform the following activities:

1. Supported the implementation of the plan for the event to meet agreed objectives

2. Contributed to identifying resources and support needed for organising an event

3. Contributed to identifying and costing suitable venues

4. Contributed to arranging resources and the production of event materials

5. Contributed to preparing and sending out invitations to delegates

6. Contributed to co-ordinating delegate responses

7. Contributed to liaising with the venue to confirm event requirements

8. Contributed to providing delegates with joining instructions and event materials

9. Contributed to rehearsing arrangements to make sure the event ran smoothly, if required

10. Contributed to following all legal and contractual requirements

11. Contributed to following the relevant health, safety and security requirements for the event

You will need to produce evidence from a variety of sources to support the performance requirements of this unit.

If you carry out the 'ACTIVITIES' and respond to the 'NEED TO KNOW' questions, these will provide some of the evidence required.

Links to other units

While gathering evidence for this unit, evidence may also be used from evidence generated from other units within the Business & Administration suite of units. Below is a sample of applicable units; however, most units within the Business & Administration suite of units will also be applicable.

QCF NVQ
Communications
Communicate in a business environment (Level 2)
Core business & administration
Manage own performance in a business environment (Level 2)
Improve own performance in a business environment (Level 2)
Work in a business environment (Level 2)
Work with other people in a business environment (Level 2)
Document production
Produce documents in a business environment
Prepare text from notes
Events and meetings
Support the coordination of an event
Support the organisation of business travel or accommodation

SVQ
Communications
Prepare to communicate in a business environment
Core business & administration
Agree how to manage and improve own performance in a business environment
Undertake work in a business environment
Contribute to working with others in a business environment
Document production
Produce documents in a business environment
Prepare text from notes
Events and meetings
Support the organisation and coordination of an event
Support the organisation of business travel or accommodation

21 Support the coordination of an event

SUPPORT THE COORDINATION OF AN EVENT

'**Support the coordination of an event**' is an <u>optional unit</u> which may be chosen as one of a combination of units to achieve either a Qualifications and Credit Framework (QCF), National Vocational Qualification (NVQ) or Scottish Vocational Qualification (SVQ).

The aims of this unit are to:

*   Understand the role and purpose of supporting the coordination of an event

*   Be able to support the coordination of an event

To achieve the above aims of this unit, learners will be expected to provide evidence through the performance of work-based activities.

Knowledge
Prior to delegate arrivals
The event planner may or may not be the event coordinator. If they are not the same person, the event planner along with the event coordinator, if these two roles are separate, will be at the event to check the event plan is being implemented correctly to meet the agreed objectives. They will normally be the first point of contact in the event of any problems. Before arriving at the venue, all members of the support team will have been given tasks / activities to perform at the venue to make sure the event is a success.

The support team will arrive at the venue prior to the arrival of the delegates, and all tasks / activities will be delegated to them. The support team will make sure:

*   The **catering** is organised for the agreed times and location. If not, they will inform the Master of Ceremonies (MC) / host / chair etc., who will advise the delegates at the introduction of the event

- All of the **equipment** and **delegate materials** are in place and in working order. They will communicate with the audio-visual technician to see how they can contribute to the smooth flow of presentations throughout the event. They will communicate any changes to the speakers so they have a choice if they want to use any enhanced service

- **Housekeeping** for the day is organised. This includes informing the MC / host / chair of the following:

  - Access to toilets

  - What to do if there is a fire-alarm test, including the location of exits and the assembly point

  - Any change to the event agenda

  - To remind delegates to check that 'BlackBerrys' and mobile phones are switched off

- There is **disabled access**

- There is someone responsible for **first aid**

- There is someone on the **venue management team** to answer any queries

- There are no **transport problems** that may delay the opening of the event

The event coordinator will have **pre-planned to meet the chair** and the speakers who will be making presentations at the event. They will need to be briefed about housekeeping and any last-minute changes, e.g. changes to their presentation which may need to be formatted and an announcement made to delegates that it will be different from the material in their delegate pack. They may have a memory stick that will need to be given to the audio-visual technician to update the slide show and to make sure it is compatible with the venue's equipment. If they are to use equipment with which they are not familiar they will need to be given the opportunity to make themselves comfortable with its use.

• ACTIVITY 1

What should the support team check before delegates arrive at the venue?

Some events may require delegates to stay overnight prior to or after the event. If this is the case, check with the venue to make sure there will be enough staff to cope with the delegates' arrival and luggage. If check-in is not available until later in the day, storage for delegates' luggage will be necessary. It may be worth considering arranging pre-registration, where the venue is supplied with a list of delegates and completes registration forms for each delegate prior to their arrival. Then the delegate only has to give their name at reception to be given their key. If delegates' accommodation will not be available at the time of arrival it is essential that a luggage storage room is provided for delegates arriving by public transport or taxi.

If there are sponsors of the event who have been promised space to exhibit their stands, these will need to be placed in accordance with health and safety regulations. The exhibits should have been set up prior to the delegates' arrival.

The reception area should have been set up with delegate badges. The badges should be split alphabetically to ease any congestion as they are collected by delegates, especially if it is a very large event. Delegate sign-in lists should be arranged in the same order as the delegate badges. Support staff will have been given a certain range of delegates' badges to hand to delegates as they arrive. All members of the event support team will have been told of the running order and who to contact if there are any problems.

The event coordinator will check with the venue management team to make sure everything is working according to the agreed plan.

Delegate arrivals

Most events will tell delegates when they can register for the event. As the delegates arrive for the event the event coordinator should:

- Be on hand to greet them
- Check whether they have any additional needs
- Show them where to sign in, if necessary
- Tell them where the cloakroom is
- Tell them where refreshments can be found
- Tell them the location of the event
- Tell them where they can store their luggage
- Answer any questions they may have
- Distribute any identity badges

- Hand out delegate packs as the delegates arrive or advise them where they are to be collected, if these are being supplied
- Show the delegates where to find the seating plan, if relevant

What should be done if more than 25% of delegates have not shown up on time?

Before informing the event organiser that the event can officially start, check to see how many delegates are yet to arrive. If there are a large number of delegates yet to arrive, a delay to the opening may

be necessary. If not, arrange with the event support team managing the reception of delegates arriving at the event, to escort delegates into the event.

During the event

Once the event is under way, the event coordinator will facilitate the smooth running

of the event. All members of the event support team will need to keep one step ahead of everything that is happening. Before the morning coffee break, check refreshments are available and there are sufficient refreshments etc. Before lunch, check arrangements are in hand. Before each speaker begins their presentation, check everything is ready and working as required by the speaker.

Potential **problems** that may arise will include:

- **Speakers failing to arrive on time** - If booked speakers are experiencing travel difficulties they should telephone ahead and let the event planner know. Check with them for an estimated time of arrival so their presentation can be rescheduled and run other activities before they arrive

- **Refreshments not being on time or of an acceptable standard** - Liaise with the venue coordinator or caterer to deal with any of these problems. It may be that an individual delegate has not advised the venue of their special dietary requirement or the caterers may have forgotten to supply it. In this case, do the best to provide them with an acceptable alternative

- **Equipment failure** - Despite all checks that may have been made prior to the event starting, it is quite possible that something will fail to work when needed. If the equipment has been supplied by the venue, call the venue coordinator to deal with the problem. If the event planner has supplied the equipment, they may have an alternative piece of equipment which can be used

- **Heating, lighting or air-conditioning problems** - Every delegate will have a different comfort level regarding temperature. Some will always be too hot; some will always be too cold. Respond to individual issues but make sure the majority of delegates are happy. Make sure the equipment is functioning efficiently

Follow up with any delegates that do not arrive at all. If accommodation has been booked in their name, the venue will need to know they will not be using it. If they are able to reuse the accommodation, there may be a reduction in the cancellation charge.

• ACTIVITY 3

What kind of problems can happen at any event?

After the event - the clear up

Collect any lost property and arrange for it to be returned to the original owner if possible. If not, take it back to the office and put it in lost property. A communication could be sent to all delegates informing them that an item has been found and what they should do in the event that it belongs to them.

Sort out any equipment. Either pack up equipment that the event leader has provided from their organisation or check with the audio-visual technician of the venue to make sure everything is okay. If equipment has been supplied by the venue, hand it back in the same condition in which it was received. If equipment has been hired from elsewhere, check with the event planner to supervise its return or collection. If the organisation convening the event supplied the equipment, pack it up safely to take it back to the organisation.

If the delegates have stayed overnight, the support team will need to be on hand when they check out. Each delegate will be responsible for making sure their keys are returned and any extras paid for. The booking instructions will have clearly outlined which costs are included in the accommodation and which are the delegate's responsibility. If delegates leave the venue without settling their bill, the venue will hold the organisation responsible. Make a note of these delegates so the organisation's finance department can invoice them for these services. However, it is much easier to deal with this situation before the delegate leaves.

• ACTIVITY 4

Delegates have left many queries that need to be followed up once the event is over. How is this handled?

Collect together any evaluation forms that delegates have left. Keep them safe so they can be analysed and reported on later. There may be additional feedback forms that are sent in later, so do not forget to add these comments to the feedback analysis. It is important to look at the feedback objectively. Where individuals were less than satisfied with aspects of the event than other delegates consider whether this is simply a matter of being unable to please all of the people all of the time. Where common issues are raised, formulate an action plan to deal with them. Take on board the matters raised and resolve to do better next time. If they relate to the performance of invited speakers, pass on the feedback to the speaker, as they will be interested to learn what delegates thought of their performance. If they relate to aspects of the venue which can be improved, pass on the feedback to the venue management. If they relate to issues which cannot be changed, such as the location of the venue, make a note to take these into account when considering the venue for future events.

Thank the venue for their service and make sure everything has been cleared up, including any papers and spare delegate packs.

If there are any documents which need to be circulated to delegates following the event, arrange for them to be copied and distributed, either electronically or via hard copy. Send copies to delegates who were unable to attend who indicated they would like details forwarded.

Throughout the event there will be endless calls on the time and initiative of the support team. The support team should use their full resources to keep on top of everything, adopting a professional and positive approach, to make sure delegate expectations can be met.

Testing your knowledge

1. What activities need to be organised by the event support team to manage the arrival of delegates to an event?

2. What would be the differences between organising the opening of an event for a major and minor event?

3. What does the support team need to do at the end of an event?

4. What is 'housekeeping' used for?

5. What happens if a delegate does not have their special dietary requirements catered for?

Skills

As a member of the event support team you will contribute to the coordination and planning of an event as required by the event planner and coordinator. The tasks that you will be asked to contribute to will vary in the depth and breadth of commitment depending on the level of your skills and knowledge. These tasks will also need to be balanced against other plans of work that you have been assigned by your supervisor / manager. Your commitment to carrying out any task to do with the coordination and planning of an event may include leading on a small aspect of the event plan or contributing to a number of tasks of the event plan.

While the event plan will probably be agreed with the client before you are asked to support the implementation of the event, there is nothing to stop you from adding any comments that you think will improve the coordination of the event.

The areas of work in the coordination of an event that you will most likely be asked to contribute towards will be, though not exclusively:

- Arriving before the event starts
- Setting up the main room and break-out rooms
- Distributing delegate packs and seminar materials
- Setting up the delegate reception area
- Organising the signing in of delegates
- Handing out delegates' badges
- Directing delegates to the main hall / refreshment area
- Working with the venue's staff
- Setting up all relevant equipment
- Being on hand to assist delegates with any queries they might have

• ACTIVITY 5

You have been asked to organise the delegate reception area. You have been told the following about the event:

- Number of delegates: 300
- What further pieces of information do you need to complete this task?
- How much time do you think you will need to set up the reception area?
- How do you plan to complete this task?
- What do you need to complete this task?
- Design a checklist to work with.

As you go about your work in any of these areas, you will always be guided by the event plan. The event planner / coordinator will have worked with you to agree:

- An outline of the whole event so timings are clear
- When you need to complete the task
- The supervisor you will report to
- The team you will be working with
- What to do in the event of any problems
- Any supplementary activity to help other members of the team

For any tasks that you have been assigned make sure you design a checklist to keep track of what you need to do, if necessary. Tick off each stage of your mini plan as each sub-task is completed. This will help you in your work and build confidence with the team you are working with. Work with other members of your team to resolve any issues that you are not sure about. A last resort for clarification will be to report to the event planner / coordinator for their feedback.

• ACTIVITY 6

You are in the main hall during the opening presentation when the projector fails during the presentation of the slide show. The event planner / coordinator is not available. What do you do?

Perhaps the two most important things you need to consider for any task you will be completing during the coordination of an event is: your personal appearance and your communication skills. You are very publicly the face of the organisation. You will need to make a good impression and strive to go beyond meeting delegate expectations. You will need to wear something that is presentable.

• ACTIVITY 7

What aspects of your verbal communication skills will you need to focus on when contributing to coordinating an event?

At the end of the event make sure that the venue has been cleared and feedback forms collected. Thanks should be given to the venue support team for their professional behaviour. Thanks should also be given to presenters and the chair.

Use this opportunity to learn something new about your organisation. Make sure you have identified the new skills and knowledge that you have acquired as a result of this task in your learning / development plan.

Testing your skills

1. What did you do prior to getting to the venue to make sure you knew that you would meet the objectives of the event plan?

2. How did you prepare the event venue?

3. What resources did you make sure were in place?

4. What did you do before the event started - the first agenda item?

5. What did you do throughout the event to assist the event planner and event coordinator?

6. What did you do to make delegates feel welcome?

7. How did you respond to delegates' requests for assistance?

8. What problems did you deal with?

9. What problems did you refer to the event coordinator?

10. Why did you refer these problems?

11. What did you learn from the way the event coordinator dealt with these problems?

12. What could the event venue management have done better?

13. What did you do when clearing the event venue?

14. What follow-up activities did you do?

Ready for assessment?

To achieve this Level 2 unit of a Business & Administration qualification, learners will need to demonstrate that they are able to perform the following activities:

1. Contributed to preparing the venue, making sure all necessary resources and supporting activities were in place

2. Contributed to arranging resources during an event in line with the agreed event plans

3. Contributed to helping delegates feel welcome

4. Contributed to meeting delegates' needs throughout an event

5. Contributed to resolving or referring problems, as required

6. Contributed to liaising with the management of the venue to make sure facility resources were in place

7. Contributed to clearing and vacating the venue according to the terms of the contract

8. Contributed to preparing and circulating papers, or completing other actions following the event, if required

You will need to produce evidence from a variety of sources to support the performance requirements of this unit.

If you carry out the 'ACTIVITIES' and respond to the 'NEED TO KNOW' questions, these will provide some of the evidence required.

Links to other units

While gathering evidence for this unit, evidence may also be used from evidence generated from other units within the Business & Administration suite of units. Below is a sample of applicable units; however, most units within the Business & Administration suite of units will also be applicable.

QCF NVQ
Communications
Communicate in a business environment (Level 2)
Core business & administration
Manage own performance in a business environment (Level 2)
Improve own performance in a business environment (Level 2)
Work in a business environment (Level 2)
Work with other people in a business environment (Level 2)
Document production
Produce documents in a business environment
Prepare text from notes
Events and meetings
Support the organisation of an event
Support the organisation of business travel or accommodation

SVQ
Communications
Prepare to communicate in a business environment
Core business & administration
Agree how to manage and improve own performance in a business environment
Undertake work in a business environment
Contribute to working with others in a business environment
Document production
Produce documents in a business environment
Prepare text from notes
Events and meetings
Support the organisation of an event
Support the organisation of business travel or accommodation

22 Support the organisation of business travel or accommodation

SUPPORT THE ORGANISATION OF BUSINESS TRAVEL OR ACCOMMODATION

'**Support the organisation of business travel or accommodation**' is an <u>optional unit</u> which may be chosen as one of a combination of units to achieve either a Qualifications and Credit Framework (QCF), National Vocational Qualification (NVQ) or Scottish Vocational Qualification (SVQ).

The aims of this unit are to:

- Understand the purpose of confirming a brief and budget for business travel or accommodation

- Know the sources of information and facilities available to make business travel or accommodation arrangements

- Be able to support the organisation with business travel or accommodation arrangements

To achieve the above aims of this unit, learners will be expected to provide evidence through the performance of work-based activities.

Knowledge

Businesses are increasingly expanding their operations to offer their products and services in a globalised community. To position a business within a globalised community, an organisation may have to send their employees to attend meetings, conferences etc., beyond their local office. Employees may be expected to travel:

- **Domestically -** Within their national borders. This type of journey will not require visas or foreign currency, e.g. travelling to Scotland

- **Internationally -** Outside of their national borders. This type of journey may require visas or foreign currency, e.g. travelling to any nation within the EU will not require a visa, but foreign currency, i.e. the Euro, may need to be arranged

Business travel may be undertaken frequently or infrequently by employees within an organisation.

Depending on the length of the trip, accommodation may also need to be arranged for an employee.

An organisation may have a specific department that looks after all these arrangements, they may have employees within a team who are responsible for these arrangements as part of their job or they may outsource the work to a specialist business travel agent. It will depend on the size of the organisation and how the business is organised. However, whatever the size of the operation arranging business travel or accommodation, an organisation should have a business travel and accommodation policy which should describe:

- How this function is organised within the organisation
- The restrictions the organisation places on this function
- Health and safety requirements for employees when abroad
- The support given to employees to make the trip a success
- The information required to monitor and evaluate this function

The advantages of having a business travel and accommodation policy are:

- **Coherency** - Everyone follows the same process
- **Employee support** - Employees feel valued and looked after
- Consistent processes
- Cost-efficiencies

Planning business travel

When it has been agreed that an employee needs to travel they should approach the appropriate person with the following information:

- The **budget** for the trip
- **When** the trip is taking place. The departure date / time and the return date / time. Consideration will need to be given to the time it will take getting to and from the point of departure. This should factor in the potential for delays and the effect of different time zones, if travelling internationally
  - The destination of the trip
  - The best form of travel. This will depend on:
  - Budget

- Time constraints

- Working practice expectations while travelling, e.g. working on the train

- Access to the departure / arrival terminal

- Frequency of the travel service

- Convenience of the travel service. Ease of travel between the terminal and the departure / destination points

- Length of the journey

- Potential problems that could occur when making a journey, e.g. delays

- Amount of luggage or equipment that needs to be taken, although this could always be sent on ahead

- Weather conditions for particular times of the year, e.g. travelling to the north of Scotland in the middle of winter with heavy snow forecast may mean driving is not advisable

Employees could travel by the following systems of transport:

- Car: usually for travel within the home nation. This may be the best form of travel for destinations where there is either no access or difficult access to public transport. Decisions will need to be made if the employee is to use their own car - mileage costs - or hire one - type of car; if they can accommodate others in the car; how long the journey will take, number of breaks to take so they are not too tired when they arrive, and the availability of parking on arrival

- Rail: consideration will need to be given to the possible number of connections and if the traveller could work while travelling by train

- Plane

- Ferry

• The number of people who will be travelling

• Any **special requirements**, e.g. A seat on a train travelling in the direction of travel; extra leg room on a plane

• ACTIVITY 1

What information is required from the traveller if making a booking to travel by train?

There are many variables involved in planning and deciding on which form of transport to use for business travel. There is no right or wrong way of doing it and it will depend on what the business travel and accommodation policy states for an organisation. However, consideration needs to be given to the **personal preferences of the traveller**:

- A car journey may be the cheapest option but the traveller may not have a driving licence

- If the traveller suffers from seasickness, travelling by ferry would not be a good option

- The traveller may have a phobia about a form of transport, e.g. a fear of flying

Sometimes a cheap option may appear to be the best option regarding cost, but it may be more expensive in human terms, and this may have a knock-on effect to the success of  the business being conducted. The monetary cost may be low but the human cost may be very high. In planning the best form of travel and accommodation it is important to remember that the aim of the business travel is to successfully conduct business. This is being carried out by an employee of the organisation. The employee needs to arrive at their destination in the best mental and physical shape to conduct business successfully.

• ACTIVITY 2

A train journey is going to cost £50 less than a plane journey. The train journey will take 4.5 hours. It will take the traveller 1 hour to get to the station and 15 minutes from the station to the meeting. The plane journey requires the traveller to be at the airport 90 minutes before each journey. The plane journey will take 45 minutes. It will take the traveller 15 minutes to get to the airport and 10 minutes to get to their point of destination from the airport.

What is the most effective journey to take? Why?

Planning accommodation
Some domestic and international reasons for travelling may require the traveller to stay for more than one night to conduct their business. In this situation, accommodation will also need to be organised. An organisation's business travel and accommodation policy will advise on the type of accommodation that should be selected, which will require the following information:

*   The **budget** for the accommodation
*   **When** the accommodation is required
*   **Where** the accommodation is required
*   The standard and type of accommodation required
*   The **number of people** requiring accommodation
*   How **convenient the location** is to the travel service being used
*   Any **special requirements**, e.g. a ground-floor room for someone who suffered from vertigo

As with making arrangements for travelling, employees need to be secure in the knowledge that they will arrive for their meeting capable of making good decisions and be able to move the business forward.e.

• ACTIVITY 3

What are the most important elements to plan for when organising business travel or accommodation?

Preparing an itinerary

The traveller or their manager will identify the business travel or accommodation requirements, specifying all the requirements to be met within budget. Once all the plans for business travel or accommodation have been agreed, a search should be completed fulfilling the requirements of the travel brief.

This should present alternative routes of travel and the costs attached to each option. This will allow the traveller to make the most informed choice about which option to select. Once an option has been selected by the traveller, the organiser of the business travel or accommodation will draw up a full itinerary that clearly sets out the timelines for the full period of travel.

An itinerary sets out the entire travel or accommodation schedule prior to the trip. It helps to organise activities well in advance so time is not wasted due to unscheduled or unplanned actions. Having an itinerary helps the traveller to focus on the planned activities and purpose of the business trip rather than on the logistics of the travel arrangements. The itinerary makes sure that both the organiser and the traveller (s) are fully prepared, guaranteeing a productive use of time. The lack of an itinerary could result in last-minute activities that waste both time and money.

The itinerary should be checked with the traveller before the bookings are confirmed with the travel organiser. The traveller may have previous experience of the actual journey and be able to make suggestions about better options to explore. An itinerary could overlook certain requirements which the traveller will see when they review the itinerary. The itinerary should always be checked to avoid any possible cancellation charges.

• ACTIVITY 4

Why is a travel itinerary necessary?

Searching for travel or accommodation options

There are many sites on the Internet which can be found to help with identifying different travel services and the costs attached to them, e.g. www.travelsupermarket.com. Each of these sites will provide a cost of the travel service or accommodation being considered. Alternatively, an organisation may employ dedicated travel agents with whom they make all their travel arrangements. The most appropriate options, which fulfil the requirements of the travel brief and the agreed budget, can then be collated. This will allow a comparison to be made across the different options.

Confirming the booking

Once the itinerary and the appropriate options of travel and accommodation have been agreed, the booking can go ahead. How this is done will vary from organisation to organisation and depend on their travel and accommodation management policy. Possible arrangements that may be in place could be:

* **Special rates** with specific hotel chains. Contact the reservations department and give them the details of the number of rooms, number of nights, date of arrival and names of guests etc.

* **Online facilities** to book travel and accommodation. This will require the use of a company credit card, unless the organisation has an account or credit facility with the supplier

* A **travel agent** who will make all the travel arrangements

* Book **direct** with a hotel or travel company

* All **bookings**, once completed, will need to be confirmed with a booking reference

The traveller will need all their travel and accommodation information as soon as possible. The traveller should be given the itinerary and all necessary documents in good time prior to travelling. The traveller will need to review all the documents to make sure they not only meet the requirements of the travel brief but also conform to the traveller's requirements. The traveller should then confirm that they are happy with all the itinerary and documents that have been provided. A business trip can be very stressful, for many different reasons, some of which the organiser may not be aware of, so it is important that the traveller is confident about all their travel arrangements. If any changes are needed there will still be time to make them. Last-minute changes are much more difficult to organise and often incur additional costs.

In order to keep track of travel arrangements and deal with any queries that may arise, all agreements and bookings should be maintained accurately in a recording system. These may be electronically, in hard copy or a combination of both. Copies of all bookings made should be kept in a 'live' file for ease of reference. When the trip has been completed all records should be archived. Records should also be maintained regarding feedback received about the accommodation, facilities etc.

• ACTIVITY 5

Which are the best facilities to use when confirming a travel or accommodation booking?

Paying for the travel or accommodation arrangements

All forms of transport or accommodation will usually require payment in advance of travel. Every organisation has different approaches regarding how their travel or accommodation arrangements are paid for, which include:

- **Invoicing -** The travel company will invoice the organisation for all costs. The invoice will need to be paid within 28 days or other specific arrangement that has been agreed

- **Company credit card -** When the booking has been confirmed, the organiser will use an authorised company credit card. This offers greater flexibility when using travel websites

- **Travel account -** If using a travel agent, an account will normally be opened which will need to be paid at specific times agreed between both parties

When invoices and credit card statements are received these must be checked carefully against the bookings in the archived file. Any discrepancies should be reported to the supplier immediately. The organisation's procedures must then be followed to make sure of prompt payment. This will avoid any charges for late payment. It will also build a positive relationship with the supplier.

Some organisations will expect their employees to pay for accommodation using their personal credit card. This expense is then claimed back using an expense account. Expense accounts will normally be linked to a cost centre or specific budget code.

Dealing with travel problems

Many problems may arise in arranging travel or accommodation, some of which are listed below:

- **Tickets may not arrive -** Chase up the company in time for replacements to be sent

- **Transport may be delayed -** The traveller should be told to check travel arrangements before they travel to make sure there are no problems

- **Transport may be cancelled -** The traveller should be told to check travel arrangements before they travel to make sure there are no problems. Alternative travel arrangements may need to be made

- People travelling by car may be **delayed** by roadworks or **breakdowns**, or may get lost in an unfamiliar area. In the case of a breakdown, arrangements should be in place for a recovery service to be used or obtaining an alternative hire car

- The hotel may have made a **mistake with the booking**. Speak to the hotel and resolve the matter. Arrange alternative accommodation if necessary

- The traveller's **luggage may be mislaid** at the airport. Deal with this as the traveller gets on with the purpose of their visit. If the visit is for several days, financial assistance may need to be organised

- A **travel company may go out of business**. Travel arrangements may need to be rebooked as the original travel arrangement may not be honoured

Whatever the problem, it will require some form of communication with the traveller to make sure they are able to reach their intended destination at the required time or have appropriate accommodation. If the travel organiser cannot contact the traveller, they may have to contact the appropriate company at the destination point to let them know what alternative arrangements have been made. It is up to the travel organiser to make sure the trip runs as smoothly as possible so the traveller is in the best form to conduct their business.

• ACTIVITY 6

A trip has been arranged for a sales manager. The sales manager lives in Reading and is travelling to Paris and then Edinburgh. The itinerary is as follows:

Day	Time	Action
Mon	07:00	Train from Reading to Paddington, arrive 07.32
	07.48	Train from Paddington to Gatwick, arrive 08.45
	09:00	Check in Gatwick Airport
	11:00	Departure to Paris
	12:00	Arrival Paris
		Accommodation booked at Hotel Georges V
	20:00	Dinner with Mr Simenon, Chief Buyer
Tue	08.30	Breakfast with Mme Bardot, Designer
	10:00	Meeting with clients at Rue St. Morgue
	20:00	Dinner with Mr Jenkins, Director of Paris office
Wed	06:00	Train from Gare du Nord to Charles de Gaulle
	08:00	Check in Charles de Gaulle Airport
	10:00	Departure to Edinburgh
	17:00	Arrival Edinburgh
		Accommodation booked at The Scotsman Hotel
Thu	09:00	Meeting in Edinburgh office
	15:00	Taxi to Edinburgh Airport
	16:00	Check in Edinburgh Airport
	17:00	Departure to Gatwick
	18.30	Arrival Gatwick
	19.30	Train from Gatwick to Paddington
	20.27	Arrive Paddington
	20.53	Train from Paddington to Reading
	21.25	Arrive Reading

The sales manager telephones at 09.30 on Monday to advise that the flight to Paris has been delayed by four hours. What needs to be done? Who needs to be informed?

Testing your knowledge

1. What is the main reason for controlling the budget for business travel or accommodation?

2. How does an organised approach to arranging business travel or accommodation reduce overall costs?

3. What details are required to arrange business travel or accommodation for a colleague?

4. What records are kept on travel or accommodation arrangements?

5. How long is information kept in a 'live' file before it is transferred to an archived file?

6. What is an itinerary?

7. What needs to be done if travel is delayed?

8. What needs to be checked before paying an invoice from a national hotel group?

Skills

As a member of the support team, you will contribute to the organisation of business travel or accommodation arrangements. You will follow the plan that has been set out by the person organising the business travel or accommodation. The tasks that you will be asked to contribute to will vary in depth and breadth of commitment depending on the level of your skills and knowledge. These tasks will also need to be balanced against other plans of work that you have been assigned by your supervisor / manager. Your commitment to carrying out any task to do with supporting the organisation of business travel or accommodation may include leading on a small aspect of the travel plans or contributing to a number of tasks of the travel plan.

While the travel plan will probably be agreed with the traveller before you are asked to support the organisation of the travel plans, there is nothing to stop you from adding any comments that you think will improve the travel plans. The areas of work in the travel plans that you will most likely be asked to contribute towards may be:

- Checking that the budget has been agreed - Revisit this with the organiser or traveller if total costs exceed the budget

- Checking the travel brief with the organiser or traveller

- Checking traveller requirements

- Searching for various business travel or accommodation options

- Working with the travel organiser to find the best travel agents etc., that should be consulted or used

- Making the booking once it has been signed off

- Arranging for the payment of any travel or accommodation arrangements

- Drawing up an itinerary of travel arrangements or accommodation, which you will check with your supervisor / manager or traveller

- Keeping all appropriate records of the travel plans

- Providing the traveller with the final itinerary which you will check through with them to make sure all the travel plans have been met as agreed

• ACTIVITY 7

If you were arranging for someone to catch a flight from London to Glasgow leaving at 08.10, what time would they need to check in?

As you go about your work in any of these areas, you will always be guided by the travel organisers or the traveller (s). The travel organiser or traveller (s) will have worked with you to agree:

- An outline of the whole travel plan so timings are clear

- When you need to complete the task

- The supervisor you will report to

- The team you will be working with

- What to do in the event of any problems

- Any supplementary activity required to help other members of the team

For any tasks that you have been assigned make sure you design a checklist to keep track of what you need to do, if necessary. Tick off each stage of your mini-plan as a sub-task has been completed. This will help your work and build confidence with the team you are working with. Work with other members of your team to resolve any issues that you are not sure about. A last resort for clarification will be to report to the travel organiser or traveller for their feedback.

• ACTIVITY 8

What is the quickest and most cost-effective way to travel from Exeter to Birmingham?

Use this opportunity to learn something new about your organisation. Make sure you have identified the new skills and knowledge that you have acquired as a result of this task in your learning / development plan.e.

• ACTIVITY 9

Put together a copy of all the paperwork relating to one particular trip that you have organised.

Testing your skills

1. How do you access information on business travel or accommodation arrangements?

2. What websites would you use to look for cost-effective business travel or accommodation?

3. How do you use a rail timetable?

4. Where would you look for information about long-term roadworks?

5. How do you arrange business travel by road, rail, air and sea?

6. What are the hotel groups your organisation uses?

7. What action do you take if a travel ticket has not arrived in time for the traveller to make the trip?

8. How does your organisation deal with car breakdowns?

9. What are the payment facilities available to you when booking business travel or accommodation?

Ready for assessment?

To achieve this Level 2 unit of a Business & Administration qualification, learners will need to demonstrate that they are able to perform the following activities:

1. Confirmed the brief and budget for business travel or accommodation arrangements

2. Checked a draft itinerary and schedule with the organiser or traveller (s)

3. Identified suitable business travel or accommodation options

4. Booked suitable business travel or accommodation arrangements, following instructions to meet the brief and budget using available sources of information and facilities

5. Booked suitable business travel or accommodation arrangements, following instructions to obtain best value for money

6. Booked suitable business travel or accommodation arrangements, following instructions to make payments or agree payment arrangements

7. Obtained confirmation and collated documents for business travel or accommodation arrangements

8. Maintained records of business travel or accommodation arranged

9. Provided the organiser or traveller with an itinerary and required documents in good time

10. Confirmed with the organiser or traveller that the itinerary and documents met requirements

11. Resolved or referred problems to the appropriate person

You will need to produce evidence from a variety of sources to support the performance requirements of this unit.

If you carry out the 'ACTIVITIES' and respond to the 'NEED TO KNOW' questions, these will provide some of the evidence required.

Links to other units

While gathering evidence for this unit, evidence **may** also be used from evidence generated from other units within the Business & Administration suite of units. Below is a **sample** of applicable units; however, most units within the Business & Administration suite of units will also be applicable.

QCF NVQ
Communications
Communicate in a business environment (Level 2)
Core business & administration
Manage own performance in a business environment (Level 2)
Improve own performance in a business environment (Level 2)
Work in a business environment (Level 2)
Solve business problems (Level 2)
Work with other people in a business environment (Level 2)
Document production
Produce documents in a business environment
Prepare text from notes
Events and meetings
Support the organisation of an event
Support the coordination of an event

SVQ
Communications
Prepare to communicate in a business environment
Core business & administration
Agree how to manage and improve own performance in a business environment
Undertake work in a business environment
Plan how to solve business problems
Contribute to working with others in a business environment
Document production
Produce documents in a business environment
Prepare text from notes
Events and meetings
Support the organisation and coordination of an event

23

Support the organisation of meetings

SUPPORT THE ORGANISATION OF MEETINGS

'**Support the organisation of meetings**' is an <u>optional unit</u> which may be chosen as one of a combination of units to achieve a Qualifications and Credit Framework (QCF), National Vocational Qualification (NVQ) or Scottish Vocational Qualification (SVQ).

The aims of this unit are to:

* Understand the arrangements to be made to support the planning and organising of meetings

* Be able to prepare for a meeting

* Be able to follow up a meeting

To achieve the above aims of this unit, learners will be expected to provide evidence through the performance of work-based activities.

Knowledge
What is a meeting?

In a business or work environment a meeting is a gathering of people to present or exchange information, which may involve planning and making decisions. Almost every team activity or project requires meetings of some sort. A good meeting will help to generate enthusiasm for a project and build skills for future projects. It will also provide attendees with techniques that may benefit them in their future careers. Good meetings require good leaders who will encourage and direct attendees to achieve the purpose of the meeting.

Meetings will vary in size and frequency depending on the type of a business. Meetings can be:

Formal

This type of meeting will be highly structured with clear aims and objectives to achieve. They may be convened at specific times of the year. They will follow an agenda and may have a large number of invited attendees. All outcomes will be recorded in some way.

These types of meetings may include: board meetings; annual general meetings (AGMs); public forums, e.g. shareholder meetings; appraisal meetings; disciplinary hearings or team meetings. Generally, formal meetings are arranged for more than four people who need to inform others of decisions agreed at a meeting. The format for taking minutes will involve a lot of detail, not necessarily word for word, though this will depend on the reason for taking the minutes. This will vary, depending on the importance of attributing who said what and what actions were agreed to. In some instances, it is a legal requirement to record the outcomes of a meeting, e.g. public board meetings.

Informal
These types of meetings may include: one-to-one meetings or impromptu meetings. The format is less formal and may only record agreed actions to be taken.

Physical
All members of the meeting will be present in a room / venue. Everyone attending this type of meeting will clearly see and hear the contributions being made by other attendees at the meeting.

Virtual
Attendees will be located around different geographic locations linked up by videoconferencing or teleconferencing. This may be both cost - and time -effective for attendees. However, the technology needs to be organised and maintained throughout a meeting. Unlike physical meetings, body language can be difficult to interpret and this can compromise the quality of a meeting.

• ACTIVITY 1

Why are there different types of meetings?

Minutes may be issued and made available to the public (if this is a legal requirement for the organisation or only available as a private record, e.g. within an organisation where commercial decisions are too sensitive to share publicly. Decisions that are made and the issues discussed during a meeting are crucial to the continued productivity of a business. It is important to keep a record of decisions and discussions in an organised and methodical fashion. While it may not be a legal obligation to maintain minutes, it is considered good practice to maintain them as verification of a formal approach to the decision-making process within an organisation.

The Freedom of Information Act 2000 provides access by the public to records created by a Board and its employees, this includes minutes from a meeting. However, there are exemptions from the Act which allow non-disclosure of either full or partial information, depending on the commercial sensitivity of the information recorded in the minutes.

• ACTIVITY 2

Why should a meeting have minutes?

Types of meetings

There are many different types of meetings, including:

- **Annual general meetings (AGM's)** - All companies with shareholders are obliged to hold a meeting at least once a year which all shareholders are invited to attend to give them the opportunity to question directors and vote on resolutions

- **Extraordinary general meetings** - Additional meetings can be called if the holders of at least 10% of the shares want them to discuss issues that have arisen since the last AGM that cannot wait until the next, e.g. the change of the Board or to discuss the implications of a takeover / merger

- **Board meetings** - Directors of a company meet regularly to discuss the strategic direction and general running of the organisation's business

- **Management meetings** - Managers meet to discuss the day-to-day running of the organisation's business to decide how the strategy agreed by the Board is to be implemented

- **Team meetings** - Meetings that discuss specific issues that affect a team and integrate information decided by senior management, e.g. the sales and marketing team, the customer service team, the communications team

- **Staff meetings** - Meetings held to address issues that will affect everybody within the business, e.g. a meeting called by a public sector organisation about the requirements relating to the distribution of information prior to an election

- **Committee meetings** - There are many different types of committee meetings, ranging from the committee of a large organisation to committees of social clubs

- **Project meetings** - These meetings will be organised to catch up with and report on project milestones to make sure the project is being managed successfully

Planning a meeting

Most meetings will be organised to achieve a specific purpose. This will be agreed before the meeting takes place. Once the purpose of a meeting has been agreed, it will then need to be organised. To prepare to organise a meeting the meeting organiser will need to know the:

- **Purpose of the meeting** - A list of interested attendees will be prepared who will confirm their interest in attending the meeting. Invitations will be sent to potential attendees with an RSVP. Once the RSVPs are returned they can be collated to identify how many attendees will be attending

- **Time of the meeting** - If the meeting is relevant for a participant to attend, they will need to know if the time is convenient and does not clash with any other appointments they have in their diary

- **Location of the meeting** - This should include a map giving attendees directions to the meeting venue, showing the location of the meeting, car parks, nearest railway station etc. Once the number of attendees at the meeting has been agreed a decision will need to be made about the location of the venue. This will be based on other factors, such as:

  - The purpose of the meeting

  - The seniority of the attendees

  - The geographic location of the attendees

  - Whether it should be in-house or external to the organisation. If the meeting can be arranged in-house it will be less costly to the business in time, finances, equipment, resources and people

  - The potential disruption to the business

Once the type of meeting venue has been agreed it should be booked, identifying any specific location within a building, e.g. natural light or not; equipment, e.g. whiteboards; resources, e.g. documents and catering requirements. Different meeting venues need to be sourced to meet the agreed meeting brief and budget. Quotes for relevant meeting venues need to be obtained and a decision made on which venue will be the best to use. If possible, the meeting venue should be checked, or check with colleagues within the organisation who may have used the venue, to get their feedback. It is important to make sure the standard of hospitality and catering is appropriate. Identify exactly what the venue is providing. Check the status of equipment and catering: is it included

or do separate arrangements need to be made? Decisions will also need to be made about how the meeting room is going to be organised. This will depend on the purpose of the meeting. There are three common layouts for meeting rooms:

Classroom - This is where the speaker stands in front of an audience seated round a number of tables. This is useful if attendees are to take part in a 'workshop'

Boardroom - This is where the whole group sit round a table. If attendees are to discuss ideas, reach a conclusion or co-ordinate activities this layout may be more appropriate

Theatre - This is where a speaker stands in front of an audience seated in rows of seats. This layout is suitable for passing on information

• ACTIVITY 3

Describe other types of room layouts not mentioned above. Why would they be used?

Requirements
- **Any special requirements** - Attendees can advise the meeting organiser of any special requirements, e.g. dietary needs, if being catered for; disabled access to the meeting venue

- **Equipment and other resources required at the meeting** - Where a screen or flip chart is being used it is essential that everyone can see it. If arranging a meeting for a large number of attendees consider whether microphones are necessary. Make sure speakers are not placed where attendees may be deafened by the sound. Other equipment you may need to have available includes:

- A laptop, to allow a PowerPoint presentation to be shown

- A multi-media projector

- Whiteboards and dry-wipe markers, for brainstorming sessions

- An easel, to put the flip chart on

- Pencils, paper and maybe a dish of sweets for each table

- Duplicates of documents that attendees will need

- **Catering requirements**

  - Tea and coffee for morning or mid-afternoon breaks

  - Lunch

  - Dietary requirements of delegates attending the meeting

- **An agreed agenda for the meeting**. An agenda will usually be made up of the following minimum headings:

  - Attendees and apologies for absence

  - The minutes of the past meeting

  - Matters arising

  - Any other business (AOB)

  - Date and time of next meeting

- A week before the meeting send an agenda and copies of any meeting papers to those who indicated they would be attending. The agenda of a meeting sets out, in a logical order, what is to be discussed at the meeting

- Satisfy any health and safety regulations and security requirements

• ACTIVITY 4

What are the main elements that need to be managed when organising a meeting?

Once all these arrangements have been put in place, on the day of the meeting, to support the meeting organiser, arrive early to carry out the following checks:

- **Catering** - Is organised for the times as stated on the agenda

- **Equipment and resources** - Is in place and it works. Make sure there are spare copies of the papers sent prior to the meeting available for those who have lost them, forgotten them or claim never to have received them. There may be other items for discussion at the meeting which were not included on the agenda. If this happens, make sure there are sufficient copies of relevant papers for the meeting, because these will not have been circulated in advance. These should be collated into the order in which they will be discussed and placed in position on the meeting tables. Sorting the papers into order will enable people to follow the agenda more easily and reduce the distraction that searching through piles of paper causes. Make sure everyone has a full set of papers. Arrange for the photocopying of papers during the meeting, if required, and deal with failures of power, equipment or catering

- If the meeting is **not in-house** make sure the following is known:

  - Where the toilets are

  - Whether there is a fire alarm test arranged for that day

  - Where the fire exits are

  - Where the assembly point is

  - Where lunch is going to be served

  - If there are facilities for smokers

  - Where the disabled access is

  - Who is responsible for first aid

  - What alarm system to use

When attendees start to arrive make sure someone is on hand to greet them, sign them in and give them a delegate's badge, if necessary. Guide attendees to where the cloakroom is, where refreshments can be found, the location of the meeting room and answer any questions they may have.

Throughout the meeting make sure the meeting organiser has all the support they need so they are not distracted by unintended events. Be on hand to usher latecomers into the meeting, re-organise seating if required, make sure all attendees sign the sign-in sheet, make sure all attendees have all the required documents, obtain more documents / additional papers, resolve equipment that fails to work properly, think of alternatives to use if equipment breaks down, make sure there are sufficient refreshments for attendees etc. Make a note of any lapses in service provided by the meeting venue, which can be followed up with the meeting organiser after the meeting is over. If things have not been delivered this may be something that the meeting organiser can negotiate with the meeting venue management team. Make any notes to improve the way meetings might be organised and run in the future and share them with the meeting organiser.

Once the meeting is over, be on hand to thank attendees for attending the meeting. Make sure they know where the cloakroom is and fulfil any requests. Clear the room as required by organisational procedures. This will vary depending on whether the meeting has been held in-house or off site. It will also depend on the size of the organisation and the ancillary services that the organisation is able to provide if in-house.

Once the minutes have been agreed by the chairperson and the meeting organiser, distribute these, as requested, to attendees and those people who were unable to attend the meeting so they not only have a record of proceedings but can make any suggestions for the future.

• ACTIVITY 5

What are the differences between organising a meeting which takes place in-house as opposed to off site?

Testing your knowledge

1. What is a meeting?

2. What are the differences between various types of meetings?

3. What five items are on every agenda?

4. What is the purpose of sending invitations to potential attendees of a meeting?

5. What needs to be considered when deciding on where a meeting will take place?

6. What types of equipment may be needed at a meeting?

7. What would be the best room layout for a training session?

8. Why are minutes of a meeting taken?

Skills

As a member of the support team, you will contribute to the organisation of meetings. You will follow the meeting plan that has been set out by the person organising the meeting. The tasks that you will be asked to contribute to will vary in the depth and breadth of commitment depending on the level of your skills and knowledge. These tasks will also need to be balanced against other plans of work that you have been assigned by your supervisor / manager. Your commitment to carrying out any task to do with supporting the organisation of a meeting may include leading on a small aspect of the meeting plan or contributing to a number of tasks of the meeting plan.

While the meeting plan will probably be agreed with the meeting organiser before you are asked to support the organisation of the meeting, there is nothing to stop you from adding any comments that you think will improve the organisation of the meeting. The areas of work in planning a meeting that you will most likely be asked to contribute towards will be, though not exclusively:

- Checking that the budget has been agreed - Revisit this with the meeting organiser if the total costs exceed the budget
- Checking what the meeting plan is aiming to achieve
- Checking where the meeting is to take place - In-house or off site
- Checking the purpose of the meeting before sourcing a venue
- Checking to see if there are any travel requirements
- Checking on what kind of room layout the venue should have
- Checking if there are any equipment requirements
- Checking if any other resources are required
- Checking all documents have been agreed and prepared for the meeting, including the agenda
- Carrying out any printing that is required
- Checking catering requirements
- Checking that all organisational procedures have been followed
- Checking that all health and safety regulations have been built into the meeting plan
- Checking that all security requirements have been built into the meeting plan
- Checking, on the day, that the venue has been laid out as agreed, that all equipment is in good working order and all documents have been compiled and placed for each attendee

• ACTIVITY 6

What administration would you carry out with people who are unable to attend a meeting?

As you go about your work in any of these areas, you will always be guided by the meeting organiser. They will have worked with you to agree:

- An outline of the whole meeting plan so timings are clear
- An outline of the limits to spending on each component of the meeting
- When you need to complete the task (s)

- The supervisor you will report to
- The team you will be working with
- What to do in the event of any problems
- Any supplementary activity to help other members of the team

For any tasks that you have been assigned make sure you design a checklist to keep track of what you need to do, if necessary. Tick off each stage of your mini-plan as a sub-task has been completed. This will help you in your work and build confidence with the team you are working with. Work with other members of your team to resolve any issues that you are not sure about. A last resort for clarification will be to report to the meeting organiser for their feedback.

• ACTIVITY 7

How would you contribute to organising a meeting for a sales team of 50 attendees?

Use this opportunity to learn something new about your organisation. Make sure you have identified the new skills and knowledge that you have acquired as a result of this task in your learning / development plan.

Testing your skills

1. How did you follow the meeting plan brief?

2. What procedure did you follow to confirm a meeting room?

3. How did you organise invitations and responses from attendees?

4. What special needs did you need to make sure were organised? How did you do this?

5. How did you know what papers were needed to be organised for the meeting?

6. What did you do during the meeting?

7. What are your organisation's procedures for vacating a meeting room?

8. What health and safety regulations did you need to consider in supporting the organisation of the meeting?

9. What security arrangements did you need to consider in supporting the organisation of the meeting?

Ready for assessment?
To achieve this Level 2 unit of a Business & Administration qualification, learners will need to demonstrate that they are able to perform the following activities:

1. Confirmed the purpose and venue of a meeting

2. Confirmed a budget for a meeting, if required

3. Organised and confirmed venue, equipment and catering requirements, if required

4. Invited attendees and confirmed attendance

5. Collated and despatched papers for a meeting within agreed timescales

6. Made sure attendees' needs were met

7. Made sure equipment and layout of the rooms met the meeting brief

8. Kept records of arrangements made and services used

9. Attended to any requirements during the meeting as directed by the meeting organiser

10. Followed organisational procedures for clearing a meeting room

11. Circulated a meeting record to agreed timescales

12. Made sure arrangements for payments were met, if required

13. Contributed to the evaluation or arrangements made for meetings, as required

You will need to produce evidence from a variety of sources to support the performance requirements of this unit.

If you carry out the 'ACTIVITIES' and respond to the 'NEED TO KNOW' questions, these will provide some of the evidence required.

Links to other units

While gathering evidence for this unit, evidence may also be used from evidence generated from other units within the Business & Administration suite of units. Below is a sample of applicable units; however, most units within the Business & Administration suite of units will also be applicable.

QCF NVQ
Communications
Communicate in a business environment (Level 2)
Core business & administration
Manage own performance in a business environment (Level 2)
Improve own performance in a business environment (Level 2)
Work in a business environment (Level 2)
Work with other people in a business environment (Level 2)
Document production
Produce documents in a business environment
Prepare text from notes
Events and meetings
Support the organisation of an event
Support the coordination of an event
Support the organisation of business travel or accommodation

SVQ
Communications
Prepare to communicate in a business environment
Core business & administration
Agree how to manage and improve own performance in a business environment
Undertake work in a business environment
Contribute to working with others in a business environment
Document production
Produce documents in a business environment
Prepare text from notes
Events and meetings
Support the organisation and coordination of an event
Support the organisation of business travel or accommodation

24 Respond to change in a business environment

RESPOND TO CHANGE IN A BUSINESS ENVIRONMENT

'**Respond to change in a business environment**' is an <u>optional unit</u> which may be chosen as one of a combination of units to achieve either a Qualifications and Credit Framework (QCF), National Vocational Qualification (NVQ) or Scottish Vocational Qualification (SVQ).

The aims of this unit are to:

- Understand the causes and effects of change in a business environment

- Understand own role in supporting change

- Understand own role in responding to change

- Be able to respond to change

- Be able to support the evaluation of change

To achieve the above aims of this unit, learners will be expected to provide evidence through the performance of work-based activities.

Knowledge

The factors that affect change
Change occurs when the form of something that once was is transformed to something different. The difference may be small or large. The difference will be determined by the type and size of the change and the time it will take to take effect. Whatever the change is, it will always involve movement - the status quo will change to a new status quo.

Change can be either:

- **Active** - Change is planned in response to an agreed approach to improving how a business is run

- **Reactive** - Change is reactive and planned against external forces of change. Usually change has been thrust on an organisation, something that the organisation has not considered or planned for

• ACTIVITY 1

What is change?

Change can occur because of the following factors:

- **Politics** - e.g. A change of government will develop new policies which may have an impact on the way an organisation is run. The coalition government of 2010 decided to get rid of many of the quangos - a quango is a quasi-autonomous non-governmental organisation

- **Economics** - e.g. How a recession may impact on society. The coalition government of 2010 will increase VAT from January 2011, which will increase inflation - temporarily - and lead to an increase in prices. This may affect what customers decide to buy, which could have an effect on the products and services organisations deliver

- **Social** - e.g. Fathers being given more time to exercise their rights to paternity leave and the effect this has on an organisation. The decrease in the birth rate is putting pressures on older members of the population to stay in work longer

- **Technology** - e.g. The introduction of new I.T. programmes into an organisation

- **Legal** - e.g. Under the Human Rights Act 1998, under Article 14, 'Prohibition of Discrimination', people cannot be discriminated against on '… any grounds …' The introduction of this European convention works in tandem with existing UK legislation

- **Environment** - e.g. The introduction of a 'smoke-free' environment in business has given rise to people either smoking outside a building or an organisation having to provide a room for smokers

Most of these factors occur as a result of external forces to an organisation. An organisation will not have prior notification of these potential changes, although they may forecast for them in their business planning. An organisation will react to these external forces and plan for implementing subsequent change. Other factors that will affect an organisation will occur as a result of internal forces happening within an organisation, which can cause changes to working practices in a business environment:

- **Organisational strategy** - A new Chief Executive may decide to restructure the business, eliminating parts of the business

- **Organisation growth** - To remain competitive, an organisation may change its products and services

- **Mergers and acquisitions** - An organisation may merge with another organisation, which will probably result in redundancies - so as not to duplicate roles and realise economies of scale, the probable reason for the merger in the first place

- **Restructuring** - A manager may decide to structure the team / department in a different way, which could mean redundancies, learning new skills, losing old skills, moving to a new team / department

- **Research and development** - New products and services will be produced which may have an effect on the working practices of an organisation

- **Job redesign** - A job may be redesigned which will require learning new skills and knowledge

• ACTIVITY 2

What are the internal and external factors that can produce change?

Most change programmes carried out in a business environment will be about increasing and / or decreasing something. An organisation will generally strive to increase productivity and efficiency and to reduce costs. This may impact on the organisational culture and working practices. There should be a very clear vision for the change to be implemented:

- Improve an employee's work-life balance by offering more opportunity to work part-time, flexitime or as a job share

- Introduce flexible working practices by introducing new policies

- Introduce new knowledge and skills by attracting and retaining new talent

The 'win-win' situation an organisation should be aiming for is to achieve its economies of scale while giving its employees greater autonomy over their working lives. If employees feel that their working lives are not respected within a change programme, they can become:

- Disengaged

- Demotivated
- Disempowered
- Less committed
- Less flexible
- Less caring

Any of these changes in behaviour could lead to a negative environment and block the realisation of the aims of the change programme. Change, whether it is forced on or planned by an organisation, is usually an opportunity to improve:

- **The team**
- Size of the team
- Characteristics of team members
- Focus and direction of the team
- Position of the role of a team

- **The individual**
- Behaviours and attitudes
- Knowledge and skills through training
- Career and life planning
- Commitment to lifelong learning

•ACTIVITY 3

What can happen to individuals in an organisation if they are not consulted or included appropriately?

Supporting change
The process of change is not easy. The success of transformational change requires the assistance of many people. Employees must feel empowered to contribute to the change process which can occur through:

Open and timely communication
Effective and constructive communication should be a two-way process, someone giving out a message, the organisation and its managers, and

someone receiving that message, the employees. Employees should receive messages about change that are clear, simple, descriptive, consistent, explanatory, repetitious and can be seen to be meaningfully communicated, e.g. managers 'walk the talk' by showing by example. Employees should keep in contact with any communication directives through team meetings, the organisation's intranet - if there is one - and any newsletters that the HR department releases. Employees should actively listen to what is being communicated and question anything they do not fully understand.

Organisational structures in place to support change interventions

As employees engage with the vision for change they need to be assured that the organisation has the relevant organisational structures in place to facilitate the vision. For example, if an organisation is used to working in silos and the new working practice is to use 'matrix management', if the latter is not in place it will lead to frustration and employees will become discouraged etc., from the change programme.

Organisational structures need to change in a timely fashion to gain buy in from all stakeholders involved in the change programme. Employees should question the need for continuing structures which are a barrier to implementing a change programme, and this should be discussed with their managers.

Providing relevant training

All people in an organisation are employees despite the level of authority and responsibility they might have in the organisation. A change programme may require new knowledge and skills. In order to make sure that these are in place, training should be carried out that is timely, sufficient, relevant and followed up. Training should not only apply to the technical skills required to carry out a job, but energy must be given to social skills and attitudes as well, as these may be habits that have built up over many years of being in the same job which may no longer be appropriate within the new culture. An organisation will have systems in place for looking at an employee's development, as part of an appraisal system, which should provide the employee with the opportunity to contribute to their future development.

Aligning internal organisational systems with the change vision

Employees must feel that the systems that support their work are not a barrier to realising the changes that need to be implemented. For example, an HR department which is open to change in the way that it operates, as the HR department will be instrumental in facilitating change in most organisations. Employees should question the need for continuing systems which are a barrier to implementing a change programme, and this should be discussed with their managers.

Committed managers

Employees need to feel that they have the support of their managers. They need to feel their managers are fully on board with the change programme so everyone can stay focused and committed to implementing the change initiatives. Managers need to take a parochial interest in all their employees to encourage and maintain their commitment to the change programme. This is perhaps the most difficult situation for an employee to address. If an employee is unsure about who to discuss this issue with, the first port of call should be the HR department, as it should take an objective and unbiased approach to resolving issues.

• ACTIVITY 4

How can employees feel empowered to contribute towards the change programme?

Employees should remain open to the change programme and recognise that it may not always be easy for either themselves or their managers to cope with all the implications of change. Employees can remain committed to the change programme by taking a bite-size approach to realising the aims and objectives of the change programme. They can do this by:

- Making sure work is planned at an individual level and also merges with team aspirations
- Breaking down tasks into manageable and meaningful chunks of work
- Using SMART objectives which commit an employee to achieving agreed tasks
- Fine tuning what has to be done and when this needs to be achieved
- Providing evidence that things are changing and producing the desired effect. Undermine cynics of change with these success

stories

- Encouraging others when they have achieved incremental steps of change and sharing how this has contributed to achieving the vision for change

Using all these strategies an employee not only drives the momentum for change but builds on it.

There is great pressure placed on employees during the change programme. Support could be considered in the following areas:

- **Psychological**
- **Practical**
- **Technical**

• ACTIVITY 5

What actions could be taken to offer psychological support?

It is not always easy to be totally on board with a change programme, particularly if the change is being thrust on the organisation. There

will be little preparation that an organisation can take, e.g. coping with all the new structures and systems that a new government will have on organisational life. Try not to pre-empt what an organisation or a manager is aiming to do. Have patience and seek to be included in the planning process to contribute ideas and agree a way forward. Another aspect of change which is challenging for employees is coping with redundancies as a result of change decisions. This not only affects those who have been made redundant but also staff who have survived and will remain with the organisation. Survivors need to know that the process of redundancy selection has been fair and impartial, and seen to be; that it has been communicated to all parties sensitively; that those being made redundant are helped and survivors of the change programme are aware of the new vision for the future.

Everyone is very different from everyone else. They will go through various stages of rejection and acceptance of the change programme.

Kubler-Ross's transition (grief) cycle identified five stages in dealing with 'catastrophic news', which has been applied to recognising how employees cope with change in a business context. The five stages of performance or self-esteem experiences by employees in an organisation are:

- **Denial** - Where employees do not want to be engaged with the change programme
- **Anger** - Where employees resist the change programme
- **Bargaining** - Where employees begin to explore the implications of the change programme
- **Depression** - Where employees continue to explore the implications of the change programme and may feel overwhelmed by the change experience
- **Acceptance** - Where employees actively engage with the change programme

• ACTIVITY 6

What are the five stages of the Kubler-Ross transition (grief) cycle?

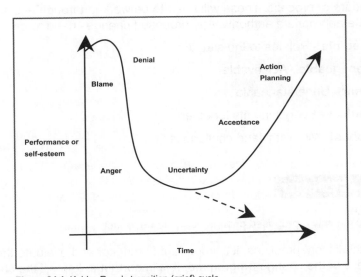

Figure 24.1. Kubler-Ross's transition (grief) cycle

It is a 21st-century mantra that the only constant in organisational life is change. Business is increasingly becoming more globalised and competitive, which will always impose on an organisation the need to re-appraise what it is doing, how it is doing it, why it is doing what it is doing, where it is doing it etc. So employees, like boy scouts or girl guides, always need to 'be prepared'. To 'be prepared' an employee should not be too fixed in their opinions or the ways that they work.

Change means change for everyone in an organisation. All employees will find that they will be asked to do things that they do not want to do or that they do not think they will enjoy doing. Remain open, not fixed, and surprise yourself. Be aware that two of the hardest things to change are behaviours and attitudes. These have been with an employee for a long time. They have been shaped by many experiences in life that may have nothing to do with work life. Recognise that there is a marriage between everyday life and work life. If these two lives have different aspirations, organisational change is an opportunity to integrate them.

While organisational change may be imposed, learn to contribute towards its positive execution. As with all work, make sure that there is a clear plan of what needs to be done. Look at what was done, what will be done and review the changes that need to take place. This may require new procedures and processes. Work through the new workflow identifying specifically what needs to be done at each stage of the procedure or process. These will need to be worked through and agreed with the appropriate authority. Any proposed changes need to be:

- **Credible** - Relates to the situation
- **Manageable** - Achievable
- **Clear** - Understandable
- **Logical** - Everything fits together
- **Robust** - Will withstand challenges

• ACTIVITY 7

Explain why a proposed change needs to be robust.

As with all work practices, it is important to monitor and evaluate the progress of the change programme. It is important to know if the change programme is achieving what it has been set up to achieve. A review will need to consider the impact that it is having on the organisation from the perspective of its structures, systems, policies and its people and the need for further incremental change. The review should ask the following questions:

- What was the change programme aiming to achieve?
- How was the change programme aiming to achieve these aims?
- How successful was the change programme in achieving its stated aims?
- What were the barriers to success?
- What were the lessons to be learned?
- Future recommendations.

A review can be undertaken in many different ways, including conducting:

- **Surveys** - Which can be done regularly with all or some employees to quantify the progress and results of change
- **Individual interviews or focus groups**
- **Turnover and absenteeism review**
- **Performance reviews**
- **Picturing of the organisation** - Where employees are asked to represent their perception of the changed organisation in images rather than words

• ACTIVITY 8

What different ways can a review of change be conducted?

Change as part of a process of continuous improvement

There is no escaping change. It is a direct and indirect organic part of any organisation's aspiration to continuously improve. This will affect the ways that an organisation operates and how its employees will operate within it. The economic environment that organisations operate in is more volatile and faces greater uncertainty than at any time prior to the 21st century. This has created the need for employees to embrace lifelong learning to keep their knowledge and skills up to date and employable. Organisations also need to be learning organisations.

Employees who learn to master operating in a volatile work environment usually develop more knowledge and skills, become more comfortable with change and may be more useful in organisational transformation. Employees not only advance organisational aspirations for growth but also improve their own development and growth, which can lead to career promotion.

Lifelong learning gives the employee the opportunity to consider how they fit their personal life to their work life. There may not always be a match between the two. There may be cultural misfits, behavioural misfits, attitudinal misfits etc. Any of these misfits may be perceived by the organisation as a threat to its continuing survival. Take the opportunity of reviewing an organisation's mission and value statements. Analyse how these statements fit with personal values and beliefs. Of course, some of these values may only be perceived when actually working in an organisation; however, an organisation's mission and value statements should give a good indication of its ethical and moral position. An employee will need to consider if they are able to work within a world of ethical or moral values and beliefs that may be very different from their own. It may require an employee to change their values to merge with expectations of business practice, e.g. an organisation may be very careful in how it makes decisions whereas an employee may have a very free and easy approach to making decisions.

Change gives the employee an opportunity either to embrace the change or reject it. Either decision will have far-reaching implications for their continued employment in an organisation. By responding positively to change, it may open up a world of future possibilities that an employee may not have considered, e.g. career progression, ways of improving leadership skills by becoming a team leader. Embracing change reinforces the belief in the successful implementation of the change programme and actively engages the employee in its implementation.

Testing your knowledge

1. Why does change occur as frequently as it does in organisations?

2. What can be the psychological impact of change to employees?

3. What should an employee do to facilitate organisational change?

4. Why should employees plan for organisational change?

5. What should an employee consider when adapting to organisational change?

6. Why is good communication so important during organisational change?

7. What strategies can an employee use to cope with organisational change?

8. How can the values of an organisation interact with an employee's personal values?

9. Why should the effects of organisational change be evaluated?

Skills

You will not be unfamiliar with change. It is something that happens in your physical body every day, in fact, every minute of the day. So it should not be a surprise to find it happening at an institutional level in your organisation. Change is something that will never stop. However, it is not always easy to cope with the affects of change. It may affect just you, it may affect the team you work in, the department you work in or the organisation as a whole. Find out what implications change will have on any of these areas of your work. Try to involve yourself in the planning of the activities that need to be undertaken to realise the aims and objectives of the change. Are you clear about what the change will mean for you? Make sure that you are. If you do not quite understand the implications, check with your supervisor / manager and go over all the communications. Go through the communications identifying what areas you do not understand and have these explained to you and your team if need be. It is important that if working as a team that all team members are in agreement with what needs to be done and how and when it needs to be done.

• ACTIVITY 9

Keep a diary over two months tracing the changes that have occurred in your area of work. What have you had to do to make them work?

Contribute towards the planning of how the change will be rolled out for you and your team. Make suggestions that you think will be helpful. Consider the impact of the change and how it will affect you. Does something else need to be done as a result of the changes being implemented? Once there is agreement on what changes need to take place, carry out your work with these new changes of practice. However, before completing these new tasks make sure that you have the knowledge and skills required of these new tasks. Go over this with you supervisor / manager either in a development meeting, team meeting or your appraisal meeting. Make any changes to your development plan. The initiative to change is also an opportunity for you to consider how you may want to make personal changes and to review your position in the organisation or beyond it.

• ACTIVITY 10

What was the most challenging change you had to cope with and why?

If you are having difficulty personally coping with change, or coping with how others around you are adapting to change, and do not know how to respond, speak to your supervisor / manager or someone in HR, as they will have an overall perspective of what is going on and what has been going on behind the scenes which they may be able to share with you; where you can support others, be of assistance and offer to help. This may be another learning opportunity to coach or mentor someone, if you have the relevant knowledge and skills to do this.

• ACTIVITY 11

What personal values and beliefs have you changed as a result of organisational change?

There is no point adapting your behaviour or work performance to the requirements of a change programme if you do not know what the impact of that change has been aiming to achieve. Work with your team to review what has been done. Identify if the change has been effective and what might need to be done to improve. Offer any suggestions that you have to improve your own work.

Testing your skills

1. What did you do to assist with organisational change in your area of work?

2. How did you contribute to the plans for change in your area of work?

3. How did you adapt to organisational change?

4. What support mechanisms did you use during organisational change?

5. What support mechanisms did you suggest were used for colleagues during organisational change?

6. How did you understand the implications of organisational change in your area of work?

7. How did you contribute to the evaluation of organisational change?

Ready for assessment?

To achieve this Level 2 unit of a Business & Administration qualification, learners will need to demonstrate that they are able to perform the following activities:

1. Identified changes needed in own area of work

2. Made suggestions for change

3. Completed own work tasks using changed procedures or ways of working

4. Identified where training or other support is needed

5. Actively sought support, as required

6. Gave support to other people during change, or sought support, as required

7. Asked questions to clarify issues

8. Gave feedback on the effects of changes in own work

9. Made suggestions for further actions, as required

You will need to produce evidence from a variety of sources to support the performance requirements of this unit.

If you carry out the 'ACTIVITIES' and respond to the 'NEED TO KNOW' questions, these will provide some of the evidence required.

Links to other units

While gathering evidence for this unit, evidence may also be used from evidence generated from other units within the Business & Administration suite of units. Below is a sample of applicable units; however, most units within the Business & Administration suite of units will also be applicable.

QCF NVQ
Communications
Communicate in a business environment (Level 2)
Communicate in a business environment (Level 2)
Core business & administration
Manage own performance in a business environment (Level 2)
Improve own performance in a business environment (Level 2)
Work in a business environment (Level 2)
Work with other people in a business environment (Level 2)
Manage own performance in a business environment (Level 3)
Evaluate and improve own performance in a business environment (Level 3)
Work in a business environment (Level 3)
Work with other people in a business environment (Level 3)

SVQ
Communications
Prepare to communicate in a business environment
Communicate in a business environment
Core business & administration
Agree how to manage and improve own performance in a business environment
Undertake work in a business environment
Work with other people in a business environment
Plan how to manage and improve own performance in a business environment
Review and maintain work in a business environment
Support other people to work in a business environment

25 Organise and report data

ORGANISE AND REPORT DATA

'**Organise and report data**' is an <u>optional unit</u> which may be chosen as one of a combination of units to achieve either a Qualifications and Credit Framework (QCF), National Vocational Qualification (NVQ) or Scottish Vocational Qualification (SVQ).

The aims of this unit are to:

*   Understand how to organise and report data that has been researched
*   Be able to organise data
*   Be able to report data

To achieve the above aims of this unit, learners will be expected to provide evidence through the performance of work-based activities.

Knowledge

Organisations gather together and research information about themselves and other organisations to maintain and build on their market share and find out what is happening in their particular sector. The amount of information that can be researched by an organisation is limitless. For example, job satisfaction, management, change, the effectiveness of a training intervention, labour market information.

An employee will be asked by their supervisor / manager to undertake a research project. They will be asked to complete this piece of research to:

*   Meet an agreed **purpose -** The aims and objectives of the research
*   Be **formatted** in a specific way
*   Be **reported** to conform to the organisation's '**house style**'
*   Be completed within agreed **time frames**
*   Meet the needs of its **intended audience**

The research project can be broken down into:

- **The research brief -** Every research brief will identify a question that needs to be answered. This will be the purpose of the research, e.g. how has the trend for absenteeism changed over the past three years?

- **Research design -** The methodology that will be undertaken to extract data

- **Data collection -** Depending on which form of research method is used for the research project, data will be collected and organised. Data will either be:

  - Numeric: this is data that is in the form of numbers, which results from **quantitative research**

  - Non-numeric or narrative: this is data that is in the form of narrative statements which results from **qualitative research**

- **Data analysis -** Data that is collected and then analysed to find causal relationships from which conclusions and recommendations about the data can be written. There are many different ways of analysing data, which depends on whether the data is numerical or non-numerical are many different ways of analysing data, which depends on whether the data is numerical or non-numerical

- **Project report -** Once all the data has been collected a report will be written which will analyse the findings and make conclusions and recommendations. This may have to follow an organisation's '**house style**'

• ACTIVITY 1

Why do organisations carry out research projects?

Data collection
To understand the implications of the research question, a research brief should be drawn up that will look at all aspects of the research. The research question needs to be fully analysed to understand clearly what it is aiming to answer. The research brief should cover:

The sources of information required
Consider different sources of information which will help to answer the research question. There are four main sources of information available:

- **Previous research carried out by the researcher or the organisation** - This will require previous research to have been stored accurately, e.g. in the organisation's library, or archived conveniently to allow easy access

- **Paper-based reference material** - e.g. Books, industry / sector magazine articles, government papers, price lists. These are shortcuts, saving time, to looking up information in reference books:

  - The preface: an initial review to see if the source will be relevant

  - The publication date: tells the researcher how current the information is

  - The index: uses keywords

  - The contents: uses chapter headings

  - The bibliography: uses other books related to the same subject area

- **Electronic-based reference material** - e.g. Using the Internet. The Internet holds information on almost everything; however, as there is so much information, it can be difficult to find exactly what is required. Use a good 'search engine', e.g. 'Google', 'Yahoo'.

To narrow the research:

  - Think of keywords that would appear in an article

  - Avoid using lengthy combinations of keywords

  - Start with seven words

  - Spell the keywords correctly

  - Use a 'thesaurus' to choose keywords

  - Use lower-case letters

- **People** - This may be an informal approach where key members of staff are asked for their opinions or a formal approach where a questionnaire is specifically designed to ask questions about the research question

The **volume** of information required - consider all types of information that will help to answer the research question; however, do not get sidetracked by irrelevant information.

- **When** the information is required
- How the information should be **formatted**
- How the information should be **reported**
- If the information is **relevant** to its intended audience

Always remain focused on the purpose of the research and what it is aiming to achieve.

All information researched should be:

- **Relevant** - Information that is applicable to the research
- **Valid** - Information is what it claims it is. It is the 'truth'
- **Reliable** - Information that is consistent

• ACTIVITY 2

What are the different sources of information which can be used in a research project? What are the most important aspects of that information, (that need to be considered as appropriate), to be included in research?

Once all information that is relevant to answering the research question has been found, it should be compiled and organised.

Organising and reporting data
However research data is gathered, it needs to be condensed, summarised and organised in a meaningful way ready for analysis and interpretation by its intended audience. Data will be collected as the results of the research question. Data at this stage will be 'raw' - it has not been collated, summarised or processed in any way. Data that is collected qualitatively should be presented graphically according to two principles:

- **Exclusiveness** - No observation should be classified into more than one category
- **Inclusiveness** - Every observation is classified into a category

This means that when organising observations there should be enough categories coded to fit all observations. This also means that each category is coded precisely so every observation can only be placed in one category, e.g. see the table below, which categorises the total revenue for each functional area within an organisation.

• ACTIVITY 3

What are the two principles for representing data graphically?

Numerical data can be presented in different graphical formats:

Tables
A list of figures or scores which give precise data, but this can be very difficult to make sense of, see below:

	2009	2010	Difference
Sales	£15,552	£20,353	-£4,801
Maintenance	£205	£584	-£379
Telephone	£315	£263	£52
Stationery	£504	£72	£432
Total expenses	£1,024	£919	£105
Sales - Expenses	£14,528	£19,434	-£4,906

Pie charts
A pie chart is the best graphical display for displaying data arranged in categories. Each category is represented by a wedge of the pie and the size of each wedge is in proportion to the percentage of each category. Pie charts should:

- Organise data in a few categories. Too many categories will make the chart difficult to interpret

- Display the pieces of the pie in either ascending or descending order of magnitude

- Be used to display percentages

In the example on the next page, the categories have been reordered so the data is presented in decreasing order of magnitude.

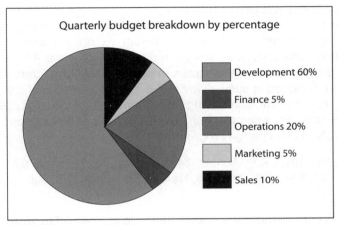

Figure 25.1. Example of a pie chart

Bar charts

A bar chart or histogram shows frequencies or percentages in a chart. Frequencies should be shown along the vertical axis of the chart and the categories on the horizontal axis of the chart. Bar charts should:

- Start the vertical scale at '0', to avoid distorting the graph
- Have rectangles constructed over each category, with the height of the rectangle equal to the number of observations in the category
- Leave a space between each category for clarity of reading

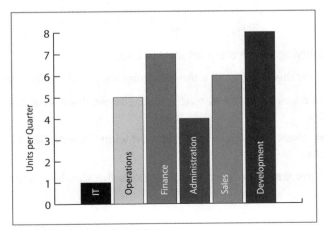

Figure 25.2. Example of a bar chart

Non-numerical and quantitative data

Non-numerical data, quantitative data, will also need to be organised. This is done similarly as with numerical data, except that with quantitative data categories are given numerical intervals. These numerical intervals are called **class intervals**. The class intervals should be designed in such a way that every measurement falls in one and only one interval, conforming to the principles of inclusiveness and exclusiveness. For example, here is a list of ages of employees that were involved in a change programme:

Stewart, 55; David, 42; Michael, 34; Veronica, 37; Susanna, 52; Thomas, 65; Kylie, 31; John, 53; Harvey, 56; Martin, 33; Robert, 43 and Charles, 48.

To make sense of this data, a table needs to be created to arrange the data by intervals. This will clearly show how many employees of each age group were involved in the change programme. In this instance, the date will be arranged in five-year intervals:

Age Group	Number of Employees
31-35	3
36-40	1
41-45	2
46-50	1
51-55	3
56-60	1
61-65	1
Total	12

When identifying which class interval to use:

- Decide on the number of intervals necessary to describe the data

- Choose class intervals with no gaps between them - As in the above example

- Choose class intervals with a common width - Using five in the above example

- Locate the first interval so that it includes the smallest score

• ACTIVITY 4

What is a class interval and what should be considered in determining which class interval to use?

Using the above example, a class interval of 3, 10, 15 etc., could have been used, which would have changed how the table could be organised. Qualitative data can also be written in the narrative, e.g.

MEMO

To: Sales Manager
From: William Weston
Date: 16 August 2010
Subject: Preston Works - Customer contact summary

01.07.10   Request for catalogue

02.07.10   Catalogue sent

05.07.10   Telephone call to make appointment for rep

06.07.10   Visit by rep

14.07.10   Order received by telephone - order number 2546448

15.07.10   Order despatched by post

16.07.10   Invoice raised - invoice number 886654

22.07.10   Payment received

• ACTIVITY 5

When should data be organised into graphical representations?

It may be appropriate to represent the data in more than one of the above formats. This will depend on the complexity of the data being presented. It may be helpful to have both a table and a graph in a report, because the effect of the data may not be apparent from a table and it may be more effectively illustrated in a chart or graph.

At this stage of the research project no decision has been made about what data will be presented in the final report. Some of the data could be inserted into the main part of a document or in an appendix. It will depend on how much detail the final report is going to present, which will depend on the audience for whom the report is being designed for.

• ACTIVITY 6

What are the different formats that can be used to organise data? What are the advantages and disadvantages of these different formats?

The presentation of the data needs to be organised in a **report**. The type of report required to organise all the data that has been collected will vary depending on the purpose of the research and the 'house style' of an organisation. A report is required to present information in a logical order. Some reports could be as simple as a memo or an email response. If the project is a complex one, a report will need to be written. If a report is to be written, an outline structure for the report needs to be agreed. Most reports will have the following headings:

- **Title**

- **Executive summary** - This is optional, depending on an organisation's requirements

- **Introduction** - This section outlines the background to the report and gives an overview of what the report contains

- **Methodology** - This section records the research methods used to collect the research data, e.g. questionnaires conducted online and over the telephone

- **Findings / results** - This section outlines all the findings from the research. This should be written in a logical way that leads the reader clearly to the conclusion (s) and recommendation (s)

- **Conclusions** - This section will present the results of the analysis, stating what the research has led to and why. Conclusions should only be drawn from the data and information presented in the report, not from any previously held personal opinions

- **Recommendations** - This section should state any action (s) that should be taken as a result of the conclusion (s)

- **Acknowledgements** - This section should thank those who have assisted with the research project

- **Bibliography** - This will include references used during 'desk' research. Source material should be referred to. This should be listed alphabetically by author and the date of publication given

- **Appendix** - This should include raw data. It may also include information referred to in the report which is too detailed to be given in full without distracting from the purpose of the report

In the first instance, a **draft report** should be written. This should identify initial findings etc. The draft report should be shown to the person for whom the report is being compiled. Agree with them that the final report will probably contain more detailed information. Agree with them what this content should be.

• ACTIVITY 7

How is a final report structured? Why is it structured in this way?

On completing a final report make sure it is proofread before having it printed and distributed. Most word-processing packages contain spell-check and grammar-check facilities. Use these first to correct any obvious mistakes; however, do not rely on them completely as they are not foolproof systems of correction. The dictionary may default to use American spelling and grammar, so will accept, for instance, 'color' and reject 'colour'. Set the default to use the English, UK, dictionary in the options a computer gives for the spell-check function.

When the automatic checking is complete, reread the document carefully to look for missed errors. Correct the document so that it is consistently formatted in the same style throughout, e.g. use of paragraphs, headings, subheadings. Take extra care when reviewing numbers, dates, times and amounts. Check for errors between similar words, such as 'affect' and 'effect' or 'less' and 'fewer'.

The researcher may have to present this report in more meaningful chunks of information to an invited audience who may not have had access to the report before attending the presentation. Create an appropriate presentation which outlines the main points of the report, e.g. the title, conclusion and recommendations. Handouts may also need to be provided.

When the final report has been completed, decide if and how it is going to be archived.

Review the information and decide whether it is worth keeping for future reference. If it is archived, review it from time to time and throw away anything that is out of date.

There are many ways of organising and reporting data. Always select the most relevant, valid and reliable pieces of information for research. Once information has been accessed and utilised, organise the extracted data in a way that meets the requirements of the person for whom the research has been completed. Create the final report in the in the most user-friendly way which conforms to an organisation's 'house style' and meets the expectations of the audience.

Testing your knowledge

1. Why is it important to agree the aims, objectives and deadlines of a research project?

2. Why should the data produced match the request for the data?

3. Why does data need to be organised?

4. How are sources of information recorded?

5. Why are the used sources of information recorded?

6. What determines the data that needs to be collected for a research project?

7. What is an 'executive summary'?

8. What is found in an 'appendix'?

Skills

Working with the person who has requested the collection of data, agree what the purpose of the research is aiming to achieve. Once this is clear you will need to agree the logistical aspects of the research, how much research is required, what sources of information should be checked, what should be extracted from these sources of information, the data and when the person for whom the report will be compiled will want it completed. In many respects, the amount of time that you are given will determine what you can do. If you have one day to provide the data, you will not have the time to write a full report. In this case, you will probably present a few tables / diagrams along with some narrative to explain them. You may even make some recommendations regarding what should be done with this data, e.g. a full report with more time to explore every aspect of the research topic.

Once the parameters of the research have been agreed, start looking for sources of information. You may have agreed with the lead person what sources you will use, so address these first. If there is more time you can widen your search and look at other means of sourcing information. Once you have the sources of information you will need to read through them and extract the appropriate data that will produce an argument which can be elaborated on in the report. Some data may already be in an appropriate format, so it can just be imported. However, other data may not be in the most appropriate format, to make it clear what the data it telling you, so this could be changed into another format. If you are not sure, discuss this with your lead researcher.

• ACTIVITY 8

The office manager is considering replacing the computers used by the department. Compile available data on the features, prices and performance of different systems. Format and organise the data.

Some data will be sourced through primary research, where data has been identified by those participants who may have completed a questionnaire, been interviewed over the telephone or been in a focus group. This data will need to be made meaningful by being formatted. Decide which format is the most appropriate. Place all the data in the appropriate format. You may want to use more than one format with the same data to allow your intended audience to explore the data from different perspectives.

Data that has been collected can be either numerical or non-numerical - which can be formatted in a narrative style, where participants who were involved in answering a questionnaire etc., have given opinions about what they think. All collected data will need to be formatted in some way to make it meaningful to the intended audience who will be looking at the data. When reporting non-numerical data it is important to look at the answers given by participants to make sure they have answered the given question correctly. Participants may not necessarily answer the question, but their answers may be appropriate to other questions that have been asked. A note of this should be made and cross-referenced. If this is a recurring theme, it needs to be reported to the lead researcher, because something may be wrong with the way the question has been written.

Looking at all the narrative answers, you will need to start assembling them into different themes or subject areas. This will allow the data to be reported in logical and meaningful ways.

Check with the lead researcher that the data that has been extracted or collected from primary research is adequate, accurate - valid and reliable - and relevant to the research topic. Remember, with research there is always a question seeking an answer. Your collection and organisation of that data will lead to answering the research question. Having satisfied all parties that the collected data is formatted and accurate, decide on what kind of report needs to be completed to present the data. Use the template for writing reports. If a full report is not required there may be elements of the report template that can be used, e.g. findings and conclusions. It will depend on the depth and breadth of the research being undertaken.

Once you have completed your report check with the lead researcher that it has answered the research question. Go over any queries they might have. Evaluate with them what they mean and answer their queries. This may require going over the data to make sure it is correct or going over the narrative of your report to make sure your report has accurately defined what the data is saying / doing.

• ACTIVITY 9

A parcel weighing 2kg needs to be sent to Singapore. Find out the alternative methods of sending the parcel, the costs of each and the delivery times. Present the data in the best format to make it meaningful to the person for whom the report has been designed. Compare the costs and times. State which method would be most cost-effective and why.

Make a final report and prepare a presentation, if one is requested.

Testing your skills

1. What types of information does your organisation have?

2. What sources of information does your organisation use?

3. What sources of information are available to you?

4. Why should you record the sources of information used?

5. How do you use a search engine?

6. What data have you organised for a research project?

7. What data was required for the research projects you contributed towards?

8. How did you design the presentation of data?

Ready for assessment?
To achieve this Level 2 unit of a Business & Administration qualification, learners will need to demonstrate that they are able to perform the following activities:

1. Collated data in a way that will help analysis

2. Organised data in a way that will help analysis

3. Checked the accuracy of data

4. Made adjustments to the data, as required

5. Presented data, that was found from research, in the agreed format and to the agreed timescales

6. Obtained feedback on data that was found from research, if necessary

You will need to produce evidence from a variety of sources to support the performance requirements of this unit.

If you carry out the 'ACTIVITIES' and respond to the 'NEED TO KNOW' questions, these will provide some of the evidence required.

Links to other units
While gathering evidence for this unit, evidence **may** also be used from evidence generated from other units within the Business & Administration suite of units. Below is a **sample** of applicable units; however, most units within the Business & Administration suite of units will also be applicable.

QCF NVQ
Communications
Communicate in a business environment (Level 2)
Core business & administration
Manage own performance in a business environment (Level 2)
Improve own performance in a business environment (Level 2)
Work in a business environment (Level 2)
Solve business problems (Level 2)
Work with other people in a business environment (Level 2)
Document production
Produce documents in a business environment
Prepare text from notes
Manage information and data
Research information
Store and retrieve information
Archive information (Level 2)

SVQ
Communications
Prepare to communicate in a business environment
Core business & administration
Agree how to manage and improve own performance in a business environment
Undertake work in a business environment
Plan how to solve business problems
Contribute to working with others in a business environment
Document production
Produce documents in a business environment
Prepare text from notes
Manage information and data
Research information
Store and retrieve information
Provide archive services

26 Research information

RESEARCH INFORMATION

'**Research information**' is an <u>optional unit</u> which may be chosen as one of a combination of units to achieve either a Qualifications and Credit Framework (QCF), National Vocational Qualification (NVQ) or Scottish Vocational Qualification (SVQ).

The aims of this unit are to:

- Understand procedures for researching information

- Be able to research information for others

To achieve the above aims of this unit, learners will be expected to provide evidence through the performance of work-based activities.

Knowledge

Organisations gather together information about themselves and other organisations to maintain and build on their market share and find out what is happening in their particular sector. The amount of information that that can be researched by an organisation is limitless, e.g. job satisfaction, management, change, the effectiveness of a training intervention, labour market information.

An employee will be asked by their supervisor / manager to undertake a research project. They will be asked to complete this piece of research to:

- **Meet an agreed purpose** - The aims and objectives of the research

- **Be formatted in a specific way**

- **Be reported to conform** to the organisation's 'house style'

- **Be completed within agreed time frames**

- **Meet the needs of its intended audience**

• ACTIVITY 1

Why does an organisation research information?

The research project can be broken down into:

The research brief
Every research brief will identify a question that needs to be answered. This will be the purpose of the research, e.g. how has the trend for absenteeism changed over the past three years?

Research methodology / design

There are four research methods that can be used to gather information:

- **Primary research -** This is research which is original and does not draw upon existing data or information. There are four widely used methods:

  - **Questionnaires:** designed to collect information from a variety of sources. This method can be conducted either face to face, includes focus groups; over the telephone; via a video facility or using a computer program. This may be a cost-effective approach and the computer program may also collate and analyse the data collected. Data from this form of primary research can be used either quantitatively or qualitatively

  - **Interviews:** using a specific script, participants are asked questions face to face, includes focus groups; over the telephone or via a video facility. Data from this form of primary research can be used quantitatively or qualitatively

  - **Observation:** the researcher observes practices and activities, without joining in, to identify what is happening and why. Observation is usually a qualitative research methodology; however, data collected from observation can be formatted quantitatively

  - **Experimentation:** using the 'scientific method', tests, or a battery of tests, are designed to see what happens under controlled conditions. The design of the experiment will usually use dependent and independent variables which the experimenter will manipulate, depending on the hypothesis they are investigating.

This method is mainly used within a quantitative methodology, but the same level of rigour will be used on the design of quantitative methodologies

- **Secondary research** - The main form of this methodology is:

    - **Desk research:** this involves investigating any relevant existing sources of information. This can be used for simple activities, e.g. finding out how the price of clothes has changed over a year in a retail store, to complex activities, e.g. using many different sources of information and extracting the relevant data

- **Qualitative research** - Does not use statistical analysis, but analyses narrative and the discourse given by participants. It lacks quantifiable evidence. It is used to explore less easily defined objectives, such as opinions. It is argued that this is a more humanistic approach to research

- **Quantitative research** - Usually uses statistical analysis to interpret numerical data collected from research. It uses large numbers of participants. It provides data in numeric terms. Data is usually obtained by asking participants to complete a carefully planned questionnaire, either directly over the telephone, face to face or indirectly - by post or email

    > Research is formalised curiosity. It is poking and prying with a purpose.
    > - *Zora Neale Hurston*

Data collection
Depending on which form of research method is used for the research project, data will be collected and organised. Data will either be:

- **Numeric** - This is data that is in the form of numbers, which results from quantitative research

- **Non-numeric or narrative** - This is data that is in the form of qualitative statements and not numbers

Data analysis
Data that is collected and then analysed to find causal relationships from which conclusions and recommendations about the data can be written. There are many different ways of analysing data which depends on whether the data is numerical or non-numerical.

Project report

Once all the data has been collected a report will be written which will analyse the findings and make conclusions and recommendations. This may have to follow an organisation's 'house style'.

• ACTIVITY 2

What are the elements that make up a research project?

Once information has been sourced it needs to be organised, analysed and presented in a way that meets the requirements of the user. Research will usually provide quantitative information, qualitative information or both, which is a very robust approach to obtaining information.

Collecting data

To understand the implications of the research question, a research brief should be drawn up that will look at all aspects of the research. The research question needs to be fully analysed to understand clearly what it is aiming to answer. The research brief should cover:

Information Sources

Consider different sources of information which will help to answer the research question. There are four main sources of information available:

- **Previous research carried out by the researcher or the organisation -** This will require previous research to have been stored accurately, e.g. in the organisation's library or archived conveniently to allow easy access. For simple research proposals, there is a good chance that most of the information will be freely available and held in a database or spreadsheet. A simple research proposal may be one that is done fairly regularly throughout a year, so it just requires updating the information. A more complex research proposal will involve more time and a greater depth and breadth of research. In a complex research proposal, research may have taken place in the past which may be a good point to start the current information research. If the research proposal is only looking at internal information it will be found within the organisation. However, a complex research proposal will normally require information to be researched both inside and outside of the organisation

- **Paper-based reference material**
  e.g. Books, industry / sector magazine articles,
  newspapers, brochures, leaflets, government
  papers. Each of these types of publication will
  have varying levels of relevance to the research
  proposal. These are shortcuts, saving time, to
  looking up information in reference books:

  - The preface: an initial review to see if the
    source will be relevant

  - The publication date: tells the researcher how
    current the information is

  - The index: uses keywords

  - The contents: uses chapter headings

  - The bibliography: uses other books related to the same subject
    area

- **Electronic-based reference material** – e.g. Using the Internet.
  The Internet holds information on almost everything; however, as
  there is so much information, it can be difficult to find exactly what
  is required. Use a good 'search engine', e.g. 'Google', 'Yahoo'. To
  narrow the research:

  - Think of keywords that would appear in an article

  - Avoid using lengthy combinations of keywords

  - Start with seven words

  - Spell the keywords correctly

  - Use a 'thesaurus' to choose keywords

  - Use lower-case letters

In all searches for information consider copyright and confidentiality.
Any published work is likely to be subject to copyright, whereby the work
belongs to the person / people who wrote it. If a quote from reference
material is going to be used it must be acknowledged, to avoid
accusations of **plagiarism**.

• ACTIVITY 3

What is plagiarism?

- **People** - This may be an informal approach where key members of staff are asked for their opinions or a formal approach where a questionnaire is specifically designed to ask questions to explore the research proposal. Talk to everybody who may have useful knowledge. Work colleagues bring lots of information from their previous experience and expertise gained in other jobs, which may be applicable to the research proposal. It may be necessary to liaise with other departments to obtain information which they may hold in databases. All personal data will be subject to the Data Protection Act 1998

Other considerations
- The **volume** of information required - Consider all types of information that will help to answer the research question; however, do not get sidetracked by irrelevant information

- The **depth and breadth** of information to be researched

- **When** the information is required

- How the information should be **formatted**

- How the information should be **reported**

- If the information is relevant to its **intended audience**

Always remain focused on the purpose of the research and what it is aiming to achieve.

• ACTIVITY 4

What are the different sources of information that can be researched?

All information researched should be:

- **Relevant** - Information that is applicable to the research

- **Valid** - Information is what it claims it is. It is the 'truth'

- **Reliable** - Information that is consistent

In undertaking the research, always be guided by the purpose of the research - what aims and objectives are to be achieved? The research proposal may range from the simple to the complex. A simple research proposal may involve looking at the number of people who have been on sick leave for more than two days over the past six months. A complex proposal may involve looking at how the market share of a particular product has changed over the past 12 months. The breadth and depth of research to be carried out will be partly informed by the deadline that has been agreed to produce the information. If there is a lot of time, more sources of information will be researched than if a short deadline had been agreed.

Designing a questionnaire

A questionnaire is used to collect data which will not be available through other sources of information. It is a primary research method.

It is simple to design, versatile and cost-effective. It needs to be designed to suit the purpose of the research question. While a questionnaire may be simple to design it is not always easy to get right. The questionnaire will need to consider:

- The research **proposal**

- The **participants** who will complete the questionnaire

- Ways of designing **questions**

- Availability of **resources** e.g. people, finance

The aim of designing a questionnaire is to gain buy-in from the participants who will be answering the questionnaire. In designing a questionnaire for a particular audience, it should target a specific cohort of people, who generally remain anonymous, unless they have granted their permission to be known. Questions should be formulated so:

- They will be **understood by the participants -** The wording of a question should be clear; simple; brief, no more than 20 words; specific, no ambiguity and relevant. Questions should not lead the participant to answer the way the researcher would like them to

- They will **encourage participants to answer the questions** - Consideration needs to be given to when participants will be approached to answer questions. Check to make sure it is convenient for the participant to respond at the time of calling - it is difficult to manage this with postal questionnaires - so they have no distractions. Participants should be given the right to withdraw from answering a questionnaire at any time

- The **participants will have the required knowledge to answer the questions** - e.g. If designing questions about hospitality, only people working in the hospitality industry should be approached to answer these questions

- They will be **easy to analyse** - The questions will produce appropriate data to analyse

There is a range of ways questionnaires may be administered, which includes:

- **Structured interviews schedule** - Face-to-face and telephone interviews. The interviewer will need to have good interpersonal skills

- **Self-administered or group-administered questionnaires** - The mechanics of how to answer the questionnaire will be explained to the participant or participants who are then left alone to answer questions. This format can also be delivered online. The researcher is able to clarify misunderstandings about the questionnaire. There is usually a high response rate

- **Postal questionnaires** - These are able to reach areas where a researcher cannot attend. The questionnaire needs to be written clearly and carefully so it is fully understood by the participants, as they will only have the supplied written instructions for guidance

	Structured interview	Self-administered questionnaire	Postal questionnaire
Completion rate	High	High	Low
Cost of data collection	High	Low	Low
Cost of data processing	High	Low	Low
Personal contact	High	Possible	Low
Correct misunderstandings	Yes	Possible	No
Controls sequence of answering questions	Yes	Possible	No
Checks for incompleteness	Yes	Possible	No
Interviewer bias	High	Possible	Possible
Wide reach	Yes	Yes	Yes

Table 26.1. Advantages and disadvantages of different forms of administering questionnaires

• ACTIVITY 5

Using information in Table 26.1 which type of questionnaire would be designed to be completed by as many participants as possible answering the questionnaire in the correct sequence?

When designing a questionnaire, make sure:

- It looks inviting and easy to complete
- It gives clear instructions

To include an introduction, if necessary

- To start with easy questions - more factual questions
- Questions are numbered
- Questions should be justified to the left and responses to the right
- Questions are sequenced to follow the same type of questions
- Questions are clear, spaced appropriately and in a large typeface

A questionnaire should be designed which sets questions that aim to meet the purpose of a research question. The questionnaire should be designed in a form that encourages participants to want to respond as truthfully to the questions as they can. Careful consideration needs to be given to designing the content of a question and the possible response the question can elicit.

• ACTIVITY 6

How should a questionnaire be designed so that it guides participants to answer questions as well as they can?

Designing Questions
Questions may be designed as either:

- **Factual -** Objective: these will have a true answer that can be verified, e.g. classification questions: age, type of organisation, job role; behavioural questions: 'Do you use the company intranet every day?' or knowledge questions: usually true / false, yes / no or right / wrong response

- **Non-factual -** Subjective: these are much harder to verify as they deal with a participant's state of mind, beliefs, opinions, behaviours or attitudes. Usually more than one of these types of questions will need to be asked to verify the response to the subject area being questioned

Questions may be designed in different ways:

Open questions
These types of questions will give the participant the freedom to **answer as they wish**. There is no set response expected from the participants when they answer these types of questions. Responses to these questions will give the researcher data about personal opinions, where they want to confirm or gain further information about one of the other types of questions below. For example, 'How do you think information flow has changed throughout the organisation?' is a type of question which can be costly to code and analyse, take time to process and is less reliable than a closed question.

Closed questions
These types of questions will give the participant a list of possible answers to select from. Closed questions are easy to process and analyse, require little time to answer and are low cost. Closed questions need to be carefully designed so they offer relevant answers to select from and do not force choices. For example:

- 'What is the most important change to affect the tourist industry in the past 12 months?' Please tick the most important change:

Change	Tick
Weather conditions	
Travel companies going out of business	
The world recession	
The lower value of the English pound	

Alternate choice questions
This type of question gives two answers: yes / no, true / false, right / wrong etc. It is fast and easy to use. For example:

- 'The new appraisal system has been a great success over the past 12 months.' Please tick one answer:

True	
False	

- However, alternate choice items may force a participant to choose an answer which does not truly fit their thinking

Multiple choice questions

This type of question gives more than two choices to answer from. The question will only have one correct answer. For example:

- 'What is the capital of Australia?' Please tick one answer:

	Tick
Sydney	
Canberra	
Melbourne	
Adelaide	

- Multiple choice questions are easy to administer and score. However, designing plausible alternative answers can be challenging

Rating scale questions

This type of question is used to rate endorsement: strongly agree, agree, uncertain, disagree, strongly disagree; frequency: never, rarely, sometimes, frequently, always or intensity: definitely true, true, do not know, false, definitely false, on a scale. For example:

- 'The new travel management policy is very clear for its users?' Please tick one answer:

	Tick
Strongly agree	
Agree	
Uncertain	
Disagree	
Strongly disagree	

- When designing rating scale questions, consideration will need to be given to:
- Content - it has to be meaningful
- Number of choices - are there enough?
- Including a midpoint or a 'do not know' response

• ACTIVITY 7

Why would an open question be used in a questionnaire?

Recording information

Each piece of information that is found should be labelled and stored in a system that enables easy access and retrieval. Notes could be made to identify how the information has influenced thinking and where they should be included in the final report. Some method for recording the information needs to be agreed. This can be done by using an electronic database designed specifically for this purpose, printing everything off in hard copy or scanning items electronically.

Information obtained either through primary or secondary research should be checked and cross referenced, when necessary, to make sure it is valid, reliable and relevant. Information should be linked to the purpose of researching information. Once all information that is relevant to answering the research question has been found, it should be compiled and organised into a final written report.

Testing your knowledge

1. Why is it important to agree the purpose, aims and objectives of researching information?

2. What is the difference between quantitative and qualitative research?

3. What are the five main research methods?

4. What is the difference between primary and secondary research?

5. What is meant by research methodology?

6. What are the implications of having a deadline for completing research information?

7. What are the different sources of information that can be used when researching information?

8. When is a questionnaire used when researching information?

9. What different types of questions can be used in a questionnaire?

10. What are the advantages and disadvantages of the different ways questionnaires can be administered?

Skills

When researching information, it is very important to identify what the purpose of the research is. If this is not clear, the way in which the research is implemented could be flawed. You could end up researching inappropriate information which has no relevance to the research proposal or questions. Work with the project leader and research team to agree what the aims and objectives of the research are aiming to find. This does not mean shaping the design of the research to reach a pre-determined outcome. The findings from your research should always remain objective. Throughout the design of the research project be careful in making sure the research is not biased in any way. This is not always easy to achieve so, if it occurs, it will need to be minimised. For example, if conducting an interview, your personal interviewing style may influence the way a participant answers your questions. Objectivity also means delivering your research and the outcomes of your research in a consistent way.

Once the purpose of the research has been agreed, agree with your supervisor / manager how long you will have to complete your required tasks. This may not always be the amount of time you would like. You will have to maximise the time given to source all the information that will be appropriate to answering the research question. The time that you are given will help you to decide the depth and breadth of your search. Decide what sources of information you will use. You should always be guided by the most up-to-date information that is available, as decisions that affect how the business will change will be informed by this research. It is important that accuracy of information and how the information is reported is observed at all times.

> Research is to see what everybody else has seen, and to think what nobody else has thought.
> - *Albert Szent-Gyorgyi*

Source information in the appropriate way given the purpose of your research questions and the time you are given to provide the research information. The information you may need will come about from the decision to undertake primary or secondary research. If it is the former, you will need to agree a questionnaire to find the information you require. You will usually use primary research if the information you are looking for is not available or if you need up-to-date information. Once this decision has been made, undertake the search for the different sources of information you think you might need. You should be open to all different types of information at this stage. In some respects you do not know what you are looking for until you find it, so be open to different types of information. Be guided by the research team you are working with, particularly if your research is a complex research question. For a simple research question you may be able to use existing procedures and data may already be available within the organisation.

You will need to make sure the information collected is relevant to the purpose of the research questions and is valid and reliable. If you are using secondary research methods, make a note of any quotes you think are relevant to and will support the research questions. Make sure you are quoting directly from source information. If you are using the material word for word, make sure it is acknowledged in the appropriate form - this may vary from organisation to organisation. If not, you could be accused of plagiarism.

As you identify all appropriate sources of information, design a method for storing this information. If necessary, map it so you know what pieces are important, and you may want to quote word for word. This can be done using hard copy or scanning electronically into your computer system. The information stored should conform to the storing procedures of your organisation, e.g. dated, so if anyone in your organisation wants to use it in the future they will know how relevant it is to their research proposal. As you work with your team, get feedback on the quality of the information that you have sourced. This will help you to stick to the purpose of the research question and keep you on track to deliver the research information within the agreed timescales.

Testing your skills

1. What types of information are available in your organisation?

2. What previous research carried out by your organisation were you able to use?

3. What sources of information were available to you?

4. What sources of information did you use?

5. If you have designed a questionnaire, how did you do it and why did you design the types of questions you have used?

6. How did you maintain a record of your findings from the researched information?

7. How did the feedback you obtained inform the way you researched information?

Ready for assessment?
To achieve this Level 2 unit of a Business & Administration qualification, learners will need to demonstrate that they are able to perform the following activities:

1. Agreed aims, objectives and deadlines for the information search

2. Identified sources of information required for the research

3. Searched for and obtained information

4. Checked information was suitable for the purpose of the research

5. Met deadlines for completing the research

6. Identified and selected relevant, valid and reliable data

7. Recorded data and stored it securely

8. Made a record of information sources used

9. Obtained feedback on what had been researched, if necessary

You will need to produce evidence from a variety of sources to support the performance requirements of this unit.

If you carry out the 'ACTIVITIES' and respond to the 'NEED TO KNOW' questions, these will provide some of the evidence required.

Links to other units

While gathering evidence for this unit, evidence may also be used from evidence generated from other units within the Business & Administration suite of units. Below is a sample of applicable units; however, most units within the Business & Administration suite of units will also be applicable.

QCF NVQ
Communications
Communicate in a business environment (Level 2)
Develop a presentation
Core business & administration
Manage own performance in a business environment (Level 2)
Improve own performance in a business environment (Level 2)
Work in a business environment (Level 2)
Work with other people in a business environment (Level 2)
Document production
Produce documents in a business environment
Prepare text from notes
Manage information and data
Organise and report data
Store and retrieve information

SVQ
Communications
Prepare to communicate in a business environment
Develop a presentation
Core business & administration
Agree how to manage and improve own performance in a business environment
Undertake work in a business environment
Contribute to working with others in a business environment
Document production
Produce documents in a business environment
Prepare text from notes
Manage information and data
Organise and report data
Store and retrieve information

27 Store and retrieve information

STORE AND RETRIEVE INFORMATION

'**Store and retrieve information**' is an optional unit which may be chosen as one of a combination of units to achieve either a Qualifications and Credit Framework (QCF), National Vocational Qualification (NVQ) or Scottish Vocational Qualification (SVQ).

The aims of this unit are to:

- Understand processes and procedures for storing and retrieving information
- Be able to store information
- Be able to retrieve information

To achieve the above aims of this unit, learners will be expected to provide evidence through the performance of work-based activities.

Knowledge

Organisations are constantly producing information. Information can be for internal, e.g. payroll, HR statistics, or external use, e.g. to formulate its business strategy - the types of products and services it should produce. Either sort of information is the acquired knowledge that an organisation needs for its survival. It will continue to use aspects of the information it has acquired which is **current**, **relevant**, **valid** and **reliable**. A lot of this information is adapted and absorbed into the organisation to form its '**intellectual property rights (IPR)**'. An organisation's IPR becomes an important product which it can either sell or franchise throughout the global economy.

• ACTIVITY 1

What are 'intellectual property rights'?

It is very important that the information that is acquired by an organisation is **stored methodically**. By employing a methodical approach to storing information the organisation profits by being able to retrieve any information easily when it is required in the future. Storage of information is about keeping information acquired today for possible use tomorrow. Part of the daily business of anyone working in any organisation will involve them filing information in some way. This will require different levels of expertise depending on the type of storage system being used by an organisation.

• ACTIVITY 2

Why should organisations have a methodical approach to storing information?

Record information

For information to be of value to an organisation, it needs to be recorded meaningfully to enable quick and easy access to it. Depending on the content of the information being stored, it will be kept for different lengths of time. If information has to be stored for a long period of time, it may have to be archived using a different system for storing information.

Electronic filing systems will have in-built sorting and storing mechanisms. Most will include a facility to store the information in folders within the main directory. Regardless of how information is stored, it needs to be coded so that it can be retrieved. Organisations may have different means of codifying their documents, however, as a rule, the following will need to be in place to access information or documents:

- **Title or subject / category** or reference number etc.

- **Dated -** Note should be taken of how a 'date' is written. In the UK, 7th September 2010 is written as 07.09.10. In America, it would be written as 09.07.10

- **Author**

- **Storage end date**

Paper records can be stored manually using different methods:

- **Alphabetical -** Information is stored in order from A-Z. Files starting with the same letter are filed in order of the second letter: Aa, Ab, Ac etc. People's names are filed by their surnames, and if more than one has the same surname, by their first names. Names starting with 'The' are filed by ignoring the 'The'. Names beginning with 'Mac' or 'Mc' come before 'Ma', 'Mb' etc.

- **Numerical -** Information is coded using a numbering system, e.g. purchase orders, invoices

- **Alpha-numerical -** Information is stored using a combination of letters and numbers, e.g. National Insurance numbers. Usually large databases hold this type of coded information, as they hold more information than numerical systems and are more flexible than alphabetical systems. The order of filing depends on the sequence of the file name. If file names start with letters followed by numbers, they are filed in alphabetical order first and numerical order within each letter

ALPHABETICAL	NUMERICAL	ALPHA-NUMERICAL
NAME: Rachel Clark Flat 6 The Bends, Weston-by-the-Sea, Somerset, WA2 9QR DOB 15.04.71 A/c No. 080521 Category Life Insurance	A/c No. 027493 Aaron Clarke 146 Brights Terrace, Holdsworthy, Middlesex, HC1 9DA DOB 13.10.51 Category Pensions	POSTCODE: HC1 9DA Aaron Clarke 146 Brights Terrace, Holdsworthy, Middlesex DOB 13.10.51 A/c No. 027493 Category Pensions
NAME: Aaron Clarke 146 Brights Terrace, Holdsworthy, Middlesex HC1 9DA DOB 13.10.51 A/c No. 027493 Category Pensions	A/c No. 080521 Rachel Clark Flat 6 The Bends, Weston-by-the-Sea, Somerset, WA2 9QR DOB 15.04.71 Category Life Insurance	POSTCODE: IM6 5QA Alan McPherson 27 Matthew Street, Douglas, Isle of Man DOB 06.10.59 A/c No. 643591 Category Mortgages

Table 27.1. Systems of storage - alphabetical, numerical, alpha-numerical

- **Chronological -** This is often used within one of the other methods. For example, customers' records are filed alphabetically, but the information within the file is stored chronologically, usually with the latest at the front. This provides a picture of the activity to be gained. It can also be based on dates of birth or start dates

- **Geographical -** This is a method of sorting by areas, e.g. North West England, East Anglia or counties, towns, cities

- **By subject or category -** Some organisations need to sort their filing under topics rather than names, e.g. a shoe manufacturer may keep files under product names such as Ladies, Gentlemen and Children

CHRONOLOGICAL	GEOGRAPHICAL	SUBJECT / CATEGORY
DOB: 29.05.85 Graham Wilcox 105 Planter Row, West Chester, Co. Durham, WC9 8DR A/c No. 090354 Category Savings	NORTH Alan McPherson 27 Mathew Street, Douglas, Isle of Man, IM6 5QA DOB 06.10.59 A/c No. 643591 Category Mortgage	CATEGORY: Life Insurance Rachel Clark Flat 6 The Bends, Weston-by-the-Sea, Somerset, WA2 9QR DOB 15.04.71 A/c No. 080521
DOB: 15.04.71 Rachel Clark Flat 6 The Bends, Weston-by-the-Sea, Somerset, WA2 9QR A/c No. 080521 Category Life Insurance	NORTH Graham Wilcox 105 Planter Row, West Chester Co. Durham, WC9 8DR DOB 29.05.85 A/c No. 090354 Category Savings	CATEGORY: Mortgage Alan McPherson 27 Mathew Street, Douglas, Isle of Man, IM6 5QA DOB 06.10.59 A/c No. 643591
DOB: 06.10.59 Alan McPherson 27 Mathew Street, Douglas, Isle of Man, IM6 5QA A/c No. 643591 Category Mortgage	SOUTH Rachel Clark Flat 6 The Bends, Weston-by-the-Sea, Somerset, WA2 9QR DOB 15.04.71 A/c No. 080521 Category Life Insurance	CATEGORY: Pensions Aaron Clarke 146 Brights Terrace, Holdsworthy, Middlesex,HC1 9DA DOB 13.10.51 A/c No. 027493
DOB: 13.10.51 Aaron Clarke 146 Brights Terrace, Holdsworthy, Middlesex, HC1 9DA A/c No. 027493 Category Pensions	SOUTH Aaron Clarke 146 Brights Terrace, Holdsworthy, Middlesex HC1 9DA DOB 13.10.51 A/c No. 027493 Category Pensions	CATEGORY: Savings Peter Matthews 33 William Street, Poole, Dorset, PD1 2PW DOB 06.08.49 A/c No. 361364
DOB: 06.08.49 Peter Matthews 33 William Street, Poole, Dorset, PD1 2PW A/c No. 361364 Category Savings	SOUTH Peter Matthews 33 William Street, Poole, Dorset, PD1 2PW 06.08.49 A/c No. 361364 Category Savings	CATEGORY: Savings Graham Wilcox 105 Planter Row, West Chester, Co. Durham, WC9 8DR DOB 29.05.85 A/c No. 090354

Table 27.2. Systems of storage

Whichever method is adopted must be stored **accurately**, to allow people to find information easily and quickly. People should find what they are looking for in the place they expect to find it. Information should be stored as quickly as possible to allow access to users within an organisation. If there is notification of a change of information, e.g. the address of an employee, it should be amended in the appropriate file

/ record. It is an offence under the Data Protection Act 1998 to store personal information that is not up to date. When amending information held electronically, saving the file will automatically update the previous version.

• ACTIVITY 3

Sort the following companies into alphabetical order:

7/11 Stores Ltd; Peterson's of York; The West Group; Megasave Superstores; 24-Hour Plumbing Co; Harvard Engineering; Singh and Danse Theatrical Agents; Reid Rentals; McHenry Shoe Co; St. Barnabas Hospital; Kingdom Plant Supplies; Mackintosh and Leverhulme; Langton's Ltd; MacIntyre and Bridgetown; Saint and Sisters Co; Patterson's Telephones; Barton Box Co; West and Hammond Ltd; Megasaver Hypermarkets; Read and Wright; Todfell and Son; Alveston Gardeners; Peter Benton Co. Ltd; Halshall of Weston plc; Parsons Stores; A & S Removals; Peter Ashton and Son Ltd and AAA1 Taxis.

Retrieving information

If a request for a document / record has been made, **retrieve** the document / record as quickly as possible. Always confirm the information required to avoid making an error when retrieving the information. Information that has been requested need not necessarily relate to the file or record name but be buried within a record of information. Know exactly what you are being asked to retrieve, to avoid delays, and always check to see if the person requesting the information has the clearance to access a document. Review the organisation's procedures for allowing access to different types of information. There may be a requirement for people to complete an information request form. It is essential that procedures and legislation is complied with, e.g. the Freedom of Information Act and the Data Protection Act 1998, for accessing information systems. Always handle 'confidential' documents with care, as other people will also want to see this information at some stage.

To make sure that a storage system is working efficiently and effectively, the administrator of the system should delete any documents / files that are agreed, from within the organisation, as no longer appropriate to store. This will free up space in the system and allow the administrator to work more quickly when storing or retrieving documents / files.

• ACTIVITY 4

Account records show annual expenditure for the following companies.
Make a list of those companies whose expenditure is greater than £4,500:

1. Alltringham Print   £17,200.47
2. Lynte   £4,479.60
3. Bulldog Holdings   £14,567.23
4. Mannering Agency   £3,364.50
5. Simon and Simon   £534,817.89
6. Adams and Sons   £4,799.99

'Confidential' information

All forms of information should be stored securely. Storing paper
documents may be secured by using keys to lock cabinets or particular
files can be locked in a filing room. Electronic documents may be
password protected. Anyone who is responsible for storing documents
should make sure only **authorised** people have access to them.
If somebody asks to see files or records, always check they are
authorised to view them before allowing them access. Always follow
the agreed procedures and legislation for maintaining security and
confidentiality. Most organisations will always have highly '**confidential**'
information that not everyone is meant to see, e.g.
payroll figures, personnel records.

'Confidential' information is information that
has great value, is considered to be of a private
nature and is only permitted to be seen by designated
people within an organisation. 'Confidential' information
can embrace commercial secrets as well as general information,
e.g. medical records. An organisation can be damaged if its privacy
of information is not upheld and respected - an organisation can be
devalued. 'Confidential' information can also be information that is not
written down. There is no single Act of Parliament defining 'confidential'
information or governing how you protect it, or setting out your rights
and obligations in respect of it. The laws on 'confidential' information are
undergoing radical change as a result of developing European and UK
legislation and decisions of the courts. Place confidentiality warnings
on standard communications, e.g. faxes or emails, to make sure if an
individual receives the information by accident they are notified of its
confidential nature. Access to information about individuals is covered
by the Data Protection Act 1998, which must be complied with when
divulging information of a sensitive nature about personnel.

It is important while preparing to store or retrieve 'confidential' information from any type of storage filing system that the 'confidential' information that it is not left in plain view so employees who may not have the authorisation to look at it can see its contents. If it is a paper document either cover it up or put it in a desk drawer. If it is an electronic document make sure that it cannot be seen on the computer screen. Always make sure that only people who are authorised to view 'confidential' information have access to it. Do not allow it to be printed without overseeing the printing and always accompany it if it is being transported, to avoid the confidential information falling into the wrong hands. If discussing confidential information, make sure that it cannot

be overheard by people who do not have access to this information. When printing copies of confidential information, make sure that any corrupted copies are destroyed.

When working on 'confidential' information, make sure the passwords or security codes that give access to 'confidential' records are not written down. Always use these passwords or codes so that no one can see what is being inputted into the computer. If posting 'confidential' information use a sticker on the envelope to identify it as 'confidential', whether for internal or external mail. Try to avoid faxing 'confidential' information. If it is absolutely essential, telephone the recipient and make sure they will be by the fax machine to collect it - this may be the form someone requesting information under the Freedom of Information Act may want it in. Try to avoid sending 'confidential' information by email, as emails are not secure. Make sure that any 'confidential' information that is no longer required is disposed of according to organisational procedures, e.g. using a specific shredder for that purpose. There may be specific bins to use which are collected separately by professional security companies.

• ACTIVITY 5

Which of the following are likely to contain confidential information?

1. HR records
2. Payroll records
3. Internal telephone directories
4. Patient records
5. Legal contracts
6. Appraisal meeting notes

Legislation regarding the storage of information

Despite the advent of the age of the computer, with its aspiration towards paperless offices, most organisations still store paper information, as well as information held on files electronically. There may be legal reasons for preserving paper copies of information, e.g. contracts. Reading information in paper form is also less of a strain on the eyes. Paper information can also be more visually appealing. However information is kept, it may require a variety of filing systems and equipment to store it and manage its retrieval.

There are a number of **Acts of Parliament** which refer to retaining and disposing of information, e.g. Occupiers Liability Act 1996, Employers' Liability (Compulsory Insurance) Act 1969, Social Security Contributions and Benefits Act 1992. There are two important Acts which all organisations will need to implement procedures to make sure they are adhered to:

Freedom of Information Act 2000

Information is stored not only because it is useful for employees to use in planning, organising and decision-making required on a daily basis, but it may be a legal or statutory requirement. Perhaps one of the most important pieces of legislation which affects the release of information is the Freedom of Information Act 2000 (FOIA), which came into force on 1st January 2005. This gives anyone the right to ask any public body for information they have on any subject they choose. This information will have to be released unless it is highly confidential, which can be exempted from disclosure. The information has to be released within one month - twenty working days. The FOIA covers almost all public authorities.

The FOIA also applies to documents produced before the FOIA was made law. Requesting information using the FOIA requires some kind of information system, as requests must be acknowledged and logged.

Private sector organisations will be affected by the FOIA to some degree. Every company is regulated, taxed or licensed by public authorities and many have public sector contracts. Under the FOIA, unless the information they hold is legally exempt, it could be open to the public and competitors. Companies carrying out public functions will eventually be covered by the FOIA, so will have to open their files to anyone who asks for information.

• ACTIVITY 6

What are the implications of the FOIA on the storing of information in an organisation?

Data Protection Act 1998
The Data Protection Act 1998 (DPA) governs the use of personal information by businesses, e.g. employee details. Personal information is information about a living individual. It includes information such as a name and address, bank details and opinions expressed about an individual, e.g. in notes relating to a disciplinary meeting. Under the principles of the Act, personal information is processed:

- Fairly and lawfully
- For one or more specified and **lawful purposes**
- Adequately, relevantly and not excessively
- Accurately
- So that it is not kept for **no longer than is necessary**
- In line with an **individual's rights**
- So that it is **kept securely**
- So that it is not **transferred outside the European Economic Area** - European Union states plus Norway, Iceland and Liechtenstein - unless there is adequate protection for the personal information being transferred

• ACTIVITY 7

Circle the correct answer. The DPA governs:

1. Company information
2. Legal information
3. Personal information
4. Technological information

There are also a large number of Statutory Instruments which set out, for specific functions carried out within an organisation, how long documents must be kept, e.g. employment records, contracts and agreements, accounts records, transport records. These will vary depending on the sector within which an organisation operates.

Handling problems

Whichever storage system, paper based or electronic based, is used in an organisation, **problems** can happen. If a problem happens, identify the cause and report the problem to the appropriate person. Two common problems that happen with storage systems are the inability to find the information or the information being out of date. If possible, suggest some solutions to the procedure:

- If the problem is misfiling, further training or further practice may be required

- If the problem is that filing is not up to date, consider if it is a resource issue or a time-management issue. If filing is done frequently, e.g. bi-weekly, it is not as daunting a prospect as it would be if it was done every month

- If the problem is not being able to find a file, e.g. it may not have been returned to the system using the correct procedure, a new system could be implemented for

- Recording who has the file and when it was returned

- If the problem is with hardware or software failure, it should be reported to the relevant department as soon as the problem is discovered

It is important to provide information in the agreed format and within agreed timescales.

> Information is the oxygen of the modern age.
> - *Ronald Reagan*

Testing your knowledge

1. Which type of electronic storage is best for transferring data?
2. What is the difference between 'vertical' filing and 'lateral' filing?
3. What are the potential sources of information?
4. What is meant by copyright?
5. What are the implications for storing information under copyright?
6. What are the principles of the DPA?
7. What issues could cause filing not to be up to date?

Skills

As someone who will look after the storage and retrieval of information, you will have different levels of authority for information that you can access. Depending on the size of your organisation and how it is organised, you may work in a department that specifically functions to store and retrieve information or you may work in a small organisation where these functions are carried out by individual members of staff. Make sure you work with your supervisor / manager to confirm the legal and organisational procedures for storing and retrieving information in your business.

Identify the types of information that you will be working with that need to be stored. If some information has to be stored because of legal requirements, make sure there is a system in place which has procedures that everyone working in the organisation can follow.

Information should be stored using a meaningful coding system, e.g. by date the document was produced. This needs to be consistent across the organisation so it can be followed by those wishing to retrieve information, or else they may not be able to find it. Having an origin date attached to a document will allow it to be more easily deleted from the information storage system at the appropriate time. This will be dictated by legislation and other organisational requirements.

• ACTIVITY 8

What legislation affects the way you store and retrieve information in your organisation?

Make sure information is stored securely either using a paper-based manual information storage system or an electronic information storage system. Have files locked away securely or only accessed through passwords.

Information is the lifeblood of an organisation. People need to know that the information they want to review is the most current documentation. An origin date could be used as part of the coding system for storing information, so people know when the document dates from. This is important when retrieving requested information, as people will want specific documents.

Access to retrieving information should only be given to those people who have permission to look at the information. Organisations store a lot of private and confidential information which can only be viewed by specifically named people within an organisation. This may be regulated by department, e.g. HR, or determined by management authority.

Retrieve information as requested, in the form that it has been requested - this may be dictated by legislation, e.g. the FOIA - and when it has been requested for. If it is 'private' and 'confidential' information make sure it is delivered to the person who has requested this information and review with them the organisation's procedures for managing 'private' and 'confidential' information.

In the event of any problems encountered while storing or retrieving information, deal with these as appropriate or refer them to an appropriate colleague.

Testing your skills

1. What are the types of storage equipment used in your organisation?

2. What types of files are stored in each type of storage system in your organisation?

3. What types of information does your organisation need to access?

4. How are passwords used to access information in your organisation?

5. Who has authority to access information in your organisation?

6. What does 'confidential' mean within your organisation?

7. What is the procedure for requesting information in your organisation?

8. How do you dispose of 'confidential' documents in your organisation?

9. How do you deal with problems if they arise?

10. What are your organisation's internal rules regarding access to information?

11. How would you deal with a request for information requested under the FOIA?

Ready for assessment?
To achieve this Level 2 unit of a Business & Administration qualification, learners will need to demonstrate that they are able to perform the following activities:

1. Identified, confirmed and collected information to be stored

2. Followed legal and organisational procedures for the security and confidentiality of information to be stored and retrieved

3. Stored information in approved locations

4. Checked and updated stored information, if required

5. Deleted stored information, if required

6. Confirmed and identified information to be retrieved

7. Located and retrieved the required information

8. Provided information in the agreed format and timescale

9. Dealt with, or referred, a problem, if required

You will need to produce evidence from a variety of sources to support the performance requirements of this unit.

If you carry out the 'ACTIVITIES' and respond to the 'NEED TO KNOW' questions, these will provide some of the evidence required.

Links to other units

While gathering evidence for this unit, evidence **may** also be used from evidence generated from other units within the Business & Administration suite of units. Below is a **sample** of applicable units; however, most units within the Business & Administration suite of units will also be applicable.

QCF NVQ
Communications
Communicate in a business environment (Level 2)
Take minutes
Develop a presentation
Core business & administration
Manage own performance in a business environment (Level 2)
Improve own performance in a business environment (Level 2)
Work in a business environment (Level 2)
Solve business problems (Level 2)
Work with other people in a business environment (Level 2)
Customer service
Provide reception services
Document production
Produce documents in a business environment
Prepare text from notes
Manage information and data
Research information
Organise and report data
Archive information (Level 2)

SVQ
Communications
Prepare to communicate in a business environment
Take minutes
Develop a presentation
Core business & administration
Agree how to manage and improve own performance in a business environment
Undertake work in a business environment
Plan how to solve business problems
Work with other people in a business environment
Customer service
Provide reception services
Document production

28 Archival information

ARCHIVE INFORMATION

'**Archive information**' is an <u>optional unit</u> which may be chosen as one of a combination of units to achieve either a Qualifications and Credit Framework (QCF), National Vocational Qualification (NVQ) or Scottish Vocational Qualification (SVQ).

The aims of this unit are to:

- Understand procedures for archiving information
- Be able to archive information

To achieve the above aims of this unit, learners will be expected to provide evidence through the performance of work-based activities.

Knowledge
It is very important that the information that is acquired by and in an organisation is stored methodically, either by using a manual paper-based system or an electronic system. By employing a methodical approach to storing information, the organisation profits by being able to retrieve any information easily when it is required in the future. Storage of information is about keeping information acquired today for possible use tomorrow.

Organisations will normally design archive retrieval systems to provide a history or collection of the sources of information that have been archived, where they are stored and who was responsible for archiving them. An archive storage system takes ownership of records of information, making sure that records are understandable to the users wanting to access them, and managing records to protect their information content and authenticity. An archived record provides evidence of the activities of an individual or department within an organisation.

What is archived information?
An archive is a record of information which is usually **preserved for a long period of time** in a safe and secure storage system. The preservation period of time that records will be archived for will vary from organisation to organisation and depend on the type of information to be archived. Information kept within an organisation will be organised as either:

- **Current information** - Required for the day-to-day running of an organisation that needs to be accessed easily and 'now'. This type of information is usually kept in a local storage system

- **Historical information** - Which may be mandatory or important to the organisation to keep. This type of information is usually archived in an archive system. It may take some time to retrieve this requested information

An archive system will be made up of records of 'historical information', records of information that are no longer current. Decisions will need to be taken about what records need to be archived or disposed of completely from a local storage system. Always confirm with the appropriate organisation authority if a record needs to be archived or disposed of. There are many records of information that are mandatory for an organisation to archive. Some **Acts of Parliament** which refer to sources of information that should be stored are:

- Occupiers Liability Act 1996

- Employers' Liability (Compulsory Insurance) Act 1969

- Equal Pay Act 2010

- Taxes Management Act 1970

- Prescription and Limitations (Scotland) Act 1973

- Health and Safety at Work Act 2005

- Sex Discrimination Act 2008

- Race Relations Act 2003

- Limitation Act 1980

- Social Security Contributions and Benefits Act 1992

- Education Act 2009

- Value Added Tax Act 2008

- Disability Discrimination Act 2005

• ACTIVITY 1

What is an archive system? Why does information need to be archived? When does a document become a record to be archived?

Some **Statutory Instruments** which set out how long documents must be kept for are:

Employment records

- **P11** - Three years
- **P38(S)** - Three years
- **Staff personal records** - Seven years after leaving
- **Unsuccessful job applications** - One year
- **Payroll** - Twelve years
- **Salary registers** - Five years
- **Tax returns** - Permanently
- **Expense accounts** - Seven years
- **Works council minutes** - Permanently
- **Wage records** - Five years
- **Medical records** - Twelve years
- **Accident books** - Twelve years

• ACTIVITY 2

Which employment records have to be kept permanently?

Contracts and agreements

- Contracts with customers, suppliers and agents - Six years after expiry
- Rental and hire-purchase agreements - Six years after expiry
- **Guarantees** - Six years after expiry
- **Leases** - Twelve years after termination
- **Licensing agreements** - Six years after expiry

• ACTIVITY 3

Which contract has to be kept for more than six years?

Accounts records

- **Limited companies** - Accounts records for six years from the end of the accounting period

- **Businesses that are not limited companies** - Accounts records for five years from 31st January following the tax year

• ACTIVITY 4

Circle the correct answer. Accounts records for businesses that are not limited companies must be stored for:

1. Six years from 31st January following the tax year
2. Six years from 30th January following the tax year
3. Five years from 31st January following the tax year
4. Five years

Transport records

- **Drivers' log books** - Five years after completion

- **Vehicle mileage records** - Two years after the vehicle is disposed of

- **Vehicle maintenance records** - Two years after the vehicle is disposed of

- **MOT test records** - Two years after the vehicle is disposed of

- **Registration records** - Two years after the vehicle is disposed of

Freedom of Information Act 2000

Information is archived not only because it is useful for employees to use in the planning, organising and decision-making required on a daily basis, but it may be a legal or statutory requirement. Perhaps one of the most important pieces of legislation which affects the release of information is the Freedom of Information Act 2000 (FOIA), which came into force on 1st January 2005. This gives anyone the right to ask any public body for information they have on any subject they choose. This information will have to be released unless it is highly confidential, which can be exempted from being disclosed. The information has to be released within one month - twenty working days. The FOIA covers almost all public authorities. The FOIA also applies to documents produced before the FOIA was made law.

The public authorities covered by the FOIA include:

- **Central-government departments** - e.g. The Ministry of Defence
- **NHS organisations** - From health authorities to hospital trusts, GP surgeries, pharmacies, dentists and opticians
- **Schools, colleges and universities**
- **Regulatory bodies** - e.g. Ofcom, the Charity Commission
- **Local authorities** - Including parish councils
- **Non-departmental bodies** - e.g. The Environment Agency

Public authorities are obliged to:

- **Maintain** publication schemes for the proactive release of information
- **Confirm** or deny to applicants whether they hold information not covered by the publication scheme
- **Disclose** the information to applicants, providing it is not exempt under the Act

A 'publication scheme' is a system for proactively releasing information. The type of information normally released via publication schemes would include:

- **Details of service** and financial performance targets and related performance data
- Board meeting agendas and minutes
- **Organisational information** - e.g. A who's who of senior staff, their responsibilities and contact details, staff rules and internal guidance
- **Financial information** - e.g. Sources of income
- Information on the authority's **decision-making** process

'Publication schemes' must be approved by the Information Commissioner. The approval time is limited to four years. The schemes should be regularly reviewed and updated.

Requesting information using the FOIA requires some kind of information system, as requests must be acknowledge and logged. If it is not clear what information is being sought, the authority must ask for clarification. If there is a cost barrier to meeting a request, the authority could outline the information it could supply within the cost ceiling. If an applicant does not respond to the authority's efforts, the authority is not obliged to take further action.

In responding to requests for information an authority must set out:

- What information it holds on the subject requested, unless it is exempt
- The information it is releasing
- The information that is exempt
- Details of the relevant exemptions

Wherever possible, the information must be provided in the manner the applicant has requested it, e.g. photocopies or computer files.

Private sector organisations will be affected by the FOIA to some degree. Every company is regulated, taxed or licensed by public authorities and many have public sector contracts. Under the FOIA, unless the information they hold on you is legally exempt, it could be open to the public and competitors. Companies carrying out public functions will eventually be covered by the FOIA, so will have to open their files to anyone who asks.

• ACTIVITY 5

What are the implications of the FOIA on the archiving of information in the public and private sector?

Data Protection Act 1998

The Data Protection Act 1998 (DPA) governs the use of **personal information** by businesses, e.g. employee details. Personal information is information about a living individual. It includes information such as a name and address, bank details and opinions expressed about an individual, e.g. in notes relating to a disciplinary meeting. Under the principles of the Act, personal information is processed:

- **Fairly and lawfully**
- For one or more specified and **lawful purposes**
- **Adequately, relevantly and not excessively**
- **Accurately**
- So that it is kept for **no longer than is necessary**

- In line with an **individual's rights**

- So that it is **kept securely**

- So that it is **not transferred outside the European Economic Area** - European Union states plus Norway, Iceland and Liechtenstein - unless there is adequate protection for the personal information being transferred

• ACTIVITY 6

Circle the correct answer. The Data Protection Act 1998 states that personal information should be:

1. Kept in line with an organisation's rights
2. Kept for as long as is necessary
3. Kept securely
4. Kept until the day the person leaves the organisation

Archiving records of information

There should be an organised system in place to decide and agree which documents an organisation is going to archive. Beyond those records, which may have a legal or statutory requirement to store them, an organisation must decide what other records it wishes to keep - whether it may be a manual paper-based system, an electronic-based system or both. Consideration needs to be given to:

- The level of importance of the document, e.g. documents that relate to the research and development of products and services

- The confidentiality of the document

- The size of the archive system

- The access to the archive system

Archival records are managed using a record-keeping system used to create them. The system in which information is organised should provide access to meaningful information. Records can be tracked down using a range of guides, inventories, indexes and other resources. The system for archiving records of information should match, or be closely related to, the way 'current information' is stored in the local storage system. This will allow for continuity of practice. A record of information that is archived can be:

- **A physical textual document** - e.g. A letter or fax
- **A visual document** - e.g. A photograph
- **An audio document** - e.g. A tape recording
- **A digital document** - e.g. An email

• ACTIVITY 7

What needs to be considered when deciding which documents will be archived?

A person who is responsible for archiving records of information should have a system in place with procedures which can:

- Help employees to find and use requested sources of information, maintain a record of which records have been accessed and by whom

- Organise and provide descriptions of the records of information that have been archived. Records should:

  - Be **titled** correctly or **coded** to enable organisation of the archive system so that it is meaningful to users of the archive system

  - Show the **creator** of the source of information

  - Have an **origin date**

  - Have an **expiry date**, where necessary. This will assist with the disposal of old records of information. If there are too many records in a system it may overload it and make it very hard to organise and manage. Procedures should be in place with retention time limits. This will assist in helping to organise an archive system to make sure it is up to date and it is easy and quick to navigate. Once a record has gone past its sell-by date it can be deleted or destroyed in a secure way, following organisational procedures

  - **Be stored appropriately** e.g. alphabetically, chronologically. This will be determined by how the records of information are coded

  - Have agreed **levels of access** to retrieving sources of information, including confidential information. Confidential sources of information should be coded so that they are only accessible to those people identified within the archive system

- Be **disposed** of at the agreed time for a particular record of information. When disposing of confidential information, it should be destroyed using organisational procedures

By organising the above elements of an archive system, it will allow easy access to requests for retrieving records of information.

- Conduct a variety of activities to preserve the material in the archives **safely and securely** - make sure that the records of information are stored in appropriate, safe and secure locations, e.g. a paper-based system should be stored free from danger of fire and water

• ACTIVITY 8

What needs to be considered when deciding how long a document will be retained in an archive system?

The design of an archive system should provide a means of:

- **Logging** to identify which documents have been archived
- Identifying the location of the documents
- Recording the person responsible for archiving the documents
- **Recording the cycle of dates** when documents have entered the system and when they have been destroyed
- **Recording the person to contact** for retrieval and their contact details

A methodical and robust archive system needs to be in place to help organise archived records stored within the system. A methodical approach will allow the retrieval of records to happen as requested and meet agreed timescales. For example, if someone requested information under the FOIA from more than seven years ago, this could be found in a timely fashion, if it was not exempted from disclosure.

Using an external archive system
Many organisations elect to archive their records off site. An organisation uses an archive system off site to manage:

- Costs
- Space
- Accessibility

- Maintenance
- Time
- Technology
- Legal requirements
- Security - particularly of confidential or vital records

An off-site archive system can be used for either a manual paper-based or electronic-based system, e.g. computer disks and tapes, microfilm and microfiche, master audio and video tapes, films and optical disks, X-rays and blueprints. If outsourcing a paper-based system, the organisation will need to agree with the external contractor the levels of responsibility:

- Coding of documents into records
- Creation of inventories of records
- Pick-up of records
- Records stored according to organisational / legal / statutory requirements
- Boxing and storage of records
- Time to retrieve records, e.g. same-day pick-up service, a rush service
- Retention schedule guidelines
- Destruction of records at the right time

Usually the external contractor will need to provide service level agreements which have been agreed with the organisation to manage the archive system and its procedures so users will have easy and quick access to records as they require them.

With the creation of so much digital information, electronic archive systems can provide:

- A self-contained secure database of digital records
- Quick and convenient access to archived digital records
- Viewing, searching, retrieving, editing and printing all digital records from virtually any personal / company computer, anywhere

External contractors who manage the archive system:

- Can create and maintain the company document web and digital document file storage space

- Host documents on a server, computers and / or CDs or DVDs for instant access anywhere in the world

- Save on time, resources and document storage space and 'state-of-the-art' document scanning

Archive systems which are managed externally from the organisation need to provide quick, accurate information decisively and competitively. It is important that the archive system is structured as efficiently as possible and is used to maximum economic benefit. The system should provide users with access to records quickly if they have been given the appropriate authorisation.

• ACTIVITY 9

What are some of the benefits of having an outsourced archive system?

Confidential records of information

'Confidential' information is information that has great value to an organisation, is considered to be of a private nature and is only permitted to be seen by designated people within an organisation. Most organisations will always have highly 'confidential' information that not everyone is meant to see, e.g. payroll figures, personnel records. 'Confidential' information can embrace commercial secrets as well as general information, e.g. medical records. An organisation can be damaged if its privacy of information is not upheld and respected - an organisation can be devalued.

There is no single Act of Parliament defining 'confidential' information or governing how to protect it, or setting out the rights and obligations in respect of it. However, the law on 'confidential' information is currently undergoing radical change as a result of developing European and UK legislation and decisions of the courts. Place confidentiality warnings on standard communications, e.g. faxes or emails, to make sure if an individual receives the information by accident they are notified of its confidential nature. Access to information about individuals is covered by the Data Protection Act 1998, which must be complied with when divulging information of a sensitive nature about personnel.

Always follow the agreed procedures and legislation for maintaining security and confidentiality.

Problems with archiving records of information

There are a lot of sensitive and complex decisions that are made within organisations that may rely on having access to sources of information that have been archived. The success of a whole organisation may depend on access to reliable and up-to-date information. Only if the archive system is efficient will it be possible to find information quickly. For example, if information is requested by someone enforcing the FOIA. Also, failure to comply with requests for retrieving archived information on time could have serious consequences for the organisation.

As with any system that is designed for functional use within an organisation, it is prone to problems from time to time. Some problems that may occur with an archive storage system are:

Design
- Stored information has been coded incorrectly and inconsistently which either delays access to it or denies access to it completely

- Stored information may not have been fully archived so pieces of information are missing from the record

- The archive system, either manual paper-based or electronic-based system, has been placed in an insecure and / or unsafe location. As a result, the system may get damaged, corrupting files which become illegible and consequently lost to users

Administration
- Written guidance on how to use the system has not been agreed or signed off. This could lead to different processes being adopted by different administrators of the system

- Absence of the administrator to administer requests for records of information, with no one else to undertake this role

- The time it may take for records to be retrieved, especially if a manual paper-based system is located off site. In this case, transport problems could also interrupt the administration of requests for records

Maintenance

- The records are not kept up to date. Records are not deleted, so they clog up the system and make it slower to operate, or records are deleted which should have been kept

- Users are slow to implement any agreed changes to the system

> (Archives are)… reminders of order, calm and continuity, lakes of mental energy, neither warm nor cold, light nor dark.
> - *Germain Greer*

Testing your knowledge

1. Explain what records of information are archived?

2. What is the difference between 'current information' and 'historical information'?

3. Explain why records of information should be archived, where practicable, using the same method as storing 'current information'?

4. What effect could the FOIA have on an archive system?

5. Why are 'publication schemes' used in the FOIA?

6. What are the principles of the Data Protection Act 1998?

7. How is an archive system made safe and secure?

8. How should confidential information be archived within an archive system?

9. What kinds of problems could happen 'maintaining' an archive system?

Skills

You may be delegated partial or full responsibility for the administration and maintenance of your archive system. Confirm with your supervisor / manager what it is you are expected to do. Look over any guidelines that have been written for archiving records. Spend some time with someone who has been archiving records to watch what they do and how they carry out this function.

Depending on the size of your organisation and how it is organised, you may work in a department that specifically functions to archive and retrieve records; you may work in a small organisation where these functions are carried out by individual members of staff or you may work with an external contractor who supplies either some or all of the functionality of your archive system. Find out the procedures which are appropriate to the type of system (s) your organisation uses and make sure you are familiar with them. You will need to work within and deliver the service level agreements between your company and the external contractor. Work with your supervisor / manager to confirm the legal and organisational procedures for archiving and retrieving different types of records of information in your business. You need to understand the expectations of your internal customers, your users - when do they expect a document to be recorded, retrieved, deleted or destroyed etc? Users will present you with a brief of expectations for an archived record. This could have important implications for decisions that need to be made within a business which has time considerations. So understand what, how and why your archive procedures have been agreed.

• ACTIVITY 10

How does your organisation organise and manage its external archive system?

Identify the types of information that you will be working with that need to be archived. If some records have to be stored because of legal requirements, make sure that there is a system in place which has procedures that you can follow.

Find out the coding systems that need to be used to maintain an archive system. Records of information should be archived using a meaningful coding system, e.g. by date the document was produced. This needs to be consistent across the organisation so it can be followed by those wishing to retrieve information, or else they may not be able to find it. Having an origin date attached to a document will allow it to be more easily deleted from the archive system at the appropriate time. This will also be dictated by legislation and other organisational requirements.

Make sure that information is archived securely, either using a manual information storage system or an electronic information storage system. Make sure records are locked away securely or only accessed through secure passwords.

Access to retrieving archived records should only be given to those people who have permission to look at these records. Organisations archive a lot of private and confidential information which can only be viewed by specifically named people within an organisation. This is probably regulated by department, e.g. HR, or determined by management authority. Find out if a list of authorised people has been created who will have access to 'private' and 'confidential' records of information.

Retrieve records as requested, in the form that it has been requested - this may be dictated by legislation, e.g. the FOIA - and when it has been requested for. If it is private and confidential information make sure it is delivered to the person who has requested this information and review with them the organisation's procedures for managing access to private and confidential information. Make sure when you receive a request to retrieve an archived record that you fully understand what it is you are being asked to retrieve and when the person requesting it is expecting to receive it. Many requests for archived information can be time sensitive because the information may be needed to inform making a decision. If in doubt, consult your supervisor / manager.

In the event of any problems encountered while archiving or retrieving archived records, check with archive guidelines or refer them to an appropriate colleague.

• ACTIVITY 11

What do you think are the most important elements required to administer and maintain an external archive system, and why?

Testing your skills

1. How are records of information agreed to be archived in your organisation?

2. How are records of information agreed to be destroyed in your organisation?

3. How do archive systems, if different types, work in your organisation?

4. Who, either people or departments, uses your organisation's archive system most often, and why?

5. How long are records kept before they are destroyed, and why?

6. What are the guidelines for administering your organisation's archive system?

7. How does you organisation deal with requests for information under the FOIA?

8. What security is in place for your archive systems? Why have the security systems been designed in this way?

9. What kind of problems have you had to deal with administering and maintaining your organisation's archive system?

10. Does your organisation outsource its archive system?

11. What types of archive systems does your organisation have?

Ready for assessment?
To achieve this Level 2 unit of a Business &
Administration qualification, learners will need to
demonstrate that they are able to perform the following
activities:

1. Identified and agreed on the information to be archived

2. Identified and agreed on the retention period for information being archived

3. Archived information to the agreed brief and within agreed timescales

4. Followed requirements of external archive systems, if outsourced from the organisation

5. Archived information to comply with organisational policies and procedures and legislation requirements

6. Maintained and updated a record of archived information

7. Retrieved archived information on request

8. Followed agreed procedures for deleting information from the archive system to comply with organisational policies and procedures and legislation requirements, if required

9. Resolved or referred problems that occurred with the archive systems

You will need to produce evidence from a variety of sources to support the performance requirements of this unit.

If you carry out the 'ACTIVITIES' and respond to the 'NEED TO KNOW' questions, these will provide some of the evidence required.

Links to other units

While gathering evidence for this unit, evidence **may** also be used from evidence generated from other units within the Business & Administration suite of units. Below is a **sample** of applicable units; however, most units within the Business & Administration suite of units will also be applicable.

QCF NVQ
Communications
Communicate in a business environment (Level 1)
Core business & administration
Manage own performance in a business environment (Level 1)
Improve own performance in a business environment (Level 1)
Work in a business environment (Level 1)
Work with other people in a business environment (Level 1)
Manage information and data
Use a filing system

SVQ
Communications
Prepare to communicate in a business environment
Develop a presentation
Core business & administration
Accept instructions to manage and improve own performance in a business environment
Support work procedures in a business environment
Contribute to working with others in a business environment
Manage information and data
Use a filing system

29

Support the management and development of an information system

SUPPORT THE MANAGEMENT AND DEVELOPMENT OF AN INFORMATION SYSTEM

'**Support the management and development of an information system**' is an <u>optional unit</u> which may be chosen as one of a combination of units to achieve either a Qualifications and Credit Framework (QCF), National Vocational Qualification (NVQ) or Scottish Vocational Qualification (SVQ).

The aims of this unit are to:

- Understand how to contribute to the management of an information system

- Understand how to contribute to the review and further development of an information system

- Be able to contribute to the management of an information system

- Be able to contribute to the evaluation of an information system

To achieve the above aims of this unit, learners will be expected to provide evidence through the performance of work-based activities.

Knowledge

What is an information system and how is it designed?

An information system or management information system (MIS) refers to the wider systems of people, data and activities. An information system should be designed to provide solutions to business problems. An information system can be:

Computer based

Has the following components:

- Hardware

- Software

- Database - An organised collection of related files or records that stores data

- Network - A system that connects different computers to enable the sharing of resources

- Procedures - The strategies, policies, methods and rules for using the information system
- People - Perhaps the most important aspect of an information system

Manual

The focus of this chapter will be on computer-based information systems.

There are many different ways of designing a computer-based information system, which can be found in the following table:

Information System	Description
Executive Support System (ESS)	Designed to help senior management make strategic decisions. This system gathers, analyses and summarises the key internal and external information used in the business
Management Information System (MIS)	Mainly concerned with internal sources of information. A MIS usually takes data from the TPS and summarises it into a series of management reports. Used mainly by middle management and operational supervisors
Decision-Support System (DSS)	Designed to help management make decisions in situations where there is uncertainty about the possible outcomes of those decisions. A DSS often involves the use of complex spreadsheets and databases to create models
Knowledge Management System (KMS)	Helps businesses to create and share information. A KMS is built around a system which allows efficient categorisation and distribution of knowledge, e.g. in word processing documents, spreadsheets and PowerPoint presentations. Information using a KMS would be shared using an organisation's intranet
Transaction Processing System (TPS)	Designed to process routine transactions efficiently and accurately, e.g. systems that deal with: • Sending invoices to customers • Calculating weekly and monthly payroll • Production and purchasing to calculate raw materials • Stock control
Office Automation System (OAS)	The aim of an OAS is to improve the productivity of employees who need to process data and information, e.g. systems that allow employees to work from home

Table 29.1. Different information systems

An information system can be a combination of hardware and software used to process information automatically. However, an information system is more than just a computer system. The heart of a computer system is the people who maintain and use it. An information system is an integrated set of components for collecting, storing, processing, analysing and communicating information. In most cases, the MIS operates behind the scenes.

• ACTIVITY 1

What is an information system and what is it used for?

An information system uses inputs and outputs. It processes the inputs and produces outputs that are sent to the user or the other systems. An information system works within an environment, e.g. an individual organisation, governmental departments, countries. When looking at information systems, it is important to note the differences between data, information and knowledge:

- **Data** - Is **raw facts** that are captured, recorded, stored and classified, but not organised to convey any specific meaning, e.g. flexitime, bank balances

- **Information** - Is a collection of facts / data, organised in a manner that is **meaningful** to a recipient. Information comes from data that has been processed, e.g. employee wages with hours worked, customer names with their bank balances

- **Knowledge** - Is information that has been organised and processed to convey **understanding**. It can include experiences, accumulated learning or expertise, as it applies to a current business problem or process. Information can be processed to extract critical implications and to reflect past experience and expertise for employees within an organisation. This knowledge may prevent managers from making the same mistakes other managers have made

Information systems are used within organisations to allow its employees to access and modify information. Because of the speed of technological change and globalisation of markets, organisations increasingly need an information system to manage their operations, compete in the marketplace, supply services and augment personal lives, e.g. organisations use computerised information systems to process financial accounts, manage HR and market its products and services; government departments use information systems to provide services to their citizens, e.g. computerised access to calculate and submit yearly tax returns. An information system can be a website that processes transactions for an organisation or responds to requests for information from its customers. Most organisations will have a website which allows its customers or potential customers to communicate with it and gain access to information or services.

• ACTIVITY 2

What is the difference between data, information and knowledge?

What should an information system provide?

To compete effectively and solve business problems, information systems should be designed to provide the following capabilities:

- **Processing fast and accurate transactions -** Events that occur in a business are called **transactions**, e.g. the sale of products and services, issuing a pay cheque. Every transaction generates data which must be captured accurately and quickly. This data is usually processed through **transaction processing** and is processed in a **TPS**

- **Large capacity fast access storage**

- **Fast communication: technological and human -** Networks enable employees and computers to communicate almost instantly around the world. High-transmission-capacity networks, those with high bandwidths, make fast communications possible. They also allow data, voice, images, documents and full-motion video to be transmitted simultaneously. Instantaneous access to information reduces lag time for decision-makers

- **Reduce information overload -** Information systems, particularly networks, have contributed to managers having too much information. The amount of information on the Internet increases at an exponential rate each year. Managers can feel overwhelmed with information and unable to make decisions efficiently and effectively. Information systems should be designed to reduce information overload, e.g. a system with software that prioritises managers' emails according to criteria

- **Span boundaries** - Information systems span boundaries inside organisations as well as between organisations. Inside the organisation, boundary spanning can facilitate decision-making across functional areas, communications etc. Boundary spanning facilitates can shorten cycle times for product delivery etc.

- **Support for decision-making**

- **A competitive weapon** - An information system can give an organisation an advantage over its competitors

• ACTIVITY 3

What should an information system be designed to be capable of delivering?

Training for users

For an organisation's employees to deliver 'on-time' or 'real-time' information, they must be able to access the information system within their organisation with the required level of expertise. Not only must an employee develop the expertise but they must also factor in the time required to keep up to date with how their organisation's intranet and Internet develops. The intranet will hold all information that relates to how an employee, the internal customer, can work within their organisation. The Internet presents the vision of their organisation's internal world to their external customers.

For an employee to use an information system effectively to provide solutions to business problems, they will need to have the required training to add further value to an organisation. However, it is worth remembering that, allied with training, an employee will need to have adequate supervision, procedures in place, job aids, briefings and an awareness of management expectations to make sure they fully embrace their understanding and applications of an information system. Training should come in the form of:

- **Induction to new recruits -** It is imperative that when an employee starts their new role that their supervisor / manager checks that they have had the relevant induction training for the systems that they have access to and will use. Make it **simple**

- **Ongoing training needs analysis -** This may be isolated training given to an employee who moves to a new department where they will have added responsibility to use functions in an information system that they have not had before, e.g. being promoted from one department to a new department. Make it **routine**

- **System updates or replacements -** This may be conducted as an information system is overhauled in an organisation and every employee needs the training to work the system correctly. Make it **timely**

It is important for all employees to have the required training for them to be able to carry out the responsibilities of their role with confidence and expertise. This is allied to the positive impression an employee will want to communicate to both internal and external customers.

Employees should be supported by the needs of the business of an organisation to make sure that their skills and knowledge are at a level where they can contribute effectively to the successful dissemination of information and application of functionality within their job roles. This should be administered by managers from across the organisation who are responsible for the development of new systems and policy. It should be delivered on demand, on time and in the best form to engage learning.

It is important that an employee is able to use an information system effectively and not to abuse it either accidentally or by design. Employees should use the information system within the guidance set out by their organisation and any legal constraints, e.g. when it comes to the security of use to:

- Protect their user id and system from unauthorised use

- Access information with the correct authorisation or clearance level, or that is publicly available

- Use only legal versions of copyrighted software in compliance with vendor licence requirements

- Be responsible for all activities on their User ID or that originate from their system

- Not monopolise systems, overload networks with excessive data, degrade services or waste computer time

Failure to comply with these requirements could lead to unnecessary waste, increased financial costs to the organisation, reputational costs to the organisation, undermining an organisation's competitive edge etc. It could also affect the motivation of employees.

All training should contribute to fulfilling company aims and objectives. The training mission must be clear and individual roles and responsibilities need to be clearly defined to produce competent and professional employees. Training facilities, equipment and materials should be supplied to effectively support training activities. Training records should be maintained to support management information needs and provide required historical data. The training staff should possess the technical and instructional knowledge, skills and attitudes to fulfil their assigned training duties. Trainers should maintain and improve the technical and instructional knowledge and skills. Training should maintain and improve the knowledge and skills of employees. It should be based on evaluation feedback, changes in regulatory requirements, changes in job scope, results of external evaluations and inspections, changes in operational procedures and changes in operational systems and equipment etc. A systematic process should be used to determine job performance requirements to specify training content, prepare training materials and maintain required training. Training should be conducted in a setting suitable for the training content. Training delivery and employees who have undertaken training should be evaluated to make sure that they have met the aims of the training and improved the bottom line of the organisation.

• ACTIVITY 4

Why is it important to support the training of staff to use information systems effectively?

Monitoring an information system

Once an information system is in place, it will need to be monitored to make sure that it is fit for purpose and is able to continue to deliver its business visions successfully to achieve its goals and objectives. The information system an organisation uses will need to be reflexive and respond to business pressures for an organisation to maintain its competitive edge and vision. An organisation needs to consider that its information system remains:

- **Strategic -** An information system should impact on an organisation's operations, its success and its survival. An organisation's information system should meet organisational objectives, enabling the organisation to increase its market share, to better negotiate with its suppliers or to prevent competitors from entering or dominating its markets. However, as a system is updated, competitors will also adjust their systems to remain equally as robust and responsive to customer needs. It is a never-ending practice

- **Customer focused -** More attention has to be paid to customers and their preferences. The organisation may decide to re-engineer its operations to better meet consumer demands. This may result in information technology (IT) systems being upgraded to provide troubleshooting advice or helplines or upgrade the organisation intranet / Internet to support both their internal and external customers

- **Up to date, through continuous improvement -** Many organisations make continuous efforts to improve productivity and quality in response to business pressures. Continuous improvement will also impact on an organisation, developing better decision-making

The above three elements will also be driven by an organisation's need to:

- **Re-engineer business processes -** This involves an organisation innovating or restructuring its business operations. This may result in major changes to an organisation which will affect its technology, HR and the general way an organisation conducts it business. This may include mergers, selling off part of a business etc. Reducing the business process time is important for increasing productivity and competitiveness

- **Improve IT systems**
  - Provides increased automation in an organisation
  - Provides increased spread over different geographical locations
  - Provides flexibility in manufacturing
  - Provides quicker delivery to customers
  - Supports rapid and paperless transactions among suppliers, manufacturers and retailers

An information system should be monitored against these considerations to make sure that it is able to continue to deliver its vision in a highly globalised and competitive market.

• ACTIVITY 5

What is the aim of monitoring an information system?

Maintain and update an information system

An organisation is only as good as the information services it provides - so that its internal and external customers know what it is doing and how it is responding to change. As the principle means of communicating its vision, an organisation's information system must be responsive to the changing needs of its business environment. Employees who have the responsibility of maintaining and updating an information system will need to troubleshoot and repair computers and computer systems. They will also need to operate help desks or have voice and data networks to respond to customer enquiries.

As information systems become more complex and are expected to be more responsive to the changing needs of an organisation, programmers will need to rewrite programs to increase the functionality of information systems to meet customer needs. Employees who are involved in maintaining and upgrading information systems will need to be familiar with incident, problem, change and release management. Specific areas that they will need to cover include:

*   **Systems planning**
*   **Project management**
*   **Network administration**
*   **Network engineering**
*   **Systems integration**

• ACTIVITY 6

What are the five areas that someone maintaining an information system will need to cover?

Network management has many tools, applications and devices which can be used to monitor and maintain a network. In network management, workstations send alerts when they encounter any problems to the management entities - management entities react to an alert by logging the event, notifying the operator, either shutting down the system or automatically clearing the fault. The management entities also poll the workstations or end systems to check periodically whether they are running properly. Polling can either be automatic or user initiated. The responses received as a result of polling are stored in the computer or a database for later analysis. The five conceptual areas of the network management are:

- **Performance Management -** This measures the various aspects of the network performance. It can measure network throughput, user response times and the line utilisation. Collected data is analysed and, if the analysed data is above the threshold value, it indicates that the network needs attention and corrective action

- **Configuration Management -** This monitors the system configuration of the network computers and the various hardware and software that are used in the network

- **Accounting Management -** This measures the network utilisation parameters in such way that the users of the network are regulated properly

- **Fault Management -** This is a way to keep the network working effectively. Faults are detected, logged and the users of the network are notified of the fault. Sometimes measures are taken automatically to fix the fault. Fault management is very important in the network, since this will lead to a resource being idle and will also lead to network degradation

- **Security Management -** This controls access to the network. This is a very important part of the network management, since not all users will be given access to all the information on a network. Appropriate rights should be given to users to access the resources that are needed by them only

Organisations will create new products and services that may require adapting / improving or current information systems which may result in a major overhaul implementing a new information system. It is very hard to anticipate the impact of emerging technologies. Depending on the size of an organisation, information systems may be monitored and maintained by either a dedicated I.T. team or, as may be the case with smaller organisations, this function may be outsourced and supported by I.T. consultants. External I.T. consultants will probably provide a wider perspective of the technology requirements managers need to be aware of and decide to implement.

> Foolproof systems don't take into account the ingenuity of fools.
> *- Gene Brown*

Information system problems

There are increasing demands placed on an information system to remain up to date and implement the advantages to be achieved from emerging technologies. An organisation also needs to respond to the changing demands of its business needs. These demands in themselves can create problems with an information system, as there may be insufficient time to redevelop aspects of the information architecture to meet user needs: there may be insufficient financial resources to implement required changes etc. The problems that occur with information systems can be categorised into the following areas:

Technical

The main problems may occur in one of the following areas:

- Hardware

- Software

- Database

- Network

Problems may occur as a result of the original design or continuing development of the information system. There may have been insufficient time to make the necessary changes to a system which has led to further problems with the system. Given the pace of change, changes which have been agreed and implemented may be out of date. The original requirements of the system may have been incorrectly analysed which lead to incorrect or incomplete implementation of the system. The system may conflict with the business strategy of the organisation. The system may respond slowly to users' needs. Data may be lost or the outputs requested from the system may be inaccurate. While many of these problems may occur because of the demands of the internal environment of an organisation, problems may also occur as a result of the demands placed on an organisation from its external environment, e.g. legislation may require the specific redesign of an information system. Also, users may use the system incorrectly, introducing viruses into the system.

Economical

The cost of achieving change may limit an organisation's ability to make the necessary changes required of its system, leaving it in the technological 'dark ages', frustrating its users and making other problems for users.

Behavioural

There might be legitimate or illegitimate reasons for a user's inability to use the system. While a system might work, it may not be comfortable to use. The installation of a system may have taken place but it was such a mess that users do not trust using it and seek alternative systems for undertaking their work. The culture of an organisation might change which is not taken into consideration in the redesign of the system, which should have taken place but which may not have. A team of users may be poorly skilled or they may be inadequately technologically resourced.

• ACTIVITY 7

What are the three categories where problems may occur with information systems? Give an example from each of the three categories.

For organisations to be effective and maintain their competitive edge, they will need to continue to develop new products and new technologies. It can be tricky trying to keep track of what technologies are available within an organisation and, therefore, it is imperative that there is a clear management system in place to monitor technological developments and the evolving needs of an organisation's internal and external customers. The most important aspect of an information system is the ease with which its user can use it. This should always be the benchmark for making any changes to an information system.

Not everything that can be counted counts, and not everything that counts can be counted.

- Albert Einstein

Testing your knowledge

1. What are the components of a computer-based information system?

2. Why does information need to be managed to meet requirements?

3. What is the purpose of having different types of information systems?

4. What is the difference between an ESS and MIS?

5. What types of information system would be used to invoice customers?

6. What are the three forms of training that should be undertaken in an organisation?

7. What are the five conceptual areas of network management?

Skills

You will be working with a team as you contribute towards the management and development of various information systems that your organisation has produced or may wish to produce, or you may work with an external consultant who has been employed by your organisation to undertake the work of developing, maintaining, monitoring and evaluating the effectiveness of your information system in a small organisation. Work with your team to understand what information systems you will be using. It is important to understand from your supervisor / manager the exact responsibilities you will have. This will not only help you to plan and organise your work but allow you to plan your learning and development.

Gain an understanding of what the information system (s) you will be working with have been designed to deliver for the organisation and for its users. Does it meet the design features? What could be done to improve the system? Does new or additional training need to be put in place to make sure the required skill (s) are there? How able is the system in responding to the bottom line of the organisation's needs? Remember an information system is there to solve the problems of a business! Is your system able to do this? How well does it provide solutions to users' needs and requests for information?

There are major ethical implications in working with an information system that need to be followed. An information system should remain pristine, that is, free from problems, and not corrupted by incorrect use or incorrect access to information or external websites. Users must make sure that they follow organisational procedures so that they do not introduce viruses into the system, which can cause catastrophic consequences to the running of a business.

Work with your supervisor / manager to understand the types of report your team work with to monitor the effectiveness of the system and how the users are using the system. How often are reports run? What is the expectation of analysing a report - who do you need to report your findings to, and by when? Undertake to gain knowledge of how you will contribute to the training requirements to realise all the functions that an information system can deliver to its users. Look at where gaps in skills and knowledge exist in the way users use the system - is there anything you can suggest that will improve users' performance and the system? Clarify what the level of contribution is that you will be expected to deliver in the training. You could undertake the training needs analysis and determine from this who needs to be trained, what the training needs to cover and when it should take place. Once any training has been delivered it is useful to determine how effective the training has been to the users, the team they work in and the organisation as a whole.

• ACTIVITY 8

Keep a diary of the training activities you have contributed to. How did you evaluate the training delivery?

Your involvement with the training aspects of the information system will alert you to the different ways you can contribute towards identifying how the information system could be maintained and updated. Keep a notebook of ideas you have and share these with your supervisor / manager to see which ones will work and why.

Work to contribute to resolving problems. If you are able to solve problems independently make sure you confirm this with your supervisor / manager. Continue to monitor the effectiveness of the information system for which you have responsibility. Try to understand how the information system is working and achieving the targets and functionality for which it has been designed.

Contribute to the evaluation of feedback and identify any potential way of improving the system, if appropriate.

Testing your skills

1. What types of information systems does your organisation use, and why?

2. What training have you had on your organisation's information systems?

3. How have you contributed to the training needs of a part of your organisation? What did you do?

4. What have you used your organisation's information system for?

5. How did you make sure that the legal requirements for handling information were followed?

6. What are the organisational requirements for handling information in your organisation, if any?

7. How did you contribute to maintaining and updating your organisation's information system (s)?

8. What kinds of problems did you resolve or refer?

9. What feedback have you given about the performance of your information system?

10. How did you contribute to the evaluation of your organisation's information system?

11. What development priorities did you identify?

12. How did you contribute to identifying future system development?

Ready for assessment?
To achieve this Level 2 unit of a Business &
Administration qualification, learners will need to
demonstrate that they are able to perform the following
activities:

1. Contributed to training on the use of an information system

2. Contributed to supporting users, if required

3. Monitored own use of an information system

4. Confirmed legal and organisational requirements for handling
    information were followed

5. Made sure a system was maintained and updated, within limits
    of own authority

6. Identified and reported problems when they occurred

7. Resolved problems, within limits of own authority

8. Provided feedback on the performance of an information system

9. Contributed to the evaluation of feedback and prioritised
    development needs, if required

10. Contributed information to enable further system development

You will need to produce evidence from a variety of sources to support
the performance requirements of this unit.

If you carry out the 'ACTIVITIES' and respond to the 'NEED TO KNOW'
questions, these will provide some of the evidence required.

Links to other units

While gathering evidence for this unit, evidence **may** also be used from evidence generated from other units within the Business & Administration suite of units. Below is a **sample** of applicable units; however, most units within the Business & Administration suite of units will also be applicable.

QCF NVQ
Communications
Communicate in a business environment (Level 2)
Develop a presentation
Core business & administration
Manage own performance in a business environment (Level 2)
Improve own performance in a business environment (Level 2)
Work in a business environment (Level 2)
Work with other people in a business environment (Level 2)
Document production
Produce documents in a business environment
Prepare text from notes
Manage information and data
Research information
Store and retrieve information
Archive information (Level 2)

SVQ
Communications
Prepare to communicate in a business environment
Develop a presentation
Core business & administration
Agree how to manage and improve own performance in a business environment
Undertake work in a business environment
Work with other people in a business environment
Document production
Produce documents in a business environment
Prepare text from notes
Manage information and data
Research information
Store and retrieve information
Provide archive services

30

Support the design and development of an information system

SUPPORT THE DESIGN AND DEVELOPMENT OF AN INFORMATION SYSTEM

'**Support the design and development of an information system**' is an <u>optional unit</u> which may be chosen as one of a combination of units to achieve either a Qualifications and Credit Framework (QCF), National Vocational Qualification (NVQ) or Scottish Vocational Qualification (SVQ).

The aims of this unit are to:

- Understand the purpose of supporting the design and development of an information system

- Understand how to contribute to the design and development of an information system

- Be able to contribute to the design and development of an information system

To achieve the above aims of this unit, learners will be expected to provide evidence through the performance of work-based activities.

Knowledge

Information systems are used within organisations to allow its employees to access and modify information and provide information to its external customers in whatever form is most appropriate for an organisation to organise and manage. Because of the speed of technological change and globalisation of markets, organisations increasingly need an information system to manage their operations, compete in the marketplace, supply services and augment personal lives, e.g. organisations use information systems to process financial accounts, manage human resources and market its products and services; government departments use information systems to provide services to their citizens, e.g. computerised access to calculate and submit yearly tax returns. Therefore, for an organisation or business to remain competitive it needs to make sure that its information system optimises all processes to provide the required data, information and knowledge to both its internal and external customers in a timely and required format. An organisation will store information on a variety of subjects, including:

- Sales
- Purchasing
- Accounts
- Personnel
- Payroll
- Stock
- Customers
- Suppliers
- Technical specifications
- Legislation
- Competitors
- Production
- Despatch
- Transport
- Company assets
- Insurance
- Archived records

An information system or management information system (MIS) refers to the wider systems of people, data and activities. An information system should be designed to **provide solutions to business problems**. An information system can be:

- **Computer based**, which has the following components:

  - **Hardware** – is the physical medium, e.g. circuit boards, keyboards, processors

  - **Software** – is a computer program, e.g. an operating system, an editor, which vary in size and complexity. Software allows the hardware to be used

- **Database** – an organised collection of related files or records that stores data

- **Network** – a system that connects different computers to enable the sharing of resources

An information system can be a combination of hardware and software used to process information automatically. However, an information system is more than just a computer system. An information system is an integrated set of components for collecting, storing, processing, analysing and communicating information. In most cases, the MIS operates behind the scenes.

An information system can be a website that processes transactions for an organisation or responds to requests for information from its customers. Most organisations will have a website which allows its customers or potential customers to communicate with it and gain access to information or services

- **Manual** based, which use physical components and resources, e.g. cupboards, index systems, to manage the information that flows to and from an organisation. Where data and information is held in manual files which are the responsibility of different departments within an organisation, there is a risk of  inconsistency where one department is more efficient than another in updating the data and information. A manual-based information system does not have the flexibility of retrieval and reporting facilities as a computer-based information system. However, the focus of this chapter will be on computer-based information systems

Common to both systems is the need to employ:

- **People** – perhaps the most important aspect of any information system. At the heart of a computer-based information system are the people who maintain, monitor and use it

- **Procedures** – the strategies, policies, methods and rules for using the information system

• ACTIVITY 1

What is an information system?

An information system uses inputs and outputs. It processes the inputs and produces outputs that are sent to the user or the other systems that interface with the main systems of the information system. An information system works within an environment, e.g. an individual organisation, governmental departments, countries. When looking at information systems, it is important to note the differences between data, information and knowledge:

- **Data** – Is raw facts that are captured, recorded, stored and classified, but not organised to convey any specific meaning, e.g. flexitime, bank balances

- **Information** – Is a collection of facts / data, organised in a manner that is meaningful to a recipient. Information comes from data that has been processed, e.g. employee wages with hours worked, customer names with their bank balances

- **Knowledge** – Is information that has been organised and processed to convey understanding. It can include experiences, accumulated learning or expertise, as it applies to a current business problem to help inform the decision-making process. Information can be processed to extract critical implications and to reflect past experience and expertise for employees within an organisation. This knowledge may prevent managers from making the same mistakes other mangers have made

• ACTIVITY 2

What is the difference between data, information and knowledge?

Information systems store data and information in a form that enables it to be retrieved on demand and used to produce targeted information knowledgably for a variety of purposes. Organisations require an information system that can:

- **Classify data and information** – e.g. name, address and National Insurance number

- **Sort data and information** – e.g. into male employees and female employees

- **Summarise data and information** – e.g. number of full-time and part-time employees

- **Manipulate data and information** – e.g. calculate the total wage cost

- **Identify appropriate data and information** – e.g. provide a list of employees earning over a selected figure

While these systems may be manual or electronic, electronic systems are easier and quicker to monitor and update and information is more quickly retrieved. To make data available it is important that it is retrievable from the application in which it is created. Most organisations will probably use a variety of database programs. Each database will have been selected to meet the needs of the individual user department; however, data produced by one database may not be compatible with data produced by other databases within the organisation. The solution to this situation is to create and design an information system which is able to download data from all the databases and manipulate it to produce the required management information. Small organisations may select an information system 'off the shelf' to meet its requirements

or an information system that can be adapted to do so. Larger or more complex organisations will need to have a tailored bespoke information system designed specifically for their needs.

Any information system needs to be designed to meet the identified needs of the end-users. Specialist system analysts will be involved in designing the necessary program. A specification will be written listing the hardware, software, data storage requirements and future proof the information system to delay the obsolescence of the system. Once the information system has been designed and installed, the data will be uploaded. The system will be tested by manipulating data to create potential problems and any necessary adjustments made to it. An information system must be capable of analysing uploaded data and producing usable results.

All information systems will need to be continuously monitored to make sure they access data and information for the end-users accurately, in the format requested and on time. As data and information changes and evolves over time, it is important that the information system is designed to be capable of being continuously improved and updated to meet the changing demands of an organisation or business.

• ACTIVITY 3

What should an information system do for an organisation?

Computer-based information systems

There are a number of reasons for designing a computer-based information system, which include:

- The current system is **incapable of coping** with either the changing requirements of the business or the increased volume of data that needs to be processed

- **Cost savings** – a manual information system can be labour intensive, which a computer-based system will reduce. An electronic information system will also free up office space used by any additional clerical staff

- Senior management have identified a need for **better or faster management information** in order to enable more effective decisions to be made

- **Loss of competitive edge** to other organisations who have installed computer-based information systems, who are able to react more quickly to changes in the market and provide more efficient customer service

- **Investment** in more up-to-date technology to benefit the organisation

- **Branding** of an organisation to project itself as being at the cutting edge of technology

- **Changes in legislation** requiring organisations to produce greater amounts of information, e.g. Freedom of Information Act 2000

• ACTIVITY 4

Why are computer-based information systems designed for an organisation?

To decide on the design of a computer-based information system the following stakeholders should be involved in the decision-making process:

- **End-users of the existing information system** – who will be able to explain exactly what the current system is able to provide and the input involved. They will also define what it is they would like the new information system to provide and where they see the opportunity for reduction in the input

- **Computer programmers** – who take the information provided by the end-users and turn it into applications that will produce the outputs required

- **System analysts** – who interpret the information provided by end-users and the computer programmers. They are able to understand the needs of the end-users and explain them in terms that the computer programmers can recognise. The responsibilities of the systems analyst are to:

  - Analyse the existing system to determine its information use and its requirements

  - Assess the feasibility of replacing the existing information system with a computer-based information system or upgrading the existing computer-based information system

  - Design a new computer-based information system specifying the programs, hardware, data, structures and controls required

  - Test the new computer-based information system to make sure it delivers the requirements

  - Oversee the installation of the new computer-based information system

  - Create the necessary user manuals and technical guides

  - Evaluate the computer-based information system

• ACTIVITY 5

Who should be involved in the design of a computer-based information system?

The implementation of a computer-based information system will pass through a number of different stages:

- **Stage 1** – agree the overall scope of the project. At this stage terms of reference are agreed:

- Which departments of the organisation need the computer-based information system?
- What are the problems that the computer-based system is required to address?
- When is the feasibility report to be delivered?
- What is the budget for producing the feasibility report?

- **Stage 2** – systems analyst to investigate the current information system. System analysts will interview end-users of the information system and look at the documentation currently in use. End-users will have the opportunity to explain how the current information system works in practice, as opposed to how it is supposed to work in theory. A feasibility report will then be produced which indicates:

  - A number of alternative solutions to the problems that the system is required to address
  - The benefits and feasibility of each alternative and a broad estimate of the costs involved

- **Stage 3 – management review the feasibility report and make a decision whether to authorise more detailed analysis of the proposed solutions.** If the go-ahead is given the systems analyst looks in detail at the process necessary to satisfy the objectives and functions of the system. This is called 'process analysis'. The systems analyst will then look at the data required to feed the process. This is called 'data analysis'. The result of stage 3 will be a logic model of the system, not in any way a physical representation

- **Stage 4 – end-users review the logic model and agree that it is capable of resolving the problems identified in stage 1.** The systems analyst then designs the physical aspects of the system and suggests alternative designs based on different cost solutions with corresponding levels of benefit. Alternative solutions will be presented to management to commission one of them

- **Stage 5** – detailed specification is written which provides a more accurate estimate of total costs. Management sign off this estimate and purchase orders can be raised for hardware and software and contracts written for programmers' time. Programs are commissioned, hardware is specified, the structure of the databases is specified and a schedule of implementation created

The systems designer and analyst will be particularly concerned, at this stage, with:

- Making the computer-based information system secure
  – Security of the system involves making sure that it is protected from corruption, that it is complete in that it delivers all of the stated requirements, that the data it produces is accurate and that it can deliver continuous outputs

- Making sure that the computer-based information system is user-friendly – At each point at which the end-users come into contact with the information system it needs to be easy to use

Once all five stages have been completed, then:

- Hardware is purchased and installed
- Programs are written and tested
- Databases are created
- Historic data is loaded onto the databases
- Procedures are drafted
- Paperwork is designed
- Staff are trained in the requirements of the new procedures
- Security of the existing files is maintained
- The new system is tested
- The system is handed over to management

• ACTIVITY 6

What are the stages for implementing a computer-based information system?

There are many different ways of designing a computer-based information system, which can be found in the following table:

Information System	Description
Executive Support System (ESS)	Designed to help senior management make strategic decisions. This system gathers, analyses and summarises the key internal and external information used in the business
Management Information System (MIS)	Mainly concerned with internal sources of information. A MIS usually takes data from the TPS and summarises it into a series of management reports. Used mainly by middle management and operational supervisors
Decision-Support System (DSS)	Designed to help management make decisions in situations where there is uncertainty about the possible outcomes of those decisions. A DSS often involves the use of complex spreadsheets and databases to create models
Knowledge Management System (KMS)	Helps businesses to create and share information. A KMS is built around a system which allows efficient categorisation and distribution of knowledge, e.g. in word processing documents, spreadsheets and PowerPoint presentations. Information using a KMS would be shared using an organisation's intranet
Transaction Processing System (TPS)	Designed to process routine transactions efficiently and accurately, e.g. systems that deal with: Sending invoices to customers Calculating weekly and monthly payroll Production and purchasing to calculate raw materials Stock control
Office Automation System (OAS)	The aim of an OAS is to improve the productivity of employees who need to process data and information, e.g. systems that allow employees to work from home

Table 30.1 – Different information systems

• ACTIVITY 7

What is the difference between a Transaction Processing System (TPS) and a Decision-Support System (DSS)?

What should the design of an information system provide?

To compete effectively and solve business problems, information systems should be designed to provide the following capabilities:

- **Processing fast and accurate transactions** – Events that occur in a business are called transactions, e.g. the sale of products and services, issuing a pay cheque. Every transaction generates data which must be captured accurately and quickly. This data is usually processed through transaction processing and is processed in a TPS

- **Large capacity fast access storage**

- **Fast communication, both technological and human** – Networks enable employees and computers to communicate almost instantly around the world. High-transmission-capacity networks, those with high bandwidths, make fast communications possible. They also allow data, voice, images, documents and full-motion video to be transmitted simultaneously. Instantaneous access to information reduces lag time for decision-makers

- **Reduce information overload** – Information systems, particularly networks, have contributed to managers having too much information. The amount of information on the Internet increases at an exponential rate each year. Managers can feel overwhelmed with information and unable to make decisions efficiently and effectively. Information systems should be designed to reduce information overload, e.g. a system with software that prioritises managers' e-mails according to criteria

- **Span boundaries** – Information systems span boundaries inside organisations as well as between organisations. Inside the organisation, boundary spanning can facilitate decision-making across functional areas, communications etc. Boundary spanning facilitates can shorten cycle times for product delivery etc.

- **Support for decision-making**

- **A competitive weapon** – An information system can give an organisation an advantage over its competitors

• ACTIVITY 8

What should the design of a computer-based information system provide?

Testing a computer-based information system
The system will be tested by manipulating data to:

- Make sure that the needs of the organisation or business outlined in the agreed specification meet the required functionalities

- Create potential problems and resolve them with necessary adjustments to the information system

An information system must be capable of analysing uploaded data and producing usable results for the organisation to function competitively. The testing of any information technology project should be undertaken to meet the four following categories:

- **Business** requirements that define the goals and objectives that any IT solution has to support

- **Stakeholder** requirements that specify the needs of end-users

- **Solution** requirements that describe functions, information and specific qualities that the delivered technology has to provide

- **Transition** requirements that define behaviours to facilitate moving from the 'as-is' to the 'to-be' state of the project

• ACTIVITY 9

What are the four categories an information system should meet?

There are three stages involved in the testing of an information system, namely:

- **Plan testing activities** – a test plan should be drawn up which answers the basic questions about the testing to be undertaken. Ideally, it should be drawn up in parallel with the agreement of the specification for the information system. Having a test plan will make sure that testing is structured and scheduled. A test is an integral part of the coherent requirements of an information system management process, which should:

  - Enable a more reliable estimate of the testing to be undertaken

- Allow the project team time to consider ways to reduce the testing effort realistically

- Help to remove misunderstandings between developers and end-users before the solution is developed

- Create a verifiable system component that will become part of the specification

- Help to identify problem areas and focus the testing team's attention on the critical paths

- Reduce the probability of implementing non-tested components

Testing usually accounts for 45–75% of the time taken on the design and development of an information system. The responsibility for planning testing activities is different for unit, integration and acceptance testing. Testing will involve developers, managers, project leaders and end-users. Some organisations may have a quality assurance / testing group which will be involved in the testing process.

Test plans can exist on many different levels. There may be a test plan for the whole project or there may be individual test plans for different components of the information system, e.g. unit testing, acceptance testing, integration testing. Test plan activities may include:

- **Determine objectives of the test** – the what and why of tests

- **Determine testing techniques to be used** – the kind (s) of testing to be done, e.g. reviews, walk-throughs, walking data through code, computer execution

- **Select appropriate test cases** – the test cases to include in the test plan

- **Maximise scheduling of test runs** – this will vary according to the type of testing being done

- **Identify needed resources** – the kinds of resources needed, how many and for how long

- **Establish start and end dates** – based on the specification

- **Secure the test environment** – make sure everything: people, machines, time, needed is available when the test (s) is run

- **Write up a formal test plan** – place all relevant information into a document

- **Review the test plan and obtain necessary approvals** – review the test plan with relevant stakeholders

Each test plan should contain a set of activities which define strategic and scheduling components:

- **Strategic components should include:**
  - Agreement of test plan objectives
  - Description of potential risks to the organisation if test objectives cannot be achieved
  - Definition of the planned approach to achieve the test plan objectives
  - Scope of application components to be or not to be tested
  - Testing techniques, e.g. baseline testing, parallel testing
  - Resources required, e.g. hardware, software, people, training, testing tools, including when and why they are needed
  - Completion date, to avoid endangering the planned delivery date
  - List of those involved in the test plan, including a project manager
  - Instructions for reporting problems – how discrepancies will be recorded, reported and tracked

- **Scheduling components should include:**
  - Critical assumptions which, if not met, will influence the effort, duration or dates of testing
  - Planned date to begin testing
  - Planned date to complete testing
  - Estimated work required to execute tests
  - Expected duration of testing
  - Actual date to begin testing
  - Actual date to complete testing

• ACTIVITY 10

What is the difference between strategic and scheduling components?

Errors that may occur could include some of the following:

- **System works but the user dissatisfied** – the system may not be aesthetically pleasing; have no functional impact; may be misleading or redundant offering a small impact on performance; be dehumanising; have counter-intuitive sequences

- **System does not work correctly** – the system refuses legitimate transactions; loses track of transactions, losing accountability; or transactions are incorrectly processed

- **System is inherently unreliable** – the system has frequent and arbitrary occurrences of the above-mentioned errors; irrecoverable corruption of database occurs, serious thought to shutting system down; system fails, shuts down itself

- **System is out of control** – the system corrupts other systems without failing itself; influence exceeds system scope

- **Engineer test data** – focuses on selecting data values that have a higher probability of identifying an error than any similar set of data values. Whether the test data comes from production files, existing tests or is created by the tester, properly engineered data reduces the number of required test cases. The engineering of test data is undertaken to:

  - Reliably predict the expected results in sufficient detail to avoid misinterpretation of the test results

  - Create data that is more likely to find errors in the solution

  - Establish a baseline for test coverage metrics

  - Reduce the number of test cases needed to achieve testing goals

  - Exercise the system components at their boundary points

  - Make sure that the most likely causes of failure are avoided

  - Establish a baseline for repeatable tests that deliver consistent results in regression

Data values that test system rules should be engineered once business rules have been established that define data constraints. Before starting unit, integration, system, performance, configuration, end-user acceptance or any other form of testing, the appropriate data should be engineered. Developers need to engineer the test data they use in unit and integration testing. Quality assurance, or any other test group, should engineer the data they need for system testing. End-users should engineer their data for effective acceptance testing.

Sometimes it is difficult to identify test cases or scenarios. If there is no system documentation, focus on business expertise, the imagination of members of the project team and ask questions. To help identify test cases or scenarios:

- **Brainstorm a list of business events** – something that happens outside the control of the information system creating a reaction from the system – that the target application responds to, e.g. to test an accounting application identify the events required: customer pays invoice, customer does not pay in time, supplier delivers goods, marketing launches new product, end of fiscal year

- For each identified event, **select variations that need to be tested**. Identify what strange and unusual things might happen that are related to the business event. These variations will be the test scenarios, e.g. following the previous example, if the customer pays the invoice, scenarios to be tested could include, do they pay the correct amount, underpay or overpay?

- For each test scenario, **identify the expected system response** by creating **global responses** – responses triggered for all of the identified test scenarios – or **specific responses** – triggered for selected test scenarios, e.g. if a customer pays the correct amount, the global response could  be to update the customer's account and post payment of the ledger accounts; however, there would be no specific response

- For each identified response, **identify the appropriate test data fields**, **inputs**, expected **outputs** and **stored data values** that will be affected. Equivalence class identification and boundary value analysis will identify the optimal values that need to be tested, e.g. when updating a customer's accounts, input data could include customer account number, payment amount, payment date; stored data could include previous amount due, current payment due date; and output data could include, new open balance, new due date

•ACTIVITY 11

How can test cases or scenarios be identified?

- **Execute tests** – there are two ways to conduct tests: on a computer by executing selected programs or modules under controlled conditions and in the form of quality assurance walk-throughs.

In either case, test execution is not complete until identified discrepancies have been documented in a problem report and distributed to the appropriate parties for resolution. Effective test execution:

- Is the only alternative to production disasters
- Reduces the cost of failure
- Decreases the probability of failure in production
- Increases the end-users' confidence that the solution works as designed
- Increases the developers' confidence in their solution
- Creates problem reports that pinpoint the work that developers have to do
- Captures statistical information that can be used to improve the overall development effort

Testing is needed throughout the system development life cycle. During the analysis and design phase, the most common form of testing is a quality assurance walk-through. A separate quality assurance group should be responsible for testing. The most commonly accepted practice is for developers to test their components while end-users test for business acceptance. The need for impartial testers increases as the complexity of the components or the need for quality increases. Techniques to execute tests include:

- **Problem reports** – A problem report is a document that records the discrepancy between an expected result and an actual result observed during test execution. The problem report needs to be documented to enable problem tracking and resolution; to establish a basis for quality metrics; and serves as a learning tool for developers and end-users. Potential components that can be used to evaluate problem reporting mechanisms include:

Problem report item	Definitions and examples
Problem report ID	Unique identifier for the problem report
Description of the problem	Short explanation of identified discrepancies
Test case ID	Unique identifier of the test case that was executed
Test plan name	Name of the test plan
Tester comments	Notes from the test executor regarding reproduction of the error
Test execution document reference	Identification and location of relevant documentation produced by the test
Requirement ID	Requirement statement regarding system behaviour that has been violated
Severity of error	Use software error categories
Who is assigned to resolve discrepancies	Project team member assigned to resolve reported discrepancies
Expected repair completion date	Estimated date defective components will be available for retesting
Status	Open: assigned; in progress; repaired Closed: deferred; fixed; non-reproducible
Problem resolution	Actions taken to resolve discrepancies
Actual repair completion date	Date defective components will be available for retesting

- **Walk-through** – an effective walk-through, a specific meeting, requires advanced preparation by the participants, a clear set of rules and the commitment by the organisation to utilise the results to improve the product and the process. The walk-through should involve the following roles:

  - **Moderator** who runs the meeting making sure everybody is heard and keeps the meeting focused on identifying errors

  - **Presenter** who presents the product being evaluated and responds to questions

  - **Reviewers** made up from all stakeholders who will use the information system

  - **Recorder** who captures identified issues, concerns and discrepancies

The critical success factors for a walk-through are:

- Prior to the meeting, expectations of the walk-through are established and managed throughout the session
- Prior to the meeting, all participants have access to the product or deliverable that is being evaluated for a sufficient period of time
- Prior to the meeting, all participants have been given the necessary tools and prerequisite knowledge to be able to evaluate the product
- There is a set time limit to any scheduled walk-through
- The emphasis of the meeting is on finding errors and *not* defining solutions

• ACTIVITY 12

What is the difference between a 'problem report' and a 'walk-through'?

As a result of testing, errors will be identified. The project team and end-users need to agree a range of **severity levels** that represent the relative severity, in terms of business / commercial impact, of a problem with the system found during testing. For example, the following description of problems ranges from most severe to least impact on the business:

- **Show stopper** – the error / bug is too severe to continue testing
- **Critical problem** – testing continues but cannot go live with this problem
- **Major problem** – testing continues but the problem will cause severe disruption to business processes in live operation
- **Medium problem** – testing continues with the system going live with only minimal departure from agreed business processes
- **Minor problem** – testing and live operations may progress. The problem should be corrected, but little or no changes to business processes are envisaged
- **Cosmetic problem** – e.g. colours; fonts; pitch size. If such features are key to the business requirements they will warrant a higher severity level

The users of the system must agree the responsibilities and required actions for each **category of problem**, e.g. problems that are most severe receive priority response and all testing will stop until this category problem is solved. Stakeholders and the project team must agree the maximum number of acceptable outstanding problems in any particular category.

The documentation of test cases makes them repeatable by people other than the person who designed them. The following table represents a list of potential components that can be used to evaluate a test case design:

Test Case Item	Definitions and Examples
Test case ID	A unique identifier for each test case
Test case description	A name or short sentence describing what this test case does
Purpose of the test	A short answer to the question, 'Why is this test needed?'
Resources required	List of all resources, e.g. hardware, software, people, training, testing tools, needed and why – role of the resource
Reaction to defects	Specific description of how the project team will react to reported discrepancies between expected and actual results
Risk category	Required to minimise the number of test cases
Interfacing systems	List of all systems that provide information to or receive information from the system in which the test is executed for this set of tests
Prerequisite test cases	List of test cases that must be successfully completed prior to executing this test case
Required data content	Data content that is required for test execution – set-up requirements
Estimated effort	Amount of work time required to execute the set of test cases
Expected duration	Amount of calendar time required to execute the set of test cases
Set-up steps	Audience-level detailed instructions for set up of the test
Execution steps	Audience-level detailed instructions for execution of the test
Evaluation steps	Audience-level detailed instructions for evaluation of the test results
Expected result	Verifiable result that should be achieved when this test is executed

Execution date / time	Date and time the test was executed
Executor ID	Name of the person executing the test
Actual result	Actual result achieved if it is different than the expected result
Actual effort	Amount of work time that was required to execute the test
Actual duration	Amount of calendar time that was required to execute the test
Test run status	Indicates whether the test was completed, interrupted, passed or failed

• ACTIVITY 13

What are the components of a test case design that can be used to repeat test cases?

Testing Your Knowledge

1. What is the purpose of an information system?

2. What subjects is an organisation likely to use an information system for?

3. What is the difference between a manual and a computer-based information system?

4. What are the components of a computer-based information system?

5. What is the difference between hardware and software?

6. What activities could be included in a test of an information system?

7. What are the two components a test plan should define?

8. What errors could occur when testing an information system? Why is the engineering of test data undertaken?

9. What is the purpose of test execution?

10. Describe a way of identifying the severity of information system errors?

11. What are the three stages involved in the testing of an information system? Describe what each stage entails.

Skills

The first thing that needs to be done before an information system is tested is to agree what the information system is being designed to deliver. This will probably be a project-based activity which will be run by a project manager. You will have been selected because of your skills and knowledge to contribute to this project. You may be involved in either the design or development of the system or the testing of the system. It is generally good practice to separate the members of the team to deliver these two functions before an information system can be signed off as meeting the agreed specification. However, no information system is every really complete as technology is constantly changing, as are the needs of organising, storing and providing data and information to the various stakeholders of any organisation.

To design an information system you must find out what data and information the organisation wants to have available to its various stakeholders. You may be involved in identifying the documentation required for the system and how this needs to function. This will require you to focus on your business expertise and knowledge of the organisation and how it functions and the purpose that it has been designed to deliver to its customers. You will need to use your imagination and think about functionality and the possible requirements that the functionality must provide for end-users. Finally, you must interrogate as many stakeholders as you know to find out what their expectations are for how the system should work for them. It is helpful when asking such questions to preface them with, 'what if …?' This will allow your imagination to establish different types of scenarios that a system may need to respond to.

• ACTIVITY 14

How have you contributed to the design of an information system? Outline what you did, why you did it and the impact of what you did?

Throughout all of your work, as you contribute to the design and development of information systems, is the importance of involving the end-user for whom the information system is being designed. If the system does not work, i.e. does not provide all the functionalities required of the system, because it has not been thoroughly investigated, the system is out of date already and will not be able to provide the organisation with the data and information its stakeholders require. While it might appear that the end-user knows all that is required, sometimes they do not. This is why it is important to continually interrogate the requirements of information systems by asking end-users: why?, why?, why? This will not only give you an understanding of the requirements of information systems but challenge end-users to make sure that the functionalities that they require of systems is being developed.

Once it has been agreed how the design of information systems is developed, you will be asked to contribute to the testing of the system to make sure that it works. At this stage you will want to establish if the end-users are happy with what has been developed; that the system is working as it has been designed to provide; that the system is working reliably; and that the system is not out of control. You will be asked to test scenarios to establish system errors and resolve these. Once an error has been discovered it should be assessed to identify the level of risk it presents to the system. Errors should then be prioritised to enable their resolution depending on how severe they are. At all stages of testing you should be supported by your project manager. You should make sure that you have devised relevant documentation to guide the testing of the system, so these can be signed off by the project manager.

• ACTIVITY 15

How did you contribute to the development and subsequent testing of an information system?

Testing Your Skills

1. How did you involve stakeholders in the design of an information system?

2. What did you contribute to the agreement of the specification of the design of the information system?

3. What did the specifications for the design and development of information systems that you were involved with cover?

4. How did you support the development of information systems?

5. How did you support the testing of information systems? Which tests did you carry out?

6. What kinds of errors did you find when testing information systems?

7. How did you contribute to resolving information system errors?

8. How successful were information systems that you have worked on in achieving the agreed design specification?

9. What kind of legal constraints did you have to work under, if any?

Ready for assessment?

To achieve this Level 2 unit of a Business & Administration qualification, learners will need to demonstrate that they are able to perform the following activities:

1. Identified and agreed the information to be managed

2. Contributed to the design and development of an information system that met agreed specification requirements

3. Supported testing of the information system

4. Identified and reported faults of the information system

5. Remedied faults of the information system, within limits of own authority

You will need to produce evidence from a variety of sources to support the performance requirements of this unit.

If you carry out the 'ACTIVITIES' and respond to the 'NEED TO KNOW' questions, these will provide some of the evidence required.

Links to other units
While gathering evidence for this unit, evidence may also be used from evidence generated from other units within the Business & Administration suite of units. Below is a sample of applicable units; however, most units within the Business & Administration suite of units will also be applicable.

QCF NVQ
Communications
Communicate in a business environment (Level 2)
Core Business & Administration
Manage own performance in a business environment (Level 2)
Improve own performance in a business environment (Level 2)
Work in a business environment (Level 2)
Work with other people in a business environment (Level 2)

SVQ
Communications
Prepare to communicate in a business environment
Core Business & Administration
Agree how to manage and improve own performance in a business environment
Undertake work in a business environment
Contribute to working with others in a business environment

INDEX